ARRESTED ADOLESCENCE

ARRESTED ADOLESCENCE

The Secret Life of Nathan Leopold

ERIK REBAIN

ROWMAN & LITTLEFIELD
Lanham • Boulder • New York • London

Published by Rowman & Littlefield
An imprint of The Rowman & Littlefield Publishing Group, Inc.
4501 Forbes Boulevard, Suite 200, Lanham, Maryland 20706
www.rowman.com

86-90 Paul Street, London EC2A 4NE

British Library Cataloguing in Publication Information Available

Library of Congress Cataloging-in-Publication Data

ISBN: 978-1-5381-5860-9 (cloth)
ISBN: 978-1-5381-5861-6 (electronic)

CONTENTS

ACKNOWLEDGMENTS

Big thanks goes to my agent, Lauren MacLeod; she has consistently gone above and beyond for this project. I'm indebted to all of those who gave notes on the book as it progressed, especially Joel Greenberg, Blake Hammond, Greg King, Kathie Rebain, Patricia Tierney, Reece White, and Penny Wilson. Thanks also goes to Kristin Pérez, for her help with Spanish translations, and Katie and Christian Flickinger for a very fun photo shoot. Of course, this book couldn't have been completed without many amazing librarians and archivists, so my gratitude goes out to Bill Kostlevy, Jason Nargis, Catheryne Popovitch, Nancy Webster, and everyone who has helped share their institution's archival collections with me. Thank you as well to all those who shared their memories, letters, photos, and research. This book truly was a group effort, and I couldn't have done it without a monumental amount of help.

INTRODUCTION

L ate on a Sunday evening in 1963, within the pale stone walls of Florence's Palazzo Pitti art gallery, a string quartet began to fill the air with
music. Selections from Vivaldi and Beethoven surrounded a crowd, and
among them a man sat and listened, his wife by his side. Their green concert tickets, stamped and torn, were tucked out of sight.[1] After the concert
the couple made their way back to their four-star hotel, the Berchielli, just
on the other side of the Arno River.

The man would have been unremarkable to most: middle-aged, with
sharply receding dark hair and a paunch. He looked like any other American tourist, though if he happened to get into conversation with a local,
they may have been surprised that he could speak passable Italian, albeit
with a flat, Midwestern accent. The man was fifty-nine-year-old Nathan
Leopold Jr. He and his wife were nearing the tail end of a four-month
international vacation, and for the first time in almost forty years, he was
grateful to be alive.

His had been an auspicious beginning. He had been born to a wealthy
family in Chicago and was incredibly intellectually precocious, a published,
polyglot college graduate by the time he was eighteen. In the spring of
1924 Leopold seemed to have the world at his feet; he was happily anticipating a three-month European vacation followed by his entrance into
Harvard Law School, his adulthood finally about to begin. That is, until the
body of a fourteen-year-old boy was discovered in a culvert outside of the
city. Leopold, along with his friend Richard Loeb, confessed to his murder.

The European tour was hastily canceled, and Leopold instead spent his
summer in the crumbling Cook County Jail, at the center of a maelstrom
of media attention. Everyone was fascinated with the killers, who seemed
to have no motive or remorse. After a month and a half Leopold and Loeb

were saved from the gallows and sentenced to life and an additional ninety-nine years in prison. When writing to his lawyer, Clarence Darrow, after the sentencing, Leopold said that he didn't "know whether to thank you or to <u>forgive</u> you!"[2]

Leopold served thirty-three years, losing Loeb to a prison stabbing along the way, and then was paroled in 1958 to the tiny village of Castañer in the mountains of Puerto Rico. After five years on the island, he was released from parole and granted absolute freedom. He celebrated by taking that European vacation that had been delayed for nearly four decades.

During the last thirty-nine years of his life, Leopold had contemplated suicide many times and often wondered if a death sentence in 1924 would have been preferable. But now, traveling around Europe after months of the best hotels and the hospitality of his many friends, filled with the sights and experiences he had only dreamed of for decades, he had at last reached his conclusion. He estimated by "certain esoteric calculations of my own," that on September 15, 1963, the day of the concert, life's pleasures had finally made up for the hardships he'd experienced. In a letter to a close friend, he attempted to explain his logic:

> I've been pretty ambivalent about whether it was <u>worth</u> doing the 33 years, six months, and two days. That is, could I have known early in my imprisonment just what lay ahead of me, would I, or would I not, have been wise to sit down and do it. I've never been sure.
>
> Until now!
>
> During the five and a half years since my release, I've lived rather fully. I've had a good many different kinds of experience, a good many varied pleasures—Castañer, the University, marriage, friends, even a touch of "high life" now and again. And now this indescribably wonderful trip.
>
> So now I'm definitely and finally sure: it <u>was</u> worth doing all those years and I did the wise thing in doing them rather than doing away with myself.[3]

Many would have disagreed with him had they known of his inner musings. In Italy, Leopold was thousands of miles from his most outspoken critics, those who still vividly remembered the days following his crime and the long summer of his sentencing hearing. These people could recall the cold teenager Leopold had been: laughing in court, joking with reporters, and his small smug grin as he peered from the front pages of newspapers day after day. They remembered the grief of a mother who had lost her child one sunny May afternoon and a father who looked at his son's murderers with incomprehension, stunned at their ability to show so little remorse.

Lounging in his hotel in Florence, Leopold had seemingly come far from that day when he took a child's life. He had founded a school and a charity foundation, had a hand in developing a malaria cure, and raised tens of thousands of dollars to build a hospital. He'd recently been described as "a leading example of prisoner rehabilitation."[4] Still, some questioned the motivation behind his actions and wondered if he had actually changed or felt sorry for the life he had taken all those years ago.

I

CHILDHOOD

1

GROWING UP

After living among inmates for over a decade, Nathan Leopold was tasked with writing a speech on the causes of juvenile delinquency and how to curb it. With a prison warden as his mouthpiece, Leopold warned penal officials that, for the average criminal, "his petty thefts as a baby and his serious crimes as a man is bridged by a long series of little tiny steps; one thing follows another almost inevitably."[1]

Tracing the steps Leopold took to get from stealing stamps to murdering a teenager in cold blood is a monumental task. Far from the disadvantaged delinquents he focused on in his speech, Leopold was born into utmost luxury. He was the descendant of men who had established companies that would live on for generations, and women who helmed social service organizations that offered aid to thousands across Chicago.

Leopold's mother, Florence, was the eighth child of Gerhard Foreman, president of the Foreman State National Bank.[2] Known for her gentle and empathetic nature, Florence gave her time primarily to Jewish and children's charities and was treasurer of the South Side Ladies' Sewing Circle for many years.[3] Leopold's father, Nathan Leopold Sr., was the heir to one of the premier shipping companies on the Great Lakes, director of Inland Steamship Company, and a frequent investor in copper mines across the country.[4] Nathan was thirty-one when he married Florence in June 1892, a few days away from her twenty-fourth birthday.[5] As a wedding gift, Nathan presented her with a pearl necklace, adding a pair of pearls every year on their anniversary.[6]

Following their wedding, the couple moved into Florence's father's home, which they shared with several of her siblings and their families. The house was filled with children when Florence and Nathan's son Foreman "Mike" Nathan Leopold was born in 1895 and their second son Samuel

"Sam" Nathan Leopold was born in 1899. In 1902, five years after Gerhard's death, Florence and her sister, Birdie Schwab, sold their father's home and bought houses next door to each other on Michigan Avenue.[7] The sisters were so close that Leopold considered them one soul split between two bodies.[8]

Florence was thirty-six when she became pregnant with what was to be her final child. She had had several miscarriages, so she spent most of this pregnancy in bed, determined to avoid another.[9] During her convalescence, she developed nephritis, characterized by kidney inflammation, which ran in her family and required careful monitoring.[10] Finally, on the afternoon of November 19, 1904, the newest member of the Leopold household was born. Nathan Freudenthal Leopold Jr. weighed six pounds and four ounces, had gray eyes, and would soon sprout a thick head of dark brown hair.[11]

Florence was quite weak after his birth, and her kidney inflammation was now a chronic issue. With Florence frequently ill and Nathan Sr. busy supervising his shipping company, the Leopold boys were often watched by their Aunt Birdie, along with hired help. When Leopold was six months old, he was put under the supervision of his first governess, a German woman named Marie "Mimie" Geisler.[12] She taught her charge to speak German, and though the family primarily spoke German at home,[13] he eventually learned enough English to tutor his nurse in the language, allowing him to become bilingual at an early age.[14]

While growing up Leopold was small and had several childhood illnesses, including measles, whooping cough, and gastrointestinal trouble that sometimes kept him on a restricted diet.[15] Though normally fully capable of physical activity, he was disinclined to play rough and competitive outdoor games with other boys, fearing injury or humiliating defeat. Despite his lack of physical strength, it was not long until Leopold's family noticed a mental precocity in their youngest member. Eager to support their budding genius, the family praised and encouraged any interest Leopold expressed in intellectual pursuits. Leopold recalled: "Ever since I can remember I have heard how bright I was."[16] Chasing this praise, Leopold spent much of his childhood undertaking solitary pursuits that he hoped made him seem unique when compared with other children, taking special delight in collecting and organizing.

His collecting began with coins and a book of stamps handed down by an older cousin, but Leopold quickly refocused on the natural world.[17] When he was five years old, he took an interest in the butterflies and beetles he found around the house and yard.[18] Hoping to keep them, he learned that amateur naturalists advised putting the desired insect in a jar with a coating of cyanide along the bottom, waiting for it to die, then carefully mounting the body. Denied the cyanide by his understandably cautious parents, he instead put gasoline-soaked cotton in a jar, as suggested by his brother Sam. This insecticide was affectionately nicknamed "Samonide," and marks one of the seemingly few happy childhood memories the two shared in their long, antagonistic relationship.[19]

Noting his son's interest, Nathan Sr. took Leopold to visit his friend Henry Coale. Coale, an avid collector of birds, regularly published ornithological articles and eventually donated thousands of specimens to the British Museum and Chicago's Field Museum. But in 1910 Coale's collection remained in his home, and once he saw it, little Leopold was enthralled. Coale gave his new patron some specimens, allowing Leopold to begin a small collection of birds for himself.[20]

This introduction to the avian world swiftly became Leopold's central focus, and at first the family didn't know what to make of his obsessive interest. When he asked to attend an ornithological convention when he was still a child, his father jokingly agreed, but only if Leopold would wear the much too large Prince Albert coat Nathan Sr. had been married in.[21] Not deterred, Leopold continued to pursue ornithology and by the time he was nine or ten, most of his family supported him. Too young to collect specimens himself, his older brothers shot and brought him birds, as did the captains of his father's ships.[22]

Along with a seemingly innate interest in nature, Leopold was fascinated with classification and comparing data.[23] He sought to learn the word "yes" in as many languages as he could and was disturbed when he was told that Latin had three words for it.[24] Mike recalled that around age five Leopold was also "extremely interested in seeing all the churches in the neighborhood, in knowing their names and knowing all about them."[25] Once his family got their first car he tagged along on drives so he could see, catalog, and, in his own six-year-old way, collect new places of worship.[26] Leopold felt that "To classify, to study non-emotionally was . . . the hight [*sic*] of knowledge. Things which could not be classified had no proper place in the universe."[27]

As was typical of upper-class children, Leopold was also trained to appreciate the arts, but he was often uninterested in them. When asked why he had pursued hobbies he didn't like, he explained "because it is considered the thing to enjoy, music, literature and painting. . . . I was trying to attain perfection, or what people around me think to be perfection."[28] He did learn to play the piano and developed a taste for opera and classical music. He would even "collect" his favorite poems by committing them to memory.

Leopold's parents were proud of their youngest child, his father remembering him as a boy with a good disposition, who was always well behaved in front of company and easy to bring up.[29] Leopold said his mother "was disgustingly and inordinately proud of me."[30] According to Leopold however, he had "a violent temper as a child," and "believed that if he wanted anything bad enough, if he would cry enough his parents would give it to him."[31] Still, he was devoted to his parents, saying they were friends more than authority figures, and remembering his mother especially fondly as "lovable and loving and a champion of the weak. She doted on her own children. It was a wrench for her when one or the other of us was away from home."[32]

Leopold's relationships with his brothers varied widely. Five years separated each of them, and tension brewed among the trio. Sam felt resentful and left out among the family—the middle child who was overshadowed by Mike, as the oldest, and Leopold, as the prodigy.[33] It didn't help that Mike was charismatic, intelligent, and a collector who focused on historical manuscripts relating to Abraham Lincoln and the American Civil War. Unlike his brothers, Sam was shy and uninterested in intellectual pursuits.[34] While Leopold respected Mike's traits, he disparaged Sam's, downplayed his intelligence, and took little notice of his advice, explaining:

> I hate to be patronized . . . it invariably arouses the negativism in me. I see it as a challenge, and, almost compulsively, I feel constrained to give you something to worry about. [Sam's] patronizing of me, certainly since 1924, and, I think since 1909, is one of the things that makes it so hard for me to accept any suggestions, even a good one, from Sam. Contrarily, I was inclined to accept without question anything Mike told me.[35]

Nearly as important to Leopold as his immediate family were his extended family members, many of them clustered together in the same neighborhood and frequent visitors to each other's homes. In the following decades, the Leopolds would share their home with family members for months and even years, if they had fallen on hard times or needed a place to stay while moving.[36] Leopold was the baby in this tight-knit group, the youngest child of his generation on both sides. From this came his nickname, "Babe," used by family members and close friends for the rest of his life.[37]

The nineteen grandchildren of Gerhard Foreman. (l-r) Bal, Mike, and Sam are on the right side of the second row. Baby Leopold is behind them, held by his cousin Beatrice Rosenberg. Highland Park Historical Society Wildwood Exhibit, 2015. Curated by Elliott Miller.

The extended family was so entwined they had created a communal vacation haven to escape the heat of Chicago summers. In 1901, Leopold's father and his uncles Oscar Foreman, Henry Steele, and Alfred Schwab bought a lot in Highland Park, some thirty miles north of the city and the Leopolds' home on Michigan Avenue.[38] The families each constructed a mansion for themselves, as well as a Germanic-inspired central clubhouse where meals could be shared beneath walls lined with hunting trophies. The grounds were teeming with life; a ravine running behind the houses offered endless exploratory opportunities for young children, and fruit and vegetable gardens were in abundance around the brightly painted "cottages."[39] They named their vacation getaway "Wildwood."

Though initially there was some pushback from permanent residents of the suburb about the Jewish families moving in, a local newspaper made it clear that hostility toward their new neighbors would not be tolerated. "Tastes do differ," one reporter conceded, "but why object to the sons and daughters of Abraham." After all, the families paid their bills promptly and "That kind of a thing goes a great way with us. We will welcome the Hebrews here."[40]

Despite the mixed feelings from the community, within the gated world of Wildwood itself, Leopold remembered his childhood vacation home as something of an idyll. Many of his cousins had finished their schooling before he was born, but there were enough children around his age as well as family friends and governesses to keep him happily occupied. The adults were just as likely to cut loose as the children; as their broods put on plays, competed in three-legged races, and rode horses, the adults brought out phonographs to dance on the lawn, and Florence was taught to ride a bike, her husband and brothers-in-law running alongside to steady her.[41]

Of course, for Leopold this also included excellent opportunities for ornithological study. Decades later he wrote: "I can never hear [a Wood Thrush] without being carried back to my early childhood, spent in Highland Park . . . where the Wood Thrush nested on our property. Surely there is nothing more beautiful than those three ringing notes."[42] He referred to the property as the setting for all of his "Alice-in-Wonderland imaginings."[43] But the fantasy would soon come to an end; in 1914 the Schwab home and clubhouse burned down during the off-season and the aging families began to spend their summers elsewhere.[44] The Leopolds sold their share of the property in 1920.[45]

During the school year Leopold spent his time in a series of institutions around the city. He entered elementary school right before his sixth birthday, attending the private Miss Spaids' School, less than half a mile from home.[46] A few years previously, Spaids' had classes for boys in lower grades but had transitioned into an all-girls school, though Leopold and another boy were allowed to enroll.[47] While Leopold didn't mind or take much notice at the time, this would lead to teasing in the years to come.

Halfway into his first year at Spaids', Leopold's uncle Jules Ballenberg died, leaving his seventeen-year-old son, Adolf Gerhard "Bal" Ballenberg, an orphan.[48] Bal, who had spent the first four years of his life living with the Leopolds and was close with Mike, was informally adopted by the family. Aside from time spent in college and the army, Bal would live with the Leopolds until his marriage, fifteen years later. Leopold quickly accepted Bal as a part of their immediate family, referring to him as his foster brother or simply his brother for the rest of their lives.

During the summer vacation between his first and second years at Spaids', Leopold's final governess was hired: Miss Mathilda Wantz.[49] Wantz had recently immigrated from Germany, and she was given charge of six-year-old Leopold and eleven-year-old Sam. At first Leopold resented her presence and taught her that in English "Go to Hell" meant "Good morning."[50]

Despite the initial friction, Leopold soon warmed to Wantz. For several years they spent much of their time together and he became closer to her than his parents. He and Sam nicknamed her "Sweetie," and she encouraged her charges to ignore the other servants, gossiping that the maids were "hores [sic]."[51] Looking back on the relationship, Leopold recalled that she had "a very great influence over my brother and myself. She displaced my mother. She was a scheming woman, who used the children as a barrier to shield herself. . . . I was thoroughly devoted to her."[52]

When he was eight, Leopold left Spaids' and entered third grade in the Douglas Branch of the Chicago Public School, where he would remain for four years. Immediately Leopold felt that he was different than the other kids in his class. "I had wealthy parents," he explained, "I lived on Michigan Avenue and had a nurse who accompanied me to and from school."[53] This obvious wealth disparity did not endear him to his classmates. He also refused to play sports, and a classmate commented that because of this "most boys thought he was crazy."[54]

While recognized as intelligent, Leopold proceeded normally in school until his fifth grade teacher encouraged him to skip several grades.[55] This heightened the growing conception of his own superiority when compared to other children. During this time, he was beginning his journey toward the philosophy that would eventually consume his life. "Up to the age of eight years," Leopold said, "conscience was drilled into me, but after the age of eight I drilled that conscience out."[56]

As Leopold raced through school, his father began making big changes in his life. According to Leopold, Nathan Sr. had become increasingly worried about harm coming to the crews of his ships in the unpredictable and deadly storms that often hit the Great Lakes in the winter.[57] In 1916, seeking a more stable business to pass on to his sons, Nathan Sr. bought Morris Paper Mills, a floundering one-year-old company located sixty miles south of Chicago, which produced folding paper boxes and containers.[58] This was supplemented, in 1919, with the Fibre Can Corporation, which produced plant-based storage items including cans, kegs, and oil drums. Family legend offers another motivation for the shift in professions.

Bal and Mike had both attended the Michigan College of Mines and when they graduated with engineering degrees both went to work for Inland Steel in Michigan. Wanting her boys closer to home, Florence allegedly asked Nathan Sr. to buy a business for them in Illinois.[59] It worked: both became directors at the mill and moved back home in 1916.[60] During the next four decades, the mill's products could be found everywhere, from the clothing department at Sears Roebuck to local drug stores, where brightly colored Morris Paper containers held everything from scotch tape to Budweiser six-packs.[61]

Around that time, the North Side neighborhoods were becoming unfashionable, and many wealthy Jewish residents were resettling on the South Side. The Leopolds followed, trading their Michigan Avenue home for a larger corner lot on Greenwood Avenue in the neighborhood of Kenwood.[62] The three-story Tudor home had been designed in 1866 by architect George Edbrooke.[63] The carriage house, which used to bed horses, had been converted into a garage and living quarters for their chauffeur and his family, and the main house was updated from gas to electric lighting as the world turned toward the future.

At their new home, though he shared a bedroom with Sam, Leopold quickly found a way to make a space that was all his own. A large room on the third floor was converted into a combination study and museum for his natural collections.[64] The year 1915 would introduce another big change for Leopold: one day when he was sick, he lay sprawled across his and Sam's beds. Seeing this, Wantz jerked the beds apart and Leopold fell to the floor. Unluckily for the governess, Florence saw it as well, and Wantz was dismissed.[65] Leopold was without formal supervision just in time for the start of his high school career.

His new school, just a few blocks away, was the prestigious college preparatory Harvard School for Boys. Founded in 1865, the school moved several times, absorbing other prep schools along the way, before it found a permanent home at 4731 South Ellis Avenue.[66] Completed in May 1917, Leopold would be among the first students to walk this iteration of Harvard's newly constructed halls.[67] He entered ninth grade at twelve years old and was well up to the academic challenges of the institution.[68] He earned As and Bs and took the basic school curriculum along with his choice electives of French and Greek.[69]

Despite his scholastic achievements, this was not an especially happy time for Leopold. Mockingly called "Flea" for his small stature and interest in entomology, his classmates described Leopold as "the crazy 'bird' of the School, the avicular member of the Fifth Class is forever harping on birds. . . . A favorite remark of this praised genius every other Monday morning: 'Oh—! Only sixteen A's.'"[70]

The derision of his peers even carried over into Leopold's time at summer camp. During his first summer away from Wildwood in 1917, Leopold was sent to Camp Highlands in northern Wisconsin. In the camp yearbook, his fellow campers wrote: "One of the busiest bodies in Camp is 'Gnat' Leopold. Gnat's favorite pastime and hobby seems to be biting and bugology. He often knocks you flat with some of his biting remarks."[71]

Apparently unwelcome among the other children and disinterested in the team sports that the camp highly valued, Leopold wanted to take Greek lessons, but didn't because he thought his father would object. "My parents felt I went to camp to fish and swim, not to study," Leopold explained.[72] Despite being out of his comfort zone, Leopold eventually made some friends and participated in camp activities, once chasing down a swimming loon in a canoe.[73]

Though unpopular among his peers, at eleven Leopold made friends with teenage bird-enthusiasts Locke Mackenzie and Sidney Stein Jr., who showed the boy the ins and outs of field ornithology.[74] For Leopold, who had up until then simply bought specimens and relegated his observations to his neighborhood, a door was opened into a new world. It was with these new guides that he first explored the marshes and plains around Hyde and Wolf Lakes, a region south of the city along the Illinois-Indiana border.

Leopold's classmates perceived him as uncomfortable around girls, but in reality he was misogynistic and regarded them "with much contempt as intellectual inferiors."[75] Still there were some exceptions, and ornithology allowed him to bridge this gap as well. When he was about fifteen Leopold became friends with thirteen-year-old birdwatcher Katherine Friedman. They went on nature walks, Leopold translated her Latin homework, and he drew her a diagram of "Freud's theory of the ego, the super-ego, the id and the libido" on a restaurant tablecloth.[76] Yet among his birding companions, many respected Leopold's talents, but not his personality. Colin Campbell Sanborn, who often went birding with Leopold, recalled him as "an obnoxious young man. In his studies he was very brilliant, and knew it too."[77]

Leopold's ornithological habit was wide-reaching. As he grew more adept at field observation, he began to shoot his finds and make study skins. This is a relatively simple procedure, favored by naturalists and museums, which involves removing a bird's skeleton and organs and filling the body with cotton. For more impressive displays, he brought his kills to taxidermists to be professionally mounted and continued to buy already mounted birds. As his collection grew, so did the number of display cabinets lining the walls of his study, and a table was placed in the middle of the room for examination and the making of study skins.[78] Leopold recalled that Florence was less than thrilled: "I'd bring a rare bird home and she could barely bear to look at it."[79] Over the years Leopold joined a multitude of national ornithological clubs, including the American Ornithologist's Union.[80] Leopold often stood out in these groups; when he was twelve he went to a meeting where "I suppose the next youngest member was 45."[81]

At thirteen Leopold was first published in the national ornithology magazine *The Auk*.[82] Initially he submitted short descriptions of rare birds he had seen around the Chicago area but soon became more ambitious. In 1920 Leopold and his friends James D. Watson and George Porter Lewis pooled the yearly lists they had kept from 1913 to 1920 of their ornithological sightings and privately published a booklet of the 237 species they had seen.[83] The booklet earned the young birders a mention in *The Auk* as being "very carefully prepared" and "of much interest to other bird students of the district."[84]

As he entered his teenage years, Leopold's sexuality gradually began to manifest, though it was apparently not his first introduction to that world. According to Sam, during the six years that their governess Mathilda Wantz was employed by the family, she bathed with the boys when their parents were away from home, undressed in front of them, showed them her used menstrual products, and fondled them.[85]

When examined by psychiatrists in 1924, Leopold said he had almost no memory of these occurrences; the only questionable parts of the relationship he could recall were that Wantz had a nickname for her nipples and that she had used the prospect of "wrestling" with her as a reward for good behavior.[86] In later life Leopold claimed the abuse had been made up by psychiatrists in an attempt to make sense of his pathology, not realizing that the stories had come from Sam.[87] Because Sam gave detailed descriptions of the abuse and corroborated what little Leopold did remember, it seems likely that it did happen, though Leopold either lied about not remembering or had repressed the traumatic memories. Regardless of his ability to remember it, this abuse seemed to leave a permanent mark and would unconsciously color his burgeoning sexuality.

A year after Wantz left, Leopold was first introduced to masturbation. A boy named Henry, a bit older than Leopold, masturbated in front of him, and Leopold was fascinated by the act and ashamed that he could not mimic it.[88] But he continued to try and as puberty set in, Leopold found success in the pursuit as well as a fantastic new hobby.

Around this time, it must be assumed that Leopold realized that he was different from other boys his age. His first crush had not been on a young girl, but on a well-built, eighteen-year-old camp counselor named Bill. And not only did his tastes bend toward men, but they were often dark and sadistic.[89] During his masturbation sessions he imagined not that Bill was his companion, but his slave. Leopold began to construct a universe of sexual fantasies, populating it with strong young slave men who were intensely loyal to him as their King. Mentally he developed "an elaborate system of capturing them and even of branding them," with a crown on their inner calf, to leave no doubts as to whom they belonged.[90] As his fantasy life flourished, nearly every boy and young man he came across would be evaluated for his place within Leopold's imaginary slave hierarchy, with his oldest, strongest slaves like Bill at the top, and the others below in deeper subjugation.[91]

In addition to his frequent bouts of self-aggrandizing self-love, Leopold was beginning to explore less solitary sexual pursuits. When he was around thirteen, he was sleeping in the same room as his friend Henry and the boys rubbed their crotches together until Leopold ejaculated.[92] Together he and Henry would entice a third, somewhat younger friend, Joe, into one of their homes. Once there they would tie him up and assault him, masturbating the protesting boy and making slight forays into the sadism that had come to color Leopold's sexual fantasies.[93] Once, going off a story another boy had told him about oil of wintergreen burning when dropped on himself, Leopold "threw Joe down and undressed and tied him and put oil of wintergreen on his genitals."[94] It's possible that Leopold's abuse of a younger child may have been subconsciously tied to his own experiences of abuse, as sexually abused children have higher than average rates of anger issues and acting out sexually.

Joe was not the only one suffering at the hands of Leopold's blossoming sexuality. Though it introduced Leopold to new pleasures, he realized that he had to hide this side of himself from the rest of society. Poetically put by a psychiatrist in 1924, Leopold felt "the painful conviction that he was not constituted sexually like other men, that this difference in makeup led him to a type of aberrant and perverse sexual activity which he keenly felt was despised by humanity as something very disgraceful and revoltingly shocking."[95]

And despised by humanity it was. In 1911, Chicago's Vice Commission advised that laws against homosexuality be made stricter, "to make it clearly understood that society regards these abhorrent deeds as crimes."[96] Despite oppressive laws, communities of gay people did exist in America at the time, even in Chicago's "Towertown" neighborhood. The area was a gathering place for intellectuals and artists and characterized by a looser sexual attitude that allowed sexual minorities a certain amount of freedom.[97] Speakeasies and dance halls popped up around the city where back rooms allowed same-sex couples to dance together, private rooms in bathhouses led to trysts, and male prostitutes competed for attention with their female counterparts.[98] But to a young teenager surrounded by family, friends, and a culture so far removed from an acceptance or understanding of homosexuality, this hidden world was likely of little comfort if he even knew of its existence.

The modern books Leopold read on the topic, including Havelock Ellis's *Sexual Inversion*, and several books by and about Oscar Wilde, couldn't have been especially comforting.[99] While more open-minded than previous literature on the topic, Ellis's book was clinical, offering case studies of homosexual men which often tied their sexuality to abuse or familial problems. And Wilde's homosexuality had recently led to his imprisonment and disgrace during a very public trial. Positive, nuanced examples of homosexuality were available if he looked for them, but most of the messages about homosexuality he received would have been exceedingly negative.

While Leopold felt free to engage his friends and family in conversations about the hedonism and lack of conscience he was actively cultivating, he kept his sexuality a carefully guarded secret. Luckily for Leopold, with the dawning of World War I, his family had bigger problems to concern themselves with.

In 1917 both Mike and Bal were in the Reserve Officer's Training Camp at Fort Sheridan when they registered for the draft and enlisted to serve.[100] Both were sent overseas,[101] and though Sam wasn't drafted, he was a member of the Student Army Training Corps during his time at the University of Michigan.[102] Up to this point, the family had been attending Chicago's Sinai Reform Temple, but Nathan Sr. thought the rabbi had pro-German leanings, and with his sons in the army, he decided he didn't want the family to attend services.[103] Leopold likely had no objection, as he had stopped attending religious studies when he was eleven and was reading up on atheism instead. Both brothers returned home safely in 1919 after seeing action in France, Bal distinguishing himself as a captain and Mike as a first lieutenant.[104]

Though worried about his brothers and ashamed that he was too young to help in the effort, the war years were not a complete wash for the growing Leopold. An infatuation with the military had started early: Mike had attended the Northwestern Military Academy from 1908 to 1910 and when looking at his picture Leopold "experienced vague sexual excitation.

The idea of a lot of boys gathered together and wearing the same uniform appealed to him strongly."[105]

The new tumult gave him easy access to twisted stories: anti-German propaganda meant to inspire patriotism was rampant across the United States. War posters depicting German soldiers on the verge of attacking women were matched with the text: "BUY BONDS" and "HALT THE HUN!" These and more explicit rape stories gave Leopold plenty of material to mull over as his sexual fantasies continued to darken.

By the time he graduated high school at fifteen, Leopold was a dangerous mix of arrogance and insecurity. He considered himself better than others because of his family's enormous wealth and his intellectual gifts, but he was also deeply self-conscious of his looks, sexuality, and lack of athletic ability. He was even ashamed of his own name, despairing of the then-uncommon name of Nathan and wishing for a simple, strong name that he considered more masculine and appealing.[106] To hide these insecurities, he projected a confident and arrogant outer shell, pretending to be beyond the scorn of others.[107]

He was helped in this mindset by a consuming interest in radical philosophy. As he read an assortment of philosophers from across the centuries, he systematically tried to unlearn all he knew of religion, conscience, sympathy, and social responsibility.[108] Nothing was safe from Leopold's philosophical purge; he was determined even to eliminate all ties of sentimentality he had to his family members.[109] At the center of it all was the ideal Leopold would come to base his entire life around: individual hedonism. Hedonism is the philosophy of maximizing pleasure and minimizing pain as the ultimate goal in one's life, and it made perfect sense to the privileged and self-centered teenager. As he would come to believe, his personal pleasure mattered more than any pain he caused others. Marinating in this dangerous mindset, he would soon meet the boy who would inspire him to push his philosophies into action.

2

A NEW RELATIONSHIP

Nathan Leopold was fifteen when he became friends with the boy whose name would be forever tied to his own. The pair had been passing acquaintances since they were children, both moving in the same upper-class German-Jewish social circles, their parents attached to the same clubs and causes. While they had sometimes mingled during social events, Leopold really got to know Richard "Dick" Loeb in the spring of 1920, just after Leopold graduated from high school.[1]

Loeb was a slim, brown-eyed, brown-haired boy of fourteen who had already finished his freshman year at the University of Chicago. He had been born on June 11, 1905, the third of four boys. By then, Loeb's father, Albert, was steadily making his fortune, having left his legal practice two years earlier to work for Sears, Roebuck and Co. As his family grew, Albert moved up within the company and eventually became vice president.[2] Unlike the more reserved Leopolds, Albert and his wife, Anna, fully embraced the role of a high society family. During Loeb's childhood his parents regularly opened their home for events, hosting concerts,[3] lectures on Palestine[4] and women's suffrage,[5] and throwing elaborate parties with hundreds of guests, their enormous lawn transformed with flowers, live music, and a dance floor.[6]

In accordance with this elevated visibility, Loeb was raised to behave in ways that would reflect well on his family. He grew up well-mannered and cultured, taking French and piano lessons and competing in horseback riding competitions on a mare he named "Peg O' My Heart" after a then-popular play.[7]

When he was four, Loeb's care was turned over to governess Anna Struthers, who was strict but loving toward her charge and he came to care for her deeply.[8] She homeschooled Loeb until the third grade, and under her guidance, he became intensely studious, a child eager to receive a desk for his birthday, who enjoyed playing chess and built a chemistry lab in the basement.[9] After he was sent to bed, Loeb liked to read late into the night, everything from classics and historical texts to crime novels in which famous detectives and master criminals matched wits.[10]

His family and governess were impressed by Loeb's gentle, empathetic nature as well as his intelligence and drive. When he was ten Loeb created and became the editor of a very short-lived periodical, aptly named *Richard's Magazine*. In an editorial written for the work's first issue, Loeb mused on the barbaric new nature of the first world war, which his elder brothers were serving in: "Daily millions of dollars are being spent in the purchase of ammunitions and weapons. Think if that amount of money was spent daily in the beautifying of the world. Think if all lives that have been lost in this war could have been spent in peaceful labor and happiness."[11] Albert Loeb's friend and coworker Julius Rosenwald sent a copy of this magazine to Theodore Roosevelt and the former president praised Loeb's efforts, telling him: "It does me good to see young men of your stamp growing up in this country."[12]

Despite the appearance of a serene childhood, Loeb often felt disconnected from his family and other children. His older brothers were closer with each other than with him and his younger brother was nine years his junior.[13] Unlike Leopold, he wasn't close with the few cousins who were around his age, and Struthers usually kept him away from friends and frivolous games. Julius Rosenwald's daughter recalled that "Dick Loeb was always held up to us as an example of what a child should do. He didn't play outdoors. He didn't play baseball. He read books. He studied. He was brilliant. . . . My father was jealous because his children were just ordinary kids."[14]

Isolated and placed on a pedestal, he felt he had no one he could open up to. If he couldn't confide in his family, Loeb decided he would strive to seem like an ideal child by hiding all his bad habits, especially the small thefts he had begun perpetuating around the neighborhood.[15] Small change from his friend's homes, cookies from his summer camp—eventually anything small enough to slip into his pocket was at risk of being picked up. Despite, or perhaps because of the risk involved, Loeb found he enjoyed getting away with these thefts and felt pride when he was able to successfully convince others of his innocence.[16]

Richard Loeb entered the University of Chicago High School at twelve years old, and one classmate recalled that he "was very active and everybody liked him, he was a very brilliant boy."[17] Despite being the youngest in his class, he received the highest grade both semesters when he took fourth-year French as a freshman.[18] He joined clubs, played golf and tennis, and became freshman class treasurer. In between more serious rounds of debate and speeches about the war in his discussion clubs, he led cheers during public speaking contests[19] and performed in comedy skits.[20] One article joked that Loeb's family was relieved when he accidentally inhaled chlorine gas and couldn't speak for eight hours.[21]

While Leopold held himself aloof and alienated his peers, Loeb appears to have been an integrated and well-liked member of the student body. "There wasn't a sunnier, pleasanter, more likable fellow in the world," Leopold recalled. "He seemed to have the inborn knack of making friends, of winning everyone's affection."[22] That he sometimes liked to show off to his friends by picking his classmates' pockets and stealing from shops was not seen as anything more than a penchant for schoolboy pranks.[23]

During his sophomore year, however, things began to change. While Loeb was still a member of the school's Literary Club, he no longer often spoke at meetings and seemed to have run out of time to make other commitments. He was focused instead, with the help of his governess and French teacher, in cramming three years of schooling into one so he could graduate as a sophomore.[24] Loeb received his high school diploma in 1919, just a couple of weeks after his fourteenth birthday.

After graduation Loeb enrolled in the University of Chicago and continued living with his parents, with Struthers staying on to tutor him. Loeb did little to distinguish himself academically that first year in college, making only middling grades, but he did join a newly formed group called The Campus Club, where he helped arrange dances and social events for students not associated with fraternities.[25] Outside of school, he continued committing small thefts and enjoyed following people on the street, pretending he was a police detective or a criminal giving covert hand signals to gang members about which houses they should rob.[26]

But the play-acting and petty crimes were growing stale, and he longed for a partner to confide in and commit more ambitious crimes with. At the end of the year, as Loeb had grown past the point where most children had governesses, Struthers was let go by the family.[27] It was then, in the spring of 1920, newly freed from Struthers's close watch and ready to embrace the drinking, sex, and wildness of his much older classmates, that he got to know Nathan Leopold Jr.

The beginning of their relationship was hardly auspicious; psychiatrists noted that "at first [Leopold] detested [Loeb], and he thinks this feeling was mutual."[28] Despite the initial animosity, they came to know each other well in the long hours spent hanging around with a group of mutual friends and attending college football games together.[29] By the time classes started in October they were friendly enough that Loeb would drive the few blocks that separated his home from Leopold's and take him to school.[30] "It's true I was drawn to him because I felt he was superior," Leopold recalled. "Dick was a sophomore when I was a freshman . . . he had a car when I didn't. He was a better athlete and had more social graces and was a better dancer. He bragged about his girls."[31]

While much has been made of the differences that existed between Leopold and Loeb, it is not hard to understand why the teenagers became friends. The relative similarities in their intelligence, upbringing, and social status made them at least superficially compatible, but the biggest reason why the fifteen-year-olds may have bonded was because of their ages relative to their peers. Surrounded by classmates who were all at least three years older than themselves, it may have been a comfort to commiserate on the unique circumstances they shared.

The data around accelerating children through school remains extremely subjective; while some children excel, happy to finally have intellectual stimulus, others flounder self-consciously and put increasing pressure on themselves to maintain their status as smartest in the room, though it may no longer be the case. Loeb appears to have suffered some of the insecurities associated with the latter group, admitting that after his early high school graduation he felt he began losing intelligence and would lie to friends about his grades to seem more scholastically successful than he was.[32] Leopold was an outlier in the equation; his brilliance continued to be recognized and he found his classwork simple, but he struggled in other ways. Decades later, when Leopold was asked whether a friend's son should be allowed to skip grades, he replied:

> If [he] skips a grade, and later more grades, he will be associating with kids several years older than he. Intellectually he will be at least their equal; physically and socially, he will not. Further, being younger than all the rest puts a kid in a challenging position. He has to prove, over and over, to himself and to the others, that he is as far advanced as they. . . . Whatever the other kids consider smart and sophisticated, [he] will have to do more and better! Since this will undoubtedly involve some socially undesirable things: drinking, staying out late, going with girls, etc., it may prove dangerous. I know what I'm talking about here; I've been thru it. If I had not been three or four years younger than the kids I palled with (I entered college at 15), I might not have ended up where I did![33]

Tossed headfirst into college life during the Roaring Twenties, Leopold did his best to prove himself. Though he did not like being drunk or the taste of alcohol, he began to drink socially "first to conform, and then to outshine," in the speakeasies and black and tan clubs that dotted Chicago's South Side.[34] In Leopold's opinion, testing the laws of Prohibition was just part of the college culture he found himself in. "We were the lost generation, the kids that grew up during Prohibition," he said. "We found that to drink was a challenge. If you were without a hip flask you were nobody."[35] Leopold's first year of college was spent chasing a dizzying high, maintaining his schoolwork with ease while exploring the shadowy world of Chicago's nightlife for the first time, his new friend by his side.

As the pair grew more comfortable with one another, Loeb began to wonder about Leopold's potential for criminality. One day, while walking through Marshall Field's department store together, Loeb stole some pipes and other small items in front of Leopold. When Leopold joined in to help, Loeb rejoiced and quickly brought Leopold into his confidence, speaking freely about the other petty crimes he had committed.[36]

When Loeb stole the pipes to test Leopold—a test which would come to have much deeper ramifications than either of them could know—it was unlikely that Leopold would have done anything other than to go along with him. Leopold had also committed petty theft as a child, stealing stamps and ties from his relatives without guilt, but Leopold had a much simpler reason for accepting his friend's lawlessness: an overwhelming admiration. Leopold recalled that "the attraction was physical, but it was far more than that. It rested on extravagant admiration for his athletic ability, his academic precocity, his wealth and the advantages it gave him, and, above all, his social graces. In a word, it rested upon what, in my eyes, was his enormous sophistication."[37]

By the time winter blew in, Leopold was infatuated. Inspired by the philosophy he was reading, he began to see Loeb as nearing Friedrich Nietzsche's concept of the übermensch or superman, one who transcends humanity and is the next step on the evolutionary chain. One friend testified that Leopold spoke openly even of this, saying that "in his estimation there was one man that he knew that approached the superman stage and that man was Richard Loeb."[38] Leopold was no stranger to crushes, but this level of interest went beyond anything he had experienced before. When Loeb invited Leopold to spend some vacation time at his family's home in Michigan that winter, he eagerly accepted.

In 1917 Loeb's parents, Anna and Albert, began buying hundreds of acres around Charlevoix, Michigan, which they developed into a farm and enormous private estate. Their mansion was fondly called "The Big House," and sat on a hill overlooking Pine Lake. Made of local stone from the surrounding fields, the house's U-shaped design opened up to a large courtyard facing the lake and offered occupants of the bedrooms on the second floor a gorgeous view.

In February Leopold and Loeb left Chicago together on an overnight train toward Charlevoix, sharing a private compartment for their long journey. In the steadily rocking train car they passed the time playing cards and chatting. At Loeb's suggestion they spent part of the evening devising a series of signals they could use to cheat while playing bridge, which they could test out on Loeb's family. During the night, when the subject of conversation turned to sex, Leopold decided to take a chance. Within the privacy of their room Leopold told Loeb not only that he was homosexual, but also of the intense feelings he had developed for Loeb.[39]

To Leopold's delight Loeb accepted this revelation and admitted he had one of his own, confessing that beyond the petty crimes Leopold knew about, Loeb was also harboring dreams of becoming a "master criminal," and committing far more dangerous offenses. This fit perfectly with Leopold's burgeoning understanding of the superman, as one of his friends described: "He felt that the superman should be the law giver, because after all he had the super intellect, he knew more than the other men . . . therefore he should make laws to suit himself, to satisfy his own needs regardless of man made laws."[40]

They began their sexual relationship that night when Loeb joined Leopold in his bunk within their sleeping berth. Leopold described this to psychiatrists as the most thrilling experience of his life, which "gave him more pleasure than anything else he had ever done."[41] The psychiatrists were skeptical of this hyperbole, as their first sex act did not involve penetration, but intercrural, with Leopold rubbing his penis between Loeb's thighs to climax. Despite their incredulity, this was to become Leopold's favorite and almost exclusive sex act with Loeb.[42] According to Sam, it had also been their governess Mathilda Wantz's position of choice.[43] Once they arrived, they spent the vacation attempting to cheat the Loeb family at cards between frequent rounds of mutual masturbation and sexual exploration.[44]

The rest of the winter Leopold was confined to bed with chicken pox followed by measles. Upset that he was being kept from the university (and, it may be assumed, from Loeb), Leopold vacillated between depression and fervent bouts of studying, often refusing food until he finished the subject he was working on.[45] But Leopold couldn't be kept down for long; when he recovered in the spring he was finally able to join Loeb on his criminal exploits. The two began with relatively harmless acts that any juvenile might engage in: cheating at cards, calling in false fire alarms, and prank calls. These dalliances started small, but it didn't take long for them to escalate to seriously dangerous felonies.

That spring Loeb discovered that the keys to his mother's Milburn Electric car, through an incredible example of manufacturer oversight, would fit any other car of the same make and model. One day when they had been drinking Loeb convinced Leopold to steal one with him. Cruising around in their stolen car they called in false fire alarms, sometimes parking to talk and drink along the way.

During one of their stops, they noticed a truck from the garage where they had stolen the car from appear behind them. They drove away and when the truck followed, they became frightened and leaped from the moving vehicle. When they made it home Loeb tried to convince Leopold to change clothes and come look at the wreck they'd left behind, but Leopold refused on the grounds that the danger of apprehension was greater than any possible thrill that seeing the car would bring.[46] This was the principle on which Leopold's entire hedonistic life rested: weighing potential pleasure against potential pain and choosing the option that would make him the happiest.

Evidently neither was too deterred by the near miss, as their joy riding soon escalated further. In an ever-changing menagerie of stolen cars, Leopold would drive Loeb around town while he threw bricks through the windshields of unoccupied parked cars.[47] They also graduated to arson, waiting until dark and setting unoccupied buildings ablaze. The teenagers would then drive away, change clothes, and drive back in a different car so they could mingle among the crowd and speculate on the cause of the inferno.

The pair would plan each escapade carefully, speaking in French or coded English on the phone in case they were overheard. Once everything was set up, they would make a big show of going to bed early, then sneak out of their rooms, cause mayhem, and return quietly in the early hours of the morning. Though Leopold did not initiate these crimes, a psychiatrist noted that "in order to maintain this relation [Leopold] was willing to steal, lie, burn, rob and even commit a homicide, with but little if any consideration for the feelings of others. . . . Loeb was pictured in his mind as the only one who made life worth while."[48]

His family seemingly had no idea about the double life Leopold was leading, and from the outside he must have appeared as a model son. That spring he gave a speech before the Chicago Ornithological Society,[49] received As in all his classes, and volunteered at a hospital dispensary.[50] While Leopold was outspoken and made no secret of his fondness for radical philosophies, his intelligence meant that his family was willing to overlook some peculiarities. Reflecting on this period in his life, Leopold acknowledged:

> I'd never had to work, never had to look out for anybody but myself, I was expected to make a passable record in school and to be courteous to my family—that was all that was demanded of me. Most of my energies were directed toward myself. I was never called on to think of anyone else, never asked for any sacrifices.[51]

It was this selfishness, masked by intellectualism and good works, which allowed him to descend further and further into amorality.

After Leopold's first year of college, he spent part of his summer back in Charlevoix with the Loeb family. In late June Anna Loeb's friend Jesse Lowe Smith was also invited to spend some time at The Big House. Smith noted in his diary that his vacation began when "Richard Loeb and Nathan Leopold & a young man whom they nicknamed 'the Count' met at the Belvidere station and drove me out to the Loeb Farms."[52] Leopold very likely already knew Smith, as he was vice president of the Illinois Audubon Society, and made sure to spend time with the naturalist, one morning waking at 4 a.m. to go birding with Smith and "the Count," and spending another day with Anna and Smith as they "explored the woods and bogs & flats" around the Loeb property. Anna Loeb was a kindred spirit; she shared Leopold's love for nature and had a bird garden in the yard of her Chicago home.[53]

Not all of Leopold's time could be spent birding, however. He and Loeb were sharing part of their summer with Hamlin Buchman, another University of Chicago student. The three had driven up to Charlevoix together, and along the way, they had stopped in a hotel for the night. Buchman was nonplussed when the next morning he found out that the pair had climbed out of a window to avoid paying the bill.[54] Buchman recalled of their dynamic that "Loeb was the bright, initiative one, always planning little stunts to injure someone, while Leopold, calm and really the superior in intellect, followed along because he worshiped Loeb's individuality."[55] It would not take long before Buchman's strained relationship with the pair would be pushed beyond the breaking point.

Once the group arrived at the estate, Leopold and Loeb had beds made up for them on a screened second-floor sleeping porch at the end of the boys' wing to take advantage of the cool breezes blowing in from the lake. It was on this porch that one night Loeb got up and joined Leopold in his bed. There, naked or nearly so, they were found by Buchman.[56]

According to Buchman, shortly after he saw the two in bed together, they invited him out for a boat ride. He accepted, and it is important to note, as the rumor goes, that Buchman had told them that he did not swim. Leopold and Loeb set off on the lake with their reluctant passenger and, once they determined they were far enough from shore, capsized the unstable canoe. They apparently assumed that Buchman would drown and hoped to pass off the incident as a tragic accident. But saying he didn't swim and not being able to swim were different things, as Buchman thwarted their murder plan by swimming back with them.[57]

When confronted with the story years later, Leopold said, "I had to smile over that story," explaining that Buchman had been on the University of Chicago's swim team, while he was an "abominable swimmer," which would have made for a ridiculously flawed murder attempt.[58] A reasonable explanation, except Buchman was celebrated for his victories in sprints and hurdles when he did track at the University of Chicago; he was never on their swim team.[59] Leopold's teenage prowess as a swimmer remains unconfirmed, though in later life he swam fairly often and even learned to skin-dive.[60]

Attempted murder or not, Buchman went to Loeb's eldest brother, Allan, with his story about finding the two in bed together. Loeb denied the claims vehemently, so Allan chewed Buchman out and he was ordered to leave the estate.[61] Upset by the entire fiasco, Buchman did so, but he also began to complain to his friends about the over-friendly teenagers. If the murder attempt did occur, he apparently did not mention it to anyone until after the pair made headlines for a more successful murder scheme. Perhaps he thought it was an accident until he realized what the pair were capable of. Regardless of the actions they took after they had been walked in on, the fact remained that the relationship Leopold and Loeb had been guarding had suddenly become jarringly exposed to the light.

Before the discovery, though their sexual relationship had only been going on for a few months, Leopold had become completely attached to Loeb. As one psychiatrist put it: "For Leopold, Loeb came gradually to personify the ideal object for a kind of poetic realization of his aberrant sex-drive, which would make this burden less [in]tolerable."[62] His sexuality was no longer simply a source of guilt, but also led him to intense joys shared with a boy whom he believed "not only approached perfection, but far surpassed it."[63]

The relationship was so important to him that he would occasionally tell friends and family members that if they were dying he would not cross the room to save them—that honor was reserved for only three people: his mother, Loeb, and the third he left a mystery.[64] Loeb was certainly flattered by the attention; when Leopold praised Loeb's intelligence it "pleased him tremendously and endeared Leopold to him."[65] Just as Leopold had found in Loeb a best friend and sexual partner, Loeb had found the smart and loyal confidant and partner-in-crime that he had longed for all through childhood.

3

WILD LIVES

In the midst of their summer together, marred by Buchman's discovery, the sixteen-year-olds decided to move away from home and continue their schooling at the University of Michigan.[1] Loeb was eagerly anticipating the change, as he found the University of Chicago too similar to high school and living at home under his parent's watch overly restricting.[2] As Leopold planned his transfer, some friends were concerned about his increasingly obvious obsession. When one told Leopold that Loeb was "glib, superficial, and lied to impress others. Leopold kept insisting I didn't understand Loeb."[3]

Truthfully, Leopold knew Loeb's flaws better than most. He was aware that beneath his friendly demeanor Loeb was frequently two-faced, a habitual liar and kleptomaniac who stole even from Leopold. Yet each of these facts Leopold willfully twisted so he saw only assets in these apparent defects, describing Loeb as "the most wonderful man in the world."[4]

Putting a damper on Leopold's plans, at the end of summer he developed scarlet fever and was unable to move to Michigan at the beginning of the semester.[5] He claimed that at home in his sickbed he had sex with a woman for the first time, or in his words: "I 'lost my cherry' to a trained nurse."[6] Strangely, another teenage boy in the neighborhood also reported being "sexually educated" by a nurse while he had scarlet fever around the same time as Leopold.[7] Leopold's mother also took sick about this time, so Birdie moved in to take care of her and the household along with day and night nurses.[8]

Leopold made it to school in late September, but just two weeks after he arrived Leopold returned to Chicago to be by his mother's side. He was there with his siblings and father when she died in her bedroom on October 17 at fifty-two years old.[9] Her death floored Leopold. The steady, comforting, and unconditionally loving presence she had created in his life had been ripped away, leaving him untethered. Leopold's parents criticized public displays of emotion, but after his mother's death, Leopold strove to push this idea even further.[10] As his love for his mother had made her passing that much harder, he decided that emotions only led to suffering, and as a hedonist he wanted to eliminate his emotional reactions completely.[11]

Though he had already been an atheist for several years, he attributed the death of his mother to take with it all of his considerations of the existence of God. Frankly Leopold declared: "If there were a God, he would not have taken my mother from me at the time when I needed her most."[12] He was not completely immutable in his spirituality; he consulted a medium in the hopes of communicating with Florence's spirit, but judging by his continuing disbelief in the supernatural, this was not a success.[13]

By the time Leopold returned to campus, he was surprised to find that, though they lived only three blocks from each other, Loeb was avoiding him.[14] When confronted, Loeb revealed that rumors about their relationship had spread, and this was his way of combating them.[15] This was especially important because that fall Loeb was rushing Zeta Beta Tau (ZBT), one of the few Jewish fraternities on campus.[16] It was Loeb's potential fraternity brothers who told Loeb about the rumors and advised him against associating with Leopold.

When the fraternity called him, Allan Loeb traveled to campus and assured the fraternity council that nothing untoward had happened.[17] The fraternity members largely believed that Loeb was not guilty of anything. With their limited understanding of homosexuality they assumed that since he liked sports, was not effeminate, and was always up for going out with girls, he must be straight. They decided that Leopold, who was often sullen and acted as if he were too good for them, should be avoided whether the rumors were true or not. Before he left, Allan cautioned his brother not to spend so much time with Leopold, and to be sure to avoid being seen alone together.[18]

Leopold and Loeb agreed it would be best if they were never seen in public in Ann Arbor without someone else present, so if they wanted to see a play or movie together, they would invite another friend along as a chaperone. They got drunk together several times and once Leopold rented a car and they drove to Detroit so they could have a night out away from suspicious eyes.[19] Hoping to allay the rumors and fit in, Leopold was sometimes intimate with prostitutes, but if he wanted to reach orgasm he had to fantasize that he was raping the girl,[20] or having sex with another man, typically with Loeb.[21]

Both teenagers policed themselves carefully and after several months of consideration, ZBT decided that Loeb would make an acceptable member. On February 25, 1922, Loeb and five others were initiated into the fraternity during a special ceremony paired with the tenth anniversary of the chapter.[22]

Despite the rumors surrounding his appointment, Loeb was well liked by his fraternity brothers. He lent notes to friends struggling in their classes,[23] and ZBT member Max Schrayer was won over by his eagerness to help out with household chores and participate in their social events and interfraternity sports teams. "By the time he graduated two years later, I really liked him," Schrayer admitted. "He was a wonderful kid."[24]

At sixteen Loeb was nicknamed "Drunken Dick," and bets were sometimes taken if, on any given afternoon when he stumbled into the frat house, he was drunk or not.[25] With that alcohol came belligerence; he sometimes tried to fight waiters if drunk enough, and once walked into a café, punched a customer in the stomach, knocked down another who walked with canes, and then promptly passed out.[26] Most of his brothers seemed to take this behavior in stride, but he was once censured by the fraternity council for his drunkenness.

While most of Zeta Beta Tau accepted Loeb, they were right to be wary of Leopold for reasons beyond homophobia. "There was intra-racial prejudice," Leopold explained. "Fellows like me didn't join a Jewish fraternity, we were prejudiced against the fellows who did."[27] According to Leopold, joining a fraternity that accepted both Jews and Gentiles was seen as acceptable, but usually only "socially inferior" lower-class Jews joined exclusively Jewish frats.[28]

While he considered Jewish fraternities tacky, most non-Jewish fraternities still had racial discrimination written into their constitutions.[29] Campus vaudeville shows sometimes featured "Jewish impersonations" billed alongside caricatured routines mocking the Chinese, which would have been especially topical as both Jewish and Chinese exchange students made up prominent minority groups on Michigan's campus in the 1920s.[30] With Jewish organizations out of the question and aware that he "couldn't get into a white man's fraternity," Leopold was left with few options besides the "self-satisfied clique" of other Jewish non-fraternity students he hung around with.[31]

Leopold barely took part in campus events, and classmates recalled that "he openly declared his desire to get back to Chicago," and "adopted a sneering attitude toward the university, his courses and his professors. Except for a very small circle of friends, he was disliked by most of his fellow students."[32] Brooding over his ill fortune, when Leopold needed someone to blame, he could turn to a very easy target: Hamlin Buchman. For it was Buchman, he and Loeb assumed, who must have started the rumors by telling people about finding them in bed together. He could not act out against anti-Semitism, or the quality of his education, and he had already mentally killed God, so the only other source against which he could turn his anger seemed to be Buchman.

In private retaliation, Leopold and Loeb went so far as to plan Buchman's murder that winter. Much like their preparation for a later crime, the teenagers discussed using a chisel, rope, and guns to subdue and kill their former friend.[33] Leopold hoped that he could act out some of his war-inspired fantasies by strapping Buchman to a table and raping him before his death.[34] In the end the pair didn't go through with their plans, never able to figure out a way to harm Buchman that would not immediately point back to them and their well-known motive for wanting him gone.

But life was not all murder planning and relationship drama. Outside of class Leopold connected with Michigan's museum curator, Norman Asa Wood, who in 1903 had discovered the breeding range of the increasingly rare bird, the Kirtland's Warbler, and taken some of the only known nesting specimens. As winter warmed to spring and the migration began, Leopold sometimes filled in to give ornithological lectures in Wood's place.[35] He was often in the local forests and fields, adding birds to his ever-growing collection. But birding he could do just as easily back in the Chicago parks he knew so well. Seeking to escape the scrutiny around his relationship and a campus he disdained, Leopold returned to Chicago in the summer of 1922. Loeb remained behind to finish his schooling in Ann Arbor.

Following that disastrous year, Leopold spent the summer months back home studying Sanskrit and teaching ornithology to groups of women and children with his friend George Porter Lewis.[36] Restlessly seeking some kind of change in his life, Leopold looked into beginning law school in Chicago but did not have nearly enough credits. Desperately, he asked if he could stop school altogether to spend eighteen months traveling abroad. His family denied the request and with few other options, Leopold conceded to staying home for another year.[37]

In the fall Leopold returned to the University of Chicago, and with his required classes mostly squared away he was able to focus on his interests: eleven of his thirteen classes that year related to foreign languages and he joined the university's Italian club.[38] He imagined his knowledge of several languages made him seem impressive, and if they were especially obscure or even dead, all the better. Practicality meant nothing to him: "Leopold's father tried to persuade him to study Spanish rather than Italian, pointing out that American trade with Latin America was expanding and Spanish might prove useful, but to no avail—Leopold insisted on learning Italian so he could read Dante in Italian."[39]

As Leopold adjusted to life back in the city, he was surrounded by family. All his brothers were again gathered under the same roof, and after his morning lectures he would go to Birdie's for lunch.[40] Since his mother's death "he tended to think of [Birdie] to a certain extent as replacing his mother."[41] He didn't completely forget Florence though, getting into the habit of visiting her grave before he went birding in the mornings.[42] After the continuous stressors of Michigan, he was able to relax, move forward with his studies, and take pleasure in things again.

Nostalgia can be a singularly powerful emotion, and perhaps no one was more susceptible to looking at the past through rose-colored glasses than Nathan Leopold. As he settled into old age, Leopold chose the year 1923 as the pinnacle of his life. "That year," Leopold reflected four decades later, "the year I graduated from college, EVERYTHING seemed to turn out just right for me."[43] This is not surprising when contrasted against what 1924 would bring. In 1923 he was still eighteen, free, and seemed to have the world at his feet.

Starting his year off right, he met a girl named Susan Lurie at the South Shore Country Club's Washington Prom, a formal dance held on George Washington's birthday. He had arrived with another date, but was intrigued by Lurie and called on her the following week.[44] As they became acquainted he asked her for dates with increasing frequency, and as she was also attending the University of Chicago they would sometimes meet for lunch when they were both on campus. Over their meals Leopold would explain his philosophical ideas, perform memory tricks, and practice French with his new friend.

Lurie seemed taken with Leopold as well. She was not oblivious to his lack of tact, explaining that other students "thought he was 'ritzie,' conceited. He was not too popular. I have always said that 'Babe' Leopold was 'ritzie,' but I have always added that he had something to be 'ritzie' about. His is a superior intellect."[45] She recalled that when they finished a conversation, he would often trace their way over it again, analyzing why the talk had flowed in a particular manner.

Leopold and Lurie's exact relationship is unclear; in 1924 Lurie in sisted they had only been school friends and Leopold said he had never been attracted to women, only going out with them because it was the socially acceptable thing to do.[46] But in Leopold's autobiography he claimed he had been "head over heels in love" and had made tentative marriage proposals.[47] He did develop a fixation on her that lasted the rest of his life, so maybe he really had been in love, or perhaps she became a symbol of a more conventional path his life could have taken.

On March 20 Leopold was elected to Phi Beta Kappa, an elite honor society for those with outstanding academic records. Though he claimed indifference and stated that he only applied for the group because his mother had wanted it, he was quite proud of the honor.[48] The group's motto, "philosophy is the governor of one's life," likely pleased him as well. Perhaps as a reward for this achievement, after classes ended Nathan Sr. sent Leopold to Florida and Cuba with his fellow Phi Beta Kappa classmate Henry Hirsch. Off the coast of Miami on a boat named "The Tramp," the young men went deep-sea fishing. Leopold was ecstatic when he caught a sailfish, immediately sending it to be mounted.[49] By night the teenagers barhopped and visited Cuban brothels.[50]

After his return from the sun-soaked southern beaches, Leopold graduated on May 20 with honors, Birdie and Nathan Sr. watching proudly from the crowd.[51] Despite buckling down on his studies during his final semester, Loeb was not granted any honors, but he managed to create a stir as he would be receiving his diploma just a week after his eighteenth birthday, making him the youngest graduate in the University of Michigan's history.[52]

An editorial in Michigan's student newspaper predicted: "For the next few years [the graduates] will disappear, merged into the vast personnel of an exacting society. Then gradually here and there the names of a chosen few will begin to stand out on the horizon of accomplishment, and Michigan's class of '23 will have its celebrities."[53] How true that would prove in less than a year, though Loeb would not be the kind of celebrity the university hoped to be associated with.

During Loeb's graduation ceremony Leopold was about 170 miles north, starting his summer with a discovery. After a failed trip to find nesting Kirtland's Warblers the previous year, Leopold and his friends James Watson, Sidney Stein Jr., and his cousin Henry Steele Jr. journeyed to central Michigan once again. This time it was earlier in the season, and they had plenty of time to search. After long periods of observation, Leopold located a heavily concealed nest on the ground.

James McGillivray, of the State Conservation Commission, agreed to take video footage of the birds. This video can still be seen: the group laughing and speaking silently, before cutting to Leopold laying on pine needles, feeding horse flies to a baby warbler.[54] During the trip Leopold sent a postcard to his friend and sometime ornithology class assistant Katherine Friedman, expressing his excitement that they "took a moving picture of bird feeding young and eating flies from my hand you won't believe this."[55]

On June 22 the group was "forced, much against our will, to leave the area."[56] Leopold did not explain why, but before he left he went back to the first nest they had found and collected everything: the two adults and four nestlings along with the nest itself, and a third adult warbler to make into a study skin. This was illegal, as Kirtland's Warblers were endangered, and Leopold failed to mention his prizes in the article he was to write up, though he did sadly note that "It is greatly to be feared that *Dendroica kirtlandi* may soon be another of the American birds on the extinct list."[57] Not overly put out that he had aided in that grim prediction, Leopold sent the group to Ashley Hine at Chicago's Field Museum, where Hine began making them into a taxidermy piece to rival Norman Asa Wood's group.

As a graduation gift, Leopold's aunt Rae and uncle Samuel Steele took him to Hawaii for most of August. While some of his time was spent typing up his Warbler article, he managed to fit in as many unique experiences around the island as he could.[58] He tried windsurfing and ate seaweed, which made him violently ill, but he didn't regret the experience. In his philosophy everything should be tried at least once to see how much

Nathan Leopold with a Kirtland's Warbler in 1923. Originally published in *The Auk,* January 1924.

pleasure it gave, so he could fairly judge if he should continue to pursue it or not. Needless to say, eating seaweed was not an experience he deemed worth pursuing in the future.

From the outside his life seemed on a rocket upward, with Leopold miles ahead of other young men his age who were only just graduating high school, but he felt listless. Nothing challenged him, and in his mind he had spent his college career "slopping around," pursuing subjects like languages and ornithology for pleasure with no career goal in mind. He devalued his ability in school, declaring it was "ten percent work and study and ninety percent horse shit."[59]

With another school year ahead of him he enrolled in law classes, in preparation for entrance to Harvard Law School the following year. Law was not his choice of profession, but something his father wanted, with the idea that he would become a corporate lawyer and join his brothers working for Morris Paper Mills.[60] With Leopold unable to make up his mind about his future, he acquiesced to his father's wishes. He was promised the motivating prize that before his transfer to Harvard he would be given $3,000 (equivalent to around $52,500 in 2023) to spend on a trip to Europe.

Loeb, who had spent much of his vacation in Charlevoix, returned in the fall and also reenrolled in the University of Chicago, taking graduate courses in history. There had been much publicity at the beginning of the summer touting Loeb's academic achievements, but privately Loeb wondered if his supposed intelligence was merely another piece of his façade. He received only average grades and when tested his intelligence was also average.[61] This academic year he would sign up for only four courses and receive a grade in just one.[62]

As his interest in academia waned, the only area he felt truly adept in was crime. Psychiatrists noted that Loeb felt that "the possessing of knowledge which others do not have is the most thrilling and satisfying experience obtainable because it proves his superiority and displaces his sense of inferiority."[63] Leopold felt much the same, but while he chased this feeling by accumulating languages and esoteric knowledge, Loeb committed crimes and then mingled with those trying to solve them, happy to know that he had information that others desperately wanted.

After his long drought of serious crimes during his Michigan years, Loeb was ready to reconnect with his former partner-in-crime and get back to his favorite hobby. With the bulk of the rumors about their relationship left behind them in Michigan, he and Leopold were again free to publicly acknowledge their friendship. Though Leopold wasn't a member, they both regularly attended lunches and dances at Chicago's ZBT frat house and again began gambling as partners, in addition to their less publicized activities.[64]

Once again Loeb had Leopold drive them around so they could throw bricks through windows and burn down shacks. They also began breaking into people's homes, each location carefully monitored beforehand, and stealing things they had no use for, like vacuum cleaners and piano benches.[65] Leopold gave his full participation, but began to feel that "it was rather foolish and monotonous."[66] Later Leopold would compare planning and participating in crimes with Loeb to Loeb going on birding trips with him: sometimes friendship involved doing things you weren't interested in just because your friend liked it.[67]

But even with less external pressure than before, their relationship was still far from easy. Because of their volatile personalities as well as the uncomfortable knowledge that they were so deeply in each other's confidences, each was afraid of the blackmail material the other had on him. The probability of blackmail was unlikely as they were complicit in many of each other's crimes, but it did not stop occasional flares of paranoia. Following heated arguments, they even contemplated killing each other to ensure the truth would never get out. Loeb once tried hinting to another friend about the possibility of committing crimes together, hoping to replace Leopold as his accomplice, but the friend did not take the bait and Loeb returned to Leopold. Their arguments were invariably followed by affectionate reconciliations, psychiatrists noting that "their quarrels and their makings up might easily be likened to similar phenomena between two lovers."[68]

In October 1923 Leopold and Loeb had one of these potentially relationship-ending fights, this time about New Year's Eve plans. The fight began when Leopold found out that, though they had agreed to spend the evening together, Loeb planned to stand him up for a double date with their mutual friend Richard Rubel and a couple of girls.[69] The argument was particularly ill-timed, as it occurred as Leopold was preparing to leave for Harvard University, where he would present McGillivray's film on the Kirtland's Warblers at the annual meeting of the American Ornithologists Union (AOU).

He commented somewhat understatedly of the affair that "we had had a misunderstanding, and we were very formal about it."[70] It appears he treated the entire argument as a series of legal moves, which he laid out exhaustively in a letter to Loeb the day before he left for the conference.

Whether they usually wrote like this to one another, only during arguments, or only when Leopold was starting law school and "full up to the neck with torts," is unclear.[71] He first sought to clear up a minor dispute that had occurred that afternoon. Leopold explained that he had trapped Loeb in his room because earlier that day Loeb had refused to let him out of his car. In Leopold's mind this ensured they remained on "equal footing legally."[72]

With this explained, he moved on to the real heart of his argument, which had devolved away from Loeb standing Leopold up. Loeb had accused Leopold of breaking confidence by telling Rubel that Loeb had refused to change the New Year's date with the girls when Leopold only told Rubel what he *assumed* Loeb had done. Leopold had initially apologized for this, but he had since confirmed with Rubel that he was right, so he was arguing that the apology he made was rendered void. Leopold was leaving it to Loeb to react to his retraction of the apology, telling Loeb he could "break friendship, inflict physical punishment, or anything else you like, or on the other hand, continue as before."[73]

Though the decision was Loeb's, Leopold cautioned him that if their relationship ended, they should be prepared to appear friendly when they met in public. The rumors had never completely faded, and he feared that if they shifted suddenly from regular contact to ignoring each other, their friends would gossip that there had been "a falling out of a pair of cocksuckers."[74] For his peace of mind during the conference, he requested that Loeb give his answer before he left the next day. He assured Loeb that "your decision will of course have no effect on my keeping to myself our confidences of the past."[75]

Loeb obliged the request and agreed to maintain their relationship. Leopold was able to enjoy the conference in the knowledge that a happy reunion with Loeb could be anticipated once he returned. In Harvard's Heath Hall he gave a thirty-minute presentation showing McGillivray's Warbler footage and speaking about his experience finding and interacting with the birds. The few films shown that week were the real stars; in a time before cheap commercial film equipment the AOU's secretary enthused that "It was indeed a treat to see moving pictures of such rare species as the Laysan Rail, Laysan Finch, and Kirtland's Warbler."[76] McGillivray's work was praised and Leopold's article on the warblers was published by *The Auk* in its following issue.

As Leopold received recognition for his ornithology, deeper issues simmered beneath the surface, highlighted by a letter Leopold wrote to Loeb while on a train heading to the conference:

I am going to add a little more in an effort to explain my system of a Nietzschean philosophy with regard to you. It may have occurred to you why a mere mistake in judgment on your part should be treated as a crime, when on the part of another it should not be so considered. Here are the reasons.

In formulating a superman, he is, on account of certain superior qualities inherent in him exempted from the ordinary laws which govern ordinary men. He is not liable for anything he may do. Whereas others would be, except for the crime that it is possible for him to commit—to make a mistake.

Now, obviously any code which conferred upon an individual or upon a group extraordinary privileges without also putting on him extraordinary responsibility would be unfair and bad. Therefore, an übermensch is held to have committed a crime every time he errs in judgment, a mistake excusable in others.[77]

As Leopold's letter makes clear, the ornithologist's defiant adolescent philosophies had by this time solidified into seriously dangerous convictions. As Leopold used the concept of Nietzsche's übermensch to encourage Loeb to live as if he existed outside of the law, it seems inevitable that the pair would eventuate in disaster.

II

CRIME

4

PLANNING

Shortly after their reconciliation following the fight over New Year's, Loeb proposed committing a somewhat more ambitious robbery than usual, this time of the ZBT house in Michigan. He imagined that he and Leopold would have a laugh hearing his fraternity brothers complaining about their losses and Leopold agreed to help with the stipulation that they also rob a fraternity of his choosing.[1]

On the evening of November 10, the two drove more than two hundred miles to Ann Arbor, planned specifically so they would arrive in the early morning following a home football game. They hoped that the fraternity members and their guests would be sound asleep after a night of drinking and that the guests would leave around extra money for them to steal.[2] The first house they broke into was Zeta Beta Tau, disguised with masks and armed with revolvers, rope, and a taped chisel. Their weapons proved unnecessary; everyone was asleep and they met no resistance while creeping around the house. The burglars nabbed $74 (equivalent to around $1,300 in 2023) and swiped personal items they found lying around the first floor, including watches, medals, and an Underwood portable typewriter.[3]

Once they were out, with the loot stored in the car, Loeb hesitated over attempting to rob the fraternity which Leopold had chosen. Leopold insisted they try to finish the rest of the plan and Loeb reluctantly complied.[4] They broke into the second house but didn't get far before hearing snoring and retreating, grabbing only a camera on the way out.[5] Both were in a foul mood as they returned to the car and began the long drive home.

Along the way the pair fought: Loeb upset because Leopold hadn't listened to him about calling it quits after ZBT, ruining a nice night; Leopold for what he saw as cowardice, and Loeb going back on his word for not wanting to rob the fraternity Leopold had selected. They argued heatedly and it seemed yet again that their relationship would end, but they valued the friendship too much to lose it. Instead, they decided to analyze what each wanted from the other and work out how to make sure both of their needs were being met.

Loeb suggested for his side of the bargain that Leopold would follow certain orders without question. They agreed that Loeb's commands would not be used for trivial matters and that he would never instruct Leopold to do anything that would make him appear foolish to his family or friends.[6] In return, Leopold proposed that they should have sex three times every two months. Sometime later they fought again and this term was readjusted to one round of sex for each crime they committed together.[7] This was necessary because of the very different feelings each had about the physical side of their relationship.

Where Leopold was very sexually preoccupied, fantasizing and masturbating sometimes three times a day, Loeb claimed he never masturbated, was concerned about his potency, and said of sex: "I could get along easily without it."[8] A psychiatrist noted that Leopold, "in order to assure himself of the permanency of their relationship endeavored in various ways to elicit a pleasurable emotional response from Loeb in connection with their sex intimacies. But this was never successful and only gave Loeb the added feeling that he was sexually 'no good.'"[9]

Both agreed to follow the terms until Leopold left for Europe and then Harvard. As one psychiatrist noted: "This understanding did not materially change their relations, but formulated what had practically been existing before."[10] Within the newly mapped confines of their relationship, "each came to realize that the cessation of their sexual intimacy would also put a stop to their criminal activities."[11] Though the pair may have remained friends without the criminal or sexual components, their relationship would have become lopsided if one had conceded their pleasure for the other. So they continued, each taking part in something they found somewhat unpleasant for the benefit of having a partner to share in an activity that they loved.

With the promise of an obedient partner for the foreseeable future, Loeb began to look ahead to their next big crime. As they continued driving home, "he stated to Leopold that these petty matters they had been indulging in were not sufficient to demonstrate that they were real criminals."[12] Therefore Loeb suggested that they should commit a perfect crime. One that left no evidence, would be big enough to be in the papers and so clever that they would never be caught, going down in the annals of history as a famous unsolved case.

At this point Loeb's idea was fairly amorphous; he just had ambitions to pull off a job bigger than anything he'd done before. First, Loeb proposed that they kidnap and kill a former fraternity brother named William whom Loeb disliked.[13] Loeb relished the idea, but after several discussions, they determined that William was an ill-suited victim. Logistically he didn't work well for their plan, being far away at school and larger than both of them, therefore difficult to overwhelm and carry, so they discarded him as a possibility.[14]

With a specific person out of the picture, the plan evolved on its own, with an empty spot where the victim would be. An intricate ransom scheme began to take shape, with twists and turns to avoid the police and a sizable monetary prize for each of them upon completion. The ransom aspect narrowed the potential field of victims, honing their focus on rich families. Murder was kept in for the simple reason that it would be safer for them if their victim could not identify them later. With these parameters in place, more victims were proposed, including members of their own families. Their fathers were dismissed because with them dead it would be more difficult for the families to get together a ransom. A child would be preferable, someone easy to overwhelm, with a rich family desperate to get them back.

It was only logical, to them, that Loeb's ten-year-old brother, Tommy, was next proposed as a victim. Though they reportedly didn't take this suggestion seriously, they talked through the possibility and decided that the heightened scrutiny on the family following Tommy's disappearance would not allow Loeb to come and go as he pleased. This would prevent him from enacting the ransom plan and destroying evidence, so Tommy and their other siblings were taken out of consideration.[15] Loeb suggested their mutual friend Richard Rubel as a victim, anticipating an intense satisfaction in the idea that he would likely be asked to be a pallbearer for someone he had murdered. But, as with their family members, they feared that if Rubel disappeared they may be brought in for questioning, which would again restrict their freedom of movement. And, always with an eye on the prize, because "Dick Rubel's father was so tight we might not get any money from him."[16]

During one of their discussions, Leopold suggested they choose a young girl, so he could secure her to a table and rape her before killing her. He had enjoyed ruminating on such rape fantasies since the war, and admitted that "The idea of nailing anybody to something appealed to me tremendously."[17] He believed he would get pleasure out of rape that he wasn't anticipating finding in kidnapping or murder.[18] Loeb, uncomfortable with the idea of stealing a kiss from a woman, let alone raping one, dismissed this idea and insisted that their target must be a young boy.[19] He reasoned that boys were granted more freedom than girls, making them easier to abduct unnoticed. As for rape, he said it had no place in a kidnapping plot; rape was its own crime and not a perfect one anyway.[20] Leopold would have to content himself with kidnapping and murder.

With their victim profile set, several names of young heirs in the neighborhood were batted around, including Samuel Harris Jr., Johnny Levinson, and a grandson of Julius Rosenwald's.[21] As for the method of murder, this was discussed just as thoroughly. Leopold was in favor of using ether to suffocate their victim, borrowing the same method he sometimes applied on large birds, as it would be bloodless and simple. Eventually, in the interest of keeping them equally culpable, they decided that one of them would knock their victim unconscious and then they would kill him together. A length of rope would be wrapped around the victim's neck, then each would grab an end and pull until they were sure the boy had died. They both "anticipated a few unpleasant minutes in strangling him," but it was hardly sufficient to scare them off the plan.[22]

To dispose of the body, Leopold suggested a culvert in a forest preserve on the extreme south side of the city that he often passed while birding. There they assumed the body would lie in the water long enough to completely disguise the identity, but in case it was found quickly, they would disfigure him themselves. They argued about the benefits of hydrochloric versus sulfuric acid for the task, and in addition to his face, Loeb suggested they also pour acid on his genitals. One of his brothers had a peculiarly shaped penis, and he reasoned the victim may be able to be recognized similarly.[23]

They developed their plan slowly over several months, the pair meeting up several times a week to discuss and test for weak spots in their scheme. Leopold sometimes tried to stall, introducing roadblocks and problems for Loeb to solve to keep them talking rather than acting and "showed so little interest at times that Loeb would criticize him."[24] The crime was to be risky and the killing slightly unpleasant, but keeping his agreeable relationship going with Loeb was more important than worries of apprehension. As for the value of human life, that never entered into it.[25] According to one friend, Leopold justified this planning aloud in the fall of 1923:

> He said that one could do anything as long as it gave him pleasure, as long as it would at no time prove a boomerang and give him displeasure. In fact, he made the statement one afternoon that if it gave him

pleasure to go out and murder someone it would be perfectly all right in his philosophy to go out and murder a person, provided of course he were not apprehended for the murder and forced to suffer punishment.[26]

In between all the plotting, Leopold's life continued as normal. He started law school and began receiving tutoring for the Harvard entrance exams he was set to take the following spring.[27] Making friends with other law students, Leopold hosted regular study sessions, where the group would go over cases and Leopold would produce notes that were handed out at the end of the evening.[28] With his friend Leon Mandel II, he began translating some sixteenth-century Italian smut, but they received little support from the university and abandoned the project after a few pages.[29] That winter Leopold started getting headaches and was prescribed a simple pair of tortoiseshell reading glasses to reduce eyestrain. He wore them for a few months, then set them aside once the headaches ceased. Later he said with a smile: "I wish I had not gotten them."[30] With the start of the spring migration, Leopold began teaching his annual classes a few times a week to groups of women and children around the Chicago area.

Between his studies Leopold made time for girlfriends as well; he escorted Susan Lurie to dances and visited her at swim practice. Helen Rose, future Academy Award–winning costume designer, recalled that Leopold courted her by bringing her books instead of chocolates like the other boys did, specifically a book on costumes and the poetry volume *India's Love Lyrics*.[31] She was not the only girl Leopold gifted that particular poetry book to; he advised a friend that "if properly recited it never fails to accomplish results with an impressionable young girl."[32] Despite Leopold's bravado, Rose recalled that he had always been a perfect gentleman, which she admitted in hindsight probably should have tipped her off about his attraction to women, or lack thereof.[33]

Unbeknownst to the girls, Leopold was committing petty crimes with Loeb on the nights they weren't out dancing, followed by gratification of Leopold's side of their agreement. If he was enough of a gentleman not to make advances on his girlfriends, he showed no such prudishness with Loeb. Following their crimes "Loeb would pretend to be drunk, then [Leopold] would undress him and then he would almost rape him and would be furiously passionate."[34]

Discussions about the murder continued throughout the winter and into early spring, but the challenge of how to safely acquire the ransom eluded them. Finally, in March, Loeb proposed that the father of the victim could throw the ransom from a moving train.[35] That way he and Leopold could wait in a car along the tracks and at a specific location the victim's father would throw a package containing the money toward them, and faster than the police would be able to stop the train or reach them, they would be speeding away, the money safe and their perfect crime complete.

They tested their scheme several times, figuring out which train and landmark to use so their victim's father would know when to throw the money, where it would land, and how easy that area would be to escape from once the package was retrieved. In late April Loeb brought a wad of rolled-up newspapers, about the size and weight they hoped the ransom bundle would be, onto a train to Michigan City, Indiana. He went to the back of the train, waited until he had passed a large brick factory with "CHAMPION" painted on the side, counted to ten, then threw the bundle as far as he could. Leopold was waiting in his car on a side road close to where they had anticipated the papers would land and watched the bundle sail into the grass.[36] With this last problem solved, it was time to start preparing in earnest.

They went on several dry runs as their plan was formalized, driving the entire length of their route several times, lacking only the victim to kill. They decided they would need to rent a car rather than use one of their own. For this purpose, they created the persona of Morton D. Ballard, a twenty-three-year-old traveling salesman from Peoria, Illinois.[37] Ballard would be set up with a bank account and registered to a hotel so they could enter that address on the rental car form. They also created another false identity, Louis Mason, as a reference who could back up that Ballard was reliable enough to rent an automobile to.

Ballard was named specifically to avoid sounding Jewish, to divert suspicion from the pair if the car happened to be traced. The name itself was inspired by a pocket watch Loeb had stolen from ZBT, engraved with the initials of Loeb's fraternity brother, Morris D. Blumenthal. To add an extra layer of reality to the façade, Leopold carried the watch when he pretended to be Ballard.[38] While much of this was likely unnecessary, this kind of planning was what Loeb loved best: "The more intricate and involved a series of actions was, the better he liked it," Leopold recalled.[39]

On May 7, just a little over a week after Leopold had received his passport in anticipation of his trip to Europe, he and Loeb began to set their plan in motion. While Leopold created an account at the Hyde Park State Bank, Loeb registered for a room at the Morrison Hotel, both under the Ballard alias. One hundred dollars of Loeb's money was withdrawn and placed in Ballard's account, and they sent letters and deposited a suitcase full of books and clothes in the hotel to give the appearance that the room was being used.[40]

On May 9, Leopold went back to the Rent-A-Car Company and rented a car as Ballard, with his address given as the Morrison Hotel and the mailed letters presented as proof of temporary residence. When the company called the number he'd listed for his character reference, Loeb answered. He'd been waiting in a nearby cigar store by the phone booth, snacking on a box of raisins.[41] He assured the employee that he was Louis Mason and that his associate Mr. Ballard was completely dependable. Leopold successfully rented the car and returned it later that day, mentioning that he might be back along this route again in the near future.

From there, the pair returned to the Morrison Hotel where Loeb found that their room had been tidied, his suitcase taken, and no further mail they sent had arrived. Disturbed, they left without paying and called up the rental car company, asking them to have any mail sent to the Trenier Hotel instead, where they set up a mailing account without reserving a room.[42] Loeb's suitcase, filled with four books he had checked out of the University of Chicago library, his name signed on their check-out slips, remained in the Morrison.

The night before the murder Leopold and Loeb began their final preparations. With Loeb dictating from handwritten notes and Leopold using the typewriter they had stolen from ZBT, they produced the ransom notes, additional instructions, and scripts for the ransom calls they planned to use in the following days. The notes were simply addressed: "Dear Sir," as they had no victim selected, and signed "George Johnson." They loaded their supplies into Leopold's car: sets of train timetables for the ransom, a chisel to knock the boy unconscious, a bottle of hydrochloric acid to disguise his identity, and a rope to strangle him with. All that was missing was a victim.

5

EXECUTION

The weather was cool when Leopold left home on the morning of May 21, driving to campus for a criminal law lecture at eight, then staying for a French lecture with Susan Lurie at nine.[1] At eleven, Leopold picked Loeb up and they drove together to rent their car. Leopold went in, introduced himself as the same Morton Ballard who had rented there previously, and rented a standard dark blue Willys-Knight with no trouble. They met up with both cars in the parking lot of a nearby restaurant and put side curtains on the rented Willys, to ensure them a measure of privacy for the afternoon.[2]

After lunch they drove both cars to the Leopold home where Leopold transferred their supplies from his car to the rental and informed the family chauffeur, Sven Englund, that his brakes needed oiling. Englund went to work on Leopold's car while Leopold and Loeb drove to Jackson Park in the rental to wait until the Harvard School let out for the day. Loeb sat in the passenger seat and wrapped the sharp end of a chisel in tape so he could hold it without cutting his hand when he used the blunt end to knock their victim unconscious.

At 2:15, they parked by the Harvard School and Loeb went out to talk with the playground monitor and some of the children, including potential target ten-year-old Johnny Levinson. They chatted briefly about his baseball game before Loeb went to the front of the school and talked with his brother Tommy.[3] After a few moments Leopold whistled for Loeb and told him of some children playing one street over "that he thought may be possible prospects."[4] A couple of blocks down they saw a group of boys playing in a different lot, Johnny Levinson among them. Johnny's father, Salmon Levinson, was a wealthy lawyer and philanthropist who was a frequent guest in the Loeb home and a good friend of Albert's. Sure that he would pay the ransom, they decided that Johnny would become their victim once he separated from the other boys.

From where they stood, they could not watch the kids without being seen themselves, so Leopold went home and picked up some field glasses he used for birding while Loeb went to a drug store to look up Levinson's address for the ransom note.[5] Tasks accomplished, they came back together and watched the children from the car until they went out of sight farther down an alley. The teenagers waited for them to reappear, and Loeb eventually went down the alley to look for them, but Levinson had disappeared. They drove by his house and to other lots where children played, but were unable to locate the boy again.

With their first target having slipped from their grasp, they began their hunt again. It was then, after more than two and a half hours of searching, that they saw fourteen-year-old Robert "Bobby" Franks walking down Ellis Avenue alone.[6] As Leopold would write forty years later: "Fourteen is a wonderful age to be. You stand on the threshold of adulthood, with all the experiences and all the joys of maturity ahead of you."[7] About to snuff out all those joys and experiences, Leopold turned the car around and Loeb got into the back seat, as they slowly headed down the street toward the unsuspecting boy.

Bobby Franks. Originally published in *My Blessed Little Pal* by Jack Franks, 1926.

As with most retellings of crimes, the victim tends to get lost in the intrigue surrounding the criminals, and this book is obviously no exception. Relatively little is known about Bobby Franks that survives in written record. His parents, Flora Griesheimer and Jacob Franks, were married in 1906. Like Nathan Sr., Jacob Franks had dropped out of school to start working as a teenager, and as a young man moved from New York to Chicago and opened several pawn shops with his brothers. With a good eye for real estate investment, Jacob rose from these humble beginnings, buying the Rockford Watch Company in 1901, which greatly increased his fortune and standing within the community. Sometime after the couple married, the Franks converted from Reform Judaism to Christian Science. This religion was becoming popular in America at that time, especially among women, who were allowed prominent roles in the church.

Flora and Jacob had three children: their daughter, Josephine, was born in 1906, their son Jack in 1908, and Bobby in 1909. The growing family bought property on Ellis Avenue in 1911 diagonal to the Loebs, constructing a yellow brick mansion. Bobby grew up playing around the Hyde Park neighborhood, in empty lots used as baseball diamonds and on the Loebs' tennis court, where neighborhood children often congregated to play matches. He was described by friends as a smart kid and a less than stellar athlete with a bit of an ego.[8] He was on the Harvard School freshman debate team and a month previously he had argued against capital punishment and won.[9]

On the afternoon of May 21, he hung around campus to umpire a baseball game after school. He began his walk home just before 5 p.m. and by the time he had gone a block, a dark blue car pulled up alongside him. Richard Loeb leaned forward over the passenger seat and greeted him. Bobby knew Loeb; they sometimes played tennis together, and as another potential victim said, both Leopold and Loeb were well known and held up by the neighborhood parents as role models, so "whichever one of their victims they had selected would have accepted a lift home."[10]

Loeb asked Bobby if he'd like a ride and the boy declined, having only a couple more blocks to walk. Loeb urged him to get in, saying he wanted to talk about a tennis racket Bobby had used at the Loeb tennis court recently. He elaborated that he wanted to get one like it for Tommy, who was stuck with a hand-me-down of Loeb's that he feared was too big for him.[11] Bobby obliged and slid into the passenger seat. When asked if he minded if they went around the block, he replied that he didn't.

At around five in the evening, as Leopold turned a corner leading away from the Frankses' home, "Richard placed his one hand over Robert's mouth to stifle his outcries, with his right beat him on the head several times with a chisel."[12] Though stunned, Bobby was not instantly knocked unconscious as they had planned. Instead, he started to bleed and moan, causing Leopold to panic, fearing they would be noticed and apprehended. While Leopold fretted, Loeb pulled Bobby out of view into the backseat, stuffed a rag in his mouth to silence him, and covered him in the lap blanket they had brought along. Bobby soon grew quiet, and once it was clear that he was unconscious, Loeb told Leopold that "it was all right, and joked and laughed, possibly to calm myself, too."[13] They stopped on a dirt road to turn around, and Loeb climbed into the passenger seat again, leaving Bobby, quiet and still, alone in the back.

The kidnappers and their victim drove toward Indiana, then turned down several deserted roads where they parked and Leopold removed Bobby's pants and stockings. Loeb buried Bobby's belt, school pin, spare change, and shoes. His more flammable clothing they kept in the car to burn later.[14] They then drove aimlessly for a while, waiting for dark. While passing the time, they stopped by a roadside sandwich shop where Leopold got out and bought them each a hot dog and root beer, which they enjoyed in the car.[15] Bobby continued to lay silent and motionless in the back, the floor of the car beginning to soak up the blood from his head wounds. While they were stopped, Leopold took the opportunity to call Susan Lurie, reminding her of a date they had later that week.

After dinner they drove around until they decided that it was dark enough and made their way to the spot they had scouted out weeks before. Their destination in the secluded prairie was a culvert that drained between the Hyde and Wolf Lakes and ran beneath a set of railroad tracks on the Illinois side of the Illinois/Indiana border. With the sun setting, they parked on a wide plain several hundred feet from their intended body dump site and took Bobby out of the car.

They used the blanket as a stretcher to carry Bobby closer to the water, where they took the rest of his clothes off.[16] As they undressed him it became obvious that there was no need to strangle him to death: he was already gone. His eyes stared blankly, and when Leopold poured hydrochloric acid over his face, genitals, and an abdominal scar, he lay completely still.[17] Evidently, the rag had blocked Bobby's throat, and shortly after it had been placed in his mouth, he had suffocated to death in the backseat. With one task neither kidnapper had much looked forward to out of the way, they set about disposing of the body.

Leopold put on rubber hip boots, took off his jacket, and carried Bobby's body into the water, Loeb helping to lower it down slowly so it wouldn't splash. While Loeb went upstream to wash the blood off his hands, Leopold pushed Bobby's body as far as he could headfirst into the narrow pipe. When he couldn't push any further, he kicked at the body to wedge it in deeper, then climbed out of the water and took off his boots.[18] Loeb, picking up Leopold's discarded jacket, joined him as he was putting his shoes on, and they walked back to the car together.

During the thirteen-mile trip home they stopped at a drug store to look up the Frankses' address and telephone number, and Leopold called his family to let them know he would be "a trifle late in arriving home."[19] Then they mailed their ransom letter to the Franks family. It began: "As you no doubt know by this time your son has been kidnapped. Allow us to assure you that he is at present well and safe. You need fear no physical harm for him provided you live up carefully to the following instructions."[20]

The rest of the letter forbade the family from contacting the police and detailed the method of getting the $10,000 ransom to the kidnapper, threatening that if the family did not follow the instructions, he would not hesitate to kill their son.

After posting the letter and before it could reach the Frankses' house in the 8 a.m. mail, the killers stopped at a phone booth where Leopold made the first ransom call. He informed Flora that her son had been kidnapped and that further instructions would follow on how the family could get him back. The Franks, who had spent the evening searching the neighborhood for Bobby when he failed to come home, were devastated.

The young killers returned to the Loeb mansion, where they hid the blood-soaked blanket in the Loeb's extensive backyard.[21] They then went down to the basement and burned Bobby's clothes in the furnace. They would have burned the blanket as well, but "it was too large to fit in and would have caused an awful stench."[22] After washing out some of the more obvious bloodstains from the rental car, they parked it in front of an apartment building near the Leopold home, where it would go unnoticed for the night. Leopold used his own car to drive his visiting aunt and uncle home, while Loeb stayed behind to chat with Nathan Sr. When Leopold returned, the pair had a few drinks and talked with Nathan Sr. until he went to bed. They played cards and drank for a while before Leopold drove Loeb home in his car, Loeb tossing the blood-stained chisel out the window on the way.[23] They went to bed in the early hours of the morning and slept soundly.

At eight the next morning Leopold went to class, then picked Loeb up for lunch with Richard Rubel. After lunch they grabbed a "disguise" for Loeb consisting of a dark overcoat, glasses, and his father's hat, which he wanted to wear later that day.[24] They then drove the rented car to the

Leopold garage where they cleaned it more thoroughly. When approached by Sven Englund, the Leopold chauffeur, Loeb told him that they had merely spilled some wine and needed no help in cleaning it up. Englund assumed it was Loeb's car and left them to it.

After the car had been deemed sufficiently cleaned, the pair drove Leopold's car and the rental vehicle into town and attempted to set up the next step of their plan. They had wanted to leave a note for Franks attached to a wastebasket, but the stickers they tried to use didn't hold well and they were afraid the note would be lost before Franks could get there. They threw away the note, which instructed Franks to go to a specific drug store, and decided to just tell him the information themselves over the phone.[25]

At three in the afternoon, Leopold drove Loeb to the Illinois Central train station where Loeb bought a ticket for a train to Michigan City, Indiana. Leopold recalled that on the way "Dick was bubbling over. He even insisted on trying to whistle, he felt so good. But even his good humor didn't enable him to get anywhere near the tune."[26] Loeb boarded the train, left an instruction note for Jacob Franks detailing how he was to get the ransom to them in a box reserved for telegraph blanks, and then got off.[27] As he did, Leopold was calling the Franks home, where he told Jacob Franks that they were sending him a cab and gave him the address to the Van De Bogart and Ross drug store, which he was to give the cab driver. When asked, Leopold refused to repeat the information and hung up.

Once Jacob had arrived at the drug store, Leopold planned to call him with instructions to go to the train station, board the train to Michigan City, and look in the box where he would find their instruction note. The number of notes and sending Jacob to multiple locations was designed to make it harder for the police to follow if they had been informed, and they had planned for the cab to pull up to the station with just enough time for Jacob to board the train. As they were sure that the police would not be able to guard the entire length of track and had no way to communicate to officers not on the train where the ransom was to be thrown, it seemed a foolproof ending to their perfect plan.[28]

After his call with Jacob, Leopold called a cab company and sent a taxi to the Frankses' home. Jacob, who in his distress had missed the exact address for the drug store Leopold had given him, panicked. When the cab driver arrived, he informed the family that he had only been instructed to drive to the Frankses' address, not where to go afterward. Unable to recall the address, Jacob did not take the taxi.

While walking to another phone booth to call the drug store, the murderers saw a newspaper headline announcing that the body of a boy had been found in a swamp. They quickly bought an issue and read the front-page story. A man named Tony Minke, who lived near the railroad, had been walking by the culvert on his way to pick up a watch he was getting repaired. At around nine in the morning he noticed something pale floating a few feet inside a drainage pipe. He flagged down a group of railroad men with a handcart, who helped him pull the body of a young teenager out of the water.

Because his hair covered the wounds from the chisel and the acid, so quickly diluted by water, had only left him slightly discolored, the men assumed that he had drowned while taking an unseasonable swim.[29] They searched the area and found a stocking and a pair of glasses that they assumed belonged to the boy, which they turned over to the police along with the body. Bobby, whom Leopold and Loeb had assumed would not be found for months, if at all, had been in the culvert for around twelve hours.

Loeb was in favor of calling the rest of the plan off, but Leopold "insisted that it could do no harm to call the drug store."[30] It was still possible that the Franks family had not yet identified the body, and may be waiting for further instructions. When Leopold called the drug store they had directed Jacob to, the clerk informed him that there was no one in the store. They tried again from another pay phone with the same result and gave up, their ransom attempt a failure. They returned the rental car, closed the Ballard bank account, and stopped to get a soda before Leopold dropped Loeb off at home.[31]

A few minutes before Leopold had called Jacob Franks with the address, the police called the Frankses' home, letting Samuel Ettelson, the Frankses' friend and lawyer, know that the body of a boy had been found in a swamp. Though the police reported that the boy was found wearing glasses, which Bobby did not own, Bobby's uncle Edwin Gresham went to the coroner's office with a couple of reporters to check just in case. On arrival, Gresham quickly identified the body of his nephew by sight, and more definitively by the enamel buildup on his teeth, a remnant from his childhood battle with rickets.[32] He removed the glasses, which were taken by the police as a possible clue. Jacob Franks was called to the coroner's after his brother-in-law and confirmed that the body that had been found shoved into a pipe beneath the railroad tracks was his youngest son. What had looked at first like a simple drowning had become a murder case and, with a wealthy young victim, the papers made quick work of capitalizing on it.

6

CAUGHT

The days that followed gave Leopold and Loeb the media attention they craved as the Chicago newspapers dedicated their front pages to the crime. Though most of their plan had failed, Leopold and Loeb could not help but enjoy the spectacular fallout. Leopold claimed that "nobody was talking about anything but the crime," but that hardly stopped him and Loeb from reading about it in all the daily newspapers as well.[1] They were able to watch as copycats imitated them: sending threatening letters and a sympathy wreath to the grieving family under the killer's pseudonym of George Johnson.

They were amused when one coroner, soon after the body was found, declared that there was evidence that the boy had been poisoned and raped.[2] Another coroner quickly refuted this statement, saying there was no evidence of either, and in his opinion the death had likely been accidental.[3] However, even the second coroner put into his official report the confusing statement that "the rectum was dilated and would admit easily one middle finger. There was no evidence of a recent forcible dilation."[4] In the current day, coroners understand that muscles relax after death, especially in children. One study showed that 74% of children under eighteen had dilated rectums after death when there had been no assault.[5] But as this was not understood at the time, chief of police Michael Hughes announced: "There is no question in my mind but that the boy was enticed by someone he knew very well to a room near the school and abused . . . after the act took place, they quarreled and Robert threatened to reveal the matter. This, I believe, precipitated the killing."[6]

Going off this theory, the prime suspects in the days following the discovery of the body were two teachers from the Harvard School: Mott Kirk Mitchell and Walter Wilson, both rumored to be gay. The teachers were grilled, had their homes searched, and were treated so poorly they would later sue, another in a rising series of complaints against the use of the "third degree" by Chicago police. The teachers were released after five days, but Mitchell left the school soon after and did not return.

But gay men were not the only ones the police were targeting. Because of the lack of evidence, they chased every lead they could, no matter how unlikely. Newspapers printed false clues: that Bobby had been picked up by a gray Winton, that the ransom letter had been written on a decade-old Corona typewriter, and that George Johnson was described as being very nearsighted, in his thirties, and five feet eleven inches tall.[7] Anyone reported to have been in the area by Wolf Lake, people driving slowly through Hyde Park, or acting in a way neighbors thought suspicious were brought in for questioning.

In his autobiography Leopold reflects on the fullness of his days after the murder; in addition to following the case updates, his foster brother, Bal, had recently gotten engaged, so there were many family dinners and celebratory parties to attend. On top of that were his birding classes, finals, and Harvard admission exams. He had been excited to see if being a murderer changed him, but as he went about his days as normal, he found to his disappointment that it hadn't.[8]

Around noon on the 23rd, Loeb was on campus when he ran into his friend, reporter for the *Chicago Evening American*, Howard Mayer. Newspapers were carrying stories about the botched ransom attempt, including that Jacob Franks had been told to go to a drug store somewhere on 63rd Street. Loeb suggested that they go around to all the drug stores on 63rd to see if they could find the one where the kidnappers called for Mr. Franks. Mayer was hesitant but was talked into it by James Mulroy and Alvin Goldstein, fellow University of Chicago students and reporters for the *Chicago Daily News*.

After trying several stores, Mayer and Loeb walked into the Van De Bogert and Ross drug store. The porter confirmed that there had been two calls for Franks, so Loeb shouted to Goldstein and Mulroy and the three reporters interviewed the employees. When the reporters called up their papers to give the scoop, Loeb begged them to keep his name out of it. Back in the car, Loeb was congratulated on his idea and replied: "Well, that is what comes from reading detective stories."[9]

That afternoon the coroner's inquest into Bobby's death began. Loeb tagged along with Mayer and listened as Jacob Franks, monotone in his grief, described his son's last day.[10] When asked if he had seen Bobby since his disappearance he replied, "About 5 o'clock, at the morgue."[11] Leopold was anxious about how close Loeb was getting to the investigation, but Loeb assured him that he was only having a little fun and no one would suspect him.[12] Leopold couldn't protest too much; though he wasn't leading reporters to clues, he embraced every chance he got to discuss the crime with his family, friends, and professors.

Leopold got a harsh reality check when he picked up a newspaper on the 23rd and read that a pair of glasses had been found near Franks's body. Leopold recognized the photo in the paper and when he was unable to find his pair, he felt sure they were in the hands of the police. After his headaches stopped the previous fall, Leopold had placed the glasses in the breast pocket of one of his suits and forgotten about them.[13] He happened to wear the suit on the day of the murder and either when he removed his jacket to get into the water or when Loeb picked it off the ground to bring it to him, the glasses had slipped out, unnoticed in the dark.[14]

Leopold called Loeb over to discuss if he should claim the glasses or say nothing and hope they couldn't be traced. Because the prescription was so common, Loeb advised Leopold to leave it alone. If he was called in by the police, then he could explain that he had lost them birding. There were records of his visit to the area the weekend before the murder, which Sidney Stein and George Lewis could corroborate. It seemed the safest choice and Leopold was grateful for the advice.[15]

Early on Sunday morning of May 25, Leopold and Loeb met up to destroy the evidence still in their possession. The previous day a newspaper had identified the ransom letters as having come from an Underwood portable typewriter, and it was imperative they get rid of it quickly. As Leopold drove to Jackson Park, Loeb tore off the keys with a pair of pliers. Originally called "Lake Park" because of the abundance of ponds, lakes, and lagoons, emphasizing boat travel and bridges connecting small islands, they thought it the perfect place for evidence disposal. Under cover of darkness, they threw the keys from one bridge and the typewriter in its case from another, into the lagoons below.

They then retrieved the blood-stained car robe from the Loeb grounds and drove to a secluded spot along Lake Michigan. Beneath a mass of logs along the shore was a place where trash had gathered and here the robe was soaked in gasoline and set on fire.[16] They left it to burn and, glasses aside, they assumed they had tied up all the loose ends that could connect them to Franks.

However, with the glasses still in the hands of the police, they concocted an alibi, in case they were brought in for questioning. Leopold favored using the alibi until he left for New York in two weeks, where he'd be catching a cruise ship to Europe, but Loeb believed it would be too suspicious to remember such a mundane day for that long unless they were hiding something. They capped the alibi date for just one week following the crime and agreed that if they were apprehended beyond that they would say they couldn't remember anything in particular they'd done on May 21.

Later that Sunday morning, several police officers parked on Greenwood Avenue and, shaded beneath the porch awning, knocked on Leopold's front door. "We told his father we wanted to talk with him about birds," one officer recalled, "and the father laughed and sent for his son."[17] Still in bed after his late night of evidence disposal, Leopold had to dress before meeting his guests. Once downstairs, they asked him to accompany them to the South Side police station. Hoping to avoid interrogation, he told the officers that he had a birding class to teach shortly. They were insistent, so he had Lewis take the class, but they were more sympathetic when he told them he had a date that afternoon. He was allowed to drive his own car so he could leave more quickly, but to ensure he didn't take off one officer rode with Leopold while the other drove the police car and led them to the South Side station.

Once there, things were rather more friendly. Leopold was asked by the police captain about his ornithology classes and he supplied the names of all the members as well as many of his friends who frequented the area. At the request of the officers, he produced a written statement, declaring he had been visiting the forest preserve for six years and detailed the previous weekend he had spent in the area with Stein and Lewis.[18] Satisfied, the officers thanked Leopold for his help and let him get to his date.

Leopold describes this date in his autobiography: "We rented a canoe and went out on the Desplaines [*sic*] River. . . . [Sue] had brought the blue vellum-covered volume of French poetry I had given her for her birthday the week before. As she read the liquid verses to me, I laid my head in her lap."[19] Though Lurie told reporters of dates she had with Leopold on May 22 and May 28, this supposed blissful Sunday of French poetry down a winding river was not mentioned.

The same afternoon that Leopold gave his statement and was apparently playing Don Juan, the Franks family was laying their son to rest. The family held a private funeral in their home that was nonetheless besieged by reporters and curiosity seekers. After several Christian Science readings, Bobby's classmates bore his small coffin to a waiting hearse. The motorcade journeyed to Rosehill cemetery, where Bobby became the first member of his family to be interred in the Franks mausoleum, photographers shamelessly snapping pictures of a weeping Flora exiting the tomb. While police were concentrating heavily on the case, there seemed no definite leads and no answers for the heartbroken Franks family as they said their goodbyes.

On Wednesday, May 29, after his criminal law lecture, Leopold stayed to chat with his professor, Ernest Puttkammer, in his office. Leopold, under the guise of rhetorical questioning, posed several inquiries about the Franks murder to Puttkammer: If the kidnapper took Franks with the intent to kill him, would that be murder or manslaughter? What if it was an accidental killing during a kidnapping? And what if the abductor had intended to take liberties with the boy and not kill him?[20] Puttkammer assumed that Leopold already knew the answers, but he answered anyway and the pair began to discuss the case and suspects more generally.

Talk turned to the Harvard teachers, who were still the main suspects, and Puttkammer was skeptical when Leopold claimed that Mitchell had tried to solicit students for sex—including one of Leopold's brothers. As Leopold was about to leave he said: "I wouldn't put it past that man, Mitchell; I would like to see them get that fellow." He then turned on his heel, saying "But I don't say he did it," as he walked out.[21]

After his meeting with Puttkammer, Leopold got lunch with Susan Lurie at the nearby Cinderella Ballroom. Leopold bought a couple of papers on the way and in the busy restaurant, the pair spread them on the table. Lurie recalled that as they read of the latest updates in the Franks case, "I said to Babe in a joking way that it would be a good joke for him to go to the police and confess the crime. He said it would be a perfect joke and that I would get the $16,000 reward."[22]

After lunch Leopold returned home and was upstairs when a maid told him that a man named Johnson was at the door asking for him. Leopold came down to where three officers waited and asked deputy Frank Johnson to show some identification, explaining once he had done so that he thought he may have been the George Johnson from the Franks case.[23] Unamused, Johnson informed him they had been asked to take him to talk with State's Attorney Robert Crowe. The glasses, which Leopold was so sure could not be traced, had betrayed him. Upon examination it was found that Leopold's glasses contained a new hinge mechanism that was not yet being widely distributed. Only three glasses with his exact frame, prescription, and hinge had been sold in Chicago, one to an attorney who had been out of town during the crime, one to a woman who was wearing her pair when questioned, and the final pair belonged to one nineteen-year-old ornithologist cum law student: Nathan Leopold Jr.[24]

Leopold tried to postpone the trip, again explaining he had a birding class to teach that afternoon, but the officers were adamant that he come with them now. He recruited Lewis once again and was taken to a suite of rooms the police had rented out on the sixteenth floor of the LaSalle Hotel.[25] Suspects under greater scrutiny were brought to the state's attorney's office, but minor ones were called to hotels to avoid reporters and usually quickly released. Before that, Leopold would have to run the gauntlet. State's Attorney Robert Crowe was eager to find the killer and end the expensive investigation. Aiding him were a team of assistant state's attorneys, including Joseph Savage, John Sbarbaro, and Milton Smith.

As per Leopold's agreement with Loeb to say he could not remember his actions on the 21st if brought in more than a week after the crime, Leopold remained stubbornly forgetful. His interrogators were soon suspicious of this memory lapse; in the few hours they had known him Leopold had demonstrated a truly remarkable memory. He could recall precise details of days that had occurred several weeks before and showed off his skill by memorizing a random list of words and repeating them backward and forward. When it became clear that he couldn't get away with not being able to remember, he relented and told the alibi he and Loeb had prearranged.

His story went that he and Loeb had taken Leopold's car out to lunch and then they went bird watching in Jackson Park. After that, they picked up a couple of girls who refused to put out, and so were dropped off again. They had been drinking all the while, so had dinner at a restaurant instead of going home, Loeb fearing his Prohibitionist parents would detect the alcohol on his breath.[26] They stayed out late, then went to the Leopold house around 10:30 p.m. where the story reconnected with reality.

He was asked to repeat his alibi several times as the police waited for him to trip up, and finally he was shown his glasses. He tried them on and said they indeed looked like his pair; if his weren't at home, he would have sworn that they were his. Crowe had Leopold driven back to his home to find them, and after a thorough search with no results, Leopold's brother Mike assured the officers that Leopold must have dropped them birding. Hadn't he told the family earlier that week that the body had been found near where Leopold had been birding the weekend before?[27] Hoping to get the issue cleared up, Mike said that Samuel Ettelson, the Frankses' lawyer, was a close family friend and could vouch for Leopold's character. He called his home, and when they learned Ettelson was with the Franks, the party made the four-block journey to the Frankses' home.

Trouping into the home of the boy he killed, Leopold explained the mistake the police were making.[28] Ettelson assured the officers that he'd known Leopold all his life; there was no way he was connected with the murder. Regardless, the officers insisted that Crowe was serious about tracking down every lead, no matter how far-fetched. Leopold was taken back to the LaSalle. At this point, Leopold recalled having been completely confident that he would be able to evade justice.[29] The police only had his glasses, which he had an easy explanation for losing, and many witnesses who could attest that he had been birding in the area three days before the murder. Asking for a lawyer, he felt, would only arouse suspicion, and he must continue to give the impression that he had nothing to hide.[30]

That afternoon, after Leopold implicated him in his alibi, Loeb was brought to the hotel and taken to a suite of rooms separate from Leopold's. He was asked to relate what he had done on the 21st and insisted that he couldn't remember, believing Leopold had done the same.[31] No amount of questioning or cajoling could jog his memory.

Crowe continued his interrogation and for a while the tone remained light; Leopold was still articulating himself well and joking occasionally. While his brother was being interrogated, Mike took police officers back to the house to search for more information. Officers combed Leopold's bedroom and study, taking bottles of arsenic, strychnine, and ether from his birding supplies as well as several typing and handwriting samples. When the party went outside, they saw reporters going through Leopold's car, so the police took their turn, uncovering the practice ransom package the killers had tossed from the train, a flashlight, and timetables for the Illinois and Michigan Central railroads.[32]

During their search, police found an interesting letter from Leopold to Loeb among Leopold's things; a handwritten copy of the one he had sent to Loeb after their New Year's fight.[33] The police were suspicious of Leopold's threat to kill Loeb and his assurance that he would continue to keep Loeb's secrets, as well as the references to homosexuality.

When Crowe asked Leopold to explain the use of the word "cock-suckers" in the letter, Leopold said that this referred to gossip their friends were likely to spread about them, rather than their actual relations.[34] One newspaper brushed the word aside, declaring: "A sentence [in the letter] that was regarded as at least peculiar was easily and satisfactorily explained by both. Their manly appearance and evident fearlessness was heavily in their favor."[35] Asked about Hamlin Buchman and the rumors of 1921, Leopold forcefully denied that any of it was true.[36]

After a full night of questioning, in the early morning of May 30, both suspects were taken separately to the state's attorney's office, where they recited their alibis for a stenographer. Following this formality, they were sent to separate jails for the night.[37] Placed in a communal cell, Leopold was unable to sleep. With a drunk taking up the only bench and Leopold refusing to sit on the floor, he instead used the time to take stock of his situation.[38] He reasoned that there was still only circumstantial evidence tying him to the crime and an alibi that could only be repudiated by one other person. As long as Loeb told the alibi story, Leopold reasoned, there was not much more the police could do, and certainly no way for them to find any additional clues.

At nine in the morning Leopold was taken from the cell and allowed to wash and shave before meeting with reporters. They gathered around the teenager, their first look at the figure who was to dominate their columns for the next four months. One described her first impression of Leopold as he sat in his chair before the crowd:

> Caesar-like, he answered each in turn. . . . A pause—long enough to light a cigaret [*sic*]—for Nathan has smoked without stopping—then a swift, decisive answer couched in judicial language, with perhaps a slightly cynical twist and a sudden smile.
>
> For he has a very winning smile, this slim youth of 19. . . . An atheist, yes. But he does not recommend atheism for "hoi polloi." God, he thinks, is a good thing to hold the common people in check.[39]

When asked if he was guilty, he brushed the question off incredulously, responding: "Why should I do anything like that? My father gives me an allowance and I teach three classes in ornithology."[40]

As Leopold was entertaining reporters, Loeb was taken home and his room was searched for incriminating evidence. Howard Mayer had come to cover the story for his paper and joked with Loeb about the mistake the police were making, investigating someone so obviously innocent.[41] Later, when he learned that the teenagers were telling different stories, Samuel Ettelson brought Mayer to the state's attorney's office and talked Crowe into letting Mayer speak to Loeb alone.[42] Once the request had been granted, Loeb assured Mayer of his innocence, saying: "I couldn't, Howie, you know that I couldn't."[43]

Mayer believed him and passed along a message from Leopold: to remember what happened on Wednesday.[44] Loeb, understanding that Leopold had broken their agreement and used the alibi, began to let the assistant state's attorneys draw the story out of him. He hoped that his interrogators would take his reluctance to tell the story as a sign that his alibi was legitimate and that he was embarrassed about his rowdy conduct.

The families of both killers remained in contact during the interrogations, offering fresh clothes and making sure they weren't being mistreated. A brother of Leopold's said: "The idea of Nathan having anything to do with the Franks boy's death is too silly to discuss. . . . We know our brother so well that we are in no way alarmed at his examination by police."[45] Loeb's sister-in-law assured her parents that "Everything is going to come out right, it is bound to, but I would give anything in my power if only those poor innocent boys had been spared the treatment they have received."[46]

The teenagers were interrogated all day without a significant breakthrough. Typewriters had been taken from their homes, but it was quickly proven that they were different machines than the one that had produced the ransom note. All the items taken from the Leopold and Loeb homes could be easily explained as unrelated to the crime. Even the most suspicious clue—that a night watchman had seen a bloody chisel thrown from a red car near the Leopold and Loeb homes the night of the murder—was hardly conclusive proof. According to one official:

> After questioning Leopold and Loeb repeatedly many of us believed their denials. Finally we called a conference at 4 p.m. Friday, May 30. At this conference we were forced to agree we had no evidence against the two except the finding of Leopold's eye-glasses near the spot where Franks' body was discovered. Some of us believed we were in danger of legal troubles by holding the two. But it was decided to hold the two just a few hours longer.[47]

This turned out to be a highly fortuitous decision. Less than two hours later Crowe and his team were alerted to the work of reporters James Mulroy and Alvin Goldstein. The pair had focused on the Underwood portable typewriter that had produced the ransom note, which Leopold had denied owning. The reporters talked to Leopold's study group, who remembered a single instance the previous winter when Leopold had used a portable typewriter instead of his usual Hammond.[48] Several members of the group were able to produce typewritten notes Leopold had printed from this portable and distributed to use as study aids.

Mulroy and Goldstein were taken into the state's attorney's office, and the notes they'd collected were compared by a typewriting expert to the type on the ransom note. It matched. In a single day the two reporters had gathered several witnesses and pieces of evidence linking their prime suspects with the most damning piece of evidence. The pair won a joint Pulitzer Prize for this work the following year.

Confronted with this new evidence, Leopold continued to deny ever owning an Underwood typewriter. He was taken back to his house where he went through the motions of searching for the portable, knowing that it was mangled at the bottom of a lagoon. It was here that Assistant State's Attorney Joseph Savage recalled being suspicious of Leopold for the first time—as he looked for the typewriter in places it could physically not fit, which showed that he didn't actually expect to find it.[49]

In his bedroom, with police scrutiny closing in and evidence beginning to pile up, Leopold considered a way out.

> I opened the top bureau drawer. There lay not one, but two, loaded Remington automatics: my .32 and my brother's .38. Each had six bullets in the clip, one in the barrel. Fourteen bullets in all. The thought came to me how easy it would be to pick up a pistol in each hand, wheel to my left, kneel on the floor by the side of my bed, and start shooting. I couldn't miss. I could get them all and still have more than enough bullets left to put one through my own brain.[50]

When they failed to find the typewriter and Leopold decided against murder-suicide, he was again escorted back to the state's attorney's office for further questioning. Each of the members of his study group was brought to Leopold, who interrogated them about their stories, attempting to get at least one of them to back down. None of them did.[51] When a police officer told Leopold that the family's maid, Elizabeth Sattler, had informed the police she had seen a portable typewriter in the home two weeks before he replied: "I see."[52] He changed course once more, admitting that he had probably had the typewriter in his house that recently, but couldn't remember where it was. Perhaps his friend Leon Mandel II, now on his honeymoon in Europe, had taken it. His interrogators had had enough. Police chief Michael Hughes said:

> Hughes: Now, listen; you are a fellow with a remarkable memory, better than any man I ever heard in my life. You don't think you could make anybody believe that, do you, Nathan?
>
> Leopold: Well, I—.
>
> Hughes: Do you think you could make any man here, sitting there as you are now and saying you can't remember who took it out or where it is, do you think you could make them believe that?[53]

On the evening of May 30, the Leopold chauffeur, Sven Englund, was summoned to the state's attorney's office and questioned by Assistant State's Attorney Berthold Cronson.[54] When Cronson relayed Leopold's alibi to the chauffeur, Englund corrected him; Leopold couldn't have been cruising in his car all afternoon, he had turned the car over to Englund at around 10:30 that morning. Leopold had complained that his brakes were squeaking. Englund remembered him saying "I would rather run into somebody than have that bad squeak," so Englund had worked on fixing it all afternoon.[55] This was what the police had been waiting for.

Deciding that Loeb was the weaker of the two and more likely to break, members of the prosecution filed into the room where Loeb was being held.

Assistant State's Attorney John Sbarbaro listed all the evidence they had collected: the glasses, typewriter, chisel, and now the fabricated alibi. Loeb recalled that the assistant state's attorneys "didn't fire questions at me, they talked to me very nicely, and they told me I was making a damned fool of myself, and I ought to tell what I knew."[56]

Loeb became frantic, thinking of the damage it would do to his family if the truth came out. After making up several more alibis and breaking into tears, he remained silent for a few minutes, head down, unable to look anyone in the eye. Assistant State's Attorney Milton Smith urged him to speak. Loeb recalled him saying: "You know all about it, you killed that man, or that boy, you were driving up and down the street, driving up and down waiting for it to get dark."[57] Finally, Loeb gave his official confession to Sbarbaro at 4:00 a.m.

While Loeb was confessing, Crowe sent an assistant and Chief Hughes to Leopold's room with the new information. When told Loeb was confessing Leopold apparently scoffed at what he assumed was yet another tactic to get him to talk, saying Loeb "would stand till Hell freezes over."[58] But as the prosecutors told Leopold specifics Loeb had mentioned—the Rent-A-Car agency they had used and the room at the Morrison Hotel they had booked—Leopold was forced to accept that Loeb had indeed confessed. When the police told him that Loeb said it was Leopold who had hit Bobby with the chisel, Leopold composed himself and said: "If Dick is talking I will tell you the truth about the matter."[59] He gave his statement at 4:20 a.m.

Their confessions were taken down individually by stenographers; then the murderers were brought into a room together, the first time they'd seen each other since being taken in for questioning. Loeb was furious and blamed Leopold for using the alibi after a week was up. Leopold shot back:

"I was urged to remember, quite strongly, what I had been doing, and I am sorry that you were made a fish of and stepped into everything and broke down and all that, I am sorry, but it isn't my fault."[60]

Their confessions were read aloud and the two argued about discrepancies between their statements. Under the guise of being helpful, Crowe supplied the teenagers with paper and instructed them to write down the differences in their statements as the confessions were read so they did not keep interrupting each other. These notes would make it nearly impossible for them to refute their confessions.

The two confessions were very similar; both gave details about the timeline, locations, and their minute actions on the days surrounding the murder. Most of the discrepancies the pair squabbled over were small, such as mistaking one street name for another, or who Leopold's rubber boots belonged to, but the real clash between them erupted over the question of who wielded the chisel and knocked Bobby out. Loeb, angry that Leopold had gone back on his word and hoping to ingratiate himself with the authorities, stuck to his statement that he had been driving while Leopold struck the blows.

Leopold, disgusted that Loeb would be so weak as to confess and then lie in an attempt to receive a lighter sentence, was furious right back. After he corrected the fuzzy street directions Loeb gave during his recitation of the murder he remarked to the officers: "Mr. Loeb is not very clear just how we drove out. It seems likely that he might have been doing something else at the time."[61]

They used the opportunity to dig themselves even further into a hole by incriminating each other. Leopold interrogated Loeb about his interest in detective magazines and his preoccupation with crime. Loeb told Crowe that Leopold had come up with the idea for the murder and stated: "I am fully convinced that neither the idea nor the act would have occurred to me, had it not been for the suggestion and stimulus of Leopold."[62] Leopold later referred to this meeting as a "debating society" where both he and Loeb were trying "to convince the judges to vote for our side."[63]

"I didn't think ahead to a future trial," Leopold recalled. "I didn't consider the possibility of there being more than one possible punishment. We had confessed; we would be hanged. I just didn't think any farther than that."[64]

III

SENTENCING HEARING

7

INCRIMINATION

Early on the morning of May 31, hours after their confessions, the murderers took the police on a tour of places connected to their crime. From the drug store where Leopold had bought the hydrochloric acid to the lake shore where they had burned the car robe, they systematically tied themselves to all available pieces of evidence and gathered dozens of witnesses along the way. The killers were subdued on this initial journey, running off the little sleep they had been able to get in jail cells. At the second stop along their route, Loeb was identified by an employee in the drug store. On hearing his name, Loeb paled, fainted, and was carried out by police to rest in the nearby Windermere Hotel.

After lunch, a nap, and an emotional phone call to his mother, Loeb rejoined the party, and the murderers were taken to Jackson Park where divers were searching for the still missing typewriter. Leopold stood against the railing of the bridge they tossed it from, looking out over the lagoon with police chief Michael Hughes close beside him. A nearby reporter transcribed their conversation:

> Leopold: I'd like to jump off this bridge.
>
> Hughes: If you ever went over this bridge you'd never come back.
>
> Leopold: That would suit me.[1]

Hughes quickly led him back to the car. After a few more stops, the teenagers were taken to the Windermere Hotel. It was the last night for more than three decades that either of them would sleep in the free world.

The following day Leopold was rested and significantly more animated as he continued to lead police along his murder route. To reporters and deputies, he expounded on a variety of topics, "one moment its Hawaiian sea weed; the next the philosophy of pessimism as declared by Schopenhauer."[2] When he overheard a woman identify him while he was eating in a diner, he stood up and turned to her, saying: "I beg your pardon, Madam, I am not Nathan Leopold. I have been embarrassed several time[s] by being taken for him." He sat down and turned to a police officer, asking: "How would you like to be able to lie like that?"[3] If he felt guilty or out of his element, he was doing a magnificent job of hiding it. Loeb's attitude was decidedly different. Described as visibly disturbed, pale, shaking, nervous, and depressed, he too talked with reporters and answered their questions, though he was less inclined than Leopold to pontificate for the limelight. When asked if Leopold dominated him, he replied: "Well, I wouldn't say that exactly. Of course he is smart. He is one of the smartest and best educated men I know. Perhaps he did dominate me."[4] Throughout the day, he reinforced to reporters that Leopold had struck Franks with the chisel and warmed to the suggestion of domination. He began affirming that Leopold had controlled him, checking with several reporters and police officers to see if they believed his claims.[5]

When Leopold was told of Loeb's statements, he asked reporters to deliver a message to his former friend: "Tell Loeb that my one regret is that I find him so weak as to accuse me and that I know the reason. He thinks that by proving the actual slayer to be me he will go free. Tell him that I know the law and that I am merely amused by his floundering. We are both principals in the first degree, and there is no forgiveness."[6] Leopold continued scorning Loeb's transparent attempts to endear himself to the press, not yet realizing how important public perception could be.

In between the evidence-gathering trips, Crowe brought psychiatrists to meet with the killers, shoring up ammunition against the possibility of an insanity defense. Not realizing that by talking rationally he was digging his own grave, Leopold chatted with the doctors as if they were colleagues, discussing the merits of various intelligence tests and an article he'd published on bird's ability to reason.[7] Both killers affirmed on record that they were sane, knew what they had been doing every step of the way during their crime, and could have stopped at any time.[8]

When first told the teenagers had confessed, the Leopold family refused to believe it, but when Leopold confirmed their worst fears with a matter-of-fact phone call, they were forced to confront the truth. Sam recalled: "My father was heartbroken. He just couldn't believe it. To come home and find a thing like that on your front porch on a Decoration Day weekend—you could never believe it either. My father was just thankful my mother was already dead."[9] Albert Loeb had been having heart trouble for two years and was not told of his son's confession until several days had passed and he was considered in good enough health to weather the shock. In the meantime, Loeb's uncle Jacob stepped in to make decisions in his bedridden brother's place.

Despite being blindsided by the news, the families got together and conferred about legal representation. Benjamin Bachrach was the Leopold family's lawyer; he already had decades of experience successfully defending murderers, gangsters, politicians, and heavyweight prizefighters, later becoming the Public Defender of Cook County.[10] But the families decided that for this case, Bachrach alone would not be enough. The evening that the teenagers confessed, members of both families journeyed to the Chicago home of Clarence Darrow.

Darrow, an icon in his day, is still remembered as one of the greatest lawyers and orators in American jurisprudence. Sixty-seven by the time the Leopold and Loeb families came knocking on his door, the self-taught lawyer had made a name for himself decades before. In his long career he had defended dozens of murderers and only one of his clients had been executed. He was a gifted speaker in court and out, known as a favorite among juries and often giving lectures about philosophy and agnosticism.

Though reluctant to take such a big case, especially one in which public opinion had already turned against the defendants, he accepted. Crowe had announced to reporters that he considered this a perfect hanging case, and Darrow saw it as a chance to speak out on a national, and even international, stage regarding the barbarity of the death penalty.

Bachrach and Darrow tried repeatedly to track down and speak with their clients once they had been retained, but Crowe kept Leopold and Loeb continually on the move. At 2:50 p.m. on June 1, Nathan Sr. finally succeeded in seeing his son but was denied permission to speak to him alone. Leopold asked to see Bachrach, but this was also denied. During the visit Nathan Sr. made his position clear, saying: "It is the duty of a parent to stand by his child. I want him to get every opportunity that everybody else would get under similar circumstances. If he is entitled to counsel, he should have it. If it is not proper for him to talk without counsel, then my advice to him would be not to talk."[11] Leopold, already convinced that talking more couldn't hurt him with the detailed confessions already on record, did not heed his father's advice.[12]

After it became clear that the state's attorney's office would be of no help, the defense submitted a request for a habeas corpus hearing to get custody of the killers transferred from the state's attorney to the sheriff. The motion was approved, and on the afternoon of June 1 Leopold and Loeb made their first appearances in Cook County's Criminal Court Building.

Still wearing the suits they had been arrested in, the two presented spectators with a marked contrast. Leopold was described as "swagger[ing] about the court building smoking cigarettes and chewing gum." He even wrote out a note that said: "Please give the bearer a pint of gin or whisky," which he asked a policeman to deliver to his house.[13] Meanwhile Loeb, looking "boyishly innocent," was described as nervous, compulsively combing his hair and pacing before they were led into court.[14]

In the crowded courtroom Benjamin Bachrach asked Judge John R. Caverly for his clients to be taken from Crowe's custody. When Crowe asked for more time with them, Darrow snapped: "This is an extraordinary request. The State's Attorney is violating the constitutional rights of the prisoners and asks the court to aid him."[15] "These are mere boys, minors. They have been in custody since Thursday, although you have no right to hold them, and I don't care how cold-blooded the murder, I am interested, like anyone else, in the preservation of our constitutional rights, especially in the case of minors."[16]

The judge agreed. Leopold and Loeb were turned over to the Cook County sheriff and taken to jail, to be held without bail. They were examined by the jail physician, and it was announced that there had been no abuse by the police. Loeb's clothes had become infested with bugs during his night in the cell, so he was given the jail uniform to wear while Leopold was allowed to keep his uninfested suit.[17] They were then taken to transitory cells and given the first of many dinners from Joe Stein's restaurant, located across the street from the jail.

Nicknamed the "Noose Coffee Shop," Stein's was used to catering to the needs of prisoners and the reporters covering their cases. The ability to order food was a privilege available to any inmate willing to pay the restaurant bill, and the Leopold and Loeb families set up credit so they could get three good meals a day. Leopold was said to smoke and then go to bed early while Loeb was restless and told a guard he felt "creepy in here."[18] He read a newspaper for a while until he too drifted off to sleep.

The following day Leopold had a chance to really meet Darrow for the first time. He recalled that when Darrow came up to his cell, Leopold looked out and "on the other side of the bars stood one of the least prepossessing, one of the least impressive-looking human beings I have ever seen." While Leopold had maintained his shellacked hair and well-tailored three-piece suit even in jail, Darrow stood before him with his hair mussed and egg on his shirt.[19] Their meeting was brief, Darrow merely counseled Leopold to keep his mouth shut around reporters and informed him that they planned to plead not guilty.

For the next several months, Leopold would come to completely change his opinion of the old orator. Whatever Darrow's first impression of Leopold was, he also developed a genuine affection for his clients. In his autobiography Darrow commented that Leopold "had, and has, the most brilliant intellect that I ever met in a boy . . . he was genial, kindly, and likable."[20] After meeting Darrow, both teenagers finally stopped incriminating themselves. Crowe's last attempt to get them to talk with psychiatrists on June 2 failed, as they answered all questions, even whether they wanted water or not: "I must respectfully decline to answer without consulting counsel."[21]

The following day Leopold was called for a visit with his father and Mike. As he was less concerned with legal punishment than with "the disgust of my family," it was not a meeting he looked forward to.[22] Leopold pleaded for them to disown him and let him hang with no defense, reasoning that would be the quickest and easiest course for everyone.[23] But his family hadn't given up and convinced him to let the lawyers do what they could. They continued to support him during the long summer, Mike arriving faithfully every Friday for visiting day. The Loebs also supported their son, but at the advice of their doctors his parents retreated to spend their summer in Charlevoix. Jacob was joined by Loeb's brother Allan, who moved back to Chicago from Seattle to discuss strategy with the defense team and keep an eye on Loeb in their stead.

With their futures in the hands of their lawyers, Cook County's newest celebrity residents turned their focus to life behind bars. The Cook County Jail sat squarely in downtown Chicago, attached to the Criminal Court Building by a bridge. Prisoners were segregated depending on their age and gender, with women on the third floor, and the sixth and seventh floors reserved for men under twenty-one. It was here that the "thrill-killers" were assigned to ten by five foot white-walled cells, Loeb on the seventh floor and Leopold on the sixth, each with a robber for a cellmate.

Their lives followed the strict regimentation of the other inmates: they were woken by guards at 6:15 a.m. and from 9:30 to 11:30 a.m. and 3:30 to 5:30 p.m. they were let into their floor's bullpen for exercise. At all other times they were confined to their cells unless in court.[24] Though the exercise periods in the bullpens were better than endless confinement in the cells, they offered little respite. The bullpens were nothing more than dim concrete blocks with open drains used for urination, unbearably hot and pungent in summer. With no exercise equipment available, prisoners made their own games, sometimes playing leapfrog or baseball by smacking a paper ball with their hands, but only when there was enough room. Often all they could do was form lines and walk in endless circles. An inspector commented: "The place is fittingly named: it is like nothing so much as a pen crowded with animals."[25]

Initially, the new arrivals were met with enormous interest from the other inmates, who had been avidly following their story in the newspapers along with the rest of the country. While Loeb quickly mingled with them, joining in on baseball games and dropping into the jail school to help tutor, Leopold kept to himself at first.[26] He did eventually make friends as well and even managed a reconciliation with Loeb.

After several weeks apart, Leopold and Loeb got together to discuss their conflicting stories on who killed Bobby. Loeb argued that as they were each legally culpable of first-degree murder, it didn't matter if people knew who actually struck Bobby. He reasoned that this way their families could each blame the other, and he wouldn't take that shred of comfort from his mother. Though Leopold disagreed, they made up regardless, determined to present a united front at the trial.[27]

As they adjusted to their new life, Crowe brought his case and dozens of witnesses before a grand jury.[28] The proceedings went quickly and the grand jury voted to charge Leopold and Loeb with two indictments, one for murder, and one for kidnapping for ransom. These decisions were sent to Judge Caverly of the Cook County Circuit Court so the killers could be officially charged.

These charges did not stand alone; the same day a woman named Louise Hohley claimed that a few weeks earlier the pair had kidnapped her and violated her with a pipe. Because of her unfocused and inconsistent story, police paid little attention to her claim. On June 2 a man named Charles Ream came to the Criminal Court Building and waited with newspaper photographers for Leopold and Loeb to pass in the corridor. When they did, he pointed at them and shouted: "It's them! It's them! Do you think that I could ever forget the faces of the men who have taken so much out of my life?"[29] Ream had awoken in the early morning of November 20, 1923, castrated and lying in a field.

In addition to Ream, police began tying Leopold and Loeb to other unsolved crimes, including the deaths of Freeman Louis Tracy and Melvin Wolf. Tracy had been shot in the head and his body dumped from a car on November 26, 1923. At the time, police speculated that the murder may have been gang related, connected to his labor union, or motivated by jealousy, as it was found that Tracy had been exchanging letters with many ladies.[30] Wolf had left home on April 7, 1924, and never returned. When his body washed up in Lake Michigan, his death remained a mystery: he had drowned, had no injuries, there was no sign of a robbery, and he was fully clothed. A coroner's jury was unable to guess if his death had been suicide, homicide, or accidental.[31] These seemingly random deaths were connected to Leopold and Loeb by proximity: Wolf had lived down the street from Loeb, and Tracy had been a University of Chicago student. Leopold and Loeb denied all allegations.

On June 11 Loeb and Leopold were brought to Judge Caverly's court for arraignment. The sixth-floor courtroom was stuffed with members of the public, competing for space with the reporters, stenographers, and court officials who were all intensely interested in seeing the young murderers in person. They stood in the aisles, on tables, and hung over railings in attempts to hear and get the best pictures possible.

Newspapers had been filled with stories that harped on Leopold's cold egoism; he was even said to have been a hypnotist who had led the weak and guileless Loeb to ruin. A particularly enthusiastic reporter described their entrance: "'Dickie' Loeb stepped lightly into court yesterday on the morning of his 19th birthday. . . . He looked as fresh as a May morning and as light-hearted as an innocent child. . . . Close behind him and his debonair youth and careless grace slipped Nathan Leopold Jr . . . in his cold, light, hypnotic eyes there gleamed the strange, subtle, serpentine wisdom of the ages."[32]

Removed from the more sensational wording of the reporters, the teenagers walked into the courtroom calmly, taking no notice of the crowd or the clouds of smoke that rose from the camera flashes. They stepped before the bench in their blue suits, with their hair recently cut and slicked back by jail barbers, and pleaded not guilty to both charges in unwavering voices. Judge Caverly set the dates: July 21 for motions to ask for more time, and August 4 for the beginning of the trial. After only a few minutes in court, Leopold and Loeb were led back to their cells and the eager crowd slowly disbanded.

Two days after their not guilty pleas, Darrow sent physicians Harold Hulbert and Karl Bowman to do a preliminary study on the defendants. The doctors set up camp within the jail's death cell, traditionally used to house prisoners waiting for their turn on the gallows. There the defendants were given x-rays, made to breathe into tubes for hours, their reflexes were tested, and every detail of their bodies from hair pattern to skin texture was recorded.

The doctors hoped to discover if there was a discernible physical cause that may have prompted the teenagers to commit their crime. Leopold let his examiners know: "I think this medical 'Psychiatric' stuff is all horseshit."[33] The doctors noted that he was irritable and nervous during the physical tests, especially when needles were involved. Interest in the private examinations was so great that reporters got into a building opposite the jail and tried to peer through the windows of the death cell with a spyglass.[34]

In addition to looking for physical reasons for the behavior, psychiatrists also tried to determine their sanity. Especially compared to what he considered to be the pseudoscience of the physical examinations, Leopold found the mental angle exhilarating. He hoped to make the best use of this opportunity to gain insight into his personality and enjoyed explaining his view of the world to well-respected men who were eager to listen.

After two weeks of interviews with the killers as well as their family and friends, the doctors prepared reports containing over a hundred pages of family history, childhood memories, fantasies, and other intimate details about their lives. Both doctors concluded that Leopold and Loeb were insane. While there was a difference between the legal and psychiatric definitions of insanity, Hulbert made sure to clarify that he thought Leopold

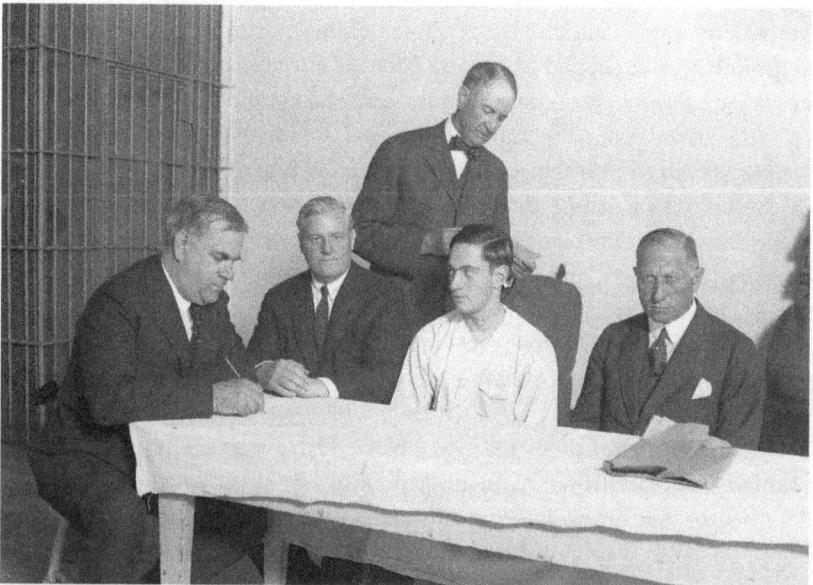

Nathan Leopold in the death cell being interviewed by psychiatrists James Whitney Hall, William Hickson, and Sanger Brown. Benjamin Bachrach sits at Leopold's right.
Chicago History Museum; DN-0078015; Chicago Daily News collection.

legally insane under Illinois law, as "his knowledge of right and wrong, concerning his actions, is insufficient to alter his conduct, and that he did react to irresistible impulses."[35] As the reports came in, Darrow debated what to do about his infamous clients. A reporter friend met up with him during this testing period and wrote in her diary that "He is brooding over this case that focuses millions of eyes upon him. Talks of pathology-philosophy etc."[36]

Following these initial exams came a barrage of other psychiatrists to provide second opinions, most notably James Whitney Hall, William White, Bernard Glueck, and William Healy. These doctors were selected by Walter Bachrach, Benjamin's brother and the final member of the defense team. Typically a civil lawyer, Walter focused on the psychiatric side of the case, coordinating the doctors and analyzing their reports. Each psychiatrist was given Hulbert and Bowman's reports to read before they started their own psychiatric probing.

During daily interviews, psychiatrists noted that:

> Throughout our contacts with [Leopold] he strove energetically to behave altogether as a purely intellectual machine, devoid of all emotions, and to dominate the situation by his philosophical rationalization. What was uppermost in his mind was very evidently a desire to make a good impression as a wholly unique being, unique in that he was not subject to the ordinary feelings which sway human nature.[37]

Through the entire process, above all else, Leopold was determined to present an unchanging face, as consistency had always been "a sort of God" to him.[38] He had to demonstrate that he was so sure of his ideals that he would not change simply because he was on trial for murder.[39] When asked if he would commit this murder again if he was guaranteed not to be apprehended, he replied that he certainly would.[40]

Asked to give his motive for the crime, Leopold explained that, as a hedonist, "Making up my mind to commit murder was practically the same as making up my mind whether or not I should eat pie for supper, whether it would give me pleasure or not."[41] There was much pleasure to be found in a successful crime of this size: the excitement it would bring and the fun of outwitting the police.[42] Still, he claimed that his ultimate reason for committing the crime "was to please Dick."[43] Loeb had wanted this, and pleasing him was more vital than the life of a child. A psychiatrist wrote that:

> He stated that the killing of one boy or one individual made no particular difference to a community. That society in Hyde Park and Chicago functioned just the same on the 22nd day of May as it did on the 20th.

He said that perhaps if he were to kill a multitude of people in a community it might make some difference, but killing one or a dozen in a large, densely populated community like this could in no way affect society. He said that if he got personal pleasure out of it that was his business and that was sufficient justification for his act.[44]

When psychiatrists asked Loeb, he produced a list of his motives in order of importance. First was the joy of planning and working out all the little details, the thrill of committing the act and the satisfaction of the successful ransom scheme. Second was the publicity he imagined they would receive and the opportunity to discuss the crime with friends and family, while understanding that he and Leopold were the only ones who knew the real truth. Third was the money received from the ransom, though it was more to complicate the plan than a desire for the reward itself.[45] One psychiatrist encouraged Loeb to probe deeper, "I would say to him, 'Why did you do it? How can you explain it?' and he would come back with the same answer, 'I did it because I wanted to, because I got a kick out of it.'"[46]

Loeb himself seemed at a loss to understand his situation. Writing to his parents, he said: "This thing is all too terrible. I have thought and thought about it, and even now I do not seem to be able to understand it. I just cannot seem to figure out how it all came about."[47] Leopold offered his own interpretation of Loeb's motive: "It was a kind of revolt—an overreaction against the strictness of the governess who had had charge of him until he was fifteen. A basic feeling of inferiority, maybe; a desire to show that he could do things and bring them to a successful end on his own."[48]

As each defense psychiatrist finished their examinations, their reports unanimously declared the teenagers were mentally ill. They decided that Leopold had dementia praecox, a mental illness attributed to a rapid mental decline in a young patient, which has since been labeled schizophrenia. They diagnosed that he was also paranoid, sexually abnormal, and was probably about to have a psychotic break.[49] Loeb provided more of a problem. While the psychiatrists agreed that he was pathological, a direct diagnosis was elusive. The defense psychiatrists opined that the state psychiatrists would likely diagnose Loeb as having a psychopathic personality disorder, but they disagreed because he was not completely self-absorbed and was still able to have an emotional life with no evidence of emotional deterioration.[50] Anna Loeb took comfort in the possibility of mental illness and hoped Loeb's mind would eventually get "straightened out." As she explained to her youngest son, "Babe and Dick are sick, mentally sick . . . they did not realize what they were doing."[51]

The defense's psychiatric reports were a nearly unprecedented undertaking for their time, but they had many shortcomings, sometimes caused by the biases of the psychiatrists. For instance: the psychiatrists had much to say about Leopold seeing himself as Christ and his mother and Birdie as Madonna figures.[52] Dr. Hulbert testified that "He does not frankly say, 'I am Christ' but he does say that he is the superior person of the world."[53] The doctor failed to see beyond his own religious beliefs to understand that Leopold, a Jewish atheist who believed in Nietzsche's superman, may not have had Christ in mind when he made such statements. Leopold himself denied Hulbert's interpretation after hearing it in court.[54]

More than perhaps any other psychiatric leaps of misunderstanding that have come to shape the interpretation of the case were the reports of the supposed "king-slave" aspect of Leopold and Loeb's relationship. When Leopold mentioned that he had sexual fantasies involving kings and slaves, psychiatrists worked overtime to find this dynamic represented in Leopold's relationship with Loeb. Hulbert and Bowman wrote that 90 percent of the time Leopold's sense of inferiority caused him to view himself as the slave in these fantasies. Leopold acknowledged many years later that the ratio was the opposite:

> I did have knowledge that the doctors in certain places had misconstrued the exact relationship that I had in my fantasies, that is, they had felt that I fantasied myself as a slave in certain fantasies, where, as a matter of fact, I fantasied myself as king. Since the trial was already in progress when this became known to me—because I heard it for the first time in court—I realized that this was very much in line with our general defense.

As the error worked in his favor, he decided "I had better just keep my mouth shut, which I have done."[55]

Their investigations were further curtailed by Loeb lying, as the psychiatrists described it:

> [Loeb] at first omitted any account of setting fires. He did this deliberately, with the feeling that it was for his own self-interest not to reveal anything about it. When confronted with the fact that he had set a number of fires he did not appear in the least embarrassed, and said "Oh, didn't I tell about that? It was one of the things I meant to tell; I didn't intend to omit it." His manner was extremely polite and courteous. He gave the impression of being absolutely frank and straightforward, and his manner was extremely convincing.[56]

The defense team was careful not to pry too deeply, to make sure nothing too damning came out. Loeb mentioned he had committed four other crimes, but Hulbert and Bowman did not pursue this because "there is a legal advantage in minimizing the broadcasting of his episodes . . . so no great effort should be made to bring forth details which he willfully repressed."[57] The public speculated that these crimes could include the castration of Ream and the deaths of Tracy and Wolf, but they have never been solved.

While the psychiatrists sometimes declined to inquire into the details of Leopold and Loeb's previous criminal escapades, many thought the defense was inventing things to make their clients seem worse than they were. Newspapers were happy to help with this angle: one paper used an inaccurate family tree to claim that Loeb and Bobby were second cousins—showing Albert and Flora Franks as first cousins.[58] Really there was only a tenuous familial connection between Bobby and Loeb: Flora Franks's uncle had married Albert Loeb's aunt in 1874. (Flora's uncle would have had to marry Albert's mother for them to be first cousins.) It's likely the families weren't even aware of the connection. Though Jacob Franks told reporters that he knew of Loeb and his reputation, a familial bond was never mentioned by either family or the psychiatrists in their extensive reports.

As snippets of the psychiatric reports were given to the press, Crowe brushed them off:

> The report that Leopold and Loeb are insane is nothing more than propaganda sent out by the defense to throw dust into the eyes of men who may be called to serve on the jury. The articles appearing in certain newspapers that they have plotted to take the lives of their brothers and fathers is nothing but bunk. I am surprised that their lawyers do not say they tried to kill each other.
>
> No reputable alienist would testify the two murderers are insane. If any of them do, it will be because they were either fools who were duped by the defendants or knaves who have profited by their gold.[59]

It was hard for anyone acquainted with either defendant to believe they had been secretly crazy all along. Salmon Levinson, whose son Johnny had narrowly avoided becoming the victim in Bobby's place, wrote to a friend: "I had quite a talk with the Loeb boy relatively a few days before the crime and he was about as insane as I am."[60]

8

THE HEARING BEGINS

In the two months since their arrest, the public fervor surrounding Leopold and Loeb had not been allowed to fade. Interest was bolstered by almost daily updates in Chicago newspapers on the legal strategies of the defense and prosecution, and when those reports became tedious they were supplemented with editorials and articles examining the minutiae of the defendants' personalities and histories. As these dissections continued into the summer, Leopold was not faring well in the court of public opinion.

A Scene in the Franks Tragedy

NATHAN LEOPOLD, JR.   RICHARD LOEB.

LOEB—You led me into this trouble. You suggested it all and you did most of the planning. I don't know why I listened.

LEOPOLD—I should give a d——! Anyway, killing in the interest of science is no worse than sticking a beetle on a pin.

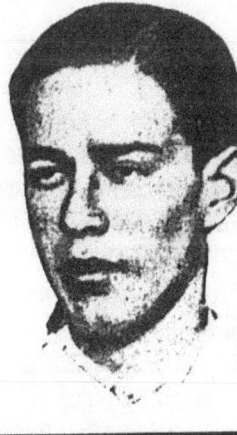

One panel of a newspaper photo comic highlighting the public's perception of Leopold and Loeb's personalities and their roles in the Franks crime. Originally published in the *New York American* on June 5, 1924.

A family friend theorized that Leopold may have chosen Loeb to corrupt because Loeb was "the most promising, admirable, lovable and naturally upright," and Leopold wanted to see if he could "poison that boy's soul and destroy it."[1] While most still saw Leopold and Loeb as one unit, to those following the case more closely it was hard not to wonder if criminologist Perry Lichtenstein was right when he declared: "If leniency is shown it should be toward Loeb. He was the tool of the moral monstrosity Leopold."[2]

While most based their takes on Leopold and Loeb's statements and personalities, undercurrents of anti-Semitism could also be detected. One reporter stared at Leopold as he reclined in his jail bunk and painted a forceful picture for his readers: "He has coal black curling hair, there is a dark touch of color over his rather prominent cheekbones. His eyebrows are thick and highly arched. His nose is distinctly Hebraic. It was not so hard, looking at him to picture him doing a cruel, wicked thing, or to believe he might be a follower of some of the unclean morbid teachings." Loeb, the reporter described as "a graceful, frank-faced blonde boy, without any line or curve which hinted evil."[3]

Despite several gold crowns and "rather bad teeth," all Loeb had to do was smile and the public seemed on his side.[4] Leopold, annoyed at the press, remarked: "I've been pictured in the public mind as the Svengali, the man with the hypnotic eye, the master mind and the brains. . . . I've been described as the devil incarnate. But Dicky Loeb, on the other hand, seems to have won the sympathy of the public."[5]

The weekend before Leopold and Loeb were arraigned, *St. Louis Post-Dispatch* reporter Paul Anderson had a chance to confront these images of the pair before their first day in court. Herded into the Cook County Jail with a group of reporters from the Chicago papers, he chatted first with Loeb, who he found in his cell fully dressed in a suit and bow tie. Loeb shook hands with each of the reporters and "with an engaging smile and intonation" bantered about the upcoming trial. After fifteen minutes the group departed and made its way a floor down to Leopold's cell.

Though Anderson was warned that Leopold "frequently waxed heavily sarcastic at the expense of visitors, and sometimes refused to see them at all," he needn't have worried.[6] As the reporters walked toward his cell, they found Leopold in his shirtsleeves standing against the bars. Anderson was surprised to note that he had an athlete's build with "none of the softness to be expected in a bookworm and esthete." Leopold regaled his crowd with bawdy stories, explaining to Anderson that he told crass jokes because the reporters "can't possibly print them. If I tell them anything respectable they write a story about it." Anderson walked away from his interviews, with the parting gift of a cigarette from Leopold, even further from understanding the killers than when he arrived.

> Any mental picture of them either as intellectual supermen or monsters is very difficult to sustain through a conversation with them. . . . The colossal egotism attributed to them was not apparent. They displayed the easy politeness natural in boys of good breeding. In fact, there is no disguising the fact that both are decidedly likable, and they are liked by virtually all the jail attaches and reporters who have come in daily contact with them for the last seven weeks.[7]

Waiting for the trial to begin, he left his readers with a chilling thought: "Both prisoners appeared to be perfectly normal, bright, well-bred, good-natured, campus youths of 19 years."[8] Perhaps this revelation was more disturbing than finding in them some obvious flaw or sign of madness. For, if Leopold and Loeb seemed no different than the thousands of other boys their age in the country, how could anyone tell which other seemingly normal teenagers had a murderous capability lurking within?

On the morning of July 21, the defendants sat in the courtroom and waited for their arraignment to begin. A few minutes after court was called into session, Darrow stood up and quietly announced that he was withdrawing his defendants' pleas of not guilty and was changing them to guilty on both charges. The trial, now a sentencing hearing with no jury, was thus slated to begin not on the original date of August 4, but on July 23, just two days later. Leopold sat motionless during Darrow's announcement and the eruption of whispers that followed, his face giving away nothing about his reaction to the turn of events. Privately he approved of the decision; he regarded himself as sane and doubted the ability of their psychiatrists to convince anyone that he was not.[9]

The defense had several reasons to adopt this legal strategy despite the diagnoses of the psychiatrists. The abrupt start to the hearing and the change in plea meant that the prosecution team would have very little time to alter the strategy they had prepared against a plea of not guilty. Because of the continuous onslaught of negative publicity, the defense team thought it best to avoid a jury of riled-up citizens, trusting in the hopefully more level-headed single authority of Judge Caverly. The lawyers also wanted to make sure that Crowe did not have two chances to hang their clients for the dual charges of murder and kidnapping that had been filed against them, as each carried the possibility of a death sentence.

Even with all this reasoning behind him, Darrow was far from confident. The day before he announced the change in plea he wrote to his son: "You have no doubt been surprised at the turn we have taken in the Loeb-Leopold case. We have concluded it is the most hopeful way of saving the boys lives. It is doubtful if any way will accomplish it."[10] Hoping to avoid "the usual unsightly court controversy between alienists," the defense lawyers suggested a neutral panel of experts evaluate the defendants, or at least that the defense and state psychiatrists should meet and come to an agreement before the hearing began.[11] Crowe refused. After court adjourned, Crowe issued a statement to the press that made his position going into the hearing clear: "There is only one proper punishment. That is death; and I shall insist on the extreme penalty." The lines were drawn and the battle set to begin at 10 a.m. on Wednesday, July 23.

After their short time in Caverly's courtroom, the defendants returned to the jail bullpen where they debriefed with reporters. These were to become regularly scheduled interviews set before and after each session in court, which Leopold claimed Darrow insisted on.[12] Forced upon them or not, the defendants entertained the reporters, telling jokes, performing skits, and telling stories about their lives in jail.

> Loeb: I'll bet we're all over the front page again. I wish they'd bring the papers up. There certainly was a commotion when Mr. Darrow moved to plead guilty.
>
> Leopold: Better not talk any more about that. Let's talk about something else.
>
> Loeb: What is it the judge says when it's all over? "The court finds you—."
>
> Leopold: Shut up![13]

Loeb obliged and the pair steered toward safer conversational waters until jail officials told the reporters it was time to leave. As they departed Leopold and Loeb stepped away from the bars and disappeared among the mass of young men circling the concrete bullpen.

The morning before their first day in court, Leopold and Loeb again greeted reporters in the bullpen. Leopold ribbed the newsmen about describing their clothes inaccurately in the previous day's papers until it was Loeb's turn to tell him to shut up.[14] Many reporters meticulously made note of their outfits the following day in retaliation. When asked if he was nervous Leopold challenged: "Do I look it?"[15] Though both teenagers appeared calm, reporters read signs of strain in their chain-smoking, but they may just have been shoring up until the court's noon recess when they would be allowed to smoke again. At 9:30 they were called away, said their goodbyes to the reporters, and went to get put into handcuffs. Led by their guards and several police officers, the defendants crossed the "Bridge of Sighs" from the jail into the Criminal Court Building, the hearing for their lives about to begin.

Long before court was in session, an enormous crowd had gathered on the street. Police officers were stationed outside the building as well as within, guarding the stairs, elevators, and the doors to the sixth-floor courtroom. The crowd around the building swelled as hundreds of well-dressed men and women arrived, all desperate for their chance to witness history. To those few who made it inside and to the sixth floor, one reporter observed: "The crowds pressing around the doors resembled those which throng many an entrance to a movie palace, and the sharp challenge of 'tickets, show your tickets,' did not detract from this impression."[16] Those lucky enough to get pink tickets, which were issued to the press, witnesses, legal teams, and family members, passed through the doors quickly. The rest had to wait in sweltering hallways and on the streets in the hopes that they may be one of the few without connections allowed in to see the show.

The courtroom had light wooden paneled walls and a white ceiling on which large fans rotated lazily to push around the hot, humid air. Several pillars helped obscure the view and a wooden semicircular half wall divided the room roughly across the middle. At the front of the courtroom, usually called the "inner ring," sat those connected with the case: the lawyers, psychiatrists, and defendants at the front closest to the judge and their family and friends sitting behind. Those for the prosecution took seats on the right side, while the defense took the left. The space beyond the dividing wall was a free-for-all. Though there were chairs set out in orderly rows, spectators grabbed additional chairs or boxes to sit on, squeezed into corners, and sat on windowsills for a better view.

The Leopold and Loeb families commandeered a bench for themselves at the back left of the inner ring, just in front of the general spectators. Both families arrived early, the Leopolds represented by Nathan Sr. and Mike, the Loebs by Allan and Jacob. Out of their sad little group, Nathan Sr. was singled out by many spectators and reporters as the most tragic. Throughout the summer he sat hunched over clutching his cane, a look of despair and confusion refusing to leave his heavy, knitted brow.[17] The father of the deceased, Jacob Franks, was also present for nearly every court session, usually sitting on the side of the prosecution and easily identifiable by the black ribbon he used as a glasses chain.

A small army of reporters and photographers from around the country took occupation of the jury box while those with typewriters and telegraph operators set up tables to hold their machines, silencers working to dampen the noise.[18] A makeshift press room with wires and telephones was set up in the jury room, so reporters could have a place to take breaks and keep in contact with their superiors while court was in session. Radio transmitters, flash photography, and motion picture cameras had been completely forbidden by Judge Caverly.

Before the first session began, a massive green filing cabinet containing the prosecution exhibits and evidence was wheeled, shuddering noisily, into the courtroom and deposited by the witness stand. At ten o'clock Caverly came out of his chambers, a short, stocky figure in his dark robe, and took his seat. At his signal the County Clerk stood up and called out: "Nathan Leopold Jr. and Richard Loeb." The spectators turned to look at the door to the courtside bullpen and waited for the stars to emerge.

Heads held high, Leopold and Loeb stepped out of the court's side entrance, a guard at each of their elbows, and walked into the hushed room. They smiled and nodded to their family members as they were led to seats behind their lawyers, three guards taking seats a row behind them. Both defendants had prepared themselves fastidiously in their summer suits, Leopold in gray and Loeb in dark blue with a dark bow tie around his neck. Their hair lay slicked back in fashion with the times and the jail barber had made sure they were neatly shaven. Darrow and the Bachrach brothers greeted their clients, then turned to face the judge as Crowe and his assistant state's attorneys waited across the aisle. The stage was set and the actors in place. It was time for the curtain to rise on the most anticipated show of the season.

Crowe kicked things off; the former judge had a taste for the dramatic, his deep voice rising during his speech as he cried "Blood! Blood! Blood!"[19] He began his statement by introducing his theory that "these two defendants entered into a conspiracy, the purpose of which was to gain money, and in order to gain it they were ready and willing to commit a cold-blooded murder."[20] He claimed that the ransom money the defendants extracted from Jacob Franks would have been used to pay off the enormous gambling debts they had amassed.

This motivation would ground the killers in a familiar reality; gambling was immoral and killing to get money, especially if a person was already rich, seemed heinous. The motives the defendants had given, that

A day in court. In the front row are (l-r) John Sbarbaro, Walter Bachrach, Clarence Darrow, and Benjamin Bachrach. Leopold and Loeb sit behind them. Chicago History Museum; DN-0078009; Chicago Daily News collection.

they had murdered Bobby Franks so they could more safely commit a perfect crime because of a belief that they were superior, was a bit too bizarre to be easily digestible. Crowe disparaged the defense psychiatrists and announced he would prove that these murderers had meticulous, intelligent minds untainted by mental illness. Leopold, watching from a few feet away, betrayed nothing during this fiery speech, staring at Crowe with an impassive face, occasionally smiling and whispering to Loeb as the thought struck him.[21]

After Crowe's long and detailed damnation of the defendants, Darrow's opening statement was fairly concise. He agreed that Bobby's murder was a terrible thing, but said that to claim, as Crowe had, "That it is the cruelest, the worst, the most atrocious ever committed in the United States is pure imagination without a vestige of truth."[22] Crowe objected to this statement and he and Darrow squabbled back and forth, setting the tone for their relationship in court for the rest of the trial, one which would be populated with plenty of sarcasm, backhanded remarks, and petty quarrels.

Returning to his speech after the verbal tussle, Darrow declared that asking for the death penalty was ludicrous because the boys were simply too young to hang. If they were sentenced to death, they would be the youngest executed in Illinois history on a guilty plea, and regardless of the outcome, their deaths would not bring Bobby back. What was the use in the deaths of two more teenagers after Bobby, just a few years younger than they, had his life tragically cut so short? At the end of his speech, he emphasized the theory that the entirety of the defense would rest on: that Loeb and Leopold's mental makeup gave them a limited responsibility for their crimes.

With that out of the way, the remainder of the day was taken up by a parade of prosecution witnesses. Crowe and his team began with a focus on the victim, calling to the stand the uncle, father, and mother of Bobby Franks, as well as two coroners. The latter brought the gruesome truth of the crime into focus by describing Bobby's autopsy in detail. Conjured before the court were mental images of the boy's copper-colored, acid-streaked face and the coroners peeling back his scalp to see the blood that had pooled there after blows from the chisel.[23] In addition to the gruesome details of the crime, spectators were particularly interested in the appearance of Flora Franks, mother of the deceased.

Following her son's death, newspapers had been filled with stories about Flora going mad with grief. It was rumored that she did not believe that Bobby was dead and sat at the window all day waiting for him to finish his walk home. In contrast to the colorful stories, she may have proved a disappointment to some trial fans. The Flora Franks who walked into court on July 23 was described as looking deeply sad, but she showed no sign of delusion. She spoke quietly and with little emotion, identifying pieces of her son's clothing and answering questions about his final days.

To touch on where this idea of Flora's madness may have come from, it is important to take into the context of her religion. The Franks family had converted from Judaism to Christian Science and Flora was apparently a firm believer, so much so that by 1930 she was working as a Christian Science Practitioner, using prayer to cure her clients' emotional and physical troubles.[24] Christian Scientists do not believe in the use of medicine or a true concept of death, emphasizing the importance of the spirit over the physical world. The religion's founder assured her congregation: "What appears to the senses to be death is but a mortal illusion; for to man, and the spiritual universe, there is no death-process."[25] Echoing this belief was the phrase chosen to mark Bobby's tomb: "Life is because God is, infinite, indestructible, and eternal."

Jacob Franks told reporters that when he tried to console Flora, all she would say was "'He isn't dead.' . . . I have leanings toward Science, but she has embraced it completely. Her faith has saved her."[26] Her statements that

Bobby wasn't dead and that she would see him again were basic tenants of her religion, but to reporters with little understanding of Christian Science, her words were interpreted as the much more sensational story of a mother going crazy over the loss of her murdered child.

After focusing on Bobby's last day and the discovery of his body, the prosecution shifted to proving that the defendants had indeed committed the murder. They called a series of employees from places involved in the crime and ransom scheme. The filing cabinet stood helpfully by, ready to produce a letter, a scrap of clothing, or a chisel as needed for identification.

Before the prosecution had gone too far down this line, the defense objected. As their clients had given full confessions and pleaded guilty, the defense lawyers argued that it was a waste of time to have several men confirm that Loeb had established a fake identity at a hotel, or that Leopold had bought the paper used in the ransom notes. To these objections, Crowe had a ready answer: "I want to show by the mountain of evidence we have piled up that when they pleaded guilty there was not anything else they could do but plead guilty. I want to show their guilt clearly and conclusively, and the details of it and ask that they be hanged."[27] Caverly agreed to let him make his case, so the procession of witnesses continued.

After Darrow attempted to quash the bulk of Crowe's case, the defense offered little resistance for the next week. They turned down most offers to cross-examine, as there was nothing in the factual evidence their clients denied. When the defense did decide to cross-examine, it was handled by defense counsel Benjamin Bachrach, with Darrow content to simply watch, listen, and advise for the time being. Despite their lack of rebuttal in court, Darrow and his team were still working feverishly behind the scenes. While the state was presenting its case, Darrow sent James Glassner, who worked in his law office, to New York and Ohio in last-minute attempts to round up more character witnesses.[28]

Leopold took the first day in stride; a reporter noticed that he often seemed to sit completely still for fifteen-minute stretches, watching the witnesses without a flicker of expression or nervous movement.[29] Loeb was more fidgety, balancing his feet on the rung of Darrow's chair in front of him and looking around the courtroom, eyes lighting on the reporters working furiously, or the crowd, who were all eager to get a glimpse of his face. While Leopold kept his impressions to himself, Loeb revealed that though he had anticipated being moved to tears by the testimony of Mrs. Franks, "I did not feel anything much. I was not sorry about any of the things I did that were wrong. I did not have any feeling about it. I did not have much of any feeling from the first. That is why I could do these terrible things. . . . There was nothing inside me to stop me."[30]

After their first day in court the defendants were led back to the jail, followed by several reporters hoping to mine them for impressions. Once in their cells both teenagers took off their jackets, complained about the heat, and requested newspapers about their big day. They joked as usual and were seemingly unaffected by the proceedings, acting much the same as they had been in the last two months that they had been imprisoned.[31]

The hearing continued on the same keel for another two days, the public still fighting to get through the doors for the privilege of straining to hear as dozens of witnesses continued the methodical buildup of evidence. A high school girl, sent to the courtroom to get her opinions for a fresh column, found herself puzzled by the other spectators. "They sit, rather uncomfortably jammed, in seats some distance from the witness stand. I doubt whether they hear anything said. I had an advantageous seat, and yet it was with difficulty that I heard. . . . I wonder why these people come day in and day out?"[32]

During court recesses, the Leopold and Loeb relatives would walk up to chat with the teenagers, Mike and Allan throwing comforting arms

Nathan Leopold talks to his brother Mike, during a court recess. Leopold's guard stands close behind him. Chicago History Museum; DN-0077985; Chicago Daily News collection.

around their brothers' shoulders. Allan relayed messages from the daily phone conversations he had with their parents and acted as a courier when they exchanged physical letters.

As the stream of witnesses continued, both defendants appeared bored by the testimony, and Loeb explained to one reporter: "It is only natural that when we hear witnesses spend fifteen minutes and more telling stories about finding a letter in a railway coach or something of the sort that we could not be exceedingly interested. We put it there and know all about it."[33] With little to occupy them, Leopold and Loeb spent their time whispering and laughing at testimony. One reporter close enough to hear the teenagers relayed that when Leopold's chauffeur described them attempting to wash the bloodstains out of their rental car, Loeb leaned over to Leopold and joked: "It wasn't good soap."[34] Following one such day in court, a reporter approached Loeb about their behavior.

> Reporter: Dick, the people on the outside are thinking you are about the coldest blooded mortal in the world because of the way you are acting in court. You laugh and josh and appear to be having a good time.
>
> Loeb: Well, what do they want me to do?
>
> Reporter: I don't know, I suppose they want you to act natural.
>
> Loeb: That's just exactly what I am doing. I sit in the courtroom and watch the play as it progresses. When the crowd laughs, I laugh. When it is time to be serious, I am that way. I am a spectator, you know, and like to feel myself as one.
>
> You can tell the people on the outside that there is no faking or pretending. I have watched you in the courtroom across the table and you laugh, smile, yawn, look bored, and all the other things. Why should I be different?[35]

The reporter was unable to answer. Much was made about the occasional laughter and smiles from the defendants, papers sometimes printing doctored or inaccurately captioned photos to make it appear as if the defendants were laughing at the Franks family or descriptions of Bobby's bludgeoning. To fit with their narrative, most of these papers failed to mention that the crowd of spectators, witnesses, and lawyers also laughed and joked during testimony until they had to be calmed down by the bailiffs. After one particularly disruptive outburst, Judge Caverly interrupted the examination to address the crowd: "If you don't stop that hilarity and laughing back there I will clean out the courtroom. This is not a vaudeville show."[36] Of course, none of the spectators had their lives on the line as they laughed over mispronunciations or sarcastic remarks.

Some thought that Leopold and Loeb had been counseled to act light-heartedly by their defense team, to better align with the narrative of their being mentally ill. There may have been some merit to that theory, as Loeb related in one letter to his parents:

> I am not really so hard hearted as I am appearing. Of course, dearest ones, I am afraid that my heart is not what it should be, else how could I have done what I did? Still, I have had time for thinking things over, and the biggest things in life are appearing to me. I am beginning to realize just what I have done and my thoughts invariably turn to you two, and the pain and suffering that I have brought upon you. As yet I cannot show any of this, for reasons Allan can best explain. One thing I have decided and that is that something must come into my life. I truly believe that religion may prove a wonderful solace and comfort . . . in my case is needed a change more fundamental than the mere adoption of a creed—a change to a person unselfish, a belief in a supreme being, and a realization that virtue is its own reward. . . . I have intentionally tried to keep away from these thoughts for the time being. However, I know that when I do let myself go that I shall see things from a different light.[37]

Though the majority of early testimony was too routine for the defense to bother cross-examining, a few occasions did present themselves. On July 24 a chauffeur named Carl Ulving testified that he had seen Loeb driving their rented car at 4:30 p.m. on May 21. To Leopold, this came too close to suggesting that Loeb had been driving at 5:00 p.m. as well and that Leopold had been the one who struck Bobby and gagged him in the back seat. He leaned forward and urged his lawyers to cross-examine Ulving to prove this wasn't true, threatening to do it himself if they refused.[38] Benjamin Bachrach did cross-examine the witness and introduced some doubt as to if Ulving had seen Loeb driving at 2:30 or 4:30, but the cross ended quickly and inconclusively, with Leopold unsatisfied by what he saw as his attorney's meager effort.

Loeb had his own objections when his reporter friends took the stand to describe the day that Loeb had led them to the drug store that Leopold had called during their ransom attempt. When reporter Alvin Goldstein testified that Loeb had said that if he was going to kidnap or murder someone, Bobby "was just the kind of cocky little son of a bitch that I would pick," Loeb's face dropped.[39] He shook his head and leaned forward to whisper

(l-r) Judge John Caverly, Leopold, Loeb, and Robert Crowe going to look at the rental car used in the murder. Chicago History Museum; DN-0078036; Chicago Daily News collection.

urgently with Darrow and Bachrach for several minutes, before sitting back dissatisfied. There was no cross-examination. Despite the reluctance of the defense team to cross-examine, the next time he disagreed with a witness, Leopold would not give up so easily.

Toward the end of the session on July 25, after another day of fairly bland testimony, police officer James Gortland testified that when he asked Leopold on June 1 what he thought his defense would be, he had replied: "Well, that will depend on the wishes of my father and the lawyers. Of course, if they wish me to hang I will plead not guilty and the jury will hang me, or I will plead guilty before a friendly Judge and get life imprisonment."[40] When Darrow asked if this was true, Leopold vehemently denied that it was.[41]

This testimony about the friendly judge came in the middle of a long recitation by Gortland of every conversation he had with Leopold and Loeb while they were in Crowe's custody. The majority of the events and quotes he related can be backed up by other sources, either in transcripts from stenographers or the printed stories of reporters. The conversation that Leopold disputed happened when he and Gortland were alone in the state's attorney's offices. Interestingly, Crowe said something very similar to

Caverly during the grand jury hearing nearly two months before, predicting that the defendants "might enter a plea of guilty before a lenient judge and escape with life imprisonment."[42] Following Gortland's testimony Darrow began a short cross-examination, but he could not get into depth before court was adjourned.

The next day Leopold and Loeb were significantly more subdued than usual. They paid close attention to Darrow's cross-examination of Gortland, often whispering to each other and their lawyers, no longer sharing jokes, but discussing legal strategy. Previously content to watch the action, Darrow, known widely as "The Old Lion," showed his teeth for the first time. He questioned Gortland into the smallest details of his story, rapidly demanding notes, dates, and clarifications from the stuttering officer. After several rounds of cross-examination and re-direct, Gortland admitted that sheets he had previously entered into evidence as notes he had taken on Leopold's conversations had actually been made as an outline for his testimony that he had written the night before his first day testifying after he had been debriefed by Crowe.[43] However, none of his testimony came close to proving one way or the other if the conversation Leopold disavowed had actually taken place.

If the conversation did happen it seems unclear why Leopold would attempt to disown this statement while letting others stand, though perhaps he thought an attack on the judge was more dangerous than one that only reflected badly against his own character. While obviously annoyed about the remark and its resistance to going away, Leopold was still able to joke about it, commenting blithely to reporters: "I'm a bit interested every time some witness testifies we said something which we never did say. In this way I learn many new things about myself I never knew before."[44]

A further day and a half was taken up by reading each defendant's confession and the statements they had made while in police custody into the record. Most of these documents had already been printed in the papers and on those days even the most die-hard trial fans began to feel their interest waver. The defense lawyers turned in their seats and chatted among themselves. Finally, on July 30, the state rested its case. The prosecution had questioned eighty-three witnesses and introduced more than one hundred pieces of evidence. Leopold acknowledged that with his exhaustively detailed argument Crowe had succeeded in his goal of proving that a guilty plea was not needed to secure a conviction, "but I wonder if he really helped his case," he mused. "I wonder if he didn't bore even the Judge just a trifle. He certainly bored me, and my life was at stake."[45]

Despite dozens of other contemporary murders and trials (including those of Belva Gaertner and Beulah Annan, known more by their fictional pseudonyms of Velma Kelly and Roxie Hart in the musical *Chicago*), something about the Franks case had caught hold of the public's attention unlike anything else. Leopold and Loeb found themselves in front-page news across the country and even in major publications around the world. They ate up the publicity, getting copies of all the Chicago papers, and even clipping pictures and articles to hang in their cells.

While many newspaper readers simply wanted to keep abreast of the details, others were using the case as a springboard to argue for their already held beliefs and causes. Editors, religious leaders, psychiatrists, and lay citizens all got their two cents in about what they thought was really to blame for the way Leopold and Loeb had turned out—pointing fingers at everything from a lack of corporal punishment in their childhoods to too many cigarettes. As one letter writer succinctly put it:

> If you have some pet theory to propound
> Or perchance some moral to unfold,
> Your perfect illustration will be found
> In the case of Loeb and Leopold.[46]

One local Communist paper (whose editor, coincidentally, was Loeb's first cousin) blamed capitalism and the boys' rich parents for how they had turned out, demonizing Nathan Leopold Sr. in a series of articles detailing the supposed conditions in Morris Paper Mills.[47] Those in favor of keeping children in the workforce, a highly debated legal issue at the time, argued that if Leopold and Loeb had done hard labor as children instead of leading pampered lives of leisure, Bobby would still be alive. Papers written by members of the Ku Klux Klan blamed their Jewishness, and Jewish publications blamed their lack of belief and training in the Jewish faith.

While many stuck to their pet causes when looking for roots in the Franks crime, the majority of the population appeared to blame the killers' colleges. There seemed to be a grave concern that Leopold and Loeb were just the first hints of what was to come with more and more teenagers moving away from their parents' homes to universities, those rumored havens of fraternity parties, bootleg liquor, and loose morals. And if the extracurricular activities didn't get them, the classes would, with a philosophy that had poisoned Leopold and talk of evolution that had turned both boys from God and, by extension, morality.

From his pulpit one reverend warned:

Go yonder to the city of Chicago and see the university students Leopold and Loeb murdering a school boy for the sake of a "thrill." There you have the ultimate logical result of the destruction of moral accountability to God. . . . Let our schools and colleges persist in teaching the theories of evolution and in the by and by we will have a country filled with Leopolds and Loebs.[48]

The first novel to discuss the case was published three days after the hearing began.[49] Titled *Sallie's Newspaper*, it mostly concerned itself with the story of a woman taking over the editing of a small-town paper.[50] The inclusion of Leopold and Loeb into the story, with the Franks murder replaced by the rape of a young girl in the last pages of the novel, seems a late, somewhat jarring addition. Author Edwin Herbert Lewis was in the process of writing the novel when the Franks case broke and was greatly disturbed by it, as he was a professor at the University of Chicago. Despite his profession he speculated that the entitlement of their upbringing mixed with the scientific, secular educations they received had led them to violence. Lewis sentenced the pair in his book to thirty years in the penitentiary as the public waited to see what fate would befall the real men who had inspired them.

9

THE HEARING ENDS

On July 30 the hearing reached a turning point: the state rested, and the defense would begin to make its case. Here was a chance for something illuminating, a peek into the minds and motives of the confusing teenage killers themselves. In the muggy courtroom, with fans and newspapers waving from packed benches, psychiatrist William Alanson White rose to his feet and ascended the witness stand. Walter Bachrach stood before him and asked some perfunctory questions—his name, place of residence, and age—but when he asked White to relay his professional experiences, Crowe stood up.

Mr. Crowe: I object to that, if your Honor please.

The Court: Why?

Mr. Crowe: It is incompetent, irrelevant, and immaterial.

The Court: Why?

Mr. Crowe: The only purpose of it would be to lay a foundation for him to testify as an expert on the question of the sanity or insanity of the defendants. On a plea of guilty your Honor has no right to go into that question. As soon as it appears in the trial, it is your Honor's duty to call a jury.[1]

White sat on the witness stand for two days waiting to see if he would be allowed to speak, as the prosecution and defense lawyers fought a battle for the trial and the future of psychiatric evidence. At the time, when psychology was still a relatively young science, the offering of psychiatric evidence to mitigate punishment was not unprecedented, but it was still new enough to be challenged. Each side read from past court cases, trying to establish a precedent to sway Caverly. In the end it was the defense who won out; on the morning of August 1, White again resumed the stand.

He started with Loeb, focusing on his dissatisfaction in childhood, his feelings of loneliness within his busy family, and the strong relationship he formed with his governess. White's testimony became a joke when he described Loeb's childhood conversations with his teddy bear and photos of him dressed as a cowboy. He meant to convey how these things showed the depth of Loeb's fantasy life and how deeply he got into character, but the public mocked him, interpreting the testimony as if White were saying that any child who talked to a teddy or played dress-up was a potential murderer.[2]

One reporter quoted a teddy bear named Jekyll-Hyde: "Where Dick gets his hot air from is past me, but I'm here to say that he can't throw mud at any Teddy Bear and get away with it."[3] Crowe remarked that his own children refused to play with their bears, and Leopold joked to reporters: "I see that Marshall Field's are to sue us for $100,000, on account of the slump in the sale of teddy bears and cowboy suits."[4]

But not all of the testimony was so easy to laugh off. White detailed Leopold's king-slave fantasies and his obsession with Loeb, quoting Leopold as saying that he "almost completely identified himself with Dickie."[5] During this testimony Leopold wrote down a couple of stanzas from the poem "Adoration" by Adela Florence Nicholson, pen name Laurence Hope, from her book, *India's Love Lyrics*. He passed it to another psychiatrist, Dr. Healy, with the message: "In re Dr. White's remarks about identification with alter ego, Dick; see poem I quoted to you."[6] The stanzas he chose were:

> Long past the pulse and pain of passion,
> Long left the limits of all love—
> I crave some nearer, fuller fashion,
> Some unknown way, beyond, above—
> Some infinitely inner fusion,
> As Wave with Water; Flame with Fire—
> Let me dream once the dear delusion,
> That I am You, oh, Heart's Desire!

This desire to be closer to Loeb, indeed for them to become one being, was echoed in later statements made by the psychiatrists, in which they testified that Leopold said he "was even jealous of the drink and food Dick ingested, because these came so much closer to Dick's person than he could ever come."[7] The doctors argued it was this uncritical and unrealistic idealization of Loeb that had inspired Leopold to follow Loeb's plan to commit murder.

On the morning of August 4, reporters found Leopold and Loeb in high spirits as they waited to be taken to court for the day. Leopold joked: "Gosh, how I would hate to walk in on a group of reporters with my hair awry. Extra! Extra! I would hear the boys cry in about five minutes. 'Leopold's hair is mussed! He is slipping!'"[8] After Loeb had regaled the crowd with an account of an argument he, Leopold, and another prisoner had gotten into about which of their alma maters was superior, they were called away, and the "indefatigable twins" departed, calling out goodbyes behind them.[9] For Leopold at least, this elevated mood was soon to disappear.

Dr. William White's place on the stand was taken by Dr. William Healy, who spoke of his own examinations of the defendants. When Crowe asked Healy in open court "How many forms of perversion did Leopold practice on Loeb?" objections were raised by the defense and this material was deemed unfit for publication. The sexual information was told by Healy in a low voice with the defense and prosecution teams crowded around the witness stand, Caverly yelling at reporters to back up if they tried to sneak closer for a listen.[10] Despite reporters being kept from specific details, Crowe's leading question meant it was clearly understood what the testimony was about. One headline hinted coyly: "Boy Slayers' Baseness Is Depicted: Leopold Loses Dignity."[11]

After the whispered conference was over, Healy testified in open court about Leopold's thoughts on the psychiatrists revealing his sexuality: "He says that there is one thing that he is afraid that he has not 'gotten across to us scientists,' . . . that the most important thing, much more important even than preserving his life, is the preservation of his dignity."[12] Dr. Glueck noted the same, writing that during the hearing Leopold

> expressed with much vehemence and in no uncertain terms, his preference to hang on the gallows rather than have his real nature revealed. . . . He said, "I can tolerate, even enjoy, to be despised and abominated by the public as a fiend. I'm still then a Napoleon on St. Helena. . . . But to reveal to the rabble my true nature" (referring to his homosexuality) "would perhaps call forth pity and disgust."[13]

Healy followed with more testimony in open court about Leopold's fantasies. He recited the poem Leopold has passed to him and stated: "Even in jail here, a look at Loeb's body or his touch upon his shoulder thrills him so, he says, immeasurably."[14] By the time court adjourned for lunch recess, Leopold was incensed. Approached by reporters as he paced in the court's bullpen, Leopold was more candid than usual in speaking against his defense team. "I seem to have about as much privacy as a gold fish," he complained. "When I said that death was less important than the loss of dignity I meant exactly what I said. When these examinations were conducted, I had no idea that every intimate detail was to be published."[15] When asked why he wouldn't want to try everything he could to avoid hanging, he replied:

> What is death? Are you afraid of sleep? Would you fear death if you were convinced that it would be merely a perpetual sleep? Well, I am just as certain of that as I am of anything. . . . I have changed my mind about nothing, and certainly not about such a measly thing as death. There has been no fundamental alteration of my philosophy in any degree, and any man whose philosophy is altered by a mere change of environment is contemptible and his philosophy is not worth a thought.[16]

Following his tirade, Leopold avoided reporters, and both killers spent the next several days somewhat subdued, listening to the testimony of Drs. Healy and Glueck. Loeb had no reaction when Glueck revealed that Loeb "told me all the details of the crime, including the fact that he struck the blow."[17] There was lengthy testimony about the various physical tests performed, and theories were supplied about what abnormal readings meant. But as the prosecution psychiatrists pointed out, the study of glands and their relation to behavior was mainly speculative.[18]

Whether the public agreed with their theories or not, the testimony of the defense psychiatrists was a welcome boost of life to the trial after the dry beginning and encouraged much debate among those following the proceedings. One man voiced his exasperation to a reporter: "It annoyed me greatly to discover that, unless I could quote correctly Loeb's words at the age of 5 to his teddy bear I was socially extinct and of no verbal importance in any discussion whatsoever."[19]

After the psychiatrists had finished their testimony, the defense got more personal by placing the defendants' friends and family on the stand. While the family members spoke almost exclusively about the amount of money each boy had saved and received as an allowance, hoping to discredit Crowe's theory about their motive, their friends were there to back up the psychiatric findings. Loeb's peers described his erratic behavior, restless energy, love for detective novels, and history of fainting spells. Leopold's friends quoted his beliefs in the hedonistic philosophy that he discussed at every opportunity.

On August 12, the state had its chance to place its own psychiatrists on the stand. Dr. Hugh Patrick testified that Leopold and Loeb were not mentally ill, "unless we assume that every man who commits a deliberate, cold-blooded, planned murder, must, by that fact, be mentally diseased."[20] While to many court spectators this was a welcome change after the defense's talk of teddies and glands, it was hard not to notice that the state psychiatrists were much less prepared than their defense counterparts. Most had only spent a few hours with the teenagers, and that time had been spent in informal conversation, listening as they were reciting their confessions or observing them while they were sitting in court.

After the defense psychiatrists had spent weeks interviewing the defendants and their families, the state could do little but try to devalue their conclusions, despite the cursory natures of its own investigations. Taking the findings of the defense psychiatrists as true, they could only state that those facts did not mean the defendants were mentally ill, and thus should have no mitigating effect on their sentence. Walter Bachrach thought that some of the state psychiatrists were beneficial to the defense, and that one had been "completely destroyed" during cross-examination.[21]

Once the state's psychiatrists had finished, all that was left were the closing arguments. First up was Assistant State's Attorney Thomas Marshall, who began his speech on August 19. Marshall exposited for a day, listing case after case in which young men had been hanged, encouraging Caverly to see fit to offer the defendants the same fate. Unfortunately, Marshall was not as adept at public speaking as he was in researching legal cases. One reporter remarked that "Marshall's high-pitched voice began almost a scream whenever his argument brought him back to the phrase he used at every opportunity—'the extreme penalty, death.'"[22] As Marshall's talk continued the next day, he bored the crowd and defendants alike; Leopold talked with his attorneys as Loeb pulled faces at a young messenger boy.[23]

In direct contrast to Marshall was Assistant State's Attorney Joseph Savage, who stepped up to speak once he had finished. Savage's voice boomed around the room and laid bare every gruesome detail of the murder with as much sensation as he could wring from it. As he described Bobby's death at length, Jacob Franks left the courtroom, apparently unable to handle the exhaustive replay of his son's last moments and what was done to his corpse.[24] Walking around and gesticulating to make his points, Savage urged Caverly toward the ultimate penalty:

> Bobby Franks, with the instinct of all boys or men, would have fought for his life, had he seen that blow coming at him. But no. The blow was struck from behind, that cowardly blow. And then, your honor, counsel come before your honor and cry out for mercy. My God, what mercy

did they show that boy? Why, your honor, it is an insult in a case of this kind to come before the bar of justice and beg for mercy.[25]

Within the growing crowd of spectators, many wept at this oration, but not everyone was so moved. After Savage had finished the first day of his speech, Loeb remarked to a reporter: "The only thing I could think of is a college cheerleader, throwing his arms around and shouting. He seemed to exaggerate it so much that I was hardly moved by it."[26]

Following the two prosecution arguments, Walter Bachrach stepped up to kick off the defense side. Staying true to his background, he emphasized the defense's position on the psychiatric elements, pulling quotes from books written by the prosecution's psychiatrists to emphasize that the defendants were clearly mentally ill. While all three speeches were important, Bachrach, Savage, and Marshall were really only the opening act for the true spectacle to come.

On August 22 the city was abuzz with anticipation, as more people than ever before congregated at the Criminal Court Building hoping for a chance to see Darrow give what promised to be one of his most memorable

(l-r) Benjamin Bachrach, Leopold, Loeb, and Clarence Darrow in court. Chicago History Museum; DN-0078021; Chicago Daily News collection.

speeches to date. This fervor is noticeable even in the trial transcript, which records Judge Caverly yelling at the bailiffs as they struggled to detain crowds in the packed hallway from squeezing into court: "Keep that door closed. If they persist in coming in bring somebody up here and I will send them over to jail. . . . No more crowding in back there. Keep quiet; keep back out of the way. Mr. Bailiffs, do not let anybody in, it does not make any difference who!"[27]

When Darrow stepped before the judge's bench, thumbs under his trademark suspenders, he pleaded for sympathy, mercy, and understanding. He stated that neither boy was entirely responsible because they had not had a say over their own upbringing. Leopold, he explained, had fastened onto the philosophy of Nietzsche, which he saw as "responsible for this boy's mad act," and influenced by his love for Loeb.[28] "He did it," Darrow declared, "obsessed of an idea, perhaps to some extent influenced by what has not been developed publicly in this case, perversions that were present," which proved that he had a "diseased mind."[29]

> Whatever madness and hate and frenzy may do to the human mind, there is not a single person who reasons who can believe that one of these acts was the act of men, of brains that were not diseased.
>
> There is no other explanation for it.
>
> And had it not been for the wealth and the weirdness and the notoriety, they would have been sent to the psychopathic hospital for examination, and been taken care of, instead of demanding that this court take the last pound of flesh and the last drop of blood from two irresponsible lads.[30]

Often Darrow turned from speaking about the case specifically, expanding his argument toward the entire American judicial system: "I am not pleading so much for these boys as I am for the infinite number of others to follow, those who perhaps cannot be as well defended as they have been, those who may go down in the storm, and the tempest, without aid."[31] Then he turned to Caverly at the bench.

> I know your Honor stands between the future and the past. I know the future is with me, and what I stand for here; not merely for the lives of those two unfortunate lads, but for all boys and all girls; all of the young, and as far as possible, for all of the old. I am pleading for life, understanding, charity and kindness, and the infinite mercy that forgives all. I am pleading that we overcome cruelty with kindness and hatred with love.[32]

Leopold claimed he nearly cried at Darrow's closing, writing, "He even made me feel with him that terrific tenderness of his for the whole undeserving human race. I wonder now if Mr. Darrow didn't that day give me the first tentative first nudge along the road to maturity."[33] Caverly was said to shed some tears as well, and many handkerchiefs made appearances among the spectators. Despite his speech stretching over three days, Darrow had only spoken for about seven hours and forty-five minutes, split into two-hour long segments, which helped keep his audience engaged. In doing so he avoided the fate of Chicago attorney Lawrence Harmon, whose twenty-four-hour closing argument in defense of "Sausage Vat Murderer" Adolph Luetgert in 1898 exhausted the judge and jury, and ended in a guilty verdict for his client.[34]

With the unfortunate position in the closing argument lineup between Darrow and Crowe, Benjamin Bachrach spoke only briefly, offering a more concise final summary of the defense's points. When he finished it was time for the grand finale: Crowe's closing argument.

Before court began on the morning of the 26th, Leopold joked to reporters about Crowe's impending argument: "I hope he doesn't talk more than three hours, as I doubt whether I would be able to stand the strain. It isn't what he says that bothers me; it is his awful mistakes in grammar."[35] Unfortunately for Leopold, Crowe's argument would also stretch over three days and be nearly identical to the length of Darrow's.

Part of his argument was occupied by his theory of motive: "Mr. Darrow says that there is no motive, that it is a senseless crime; that the ten thousand dollars had absolutely nothing to do with it. I will undertake to prove, not by argument, but by sworn testimony, that the ten thousand dollars had everything to do with it."[36] He read off a list of deposits Loeb made into his bank accounts, connecting them with miscellaneous crimes or gambling for high stakes, which Crowe claimed at some point had soured and put him heavily in debt. Both defendants scoffed at Crowe's theories, Loeb offering his explanation to reporters: "Everyone knows I have always been an ardent Michigan [football] supporter and Michigan was decidedly victorious in the Fall of 1923."[37]

Crowe also brought up the first coroner's examination, which had concluded that Bobby may have been violated. The defense objected and Caverly ordered all women to leave the courtroom, as this material was unfit for their delicate ears. Though the coroner's report said of Bobby's body "there is no evidence of recent forced entry," Crowe waved it away, saying that a night in the culvert had washed away all the physical proof. And what was to stop the defendants from doing such a thing? After all, he reasoned,

"If the glasses had never been found . . . Nathan Leopold would be over in Paris or some other of the gay capitals of Europe, indulging his unnatural lust with the five thousand dollars he had wrung from Jacob Franks."[38] And of course he could hardly finish without taking shots at his opponent:

> The trouble with Mr. Darrow is that he does not know all the facts in this case. He does not know all the evidence. I thank God I am not a great pleader, because I think that sometimes when men are obsessed with the idea that when they open their mouth words of wisdom rush out, that all that is necessary in the trial of a case is to make a wonderful argument, that that is why a great many of them fail in my judgement, because they rely too much on their oratory; they pay no attention whatever to the facts in the case, and after all I believe that courts and juries are influenced not by oratory, but by hard facts sworn to by witnesses. That is why I have paid more attention to the preparation of the evidence in this case than I have to writing a closing speech.[39]

Concluding, he warned Caverly that "Society can endure, the law can endure and criminals escape, but if a court such as this court should say that he believes in the doctrine of Darrow, that you ought not to hang when the law says you should, a greater blow has been struck to our institutions than by a hundred, yes, a thousand murders."[40]

A very brief hearing for the kidnapping charge was held after Crowe finished, with only two witnesses called. When it was over Caverly announced that as he had thousands of pages of material to go over and a very important decision to make, he was setting the sentencing for September 10 at 9:30 a.m. All there was left to do, for the lawyers, defendants, and everyone around the world following the case through the papers, was to wait.

Though the hearing had ended, reporters continued their visits, the killers laughing and clapping with appreciation when given a few verses of a song parody about themselves. They abstained from too much talk about the closing arguments, but Leopold scoffed when asked about Crowe's attempts to get them the death penalty with a nonchalant "As though it worries me."[41] Friendly local reporters who quoted them accurately and wrote positive stories were given interviews, and friends like Tyrell Krum, who would sneak bourbon from Jacob Loeb's liquor cellar into Leopold and Loeb's tin cups, were given exclusives. Though never one to admit to nervousness, Leopold confessed that "Those daily highballs before supper helped."[42]

Over the next week Leopold and Loeb kept up their playful banter with friendly local reporters, but out-of-towners were banned because the killers could not check their papers to see how they were being represented. Daily they denied that they were nervous about the sentence, both repeating that there was no point in worrying about it. "The only regret I will have in the event I am hanged will be that I will be unable to read the morning paper account of it the next day." Leopold said. "I have a curiosity to see just how badly they would handle it."[43]

But not worrying did not mean he was not planning. While Loeb "played a lot of soft ball in the bull pen [and] spent a lot of time wondering which girl, or girls, would come to see him next visiting day," Leopold used his two weeks to prepare for both outcomes: death or an extended prison sentence.[44] In either case, he wanted his ornithological specimens to find an appropriate home, and he began negotiations with Chicago's Field Museum and the Elgin Audubon Society for the honor of his collection. The museum decided they would take ten of his most rare study skins as well as the mount of the Kirtland's Warbler family once it was completed. All the rest of the collection, including thousands of birds, his sailfish from the previous summer, and various insects, eggs, and nests would be gifted to Elgin.

Leopold announced that in the event of a death sentence, he would write and sell his memoirs, and possibly a book of his philosophy, which he thought was unique enough to warrant being written down and disseminated. In addition, he planned to disprove spiritualism by failing to return and answer a series of prearranged questions from beyond the grave.[45] To another prisoner Leopold explained: "In the event that I am sentenced to death upon the gallows (as appears quite likely) I shall take steps to attempt to pierce the veil, altho I personally am convinced that no after life exists. I at least will be prepared for the exigency in case I be mistaken."[46]

Perhaps most importantly, he dreamed up a perfect finale to his life: his last words. He planned to recite a section from "Thanatopsis" by William Cullen Bryant, with minor alterations, before the bag was placed over his head.[47] His planned passage (without alterations) is:

> So live, that when thy summons comes to join,
> The innumerable caravan, that moves
> To that mysterious realm, where each shall take
> His chamber in the silent halls of death,
> Thou go not, like the quarry-slave at night,
> Scourged to his dungeon, but sustained and soothed,
> By an unfaltering trust, approach thy grave,
> Like one who wraps the drapery of his couch
> About him, and lies down to pleasant dreams.[48]

Leopold apparently would have put the poem in the first person: "I have so lived that when my summons comes," and changed one section to "although unsustained and soothed by my unfaltering trust, I shall approach my grave," to indicate his atheism.[49]

When the defendants were marched into the Cook County courtroom for the final time, Leopold was in gray and Loeb in blue. The courtroom had been cleared of spectators, only allowing in family members, legal teams, and the press, for this final installment of the drama. After waiting for the cameras to cease their clicking, Caverly stood up and addressed the room.

> Here the court will say, not for the purpose of extenuating guilt but merely with the object of dispelling a misapprehension that appears to have found judgement in the public mind, that he is convinced by conclusive evidence that there was no abuse offered to the body of the victim.
>
> But it did not need that element to make the crime abhorrent to every instinct of humanity, and the court is satisfied that neither in the act itself, nor in its motives or lack of motives, or in the antecedents of the offenders, can he find any mitigating circumstances. . . .
>
> The records of Illinois show only two cases of minors who were put to death by legal process—to which number the court does not feel inclined to make an addition.
>
> Life imprisonment may not, at the moment, strike the public imagination as forcibly as would death by hanging, but to the offenders, particularly of the type they are, the prolonged suffering of years of confinement may well be the severest form of punishment and expiation.[50]

Each was sentenced to life imprisonment for murder and ninety-nine years for kidnapping, Caverly specifying that "In the case of such atrocious crimes it is entirely within the discretion of the department of public welfare never to admit these defendants to parole."[51] Leopold remarked that after months of psychiatric examinations, "[if] the only thing that influenced him to choose imprisonment instead of death was our youth; we need only have introduced our birth certificates in evidence!"[52] Leopold and Loeb shook hands with Darrow and were hurried back to jail while reporters ran to phones and telegraph machines to relay the news.

To separate them from reporters and other inmates, the killers were placed in the jail's death cell.[53] Traditionally the cell was inhabited by men counting down the days until they would ascend the gallows, which were erected and disassembled in a courtyard visible from the cell's small window. Rarely occupied and spacious, the death cell is where Chicago's thrill killers had been given their psychiatric exams and was now where they would await their transfer to the state penitentiary. Once settled they called for a big dinner from Stein's: steaks slathered in onions, with all their favorite sides and desserts.[54]

Each of Darrow's clients sat down to write him following his plea. Before being "exiled from the country that has tabooed free speech," Leopold had thanks to give: "This one attribute of man [intellect] has always appealed to me more strongly than any other, and since you happen to possess more of it than any other man whom I have had the pleasure of meeting—this alone would cause me to bow down in abject hero-worship. It would be an inconsistent 'Superman' indeed who did not reverence his superior!"[55]

After piling on pages of praise, he concluded by declaring: "Your speech in my behalf was one of the greatest experiences of my life, and life to me seems merely to be measured in experiences."[56] As humans were changed by every social interaction they had, he hoped that his contact with Darrow had changed him for the better.

In addition to this praise, Darrow received $65,000 from the families for his efforts, with another $65,000 going to the Bachrach brothers to split between them, and several more thousands to the psychiatrists who testified for the defense. Despite equaling over a million dollars in 2023 money, Darrow complained bitterly about the payment: in his opinion, "it was about a quarter of the amount I should have received for a case of such magnitude and such exacting labor."[57]

In 1929 the average yearly income for lawyers was reported as around $5,500, eleven times less than what Darrow received for his three and half months of work on just one case.[58] The $65,000 was nearly unprecedented, close only to Darrow's last complaint about receiving less than he should, when he was given $50,000 for defending the McNamara brothers in the case that got him arrested for bribing the jury and barred from practicing law in California.

What the future would hold for the defendants once they entered prison, few could guess. While many of the defense psychiatrists predicted Leopold would only last a few years before losing his mind, Bernard Glueck thought there was still hope for the city's infamous thrill killers. "They may become crushed by the big change in their lives, and on the other hand may bring out something that will be of benefit to mankind."[59]

IV

PRISON

10

A NEW CODE

The morning after one of the most publicized sentencing hearings in the country's history, Leopold and Loeb lounged in their cell and chatted quietly over a game of cards. According to Leopold the nonchalance was not an act: "There was some slight feeling of relief, but relief from the tension of uncertainty rather than from any particular dread of the extreme penalty. . . . I had no conception of what prison would be like, nor did I make any effort to think about it."[1]

That evening at 8:30 they were handcuffed together with a three-foot chain and emerged from the jail, laughing and led by a cigar-smoking chief of police into the back of a police car. Amidst the jostling crowds of citizens kept back by mounted officers, an armed cavalcade of police cars slowly pulled away and the murderers began the thirty-five-mile journey to their new home. Along the way Leopold mimed stroking a beard and joked: "About the time we get out, fifty-three years from today, you and I'll be talking through our whiskers, Dick."[2]

Less than an hour after they had left Chicago, the faded yellow stone that made up the Illinois State Prison in Joliet appeared in the distance. Leopold, Loeb, and their escort rolled down the wide lane beside the prison and stopped before a large iron gate. Not out of the public eye quite yet, when Leopold and Loeb stepped out of the car they were met by a mass of reporters and citizens, all eagerly craning their necks to see the famed killers one final time. While police endeavored to hold the crowd back, the teenagers followed their guards up the steps and into the prison's administration building.

Historically, Illinois has not been known for its humane approach to penology. In 1898 a government board of commissioners declared Joliet uninhabitable:

When one thinks of two men spending never less than fourteen hours each day during six days of the week, and on the seventh day nearly twenty-one hours, in a space so reduced, and with a slop bucket in the cell . . . he is compelled to ask what excuse the great State of Illinois can offer for compelling the management of this penitentiary to so deal with men who are required by law to serve sentences here that they must eat, rest, and sleep in quarters so contracted, so repellant, and so utterly unfit for the purpose, that their very existence is a disgrace to the State that permits it.[3]

In the two and a half decades since that damning report, the prison population had ballooned drastically and nothing had been done to improve the cells, still small enough that all prisoners had to do to touch opposite walls were spread their arms. Adding to the problems caused by these spatial limitations, no physical recreation was available, and because of over-crowding almost double the amount of workers needed were assigned to each shop.[4] With so much idle time and pent-up energy, fights and escape attempts were frequent. Add on a prison staff that was untrained and rotated every four years with the gubernatorial elections and Joliet had earned its reputation as the worst prison in the state. Leopold knew none of this as he and Loeb followed the guards deeper into their new home, stepping forward blindly into the next chapter of their lives.

As they had arrived in the evening after the prison workday had ended, Leopold and Loeb were led to separate holding cells to spend the night.[5] The following day they were taken for their official registration and examination. There they were assigned numbers that would be used in place of their names, and to complete the transformation into inmates, 9305-D and 9306-D were shaved, disinfected, showered, and dressed in blue prison uniforms.[6]

After their registrations, the new convicts were brought to the visiting room where a bevy of reporters waited to interview them. Leopold, who had by this time become heavily disillusioned with all the publicity they had received, whispered to Loeb to keep his mouth shut.[7] Both prisoners remained silent as questions were lobbed at them, until one reporter pleaded that this was likely the last chance the press would have to speak with them. With a smile, Loeb assured him that would suit them both fine, and the prisoners were led away.[8]

Several enterprising reporters were able to get more information by hanging around the clerk's office after the aborted interview while Leopold and Loeb were having their prison records created. Leopold complained to reporters he thought were guards that "publicity has been most of our trouble."[9] Asked what their idea of education was, one of the killers replied: "Education is the ability to adapt one's self to new surroundings and conditions."[10]

After their records were completed, Leopold and Loeb shook hands and wished each other luck before they were assigned to single cells and separated, with Leopold on the west side of the prison and Loeb on the east. Prison officials reasoned that if the killers had any hope of rehabilitating it could only happen if their contact was kept to a minimum. Separated from each other and largely cut off from the rest of the world in an environment that was completely alien to them, the coming years would test just how "educated" each of them was, and how far their adaptability could stretch.

Life in prison was extremely regimented: Leopold was woken by a bell at six in the morning, dressed in the single outfit he was given, and walked in a line to work. Every lukewarm breakfast, lunch, and dinner was served in a communal dining hall in silence.[11] He worked six days a week and on Sunday, unless he attended church services, was locked in his cell alone for twenty-one hours. Once a week he was allowed a three-minute shower in the public stalls, watched over by a guard who controlled the temperature. These daily situations were depressing enough, but little could be more degrading than the morning shit run. As Joliet would lack plumbing in its cells until the mid-1950s, every morning before breakfast prisoners had to throw the contents of their toilet buckets into a large outdoor trough. Leopold recalled the experience in some detail in his memoir:

> In many ways the bucket run epitomizes prison; it is the picture that most completely symbolizes to me our life in those days. The long, silent lines streaming from both cell houses and converging on the trough; the smell; the agility required to dodge flying spray on windy days; the acrid odor of disinfectant. . . . And then the march, under leaden skies, over the seventy-year-old cobblestones in the yard, worn smooth by countless thousands of scuffing feet and seeming to reek of the human misery with which they have come in contact.[12]

After a few weeks, Leopold and Loeb learned that Stateville, Illinois's newest prison, was the place to be. In 1916 the state had begun construction on a larger prison five miles from Joliet to replace the crumbling monolith. Through poor planning, stricter parole laws, and Prohibition, by the time the new prison opened the inmate population in Joliet was so large it was decided that both prisons would have to remain operational under the jurisdiction of one warden. A transfer was still nothing but a distant hope for the notorious duo; each was told they would need to serve nine months in Joliet without a single punishment before they could be considered for a transfer. As with most things in their new lives, all they could do was wait.

Preceded for months by their reputations, by the time Loeb and Leopold arrived, the other inmates were eager to size up these child-killing millionaires' sons.[13] Leopold tried to fit in by imitating the prisoners around him, taking up chewing tobacco and using prison slang within his first week of incarceration.[14] Unable to admit unpopularity, Leopold would paint a pleasant picture of these days in his autobiography, claiming that he and Loeb were accepted instantly and that all the inmates went out of their way to be helpful to them. By all accounts other than his own, Leopold's notoriety, difference in background, and persistent arrogance kept most of the other prison inhabitants at arm's length.

Yet Leopold's infamy and wealth were not wholly negative; they also attracted opportunists eager for favors. These new allies informed him of the ways of prison and were willing to get him contraband, albeit at inflated rates.[15] One con who watched Leopold form these connections recalled that he "performed a thousand and one prohibited acts that meant punishment were he caught. . . . It usually takes the newcomer some time before he feels himself sufficiently adjusted enough to carry on the surreptitious practices that are found in prisons. Not Leopold."[16]

Along with all other new prisoners, Leopold and Loeb were given the Army Apha, a test used in World War I to determine the job each new recruit was fit for. Leopold scored a 205 and Loeb a 176,[17] placing them far above their prison counterparts who averaged a score of 70.[18] These scores should not be confused with those of intelligence tests; when Leopold and Loeb took the Stanford-Binet intelligence tests a few months prior, Leopold received a 118 and Loeb a 119, scores which were only "high average." However psychiatrists said the scores were almost as high as it was possible for people of their age to receive and not an accurate measure of their intelligence, as the tests they used were primarily built for children and the scoring scaled by age.[19] While both were obviously intelligent, what they would score on a modern IQ test is unknown.

Though his intelligence and education normally would have allowed him to work a desk job, prison officials worried that if either Leopold or Loeb were reported to be doing anything other than menial labor there would be backlash. Instead, Leopold was assigned to weave rattan chair bottoms. He was clumsy with his hands, but his proclivity ended up mattering little, as he would usually ignore the chairs to wander around the shop, not at all afraid of discipline that didn't come anyway.[20]

Soon after their confinement, Leopold and Loeb asked to teach in the prison night school in addition to their regular jobs.[21] In November Leopold began teaching, but when newspapers publicized the position, concerned citizens wrote in warning that this degenerate murderer would use his position to spread immorality. Leopold's position was revoked, and he once again had to face unproductive days followed by empty nights alone in his cell. "At no point in our lives in prison did the authorities feel that they could make a decision in our cases on the merits of particular situations," Leopold recounted bitterly, "always their main concern was what the reaction of the press would be."[22]

To help keep himself stimulated, Leopold asked his father to send him textbooks and subscriptions for weekly fiction books, magazines, and newspapers, anything that would help lessen the monotony.[23] One diversion appeared almost two weeks after they entered Joliet, when Clarence Darrow accompanied Mike Leopold into the prison's visiting room. The men talked with Leopold and Loeb across a wooden table as the prisoners devoured the home-cooked food brought for them. Between bites of peaches and squab they discussed their chances of getting out one day, and Darrow opined optimistically that they would eventually be freed, but he advised them to think of the prison as their home, without focusing too much on that still-distant future.[24]

Darrow wrote and visited his infamous clients a few more times before his death, but their families would be their real links to the outside world. Every two weeks prisoners were allowed to write one letter and have a visit with two guests, each letter recipient and visitor preapproved by the prison. For Loeb this meant his mother when she was in Chicago, and his brothers or extended family members when she was in Charlevoix. For Leopold it meant an hour with his father and Aunt Birdie discussing family gossip and Leopold's studies.

In this way the months passed, summer faded to fall, bringing a bird migration that Leopold couldn't see beyond a flock of nighthawks he managed to glimpse out a window. This was the first year since he began field ornithology that he would not be out in the fields before dawn recording their flight.[25] While he had lost most everything else, for now Leopold still had Loeb.

Although they were kept separated, they managed to send notes and share lengthier conversations during Jewish holidays. There was never a guarantee they could see each other, however, as Loeb explained to Darrow in 1926: "We had hoped to be together for a few days this Spring during the Passover Holidays, but unfortunately there was no celebration."[26] When away from his companion, Loeb managed to make other friends, but according to a prison psychiatrist who read Loeb's diary from this period, he was not mentally adapting as well as Leopold was. "Dick tried for a long time not to acknowledge to himself where he was," the psychiatrist recalled. "He relived the events in the years before his trouble and tried to 'escape' in reading books and re-reading letters from his family and friends outside."[27]

Anna Loeb visited her son for the first time almost a month after his confinement. Accompanied by her elder sons, Anna assured Loeb of the family's devotion and Loeb did as much as he could to sugarcoat his life behind bars, speaking of the ample time he now had for reading and writing.[28] Later, Loeb would say that when writing to loved ones, a good prisoner "takes his imprisonment philosophically; he does not moan and groan; he tries to be as cheerful as possible."[29] In a letter Anna wrote to Darrow after that visit, she admitted: "I try to be brave and face the situation, but no one will ever know how trying it is. Am I going to succeed? It is putting one to the severest test that it is possible to endure. To say good-bye, come home to our comforts and leave my Dicky there."[30]

It would become that much harder to bear when on October 27 Albert Loeb died, the heart problems that had plagued him for two years finally running their course. According to Leopold, Loeb took the death of his father hard, guilty about being the source of the stress and unhappiness which had overshadowed Albert's final months.[31] A guard reported that for some time after his father's death, Loeb spent his evenings sitting "on the edge of his bunk, his head resting in his hands, gazing at the floor for hours."[32]

While Loeb ruminated on his family, Leopold spent his first fall and winter in prison giving himself over to boredom. Though his father encouraged him to write a polyglot dictionary and Darrow a book on birds, he was not allowed paper or pencil, and the frequent clouds of dust that coated the cells discouraged keeping the expensive reference books he would need for such endeavors.[33] "My recollection of the whole period is one of unrelieved leaden grayness," he wrote.[34] One bright spot in those winter months appeared in the form of hesitant handwritten letters from Susan Lurie, the first arriving as a gift for Leopold's twentieth birthday.[35]

Leopold responded eagerly, sending a letter and bracelet, but Lurie forbade him from doing either again, not wanting a reciprocal relationship. She seemed unsure about writing him at all, eschewing the idea that she was a Beatrice who could guide him out of Hell. She reasoned: "If, when you had the opportunity to see me every day, and be with me, you received no inspiration to do the things which are considered fine and beautiful—how can I think that I might inspire you that way now?"[36] After four months of occasional letters, her communications ceased and she never contacted him again.

These infrequent letters did little to impress the prison population, who roundly regarded Leopold as a homosexual sex criminal. Though Caverly had ruled that Bobby hadn't been molested, the rumor that he had been proved very difficult to dispel. As true today as it was in the 1920s, criminals convicted of sex crimes, particularly against children, were the most likely to face sexual violence at the hands of their peers. His being younger than most of the other prisoners hardly helped matters. Bluntly, Leopold remarked: "Most young kids that come here get bummed, and I got propositioned more than most."[37]

As winter gave way to spring, both Loeb and Leopold found themselves jarred out of the monotony of the last seven months. In mid-May, Leopold was diagnosed with appendicitis. As Joliet lacked adequate surgical facilities, he was transferred to the hospital ward in Stateville.[38] It was fortuitous timing: while Leopold was awaiting an appendectomy, prisoners in Joliet were growing increasingly sick, many falling victim to a measles outbreak that swept through the prison's close quarters.

In early June Loeb found himself among them and along with his high fever, he began to show signs of mental disturbance. A prison psychiatrist noted that Loeb:

> Expressed the fear that an inmate attendant was planning a sexual assault upon him. Later he developed the idea that hydro-therapeutic treatment and restraint which was used to combat acute excitement, was part of an ordeal through which he was being put as a test of his qualifications for a position of trust and responsibility in this prison. He was violent, obscene, abusive in his language, [and] destructive.[39]

After several weeks, Loeb returned to reality and was allowed to rejoin the prison's general population. While Loeb readjusted to life alone in Joliet, Leopold recovered from his appendectomy and marveled at the drastic differences between Joliet and Stateville. What he could see of the prison was spacious and out the windows there stretched grassy fields, birdsong, and a blue sky.[40] According to a researcher who saw a list Leopold kept of the men he had sex with, the hospital was also where he had his first sexual experience in prison.[41] Desperate to stay, Leopold asked his father to plead his case to the warden, who consented to keep him, all the better to separate him from Loeb.

Over the next few weeks, Leopold grew increasingly charmed with his new home. While he was still relegated to a menial job, this time in the shoe factory, Stateville was not tied to the idea that because someone broke a law it meant they had forfeited the right to small comforts and basic human dignity. The food was served hot and second helpings were allowed, the green-painted cells were more than twice as large as Joliet's, and contained windows, sinks, and toilets. More than anything Leopold recalled appreciating the air and water quality, the atmosphere much healthier than the rank and dusty darkness of Joliet.

Leopold even approved of the panopticon cell houses: circular four-story structures with a single guard tower in the middle. In keeping with Stateville's interest in penal innovation, the panopticon was meant to inspire inmates to regulate their own behavior and rehabilitate themselves by implanting the idea that a guard could be watching at any time. Panopticons have since fallen out of favor for their tendency to induce paranoia, but Leopold was unaffected, noting that as the guards were also in full view of the inmates, it was easy to wait until their backs were turned to break a rule. After one day in the general population Leopold decided, "I would rather serve a year at Stateville than six months at Joliet."[42]

Desperate to fit in, Leopold learned to live by the prison code of ethics, or "hoodlum code." A criminologist observed:

> There are certain things which prisoners must do, and certain things which they must not do, if they wish to avoid the suspicions or active enmity of their fellows. Rule number one in this code of ethics, a rule which is more important and takes precedence over all others, is the one concerning the giving of information pertaining to any incident to the officials.[43]

Leopold learned to shun snitches and regarded most prison officials as subhuman. In this way he was able to gain some trust among the cons, but his personality meant he was no more popular in the new prison than he had been in the old. A reporter who spent several weeks with Leopold later in his prison life observed that his "means of adjusting to prison has been an odd combination of staying aloof from the inmates, yet trying to act like them. He is careful not to flaunt his superior knowledge before the other inmates—yet he never lets them forget he possesses it. He conspicuously obeys the hoodlum code—yet he is almost excessively polite, not only to prison officials, but to inmates."[44]

This contradictory persona meant that Leopold would never be popular, but to those who would consent to associate with him, he could be a warm and attentive friend. One con said, "I remember my birthday in 1930. I opened my locker that day and it was stacked full of stuff. Nate'd been picking it up for weeks. . . . It was the first time I had a birthday present in prison."[45]

As Leopold became more comfortable with Stateville, he was assigned his first cell partner, George Fisher, a man Leopold described as a jewel thief and "professional horse-race tipster."[46] With Fisher's help, Leopold branched out beyond inmate allies, the pair advising guards on stock market investments in exchange for better food and contraband. Bribery was hardly uncommon in the prisons: in 1928 researchers observed that in Joliet and Stateville "the position of the guard is well-nigh intolerable. His salary is ridiculously low. . . . His hours of labor are very long—sometimes sixteen hours a day."[47] Under these conditions it seems inevitable that so many were willing to take bribes, sell contraband, and let the prisoners dictate policy. After nearly two years behind bars Leopold was settling into his groove and becoming what one reverend who visited the prison called a "confirmed criminal."[48]

After Fisher was transferred, Leopold spent a brief time with another murderer named Charles Shader. They had sex, but with little in common beyond their crime, Leopold got himself transferred into the cell of Mike Dennehy.[49] The two also became sexual partners, and Leopold admired the more experienced con, praising his extroversion, intelligence, and strict adherence to the hoodlum code.[50] Leopold and Dennehy had a common affection for languages and after practicing Italian together, Leopold seemed intellectually revived. He asked his Mexican coworkers Bernardo Roa and Juan Rizzo for Spanish lessons, picked up on his neglected studies by taking correspondence courses in Sanskrit and Hebrew, considered translating philosophy texts, and began writing sentimental poetry.[51]

For a less intellectual hobby, Leopold also began breeding birds. Stateville's larger cells and yard were conducive to this, and it was common for prisoners to tame any birds they could manage to trap, keeping some for food and others for pets. Leopold was particularly fond of robins and horned larks: raising the chicks by hand, carrying them around in his shirt pockets, and training them to come when he whistled. After one of her many visits, Birdie wrote to her nephew in early 1926: "The best that is in you is coming more and more to the surface . . . and all I can say is that we always leave you content in knowing that you are <u>always</u> busy trying to <u>go ahead</u>."[52]

Yet the positive surface life Leopold seemed to be leading was called into question in early May 1926. During a routine search of their cell, guards uncovered contraband sugar, vegetables, dead pigeons, and a small grill that Leopold and Dennehy had been using to supplement their bland prison diet. Both men were sent to solitary confinement.[53]

Solitary confinement is perhaps not the proper term for Stateville's isolation ward in its early days. Much more evocative was the name inmates and guards used: the hole. Located in a building separate from the rest of the prison, inmates unlucky enough to get sent there spent ten hours a day in pitch-black cells standing with their hands chained to their cell bars. If the jailer on duty was feeling particularly vicious, he and the inmates working with him would beat the prisoners while they were unable to move. At night they were unshackled, given a small amount of bread and water, and allowed to sleep on a concrete bench.

On May 5, two days after Leopold was placed in solitary, seven inmates looking for a way out of prison went into Deputy Warden Peter Klein's office and stabbed and beat him to death with shears and an iron bar. Klein's office was located across a lobby from solitary, and after capturing a guard captain the convicts ordered him to unlock the door leading to the solitary cells, telling him that "they wished to release a fellow prisoner confined there."[54] Escapee Juan Rizzo asked which cell Leopold was in, then moved off in that direction.[55]

According to Leopold's autobiography, he was completely ignorant of the planned escape attempt and was shocked when Roa and Rizzo opened his food slot and told him "in a suave, almost courtly manner" that they were going home, wouldn't he like to come along?[56] Leopold claimed that he rejected their offer and was then visited by another escapee, covered in Klein's blood and inquiring about a medal he had stolen from the dead deputy's desk. Leopold shooed him away.[57] Rizzo returned, repeating his offer, which Leopold again refused, but he asked to have his arms uncuffed and to be given a cigarette and water. They obliged his requests and continued with their escape.

This is how Leopold reported the incident in his book, but it is not the story he told when questioned in 1926, as he had to explain a piece of evidence he would later fail to mention. When speaking to authorities in the days after the escape, Leopold claimed that when the escaping convicts came to his cell, they were aggressive and he was afraid for his life. And so, with what he thought would be his final moments, he scratched a short farewell note to his father in the cork covering his cell's cement bench:

Dear Father,

As I am about to go away I want you to know that in my last hours I acknowledge that had I followed your teachings, I would have avoided trouble. I am sorry, dear father, for the trouble I have caused you and realize that I did not do the right thing.

Lovingly, your son,

Nathan[58]

Of course, Leopold was not harmed; he was friendly with most of the escapees—six of the seven were employed in the Shoe Shop where Leopold was a clerk, including his ex-cell partner Charles Shader. As Leopold sat in his cell enjoying his first cigarette in days, the seven convicts left him behind and used the guard captain and Klein's car to make their escape. Most were recaptured quickly, but one evaded capture until 1931, and Roa escaped again in 1927 and was never caught.

The returned convicts claimed that Leopold had been their financial backer, some saying he joined the group willingly, others that he had to be threatened to give them money to help them get established once they made it out.[59] Two escapees alleged that it had been the plan for Leopold to go along with them, but when Leopold learned of Klein's death he backed out; murder had not been part of the original plan and he was unwilling to risk another chance at the gallows.[60]

When the six recaptured prisoners came to trial, it was decided that Leopold's involvement in the escape plot would not be heavily investigated. The charge the defendants were facing was for the murder of Klein, which Leopold had no part in. As for his role in the escape attempt, the evidence was deemed not enough to prosecute by, especially as the convicts had time to collaborate on a story and incentive to throw the blame on another, more notorious inmate. When called into court, Leopold refused to testify, explaining that "I am an inmate and want to live up to the ethics of the institution."[61] He was dismissed.

Most importantly, letters and ledgers were found connecting Klein and a parole official to the dubious release of over eight thousand prisoners; all it took to secure a release was buying stock in Klein's manufacturing company.[62] This revelation of corruption took much greater focus, leading to investigations and public outrage. The six prisoners on trial were sentenced to death, and four were hanged for their part in the plot.

While he got off lightly in this case, Leopold's days in court were far from over.

Shortly after Leopold and Loeb were arrested in 1924, a man named Charles Ream claimed that they had kidnapped and castrated him in November 1923. A lawsuit was filed and a case against the pair was brought to court on January 4, 1927. Transported from Stateville on a brisk January afternoon in a baggy, prison-issued suit, Leopold was escorted into the Will County courtroom while Loeb was already on the witness stand. Loeb nodded and smiled at his friend as Leopold was led to his seat.[63] When Loeb was through testifying the pair reconnected, turning and whispering to each other in their chairs as they had the last time they were together in a courtroom.

In contrast with the Klein case, there was no evidence to tie Leopold or Loeb to this crime. Several police officers testified that when they had interviewed Ream the morning of his assault, Ream said the perpetrators had their faces hidden and he would not be able to identify them. The descriptions Ream *had* been able to give of their heights and weights did not match either defendant.[64] Taking away his credibility even further, Ream was now claiming he had awoken from his surgery very near where Bobby's body had been dumped, some three miles south of the location in his original story.

After a few days of testimony, the jury returned with a split verdict, and rather than go through a re-trial, the Loeb and Leopold families settled with Ream out of court.[65] For Leopold, the trial had been a pleasant break: he had been able to dress in something other than coarse denim, have long chats with Loeb, and get away from his dull job. Not long after they had returned to their separate prisons, Loeb signed up for Latin correspondence courses from Columbia University, where Leopold was also taking courses, evidently inspired by his polyglot partner.[66]

11

TURBULENCE

In the three and a half years he'd been in prison, Leopold had done little to change his negative reputation. He was still working in the Shoe Shop and had been sent to the hole three times, and a prison psychiatrist classed him as "a psychopathic person with severe behavioral difficulties."[1] Despite this, in May 1928 Leopold's life took a definite upturn. He was transferred out of the shops and into the library. Thanks to his new position, Leopold was moved into a better cell house, had access to a more private bathroom, and was no longer required to march in line under guarded watch.[2] The combination of access and lessened scrutiny allowed him more sexual freedom, and he arranged liaisons in the shower, library, and chapel.[3]

As Stateville's library was closed to the prison's general population, Leopold was given a pass that allowed him to walk the prison so he could deliver books—as well as notes and contraband—to other prisoners. In this lawless time inmate clerks often had more power than guards, able to set cell arrangements, job assignments, and clear records when their friends got in trouble.[4] Away from many degrading prison routines, Leopold felt that "in a way, I was my own man."[5] When his family gifted him a canary that Christmas, he was even allowed to keep it in the library's attic. He named the bird "Dick."[6]

When Leopold joined the library staff, he could immediately see that its organization made very little sense. The books were sorted, not by genre or author, but by the date they had been acquired, which made finding anything almost impossible.[7] But he wasn't about to speak up and risk losing what he had so recently gained.

As the handiest with a typewriter among his coworkers, Leopold was assigned to secretarial duties for the Protestant chaplain who oversaw library operations. While assisting with the chaplain's correspondence, Leopold got his first experience with rudimentary social work as he and the chaplain sought to mitigate prisoner's sentences and find jobs and support for them once they had been paroled. Leopold wrote:

> In some ways it was discouraging, for in many cases . . . there was just nothing we could do in what appeared to be instances of real injustice. But we were able to help a great many men and I never failed to get a real, personal glow when it was possible to set somebody on his feet. It was my first opportunity to be helpful to my fellow-convicts and it certainly gave me the greatest pleasure I had known in prison.[8]

Around this time Leopold was also befriending Catholic chaplain Eligius Weir, whose background teaching philosophy, interest in criminology, and logical way of thinking meshed well with Leopold. The two would discuss a wide array of topics including Nietzsche and various religions, and while Leopold remained a hedonist and an atheist, he credited this friendship with an increase in his tolerance and maturity.

His improved mood and sense of purpose were noted when two of his old school friends, Abel Brown and Jack Long, came to visit. After the trip Brown wrote: "Jack and I were mightily impressed with your manner, alertness, development and outlook. You were an inspiration to us, you, despite circumstances tougher than we've known your physical appearance is great, your mentality keener, your sense of humor a joy."[9] Yet once again life stepped in to unravel whatever positive progress Leopold may have been making.

One morning in the spring of 1929 Leopold was called into a deputy warden's office. He re-created the conversation in his memoir:

> "Did you hear anything about your old man?" When I replied that I hadn't, he said, "Well, I hear he kicked the bucket. I ain't sure though. If I hear for sure, I'll let you know."[10]

Leopold had the news confirmed while waiting in line at the prison commissary, where he caught the headline in a copy of the *Chicago Tribune*.

Nathan Sr. had died unexpectedly following complications from gallbladder surgery, and Leopold was for a time left unmoored, getting into physical fights with other convicts and being found drunk in the library.[11] The following week Mike came down to visit and promised to take on the mantle of Leopold's care.[12] Leopold couldn't have asked for a better substitute. Exalted in Leopold's eyes since childhood, his estimation of Mike would continue to grow in the coming decades. Having no children of his own, in part because of the stigma surrounding his family's name, Mike dedicated himself to his brother, offering advice, assistance, and information on any esoteric interest Leopold happened to acquire.[13]

In the summer of 1929 after the gubernatorial election, Warden Elmer Green, who had run the prisons since 1925, was replaced with Henry Hill. While Hill had no formal experience, he was passionate about penology and eager to make changes. Believing in the theory of rehabilitation over punishment as a crime deterrent, the former postman tried to make life more humane for the convicts under his care. He introduced radios, talkies, and allowed the prisoners to write a letter every week rather than every two weeks. Hill received a lot of public backlash for "coddling the criminal," but the prisoners appreciated his efforts and showed it by pushing their expanded freedoms even further.[14] "Those were the days when anything went—when you could do nearly anything you were big enough to get away with," Leopold remembered fondly.[15]

During their years apart Leopold and Loeb rejected the idea that they must have no contact in order to better themselves. As he had been working as a clerk for the deputy warden for several years, Loeb knew in advance every prisoner who was being transferred from Joliet to Stateville. If he trusted a con who was transferring, he would give them a short, verbal message to relay to Leopold, usually no more than a coded greeting.

Once, a newly transferred con called Leopold over in the yard and told him he had a message from Loeb, then handed him a tube of toothpaste. While it may have seemed like a comment on Leopold's oral hygiene, when Leopold returned to his cell, he found the real message. Prying open the large end of the tube, Leopold squeezed out the contents and among the paste found a foil pellet made of gum wrappers. Within were several pages of a tightly folded letter. Leopold was ecstatic to have such a long message with Loeb relaying his news and experiences since they had last seen each other years before.[16] As the vast majority of transfers were from Joliet to Stateville, Loeb was able to get word to Leopold semiregularly, but Leopold was unable to answer with any frequency.

That changed completely when Warden Hill introduced a commissary system that connected the twin prisons. After the change, a friend of Leopold's who worked for the commissary would place Leopold's letters, written in a code they had created in the Cook County Jail and usually with invisible ink, underneath the revenue stamp on a cigar box. That box would be placed with the rest of the goods Loeb had ordered for the week. As a quick way to reply, they would ask each other multiple choice questions tied to commissary items neither of them regularly bought—so if Leopold wanted to indicate he was choosing the third option of a question Loeb had asked he would have the commissary send Loeb three packs of denture paste.[17]

In the summer of 1930 Loeb sent big news: he would be attempting to transfer to Stateville. For his best chance, he would wait until his mother returned from Charlevoix in the fall, so she could speak to the warden in person and argue his case. Leopold eagerly awaited more news, but he ended up seeing Loeb quicker than anticipated.[18]

On October 8, 1930, Leopold was conducting business in the library as usual when officials discovered he was in the habit of forging the chaplain's signature on call slips and arranging meetings with other prisoners in the chaplain's office.[19] This was not the first time Leopold had been punished for private meetings with other cons: in 1928 he had been demoted for going into the bathroom with another inmate while carrying contraband cash.[20] For this new infraction he was placed in the hole for six days, and when he was released the extent of his punishment was revealed: he was being transferred to Joliet.

Leopold was stunned: "This transfer meant leaving my work, leaving everyone I knew in prison, leaving my comfortable surroundings, and starting over again from the beginning. I didn't know whether I could take it."[21] On October 14, Leopold was driven to Joliet, the prison "as grimy, as dingy, as forbidding as I remembered it."[22] In the deputy warden's office Loeb was on hand when Leopold was brought in for processing. Word had come through that Leopold was to be assigned to a Fibre Shop again; with Loeb's help Leopold was assigned to the newest shop building and the only one with running water, but it did little to soften the blow. He recalled: "The first night back in the cramped, odorous cell in the old prison was the low point of my life."[23]

The next day Leopold awoke once again to a layer of dust coating the surface of his water jug and the stench of hundreds of slop pails mingling in the morning air. After breakfast he marched to his new job, where he was expected to drag chairs to and from the booth where they were painted, but there was little to keep him occupied. Lounging around the shop he reconnected with Jack Naples, whom he had met in 1924 while both were being held in the Cook County Jail. Naples got Leopold switched to an even easier assignment, where Leopold "sat around all day and helped [Naples] do nothing."[24] With little to occupy him, Leopold's already low mood sank even further.

On the 16th, Leopold was called to the deputy warden's office, where he found Loeb waiting for him. While Loeb had been promised several meetings with Leopold, they were allowed only this ten-minute visit.[25] They used their scant time to trade information about friends who would be able to see that the other was set up well in their new homes. Before they parted, Leopold told Loeb that he was considering suicide. Leopold's conviction to kill himself was sealed when Warden Hill discussed Loeb's transfer to reporters, saying: "I do not believe they should be under the same roof."[26] Save in the event of Loeb being sent back, Leopold was to be trapped in Joliet indefinitely, and death would be far better than that.[27]

Leopold decided that it may soften the blow if he warned his family. Mike and Birdie came to visit the next day, and halfway through their allotted hour, Leopold asked his aunt to step outside. When she had gone, he told Mike his plan and explained that he felt it would likely be better for the family if he was dead. Mike disagreed "violently."[28] He urged Leopold not to give up and promised to talk to the warden about the possibility of a transfer. Though far from convinced, Leopold agreed that he would postpone his death at least until they had a chance to talk again.[29]

After the visit, Birdie and Mike sent letters to Leopold expressing their worry and love for him. While Birdie offered platitudes and silver linings, Mike was more grounded: "I have no suggestion to offer at the moment, excepting to take ahold of yourself. Make up your mind to stay on top of the situation, and above all not to lose courage or heart. I recognize that things look pretty black at the moment, but out of darkness comes light, and you must keep your courage intact."[30]

Though his concern shone through, Mike couldn't help admonishing his brother for the trouble that had placed him there: "You have done a very foolish thing, and it is not the first, and I only hope, as I have done in the past, that perhaps this is the time that you will come to the realization that these indiscreet acts on your part can not be done and gotten away with."[31]

Assuaged by his family and with a promise from Warden Hill that he would consider transferring Leopold in six months, he relented. To distract himself from the constant countdown in his head, he began to work with the prison employees who had known Loeb. Loeb had been a favorite of criminologist John Larson, the inventor of the modern polygraph test. Once they became close, Loeb sat down for polygraph sessions wherein he relayed the Franks murder both truthfully and mixed with lies, to see if the detector could tell the difference.[32] Larson was much less impressed by

Leopold, who "in his egocentric, erratic, litigious fashion" made excuses and refused to be tested.[33]

Despite the stakes, Leopold did not heed Mike's advice to curtail his "indiscreet acts." While more cautious to avoid getting caught, Leopold still shirked work, bought contraband, and exchanged letters with Loeb, viewing his time in Joliet as unjust and refusing to change the actions that had placed him there. It seemed there was little incentive to change anyway; after three months Warden Hill gave Leopold a date for his transfer: February 28. Leopold sent word to Loeb that he would see him soon as he waited impatiently for the day to arrive.[34]

However, conditions in Joliet indicated that a timely transfer was unlikely to happen. Changing parole laws meant that men were kept inside longer for minor infractions, often pushing back anticipated release dates for several years.[35] The mood within the prisons was already volatile on February 22, with an event that inmates dubbed the "Washington's Birthday Massacre." Prison officials had been tipped off about an upcoming escape attempt, but rather than stopping it, guards camped across the street watching the route they'd been told the prisoners would take. When the night finally came and three prisoners began climbing over the wall, the guards machine-gunned them to death.[36] To the cons, this was murder. Rubbing salt in the wound, a coroner's jury decided to "exonerate the guards who were acting under orders, and commend them for their alertness."[37]

"There was an ugly feeling all over the prison," Leopold recalled. "For the next month you heard nothing except how we ought to shoot the screws, we ought to throw the joint up for grabs."[38] Things reached a boiling point when thirty-five-year-old con Joseph Coakley died in the hole on March 9. The rumor was that Coakley had complained several times of pain and feeling ill but was told he would have to wait for medical attention until he left the hole.[39] It made little difference when a coroner's jury ruled that Coakley's death was caused by cardiac thrombosis and was "in no way due to the punishment this man was undergoing in the Solitary cell."[40]

On March 14, a rumble began in Joliet's dining room. Men leaped from their benches, overturned tables, and flung bowls of stew at guards as crowds of screaming cons burst into the kitchen and began to destroy the appliances.[41] Leopold was in the Fibre Shop when the riot began, and inmates soon came tearing through, smashing machinery and furniture. Naples joined in by borrowing Leopold's lighter to set fire to a pile of chairs waiting to be shipped out.[42] The cons stood and watched them burn. "It wasn't our fire," Leopold explained.[43] Four other fires were lit around the prison, but they were quickly put out, and one inmate was shot in the chaos.[44]

The rest of the inmates had their cells stripped of possessions; Leopold lost his books, letters, and pictures.[45] What followed were days spent entirely in their tiny cells, with all outside communication cut off. On March 18, Leopold was overjoyed when a guard ordered him to pack for transfer and herded him onto a bus, but when they approached Stateville's gate they saw armed guards running toward the wall. The bus turned around and headed back to Joliet.[46]

What the transfer bus had narrowly avoided was a massive, well-coordinated riot, far out-scaling Joliet's. Convicts simultaneously set Stateville's shops, mess hall, and kitchen ablaze. Pouring out of the gutted buildings, the rioters ran screaming and slipping around the muddy yard, looking for anything they could take their frustrations out on. Finally, the national guard was brought in; fully armed soldiers dodged flying hammers and knives before they at last managed to corral every inmate back into their cells.[47] As embers dropped from the ceiling the cons chorused: "We want a new parole board!"[48]

12

THE PRIME OF LIFE

Two weeks after the riot, Leopold and a couple dozen other prisoners were again loaded onto a bus and driven to Stateville. The prison Leopold had left just five months before had changed radically; burned-out buildings and rubble dotted the yard, but to Leopold it was still worlds away from Joliet.[1]

Leopold was assigned to the work division, and after three months which he spent picking weeds, carrying water, and chopping wood, Stateville was beginning to return to normal. Privileges were restored slowly, and eventually authorities began letting cons outside for recreation periods again. Leopold said that the best part of June that year were the afternoons he got to spend talking with Loeb when their cell blocks were in the yard at the same time. "We hadn't had such an opportunity for uninterrupted conversation for years," Leopold recalled, "and we reveled in it."[2]

During their strolls Loeb talked about his job; though he had been in the greenhouse for only six months he was already anticipating a promotion to the top position. Working there came with some very desirable rewards; he was allowed to walk around most of the prison and even outside the gates to tend the flower beds. Perhaps most importantly, Loeb delivered fresh flowers to Warden Hill's quarters, and he quickly charmed Hill's wife, allowing him a sympathetic line to the warden.[3] Soon Leopold found himself in an equally desirous position.

In early December, after a long campaign, Leopold was allowed to take charge of the prison library. As all but a few hundred books had been destroyed when the library went up in flames, the collection would have to be rebuilt. This was the opportunity Leopold had been hoping for. Leopold threw himself into the new assignment, sending a flurry of letters to university libraries asking for book donations and buying a Dewey Decimal classification guide with his own funds, his sense of order delighted with this system in which everything had its place.[4] Leopold hired three con assistants who helped catalog and label the new arrivals that began coming in. Leopold recalled: "I definitely had the feeling that here was something constructive—here was something that mattered. That was a feeling I could never work up over weaving a chair bottom or mixing paint."[5]

It was the first time since entering prison that Leopold was given his own space to control, and he was even able to use the library's attic to start raising birds again.[6] When he first received Dick the canary in 1928, he was one of only two canaries living in the prison. By the early 1930s, thanks to Hill's many changes, there were thousands within the walls, enterprising prisoners breeding them to sell to pet stores.

After the riot, Warden Hill was replaced by Colonel Frank D. Whipp, and once the unrest was settled, prisoners were given almost unprecedented freedom. Eventually the guards "retreated to the walls," merely hoping to keep the prisoners contained without bothering to try to control what they did within.[7] Cells became cluttered with canary cages, old newspapers, easels, pinup posters, and drying laundry strung from wall to wall.[8] Walking through the yard one could see hundreds of prisoners laying in the sun, shirtless and bronzed. While they tanned, they could eat fresh fruit or smoke a joint, as inmate garden plots stretched across the grounds; watermelons and tomatoes grew beside marijuana in the open air.[9] Leopold wrote of this "golden age":

> There was big gambling in the cellhouses. A man would run the poker game, provide the cell, guarantee payment, furnish cigarets [*sic*] and refreshments and cut the pot ten percent. There used to be a game running in cell 319 in C House all the time. They rented the next cell to do their cooking in. You didn't have to go to the diningroom [*sic*] if you didn't want to so you bought stuff at the commissary and scored for food and lived like a king. A lot of the fellows made liquor from potato peelings or apples, fermented with sugar and yeast.[10]

Leopold and Loeb used the laxity to spend time in each other's company. They played handball and bridge as partners and collaborated at work, Leopold recalling: "If Dick had a big batch of young plants to transplant to the cold frame, I'd go down and help . . . if a new shipment of books came in, Dick would be there to help with the classification and marking. We spent a lot of time together."[11] This seems an understatement; they often were counseled together by Father Weir and when Leopold had his lingual tonsils removed, Loeb stayed by his side during surgery.[12] Their bond was so well known by the administration that when Leopold got sick, Loeb was also given medication as a precaution.[13]

Leopold recalled that he and Loeb were "as close as it is possible for two men to be . . . we made it an invariable practice to have a twenty-minute talk immediately after breakfast each day. We cut everything up together, whether it concerned him, or me, or both of us. We had no secrets."[14] For the first birthday they spent together in prison, Loeb gave Leopold a hand-drawn card with a poem about friendship on it.[15]

Their fellow inmates seemed unable to speak of one without mentioning the other, though this did Leopold no favors. A convict who knew both

A birthday card from Richard Loeb to Nathan Leopold, circa 1931.
Nathan F. Leopold Papers, Chicago History Museum.

noted that "Dick was much better liked. Well, maybe not better liked, but more of the fellows knew him than knew Nate. . . . You could always see Dick out in the yard, stripped to the waist, getting that tan. Nate didn't always go to the yard. He stayed inside reading more."[16] A prison official concurred that "Loeb was tremendously popular throughout the prison. . . . Leopold, on the other hand, because of his supercilious intellectual snobbery, is generally disliked."[17] Though Loeb was a voracious reader and began writing a book on the American Civil War, other prisoners were appeased by his love of sports and no one accused him of being over-intellectual.

As it had in the days before their arrest, it seemed that Loeb's pleasant disposition allowed most to wave away character traits they would turn around and damn Leopold for. A friend of Leopold's "was struck by the difference in attitudes toward the two. Many of the charges brought against Nate could apply to Dickie: He was also a Jew, rich, highly intelligent, in on the same charge as was Nate, and a homosexual, but Dickie was 'a politician,' an extrovert, handsome."[18] One prisoner, who denounced Leopold as "one of the biggest fairies in the joint," still liked Loeb, though he acknowledged that Loeb "was a wolf and went strong for kids too."[19]

Typical prison relationships at this time were symbiotic, usually with an older prisoner (called a wolf or jocker) offering a younger one (a punk or kid) gifts, money, protection from other inmates, or a good job in exchange for sex, with very clear roles for who would be penetrated and who would not. While wolves were usually considered manly and straight by other prisoners, punks were seen as socially inferior and gay, yet desirable. And the younger the punk, the more attractive they were to the older men vying for their attention. It's unclear if Leopold took on the punk role in his early prison years, but now in their late twenties, both Leopold and Loeb had aged enough to be taken seriously as wolves.

Though he never mentioned sex in his autobiography, it is not hard to read between the lines as Leopold relayed numerous instances when he and Loeb took younger prisoners under their wings. They placed them in good jobs, gave them money and legal help, and would even arrange employment for them once they were paroled, which would have made them very desirable partners, especially as the Great Depression worsened.[20]

One such inmate was Trevlyn Clinkunbroomer. Clinkunbroomer was just twenty when he came to in 1928, poor, and with little education. Leopold got him a job in the library and had him transferred to his cell.[21] Perhaps showing more dedication than existed in most prison relationships, when Clinkunbroomer was released at the end of 1934 Leopold continued to write to him, "(illegally, of course)."[22] Even after his marriage, Clinkunbroomer still sent Leopold cards as well.[23] How these affairs affected the relationship between Leopold and Loeb cannot be known, though with his understanding of prison culture, Leopold must have realized that even if he wanted a sexual relationship with Loeb, the discovery of this by other inmates would be disastrous.

As Leopold was finding fulfillment in the library, Loeb was concocting his own ways to stay constructive; in 1932 he suggested a plan to enhance the prison's school program. At the time Joliet and Stateville had a dismal education system that only went to the eighth grade and was attended primarily by illiterate prisoners and non-English speakers. Leopold and Loeb talked through the idea and decided that if they were to start a school, it should be done through correspondence rather than in-person classes.[24] That way inmates could keep their day jobs and work at their own pace, and inmate teachers could correct lessons from their cells, with no need for classrooms that would have to be guarded and create extra work for the prison administration.

Though he agreed that it would be a fine endeavor, Leopold thought "teaching was about the most boring thing I could think of."[25] But Loeb was excited about the plan, so Leopold agreed to help get it started. The pair and a couple other cons worked for months to choose their textbooks and write up lesson plans and worksheets, with Loeb handling English, history, and plane geometry, while Leopold took care of algebra and several languages. Helen Williams, from the University of Iowa's correspondence department, gave advice and examples of some of her university's courses to help them, as did several professors from the University of Chicago. When they were far enough along, Loeb broached the idea to Warden Whipp's wife, who agreed to put in a good word to her husband.[26]

In January 1933 the program was approved and opened to admit its first students. At first it was only available to a very carefully chosen group of cons who Leopold and Loeb were sure would stick with the courses and do well in them. As this test group flourished, more inmates were encouraged to enroll. Once officials were assured the school was likely to stick around, Loeb was given a converted cell in C House to work in, the bunk bed replaced with a desk and filing cabinet. Soon the office was piled high with papers to grade, extra textbooks, lesson plans, and empty workbooks. Two poems were placed beneath the glass of the desk: "Friendship's Road," a sentimental poem popular on greeting cards at the time, and "The Quitter" by Robert William Service, which encouraged the reader to continue despite adverse circumstances.[27]

On the surface the school may not have looked very successful. It was quite slow to grow, not reaching above eighty students a year until 1936, and during the school's first four years 1,043 inmates began lessons, but only 319 lessons were completed.[28] Still, this retention rate was common among distance learners, and when the school's courses were tested, they were found to be harder than correspondence courses offered by many universities. Loeb's English classes were far and away the most popular, seeing at least triple the number of students as any other courses the school offered.[29] One government official stated that "Loeb was [the school's] animating spirit and he gave to it the very best that was in him. No pupil ever had had a more precise and painstaking teacher or tutor than Loeb."[30]

After noticing the difficulty prisoners had with his beginner grammar course, Loeb decided to create his own English textbook for use in a remedial course. The homework included exercises like writing resumes and letters to employers, which would have a practical use and hopefully encourage his students to stick with the program. Loeb's personality shines through the writing, the examples often including his favorite books, sports, and historical events.[31] The book, titled *English A*, was completed in 1934 and Loeb had a copy leather bound and sent as a Christmas gift to his mother.[32]

Anna Loeb was proud of how far her infamous son had come. After a Rabbi visited Loeb in 1935, she wrote to thank him for his kindness and interest:

> Your tolerance makes me think of what an old Chinese Philosopher said when his daughter had committed an error. She was put to rest: he sat by her bier reviewing her life and his last words (when everyone was condemning her) were "Is intolerance wisdom?"
>
> I feel confident that everyone who comes in contact with Dick must realize that something in that adolescent period went wrong. He has made the most marvelous adjustment under the circumstances. He is doing a fine piece of work and if the Press would let the matter drop, or tell the truth about him and his attitude since his confinement, it would not be so difficult. In spite of everything he has forged ahead and tried to be of some help to those unfortunate inmates.[33]

Leopold enjoyed teaching and working in the library, but his heart lay within the sociological research office. Ferris Laune, a university student who headed the sociologist's office, was researching accurate ways to predict which cons would succeed and which would fail when paroled. There was a growing movement in criminological circles to develop accurate models for predicting this behavior. After several conversations with Laune, Leopold was intrigued by the possibilities.

While assigned to other jobs, Leopold, Loeb, and Clinkunbroomer also joined "the salt miners," a nickname given to the group of inmates assisting the sociologists with their research. Above their office door Leopold hung a quote from Virgil's *Aeneid*: *Forsan et haec olim meminisse invabit*, which Leopold translated as "Someday, maybe, it will be pleasant to remember even this," explaining that "tough times are pleasant to remember, if only they're far enough in the past. Well, maybe that was true of prisons too."[34]

After researching proposed methods of parole prediction, Leopold and Laune decided to try out one of their own based on the "hunches" of inmates.[35] First, Leopold and Loeb guessed if 150 inmates they knew personally would be successful on parole, then talked through their reasoning for each case.[36] After two months of these daily dissections of their prison acquaintances, they had a list of forty-two factors they thought had bearing on the likelihood of parole success.[37]

They decided that the most important factor was if the inmate had decided not to break the law, reason notwithstanding. They figured that "an individual might have no scruples against stealing, but if he had thoroughly made up his mind that stealing was a losing proposition and had definitely decided not to steal, that individual would be a good risk on parole."[38] Whether a prisoner felt true remorse for their crime, received psychiatric help, or had any other rehabilitative services were not factors they considered.

The prison administration was happy to show them off: guests on tours were shown the school and sociology offices and allowed to chat with the killers. After author and sociologist Edwin Sutherland stopped by and sent the salt miners his latest book on criminology, Leopold was quick to send him a thank you, saying he was looking forward to reading it, "just as soon as I can persuade Dick, who was slightly more agile in his grabbing when the book arrived, to relinquish it."[39]

Quickly the work absorbed Leopold, and as the testing concluded and the statistical interpretation of the data began, Loeb dropped back to focus on the school while Leopold homed in on the math. The civilian education supervisor remarked that while Leopold was always polite, "I think he would like to talk mathematics with someone, but I cannot understand him, he is so much more advanced."[40] Leopold did not take long to seek out a more advanced mathematician to fill that void.

Since 1930 Leopold had been studying math through correspondence courses from the University of Iowa, moving from analytic geometry to integral calculus.[41] Despite his busy schedule, he found time for higher math because he wanted to better understand the theories of one of his greatest living idols: Albert Einstein.[42] In 1921 the physicist had come to the United

States for the first time, going on a lecture circuit explaining relativity to raise money for the Hebrew University in Jerusalem. Leopold had attended a couple of these lectures that Einstein gave at the University of Chicago, and even met the professor briefly at a party following one of his talks.[43] After Leopold spent three years studying, a family friend who was a colleague of Einstein's agreed to introduce the pair.

In a letter, Leopold asked Einstein to recommend books and courses he might take so he could better prepare himself to study relativity. He also heaped praise on the physicist, writing: "I cannot help but feel that your work is by far the most important intellectual achievement in the past two centuries and is destined to have a profound influence upon the entire future of human insight."[44] More than actual advice, Leopold admitted that he wrote Einstein mostly out of a desire to own a letter from him.

Leopold's wish came true. Einstein replied, giving him a little advice and encouraging him to do a lot more background reading before attempting to jump into relativity.[45] Though the note was fairly short, Leopold was so excited to have a letter from his idol that he framed and hung it in his cell. In 1936 Leopold completed an essay on relativity and sent the forty-page paper to Einstein, who replied:

> I have read the treatise with interest. Apparently he has a clear and independent mind. Nevertheless, one notices that the author's scientific knowledge is somewhat superficial. The consideration of the reversibility of the cause-effect relationship is wrong, the concluding remark concerning Gauss' Law is unclear and indeed irresponsible. I believe, however, that he should be encouraged to thorough study; on the basis of subsequent scientific grounding he will perhaps be able to create something of lasting value.[46]

Leopold didn't take Einstein's suggestion—giving up his studies in higher mathematics—but despite the mix of compliments and criticism, Leopold was pleased that Einstein had bothered to read his work and his adulation of the physicist only grew stronger. Several months later, when Einstein's second wife, Elsa, died, Leopold yearned to take her place:

> I had as a dream and an ambition the wish to be in a position to do things for him like put out his pajamas and slippers, see that he never ran out of pipe tobacco or tooth paste. . . . I reasoned that if, over a ten-year period, say, I could save two hours of Einstein's time, it is conceivable that with those two hours more in his active working life, he might have presented the world with a unified field theory.[47]

Looking back, Leopold declared that "this period was a wonderful one. . . . I wasn't even conscious of doing time anymore. Living here was just a convenience for my work."[48] To Leopold, who said that "life has always appeared as a perpetual battle against boredom," the school, sociological office, and library ensured that for several years boredom was not an issue.[49]

A slight hiccup occurred on June 12, 1935, when Leopold was fired from his library position. Leopold claimed this was because the new Protestant chaplain did not want someone so notorious working under him, especially not a Jew.[50] The blow of the job loss was lessened as it allowed Leopold to move full time to the sociologist's office.

As his experiment with parole recidivism took shape, Leopold began seriously considering writing a thesis and trying to find a university that would be willing to award him a PhD. In 1933 he and Loeb wrote to the various universities Leopold had taken correspondence courses through, seeking transcripts.[51] He had Loeb discuss the idea with Northwestern University, where Laune was also pursuing a doctorate, to see if an arrangement could be worked out. He explained of his "symbiotic relation" with Loeb that "Each did the tasks for both at which he was most proficient. And it was highly successful! Tho it was I, and I alone, for example, who wanted a Ph.D. from Northwestern, it was DICK who did all the talking—not I! Why? Because he had a way of twisting people around his finger that I lacked and lack."[52]

Talks with Northwestern were going well, and as a way to begin engaging with a wider academic world, in September 1935 Leopold's article "Parole Prediction as Science" was published by the *Journal of Criminal Law and Criminology* under the name William F. Lanne. His efforts were noticed by the little community of academics studying parole prediction, inspiring a response article from Ray Huff, a member of Washington, DC's Parole Board, titled "Is Parole Prediction a Science?"[53] Leopold, seemingly enjoying the opportunity for an intellectual sparring match, responded with "The Scientific Status of Parole Prediction."[54]

His original article was cited several times in the coming decades, and Leopold claimed it was taught in colleges, though this is difficult to verify. While he was proud of his contributions to the library and school, it bothered him that anything done within the prison did not affect the wider world. With this publication and the engagement it inspired, here at last was proof that he had not completely thrown his life away in 1924. But that taste of victory would soon cost Leopold another job.

In late 1935, when newspapers revealed William Lanne's identity, Leopold and the other "salt miners" were removed from the sociologist's office and had to find employment elsewhere. Leopold was fortunate and was allowed to move full time to the school, but to say he was disappointed would be an understatement. "I'd been doing the best I could in a socially commendable cause and I got kicked in the face for my trouble," he complained decades later.[55] Cut off from the library and his research, he still had the school to cling to, but in a few months when he lost that too, it would turn out to be the least of his problems.

13

LOSS

For half a century Joliet and Stateville had been embarrassments to the state. The frequent escapes, murders, beatings, and corruption that occurred within were regular staples in the national news. But 1935 was a turning point in the history of the Twin Prisons when Joseph Ragen took over as warden. Unlike most of his predecessors, Ragen had experience in penology, as a warden and Illinois's director of public safety. While he too was subject to the party politics that had ousted his predecessors, when Ragen was replaced in 1940 following a gubernatorial election, he was back on the job in two years after a particularly violent and well-publicized escape. Aside from those two years, Ragen ruled over Joliet-Stateville from 1935 to 1961 as the head of what some called an authoritarian regime.

Once he arrived, Ragen decided he first must get a full understanding of what he had to work with, and walking the grounds in his first days Ragen jotted notes on some of the most egregious things he saw:

> Yards filled with 83 makeshift shacks, built of tar paper, tin and lumber. These are used for "entertainment" and immoral purposes on a grand scale.
>
> Signs prominently displayed on some of the shacks say, "Officers not wanted."
>
> Several of the gardens are actually cultivated weed patches. The weed grown there is obviously marijuana.

As he made his way inside, Ragen's notebook continued to fill.

> Many cells with from one to 200 canaries; others have cats, dogs and rabbits.

> Many cells dolled up with curtains concealing cell doors and more
> frilly curtains over the barred window.
> "Big Shots" have curtains plus overstuffed chairs, chests of drawers
> and dressers in cells.
> Many inmates dress in civilian clothing.
> Guards wear no uniform dress. . . . Almost impossible to distinguish
> guards from inmates.
> Some guards arrive on post drunk.[1]

Obviously, there was much work to be done. Many guards were fired, and a new hiring process was established so that guards were no longer political pawns to the governor, but were hired based on merit, had clean background checks, and were trained before they began. Truckloads of contraband were confiscated from inmates, including barrels of weapons.[2] Upholstered furniture and curtains were removed until the cells were back to their bare bones. To curtail the prison's underground economy, all physical money was confiscated, and each inmate was allowed only three dollars of credit to spend in the commissary each week. Ragen ordered the sheds on the prison grounds be bulldozed and created an inmate landscaping force so that every convict would have a job to do, even if it was only moving dirt from one part of the yard to another to level it out.

Ragen had met Leopold and Loeb in 1934 during a tour when he was superintendent of the Illinois prisons.[3] He had been impressed with Loeb's sunny disposition and dedication to the school, considering him reformed. Leopold did not make such a positive impression.[4] Ragen may not have realized it, but neither were fans of his new regime. Loeb was told he was no longer allowed to deliver and pick up lessons from his students, and they were among those hit the hardest by the commissary spending restrictions.[5] With their spending power so reduced they couldn't continue the same level of generosity to friends and punks, which may have led to increasing tension with a friend of Loeb's, James Day.

In 1931, after an adolescence spent in and out of correctional facilities, Day had been arrested at sixteen years old for robbing a gas station clerk of $26. Tired of juvenile homes, Day gave his age as nineteen.[6] He was given a one-to-ten-year sentence for armed robbery and sent to Pontiac Prison.[7] In 1934 he was transferred to Stateville, where he apparently caught Loeb's eye. Loeb got Day an office job, a transfer to C House, and supplied him with gifts of cigarettes and candy.[8] After Ragen's changes were implemented, Day allegedly resented Loeb's decrease in gifts.

The cold morning of January 28, 1936, started fairly normally for Leopold. He and Loeb bought sweet rolls from the commissary rather than going to the main hall for breakfast and shared the treats with their cell-mates in Loeb's cell. As the prisoners chatted before they had to report to their jobs, Day stopped by to have a bite. Despite the rocky weeks prior, things seemed friendly for the moment.[9] Day mentioned that he would see Loeb that afternoon and then went to his job in the front office. Leopold and Loeb spent the rest of the morning correcting papers and talking over plans for a new algebra course they were thinking of introducing. Loeb left to take a shower around 11:30 and Leopold went back to his own cell.

At 12:20, Leopold's friend came to his cell and informed Leopold that Loeb had been hurt and was in the hospital.[10] Leopold grabbed his coat and ran to the gate surrounding the hospital building. Standing in the winter wind, as Leopold was "debating whether I could kick the gate in," he flagged down Father Weir, who was hurrying in to see Loeb as well.[11] Leopold pleaded with Weir to ask for permission so he could be admitted. Weir did so, Ragen gave his consent, and Leopold rushed to the operating room, shocked by the scene that greeted him.

Loeb lay naked and unconscious on an operating table with four doctors around him. "Dick's throat was cut—a series of four deep gashes had almost severed his head from his body. His trunk, his arms, his legs were one mass of knife cuts."[12] Leopold offered to donate blood but was told that enough had already been taken from other inmates who had followed Loeb's stretcher to the hospital.

There was nothing more for him to do, but he was allowed to stand at the foot of the operating table and watch the doctors attempt to save Loeb's life. Leopold tried to speak to him, though with an ether mask over his mouth and an oxygen tube in the hole in his trachea, Loeb would have been unable to answer even if he had been conscious. When Loeb's temperature began to drop, Leopold held a blanket and hot water bottles at his feet. As it became increasingly clear that Loeb was unlikely to survive, and his family had not yet arrived, Leopold was given the responsibility of determining if last rites should be given.

Apparently, the killers had made a pact several months before, vowing "never to accept any religion, no matter what happened."[13] Respecting his wishes, Leopold denied the last rites and according to Weir, after the fact, an "inconsolable" Leopold "came to me several times, telling me how glad he was that I did not attempt to administer any Rites to Loeb, because, if I had, the public would say, 'In the end, he weakened.'"[14]

Despite the best efforts of additional doctors from Joliet and those sent by the Loeb family who added their hands to the effort, Loeb died at 3:07 that afternoon.[15] Leopold stayed behind once the doctors left and assisted the inmate nurse in stitching Loeb's wounds and washing his body. After this was done, Loeb's body was laid on the operating table and covered with a white sheet. Leopold sat beside the body and uncovered Loeb's face to get a long last look. Leopold mourned that "I had had no chance even to say good-bye."[16] He stayed with the body until it was taken away.

Leopold's cellmate, who worked as a nurse, offered to admit Leopold to the hospital to keep him away from the prying questions of the other inmates, but Leopold declined. Instead, he returned to their cell and lay on his bunk, trying to comprehend what had happened, "disjointed pictures of the horrible thing I had seen kept flashing through my mind."[17]

All that was known was that around noon that day, both Loeb and James Day had been together in a small shower off a hallway near the main dining room. The shower was part of the officer's mess hall, which was being renovated for the use of the school, and teachers were allowed to use the facilities at their leisure. A few minutes after noon Loeb had burst from the bathroom, naked and bleeding profusely, and stumbled down the hallway before collapsing. Day appeared in the doorway wearing only Loeb's shirt, the walls, toilet, and sink behind him dripping with blood.[18] He handed a straight razor to a guard captain, saying "Cap, here is what I did it with."[19]

Day was brought to Loeb's friend, criminologist John Larson, to explain himself. He claimed that Loeb had been harassing him for over a year trying to have sex with him, threatening to get him fired if he didn't give in. Finally fed up with his denials, Loeb had lured Day into the shower and threatened to rape him. When Day protested, Loeb pulled out a straight razor and Day quoted Loeb as saying: "All right, it's fuck or fight for you. Take your clothes off and keep your mouth shut."[20]

Day undressed, but when Loeb's guard was down Day fought back, seizing the razor and cutting Loeb several times, but the enraged and insatiable Loeb would not stop advancing. According to Day, the razor changed hands several times, but finally Loeb retreated, running from the bathroom and out of sight. Larson was skeptical of this story; he knew of Day's reputation and assumed that after Loeb had tired of him and moved on to a new kid, Day had murdered his former jocker in a fit of rage and jealousy.[21]

While much is still unknown, the story of Loeb's death is much clearer now than the morning it happened. Day's cellmate George Bliss admitted that he had stolen the murder weapon and kept it hidden in the Protestant chaplain's office for several months before Loeb's death.[22] On the morning of the murder Bliss carried the razor around the prison until he met up with Day on the way to lunch, who had purposely dropped to the back of his work line so Bliss could pass it to him surreptitiously. After lunch Day slipped out of his line and into the bathroom where the altercation with Loeb took place.

According to the civilian education supervisor, when he was interviewed less than a year before the attack, "Loeb is always the same and always punctual. You can tell the time of day by his movements."[23] Assuming that this was true, it would have been easy for Bliss and Day to plan their attack, knowing approximately where Loeb would be and when he would be the most isolated.

Once alone with Loeb, Day attacked; prison doctors revealed that the first wound Loeb had received was the deep cut to his throat, and they could tell that the slash had been administered from behind, not in a defensive frontal attack as Day claimed.[24] When this did not kill Loeb, Day evidently kept attacking as Loeb attempted to shield himself, judging by the multitude of bone-deep defensive wounds on his hands. According to his autobiography, Leopold felt little animosity toward Day, viewing him only as a tool used by George Bliss.[25] He declined to explain why Bliss would want Loeb dead.

After Leopold spent several hours in bed attempting to process the events, he was escorted to the cells for psychiatric patients, located away from the general population in the prison hospital. There he put up a fight, determined not to be admitted as a patient, fearing the reaction if the public thought he had become mentally unstable after Loeb's death. Against his protestations, the doctors kept him overnight and put him on suicide watch. Leopold resented the flashlight they kept shining in his face that kept him from sleeping. Though Leopold argued with the nurse again, they would not relent and he got up and paced for the rest of the night.[26]

When Darrow was contacted he told a reporter that he "felt terrible" about Loeb's demise. "[Loeb] always hoped that some day he would be set free. I have always hoped so, too. I can't conceive any reason for his murder. All the fellows down there liked him."[27] The jaded old lawyer who had fought to save him from the gallows had one final thing to say on the matter: "He is better off than Leopold—better off dead."[28]

If Leopold found any solace in sharing his grief, he could have been comforted by the reactions of Loeb's family. Anna Loeb was "grief-stricken" that she had not been able to be by her son's side during his last moments, and reporters looking for comments from the family were sent away with the statement: "We have suffered enough."[29] A private funeral took place at the Loeb home on January 29. After Anna paid Loeb's body a final visit at the morgue, it was taken to Oak Woods cemetery for cremation.

Almost everyone in Leopold's life seemed united in their concern for him. Father Weir came into the operating room while Leopold was sitting beside Loeb's body and warned him against doing anything rash, which Leopold took as advice against attacking Day or committing suicide.[30] Helen Williams, the director of correspondence study at the University of Iowa, had been writing to Leopold for five years and had toured the school and sociologist's office a year before. The day of Loeb's funeral she wrote to Leopold:

> It does not seem possible that Richard is really gone. He will be greatly missed—and I cannot agree with anyone who says, "It is better so." He was giving the world a needed service and that is as much as can be said for any of us. . . . Tho he will be missed by everybody, I'm sure you will miss him most of all. And I'm sending this note of sympathy. It is all I can do.[31]

Leopold was less than comforted, as he wrote her in 1962: "Words are weak and useless things in the face of the loss of a dear one, as you, for instance, learned when you wrote me, 26 years ago, after Dick's death."[32] Other stilted letters arrived from Leopold's family members and friends, even less sure than Williams on how to address the loss of Leopold's first love, co-defendant, and closest friend.

Neither Leopold nor the Loebs were able to mourn the loss in peace, as reporters ensured that it became national news. "Pervert Loeb Cut to Pieces by Prison Foe," headlined an article relaying Day's story of Loeb's alleged rape attempt.[33] Another columnist remarked that Loeb "lived like a beast and died like one. . . . Practical justice should see that Loeb's slayer is treated like someone who has merely cut off the head of a poisonous snake."[34]

In addition to lurid tales of his alleged sexuality, the press was also portraying Loeb as the king of the prison. Photographers snapped pictures of Loeb's cell, and reporters were quick to say the canary cages (which weren't his) and items from the commissary were luxuries exclusive to Loeb. Nearly all prison assignments had access to a small bathroom where employed prisoners were allowed to bathe, but reporters painted Loeb's "private bath" as an exception and evidence that he had unchecked power.[35]

Two assistant state attorneys were assigned to prosecute in Loeb's defense.[36] Leopold explained the decision, saying: "The Loeb family did not prosecute Dick's murderer because, like me, they felt that this could not bring Dick back and because we felt that lengthening the prison term of Jimmie Day could not serve any useful purpose. We agreed that Dick would not want us to take an active part in the prosecution of his murderer."[37] Day was being represented by lawyers Harold Levy and Emmett Byrne, who in Leopold's opinion took the case "for no cash and a million dollars' worth of publicity."[38]

As both sets of lawyers descended on the prison looking to strengthen their cases, the prosecution found little help from the prisoners who until recently had been more than happy to accept Loeb's gifts and sing his praises. Even Leopold refused to aid them, and though it may appear strange that he did not speak out against Day, it must be understood that for eleven years he had lived under the prison code of ethics and recognized how far he would fall in the eyes of his companions if he were to violate them. In Leopold's own words, written three years before Loeb's murder:

> The "Good hood" has one commandment, and only one: Thou shalt not squawk. "Squawking" is defined as the acquainting, by word or deed, of anyone in authority—police, prison officials, and the like— with anything which may conceivably react to the detriment of another individual. The commandment is categorical, and admits of no dispensation nor exception even under the most extreme circumstances.[39]

Later, Leopold would rationalize that "if Dick does not exist anywhere as a conscious entity, then nothing I might do could possibly affect him one way or the other."[40] While he refused to testify, Leopold discouraged other inmates to lie for Day, saying that though Loeb was dead, he and Anna Loeb were still alive, and they would both be hurt by such falsehoods.[41] Though he remained mute before the grand jury, Leopold did make a statement to authorities in an attempt to dispel some of the negative publicity. Brought before the director of public welfare, Leopold denied they received special privileges and said that Loeb had his job because he "was the only man in the penitentiary who had the education sufficient to develop and conduct the school."[42]

When the trial began at the beginning of June it was immediately clear which way the jury would go. The defense leaned into proving Loeb's homosexuality and the ways he wielded his influence to get jobs and cell transfers for his punks. "Dickie Loeb," Levy announced to the jury, "the big shot of cellhouse C, was permitted to run at will from cellhouse to cellhouse on the pretext of giving out education, while the only education he desired to give was one in degeneracy."[43]

When brought to the stand, Day described the fight in poetic bursts: "All I could see was a man sometimes, a pair of eyes, and hands reaching at me like claws."[44] He tried to say that during the fight all he could think about was poor Bobby Franks, but this was quickly objected to and ordered stricken from the record. In his closing argument, Levy assured the jury that if Day was not acquitted they would be "'rebuilding the walls of Sodom and Gomorrah,' and serving notice on other convicts that they could not protect themselves from a 'wolf!'"[45] He declared that "By the laws of God and man, Jimmy Day SHOULD have killed Dickie Loeb!"[46]

It seemed that the reality of the situation mattered less than Loeb's alleged homosexuality, which was more than enough to convict him on its own. The head juror for the trial later revealed that the jury's attitude had been that "Nobody liked a Queer a Homo a lesbian . . . so it was a good thing to get rid of such people."[47] After only fifty minutes of deliberation the jury returned with a not guilty verdict for Day, who was applauded by the court spectators while music from a parade on the street below floated in through the windows. The judge promised Day that "When you appear before the parole board, I will do anything I can for you."[48]

This was exactly what Day had been hoping for, his lawyers announcing their intention to apply for immediate parole after the trial's end. Warden Ragen, however, disgusted with the affair and inclined from the evidence not to believe Day's account of the attack, removed Day's good time, ensuring he would have to serve the full length of his one-to-ten-year sentence.[49] After the trial Day remained in Joliet for several years and was disciplined many times, most severely when he was caught sodomizing his cellmate just five months later.[50] He was transferred to Pontiac prison in November 1939, where psychiatrists noted that he was paranoid and sometimes hysterical. He attempted to be released early several times, but his punishment, psychiatric, and behavioral records were poor, and he had to wait until 1942.

14

DEPRESSION AND NEW HOPE

"After Loeb's death, Leopold dwelt in limbo," one reporter observed.[1] In his autobiography Leopold recalled that "The realization that Dick was dead took some time to become vivid and real to me. It just didn't seem possible. I missed him terribly—all the more so since all the years in prison we had shared everything and planned everything together. I was very lonely."[2] Leopold admitted that when he was sure he was unobserved, he had cried four times while in prison; one of those times after Loeb's death.[3]

When Loeb died Leopold said that he "felt like half of me was dead," and in a way, he was.[4] From the beginning of their relationship when Leopold said he "completely identified himself" with Loeb, he reached toward the ideal of them as two halves of a single entity. When he wrote about his relationship with Loeb in prison, he portrayed them as never in disagreement or disharmony, but this may not have been the case.

Father Weir recounted a conversation he claimed to have had with Loeb about three weeks before his death:

> [I] said to him, "I want to tell you something, Dick. You hate Leopold."
> He said, "You know too damn much, but do me a favor, and never let him know that I hate him."[5]

Though he inquired, Weir was unable to learn what the nature of the trouble between the pair was, or when the shift had occurred. This statement seems odd, given the amount of time the two spent together, but it perhaps matches the turbulence in their relationship pre-prison. Loeb admitted to psychiatrists in 1924 that "He often contemplated shooting [Leopold] when they were out together and had [Leopold's] revolvers along."[6]

151

This was when they were seeing each other regularly, and apparently on friendly terms. Perhaps the animosity was a recent development, exacerbated by their increased proximity now that Leopold was also working for the school full time. Or maybe that old ambivalence had never completely faded. Leopold may never have noticed, as he admired Loeb for being "a great diplomat . . . he never let anybody know if he didn't like them."[7]

Once Day's trial was completed, Leopold was released from the detention cells, but a guard was assigned to follow him. This was ostensibly a way to keep him safe, but it also ensured he would have a harder time talking freely with his friends, seeing his punks, or doing any of the usual prison rule-breaking that had become an integral part of his life. Even after the guard stopped tailing him in December, he was forced to cell alone for several years.

   Without Loeb and after nearly a year of close observation by officials, Leopold had become even more disinclined to talk with strangers and kept his true thoughts and emotions firmly to himself. A psychiatrist who knew Leopold after Loeb's death observed: "You can't get inside him. He has built up a barrier, a wall, around himself. I think he did it deliberately, it's a protective shell."[8] A con confirmed this, noting: "You can get just so close to Babe, and then the wall goes up, and you're on the other side. . . . I got to know the many sides of Babe: the aesthete, the scholar, the teacher, the gourmet, the philosopher, the wit, the indefatigable worker, and the dilettante, and to wonder if each facet was but another mask."[9]

   With all the negative press following Loeb's murder, added to the public scandal of Leopold publishing under a pseudonym, Northwestern cooled on their plans to allow Leopold to receive a PhD. On April 27, Leopold waived the rights to his dissertation, turning over complete ownership to Laune.[10] What they had intended to be a joint project was thus submitted for review and publication, Laune receiving his PhD and sole authorial credit for *Predicting Criminality: Forecasting Criminal Behavior on Parole*, which was published later that year.

   Despite the loss of the doctorate, Leopold found some relief in returning to the school, now more motivated than ever to keep it flourishing as a "living memorial" to Loeb. He christened the school with a new Latin motto: *Ratione autem liberamur*, meaning "By reason, however, we are set free," a phrase which was chosen both for its message and because the Latin matched Loeb's initials. The motto and emblem depicting a broken ball and chain graced the cover of the school's new course catalog, along with a likeness of Loeb sitting at a desk with an open book before him.[11]

Soon after Loeb's death, the Stateville Correspondence School (SCS) program was accredited, and Illinois colleges agreed to accept cons who carried high school diplomas from Stateville. In early 1941, with help from Helen Williams, SCS accepted its first out-of-state student, a prisoner from the Iowa State Penitentiary.[12] The student was so impressed with the school that he wrote an article about his experience for his prison's newspaper, and several more convicts from Iowa soon signed up for courses as well.[13] By the end of the year SCS had gotten requests for courses from prisoners as far as the Attica State Prison in New York.[14]

While instrumental in the school's success, Leopold couldn't help giving preference to his favorite subjects. He prepared a course on the *Aeneid* that he admitted only two or three convicts ever took, and without Loeb to balance things, by 1937 the school offered twice the number of language courses as it did all other courses combined.[15] For several years Leopold and a couple other middle-aged cons named Heinrich Hammer and Gerald Burd expanded the SCS linguistics program until it surpassed many outside universities in the variety of courses it offered.

He would never be as popular as Loeb, but Leopold's position within the school did earn him the admiration and friendship of many of his students and fellow teachers. In 1937, Leopold's students got together a booklet of good wishes for Leopold's birthday, in a mix of the languages he taught as well as English, including a note from one of Leopold's favorite students, David Fulford.[16]

Fulford was twenty-one when he was arrested in 1934 for a series of home robberies and car thefts. He had previously done time in juvenile institutions and had not had a lot of schooling. Leopold encouraged Fulford to take classes and was impressed when he "sopped up knowledge like a sponge."[17] After Fulford had taken a preliminary English course, Leopold got him a job correcting English papers, then moved him to the school office where he worked alongside Leopold and two clerks.[18] While he assisted in forming Fulford's burgeoning scholastic interest, Leopold was compensated handsomely when he took Fulford on as a punk.

Another con Leopold tried to coax into joining the school's ranks was Francis Sandiford. Shortly after Sandiford was transferred from the Pontiac prison, Leopold made his teaching pitch, but it didn't stick. Sandiford was already well situated with a job in the commissary, and it hadn't taken long for word of Leopold's reputation to reach him. He recalled:

> As soon as I hit the Big House in Illinois, I had learned that I had to hate Leopold. . . . If you could get anybody to talk about Leopold without

blowing his top, you got loaded with stories to prove he was strictly scum. Cell partners would stop [talking] with me for days at a time if my questions made them think I doubted. I had to go along, or I'd be given the same treatment as Babe. What got me was that many of the convicts I questioned had never even seen him.[19]

Wary but not scared off completely, Sandiford talked with others who did know the infamous con, and learned that Leopold worked hard, often donated blood, and helped cons cover their legal fees if they couldn't afford to pay them themselves.[20] Softened by this knowledge and curious to know more, Sandiford consented to meet weekly, ostensibly to discuss his math class, but the conversation soon branched out into different channels. According to Sandiford:

> My voracious appetite for reading brought down Nathan Leopold's guard. By giving him the role of master I became the willing pupil, fawning in his preening. At first he led me into the esoteric world of James Branch Cabell, Ronald Firbank, Suetonius, and Baudelaire, but this led to words and thoughts that couldn't reach the goal I thought he had in mind, since he celled in C House and I in D.[21]

Presumably the "goal" Sandiford mentions was a sexual relationship, but allegedly Leopold did eventually get there.[22]

Despite Leopold's habit of hiring teachers and assistants whose qualifications had more to do with their looks than their training, the correspondence school continued to grow, peaking in the late 1930s with sixteen teachers and about 440 students.[23]

In 1940 Leopold dusted off his old statistics knowledge and set to testing if SCS students violated parole at a different rate than nonstudents. After some help from Everett Lindquist, a statistician and educator who would go on to create the ACT,[24] Leopold self-published his findings, in which he proposed a tentative correlation, if not causation, between attending SCS and a better chance of parole success.[25] Aside from his school duties, Leopold edited Father Weir's book, *Criminology: A Scientific Study of Modern Crime Problem*, and ghost-wrote several articles and speeches for Warden Ragen about criminology and the correspondence school. Ever wary of publicity, none of these works carried Leopold's name, and most never made it beyond prison walls.

After five years of running the school alone, Leopold was more than ready to move on. While he wanted to help the program prosper in Loeb's memory, the lack of privileges and freedom of movement that had persisted since Ragen became warden weighed on him, and he was bored in this position he had never wanted to begin with. Over the years he made several attempts to transfer but was always denied, until finally in May 1941 his request for a job in the x-ray lab was approved.[26] Though he continued to teach and correct courses occasionally, he was far less involved in the program, and following his departure, the school gradually loosened its standards. In a few years course completions could be bought and the diplomas convicts received were basically meaningless.[27] In 1943 they were forced to discontinue the program to other prisons, though it remained running in Stateville and Joliet for several decades.

Leopold stayed for six months in the x-ray lab before he was transferred one floor up to the detention hospital where he worked as a night nurse. Though he had applied for the x-ray lab, it was here where he had really wanted to be. Within the hospital building, separated by several hundred yards from the cell houses and general population, the detention hospital housed the mentally ill inmates deemed too disturbed for the general population but not disturbed enough to be sent to the psychiatric section of Illinois's Menard prison branch.

For a time, it seemed that Leopold had found a pleasant fit for himself. Life as a nurse yielded the best living conditions he had ever had in prison, giving him all the pleasures he'd been too distracted to enjoy after Loeb's death, as well as perks patients couldn't dream of. Nurses lived on the assignment and because they were expected to be on hand whenever a patient needed something, their cell doors were never locked. Leopold could have furniture in his cell, there was always a healthy supply of drugs and alcohol available, he could bathe in the hydrotherapy tubs, eat good food, and the patients washed and pressed his clothes.[28] "There were no rules," Leopold wrote, "we were permitted to do pretty much as we pleased."[29]

Though the nursing position seemed ideal, in late 1942 Leopold asked for a transfer. In his autobiography Leopold does not address his reasons for this beyond: "Many as were the privileges on the job, there were some disagreeable features."[30] What he failed to convey was that the remoteness of the detention ward, with little supervision given to the convict nurses in charge of the sick and mentally ill, was a recipe for a breach of power.

Sandiford described conditions within the detention hospital in 1941 when he was admitted there: "What at first seemed a refreshing break from monotony became an ordeal in which the constant threat of brutality by the nurses added to an already anxious state." Instead of medication, patients got "cold and hot baths, forced enemas and starvation. Often the patients were beaten unconscious and tied into straightjackets, their moans drifting through the locked doors of their cells."[31] Leopold confirmed the abysmal conditions of the detention cells in an interview, speaking of the brutal nurses who were careless with medication and wrapped patients they didn't like in wet blankets, leaving them freezing and unable to move.[32]

It's unclear if Leopold actually objected to these treatments, as he later complained that he felt excluded from the "clique" the other nurses had.[33] It was so bad that he got into a physical fight with one of his coworkers. As to the cause, he offered only that "there was no special *casus belli*—he was drunk and I guess he just didn't like Jews."[34] Sandiford told a different story. He blamed head nurse William Madden for the fight, who had a reputation as a sadist and ruled the detention ward according to his whims. One night Sandiford said that he was called to draw smut while Madden was fondled by another patient. Coming upon this scene, Leopold allegedly mocked Madden's impotence and was brutally beaten.[35]

Whatever the exact situation surrounding the fight had been, it was clear that the position was unstable, and Leopold decided to jump to a new job, his eye on a position as a dormitory orderly.

In May 1943 he got his transfer and moved to a dormitory, which housed cons outside of the general population who worked in the front offices and the Honor Farm. These dormitories were located near the prison's entrance rather than in the regular cell houses and Leopold's only job was to keep one sixteen-man cell clean.[36] While the other men were at work Leopold had nearly unlimited leisure time, with access to a recreation room, private shower, comfortable hospital bed, and lax security. For a year he drifted along with little ambition beyond his personal comfort, but in May 1944 the dormitories were cleared out and all cons sent back to the cell houses. Thanks to the draft there was not enough staff to supervise the entire structure. With his privileges taken yet again, Leopold requested another transfer, and in August 1944 he was back in the x-ray lab.[37]

This span of years, as he drifted from one job to another, was especially barren for Leopold. His ties to the school loosened, his scholarly interest faded, and his personal connections were disappearing. Hammer and Burd were paroled, and Sandiford and Fulford were transferred to Menard. Even Dick the canary, who Leopold called "so much my pal, so much my rappartner," had to be put to sleep in 1942.[38] He was evidently quite desperate to hold onto something, as he was reprimanded for "having possession of a shirt belonging to an inmate transferred to Menard."[39] As prisoners' shirts had their numbers printed on them, he wouldn't have been able to wear it, so had likely kept it for sentimental reasons.

Despite the distance and illegality, he kept in touch with as many paroled prisoners as possible, often through Helen Williams.[40] Williams, who by this time had been corresponding with Leopold for over a decade, was touched by the level of devotion Leopold expressed for his punks. She explained that "there were a number of these boys Nathan was interested in . . . [he] wanted me to meet them if I could and sometimes write them, or send them things, which I did."[41]

It was a bit more complicated when Leopold wanted to write to Dave Fulford while he was still in Menard, but Williams wasn't deterred. She got placed on Fulford's mailing list, so when Leopold sent her letters for Fulford she forwarded them on.[42] With her address on the envelope, the prison censors had no reason to suspect the ruse. Fulford understood that any letters signed "Aunt Helen" were from Leopold, and when he was paroled the following year, they kept up this charade for a decade before they felt comfortable writing to each other directly. Williams was well used to this subterfuge; since 1936 Leopold had been writing her under the names of various prison staff members to get past the one letter a week rule.

In 1944 the world had been at war for five years, and the effects were felt even behind Stateville's walls. The prison's newspaper carried articles about patriotism and the war effort, and cons who had relatives fighting overseas waited impatiently for letters to make it past the censors for the latest news. His brothers too old and his nephews too young to be drafted, Leopold was exempt from this worry, but his daily life changed in other ways. Superficially at first: he began trying to learn Japanese in the vague hope it could help somehow and quipped to a reporter that the rubber shortage was interfering with his handball game.[43]

With hundreds of American soldiers losing their lives to enemy fire every day, there were thousands stationed in the tropics who found they had to combat an additional enemy: disease. Malaria had been especially devastating, and while there were some cures available, they produced harsh side effects and it was hoped that safer medication could be found. Looking for a large number of young, healthy, male volunteers who weren't serving in the armed forces, whose environment could be standardized, and who could be monitored around the clock, it seemed like the perfect idea to look to men's prisons as a place to test new medications. Toward this end, the University of Chicago sent Dr. Alf Alving and a medical team to Stateville.

Testing began in October 1944. Inmates were infected with malaria and then given experimental drugs in various doses to track how the disease was transmitted as well as the side effects and curative powers of each drug.

Though still assigned to the x-ray lab, Leopold worked as a nurse for the project, doing statistical analysis on the various drugs, dissecting mosquitoes, and caring for sick patients. He'd already had considerable experience nursing malaria patients from his time in the detention ward, as the doctors there treated inmates with neurosyphilis by infecting them with malaria to give them fevers hot enough to kill the infectious bacteria.[44]

His patients lay in single, metal frame beds lining the hospital wards, some shivering, wrapped in blankets with hot water bottles, others with their shirts open, exposing flushed chests as they sweated through their sheets. After half a year behind the scenes, Leopold himself was voluntarily infected on June 19, 1945.[45] Thus began Leopold's path to freedom—with a deadly virus coursing through his bloodstream.

Leopold opted for an experimental inoculation: he had the salivary glands of a mosquito inserted under the skin of his thighs twenty-four hours apart, then in another twenty-four hours the skin, tissue, and mosquito glands would be removed and implanted into other volunteers. Like the others in his experimental group, Leopold experienced chills, a 105-degree fever, and spent much of his time lying in the malaria ward in a haze. He relapsed in August, but by October he was considered cured, with no parasites found in his blood for more than eight weeks. During his illness Leopold remained on the ward to continue his work when he wasn't debilitated by symptoms.

The Stateville experiments were extremely successful: in his autobiography Leopold emphasized pentaquine as the standout discovery of the project and the cure for malaria.[46] The drug was heralded as such for several years, but it was chloroquine, one of the drugs Leopold had been administered after his initial sickness, which proved the most long-lasting and popular malarial treatment. Today it remains the most commonly used drug to treat malaria worldwide, other than in places in which it was so widely used that chloroquine-resistant malaria strains have become the norm.

It was during a war in which millions died, and criminals, Jewish, and gay people were singled out for execution, yet it gave Leopold a sense of purpose. Dr. Clay Huff, who worked on the project, reported that Leopold "was diligent in his duties and became very skillful in caring for and dissecting the mosquitoes, and in identifying the microbes in the mosquitoes and in the blood of the patients microscopically. His intelligent mind was ever searching ways of furthering the project."[47]

While many of the doctors and scientists assigned to the project admired Leopold's work ethic, project leader Alving disliked him, but needed his cooperation, as he was often a spokesperson for the other inmates and had some sway in influencing their decisions to volunteer.[48] Acknowledging that Leopold had once done good work, Alving thought that after several years he wore out his welcome and believed that Leopold stayed on as a nurse not out of a sense of patriotism or a desire to assist his fellow man, so much as for the access it gave him to other inmates as an easy pipeline of sexual partners. "Leopold had the whole thing wired to his advantage. He was brilliant at controlling people," one author summarized.[49]

The practice of using prisoners as subjects in medical experiments has become increasingly controversial, but even in the 1940s Leopold felt the need to address this ethical dilemma. In an article written for the prison's newspaper, he defended the doctor's choice of guinea pigs, writing: "The malaria project is probably the best thing that has ever happened in the Illinois State Penitentiary,"[50] asserting that each man was thoroughly briefed on the dangers and asked at least twice if they fully understood what they were risking for no promised reward. He also spoke of the altruistic reasons why some prisoners decided to undergo infection: patriotism, perhaps to benefit a relative fighting in the war, or even some with a sense of doing something for the benefit of all mankind.

> Many of us were not unmindful of the fact that for the first time in a long, long time we were being offered the opportunity of doing something which would be appreciated by society—something that would make people feel less harsh toward convicts. . . . Being present at the very birth of new knowledge is a privilege given to a few people in the world. The feeling that one has been permitted to have a small part in helping solve a grave medical problem is the source of more solid, lasting satisfaction than most of us have ever known before.[51]

But, he later admitted, there were many more common motives far less altruistic. The hope of shortening their sentence was, Leopold claimed, the "most frequent and the strongest motive. . . . A convict will do nearly anything if he thinks it may result in shortening the time he must serve." In addition he spoke of a desire for money, as each prisoner was compensated $100 (around $1,650 in 2023) for the completion of the experiment, and, as ever, using a medical experiment as an escape from the seemingly deadlier threat of normal prison monotony.[52] This kind of thinking would have repercussions far beyond what Leopold would have been able to predict.

In 1947, during the Nuremberg trials, Dr. Andrew Ivy represented Nazi doctors and argued that the program at Stateville indicated that prisoners could ethically consent to medical experiments, therefore so could those in concentration camps.[53] Ivy cited a radio broadcast that aired on

January 3, 1946, in which Leopold and several other convicts voiced their pleasure with the project and the patriotic reasons they had for volunteering.[54] Ironically, Ragen revealed that this broadcast had been scripted and that he had lectured the volunteers about how they needed to stick to their lines before they went live.[55]

After the majority of the malaria experiments had concluded in 1947, the inmate volunteers were encouraged to apply to the governor for executive clemency, and soon began to see cuts in their sentences. A parole was looking particularly appealing for Leopold in September when Father Weir stepped down from his position as chaplain after twenty-one years. After his departure, Leopold wrote the priest: "Shakespeare somewhere says 'Parting is such sweet sorrow.' I can't see it that way, Padre. Parting from you is sweet in no sense whatever. I feel as tho I were losing a dearly-loved older brother."[56]

Leopold was further grieved when on January 8, 1948, his Aunt Birdie died after a short illness.[57] Yet Leopold still had his brother Mike to bolster him, who in the same letter that he informed him of Birdie's passing, assured his brother that in regards to his obtaining parole, "I have not wavered in my faith."[58] As Mike began work on getting Leopold paroled, he wrote to his brother that he had "only one request to make in return, do not let me down."[59]

A few days after Mike mailed that letter, the division of correction received Leopold's first petition for executive clemency. It cited the constructive work he had done as reasons to reduce his sentence, before taking a more philosophical approach:

> Your petitioner strongly feels that in deciding his case, the Department is deciding between two opposing views of the purpose of incarceration. If the purpose of imprisonment is revenge on the part of society, then a man convicted of murder may never hope for release. . . . But if the purpose of imprisonment is reform and rehabilitation of the offender, your petitioner respectfully submits that the twenty-three years he has already served have effected the maximum rehabilitation possible.[60]

Leading up to his hearing, Mike reached out to professionals who had known Leopold in prison and asked them to send positive letters on Leopold's behalf to the parole board. He led the charge himself with a letter stating:

> Were we not convinced of the safety of requesting executive clemency . . . we would not be pleading on his behalf but would be urging the opposite. We have no desire to relieve events of 1924. . . . Our con-

tact with him over the last twenty-five years, together with repeated conversations with the authorities in charge, lead us to the conclusion that we are asking for something that is not only well deserved but is safe as well.[61]

In his two-page letter Mike laid out the carefully augmented list of reasons why Leopold should be freed: citing SCS, crediting Leopold with its creation, and the malaria experiments, claiming his brother "played the most important part of any inmate."[62] He also tried appealing to the board's sense of mercy by citing Leopold's increasingly frequent health problems, which would soon be partly explained when he was diagnosed with diabetes, assumedly meant to imply he would be physically unable to harm anyone and unlikely to live long after release.

After sending the petition and positive letters, Leopold could do little but keep track of the other malaria volunteers who regularly took their turns before the board as he waited to be told if he would be allowed the privilege of doing the same. On June 30, 1948, he spent his last day assisting on the malaria project before he moved back to his work full time in the x-ray lab two floors below.[63]

For nearly eight more years the x-ray lab would remain Leopold's domain. Consisting of three rooms on the ground floor of the prison hospital, Leopold had quickly made the place his own. The first room was an office, home to Leopold's desk, an x-ray machine, and a filing cabinet. In a room behind the office there was a locker, couch, and toilet, and beyond that the dark room where x-rays were developed. Looking around the rooms a reporter described the more personal touches Leopold had added:

> Leopold's books, most of them on birds and sociology, and some of them autographed, fill a bookcase. In a filing case his notebooks, manuscripts, and letters are neatly filed. On the walls hang Leopold's certificate as a medical technician and a picture of Albert Einstein, a picture of Dick Loeb, taken years ago at his parents summer home in Charlevoix, and a picture of Leopold's assistant's girlfriend.[64]

He also occasionally kept pets there, briefly a pair of hamsters he'd named Sue and Bill, and after them a canary.[65] Leopold had a fondness for these pet names, going on to own at least three more pairs of Sues and Bills. The Sues he said were named for Susan Lurie; the Bills he declined to explain. Leopold purchased a small television set for the ward so he could watch it after the other hospital workers had gone to sleep, following college football and keeping up with the world through the twenty-inch, black-and-white screen.[66] Interviewed years later Leopold acknowledged: "I have looked things over carefully in my time here, and the most valuable thing in the place is that door," as he nodded to the door of the laboratory. "I can shut that door and have my television set, my books, my notes, my privacy. It means a lot."[67]

Things seemed to be going well in Leopold's corner of the world until mid-August when one of the prison doctors walked from Leopold's office into the inner room and saw an inmate "lying naked on couch examined by NL with [a] stethoscope."[68] Three days later Leopold was ousted from the x-ray lab and back in the cell houses doing cleaning duty.[69] Leopold knew that if he was to have any chance at securing an executive clemency hearing he had to spend his time as constructively as possible, and that assuredly did not include sexually tinged punishment records and janitorial work. In just two months he managed to get transferred back to the x-ray lab, and the incident was not included on his record.[70]

The close call also did not seem to scare him away from the hunt. Twenty-one-year-old convict Gene Lovitz claimed that Leopold had attempted to seduce him in the same set of rooms the following year.[71] Lovitz recalled that for months leading up to the incident he and Leopold would walk around the yard and talk. According to Lovitz, Leopold would claim that if someone found their "alter ego," then sex with that person was normal and did not indicate homosexuality.

One day when Lovitz complained that his disability pension had been revoked, Leopold said he could get it back by fogging his x-ray to make it look like he had asthma. Lovitz agreed to the scheme, and after taking his x-rays, Leopold ushered him into the dark room. There, Leopold compared Lovitz to Loeb, who Leopold claimed as his own alter ego, saying Loeb and Lovitz had similar macabre senses of humor and easygoing attitudes. Then Leopold asked Lovitz why he didn't let the female mosquitoes bite him, referring ostensibly to the mosquitoes used in the malaria experiments and Lovitz's refusal to take part, but Lovitz recognized the double entendre.

As Lovitz began to demand that Leopold open the door, Lovitz claimed that Leopold became more overt. "'I could make it mighty nice,' I think he said . . . he says something like: 'You won't lose your manhood by letting me go down on you,' and that's a pretty goddamn exact quote."[72] Finally Lovitz was allowed to leave and the two avoided each other for the remainder of Lovitz's sentence. He never got his pension back.

When not distracted by potential sexual conquests, the possibility of parole loomed large in Leopold's mind. At last, in February 1949 it was confirmed that he would be allowed a hearing in April. When that information became public, a wave of negative publicity began and letters of protest flooded the parole board. One energized citizen sent an anonymous postcard warning that if "THE JEWISH KID ASSASSINS AND SEXY EXPERIMENTERS," were paroled "YOU'LL SET A PATTERN AND EXAMPLE THAT WILL DO MUCH TO DESTROY ALL FEAR & RESPECT FOR LAW & ORDER."[73]

Tensions were high when, backed by a small force of supporters consisting of his family and friends, Leopold came before the parole board for his clemency hearing on April 22, 1949. Leopold was led in front of the panel and asked questions relating to his role as a malaria volunteer and his prison work record. Standing before the table where three men sat in judgment, "I was nervous, of course," he recalled, "the next few minutes were the culmination of a quarter century in prison; they would determine what the next quarter century would be."[74]

"Leopold made an effective plea for mercy," a reporter observed. "Leopold displayed humor and laughed several times at his own quips. He looked anything but the pervert and murderer of 1921 [*sic*]," though he noted, "He did not, however, say he was sorry for his crime."[75]

In the long months before the verdict was announced, more of Leopold's friends began writing to the parole board in attempts to persuade the authorities in the direction of leniency. Dave Fulford added his voice to the mix, handwriting a parable about himself and the role the correspondence school had in his rehabilitation:

> Because of the interest and untiring efforts of Nathan Leopold, I am a free man—married, the father of two children and successful in business. . . . Had it not been for my coming into contact with a person so willing as he to devote his every effort to the betterment of his fellow man, it is quite possible that I would have continued to be a burden on society.[76]

After five months of waiting, in September it was announced that the board had decided to cut Leopold's ninety-nine-year sentence to eighty-five years.[77] At the time in Illinois, prisoners had to serve one-third of their sentences before they were allowed to try for parole. Under Leopold's life sentence he was parolable after twenty-five years and under his new eighty-five-year sentence he was eligible after twenty-eight years and three months. As his sentences ran concurrently, his longer sentence canceled the shorter out. That left Leopold with a date to shoot for: January 1953.[78]

15

IMAGE REHABILITATION

For a few years after his commutation, Leopold did what he thought may help him win parole without interacting with the outside world. He worked in the pathology lab at night to train himself in bloodwork, started learning Hawaiian in case he was paroled there, and obtained certification as an x-ray technician.[1] He also located the parole recidivism sheets from his earlier experiments and checked to find how many of those original hunches had been correct.[2] Unfortunately, it seemed the methodology left much to be desired: according to Leopold's calculations, the four inmates who had given hunches were wrong 26.9–34.8 percent of the time, with Leopold the second worst at predicting parole failures. Leopold published these findings under the name Richard A. Lawrence, a pseudonym that Loeb had sometimes used in their pre-incarceration days.[3]

During his forty-seven years he had accumulated a vast network of friends and coworkers and to them he sent out hundreds of nearly identical letters pleading that they write letters on his behalf:

> I cannot but feel . . . that in my case it is more or less a matter of now or never. For, from the point of view of the penalty theory, I can hardly hope that if twenty-eight years is not considered sufficient punishment, twenty-nine, or thirty, or x years will be. From the point of view of the rehabilitation theory, I think there can be little question that my ability to make a living and any possible chance I have of doing any construc- tive work are both descending curves. Since I do feel that this will, in essence, be a final decision, I naturally want to leave no stone unturned in presenting my case.[4]

Many of the resulting letters were glowing in their praise, though not every request for a letter met with a positive response. Sociologist Courtlandt

Van Vechten raised concerns about the motivations behind the jobs Leopold and his supporters touted as proof of his rehabilitation, and Leopold admitted that "the characteristic syndrome has been kicking up a job for something to do, getting started on it, finding it a challenge, and ending up by getting completely fascinated and burying myself in it. I'm afraid that, very often, altruism has not entered very heavily into my motivation."[5]

As Leopold's letter-writing campaign continued, so did the negative publicity. Journalist and author Bob Considine noted in his weekly column: "There are several moves afoot to turn loose Nathan Leopold, the queer who murdered Bobby Franks."[6] He warned readers that "perverts" like Leopold "continue their perversion in prison and emerge with the same sadistic stare—to pervert again."[7] The parole board members and governor were all publicly elected officials, so Leopold's supporters decided that even with dozens of glowing letters from people who knew Leopold personally, without wide public support his parole would never go through.

Since the circus of 1924 Leopold had maintained a hatred for reporters, but he would have to swallow his disdain if he wanted a chance at regaining his freedom. *Chicago Herald-American* reporter Gladys Erickson was deemed the perfect woman to help. She was a family friend and had always been generous toward him in her past articles. Leopold counted on her continuing kindness when he agreed to sit down for an exclusive interview in August 1952.

Erickson's four-article series introduced the new Leopold to the world. With a series of softball questions, Erickson allowed Leopold to explain his prison accomplishments, leading readers through his work with the school, parole prediction, and malaria as well as other tidbits he hoped would endear him to the public, like his pledge to fight against Communism and his aptitude with languages. Throughout the transcript of his interview, Erickson interjected compliments, claiming Leopold "has piled up a record of unparalleled mental achievement in American prison history."[8] While Leopold found the abundance of praise distasteful and initially feared a backlash, positive feedback started coming in, and nearly two decades later he credited her articles with having "started the swing of publicity from nasty to nice."[9]

After Erickson's articles other reporters began inquiring about interviewing Leopold, and he accepted those who assured him that their stories would be positive and would quote him directly as often as possible. Alvin Goldstein was one such reporter, who faced Leopold in December 1952, more than twenty-eight years after gathering evidence that led to his conviction. After agreeing to the interview, Leopold asked: "How are you going to handle this, Al? . . . After all, you are the one person alive who probably did the most to put me here. How do you feel about my getting a parole? Would you be in favor of it or are you going back over the past in your story and try to prevent it?"[10]

Goldstein promised to remain objective, though he did cover Leopold's past as well as the good prison works Leopold described to him. When his editor asked the same question, Goldstein replied: "My instinct is, to be frank, to deny parole on the ground that he should serve his sentence and compensate society to the best of his ability in prison. Again let me emphasize this is a personal reaction no doubt colored by prejudice, and I felt deeply and humbly sorry for him."[11]

Despite the hesitance of some reporters, most articles were extremely positive. Leopold learned the perfect way to answer questions, and which lies he could get away with. He began telling reporters that the last time he'd been placed in solitary was when he shook his brother's hand in the visiting room in 1946.[12] This wasn't true; the year before he'd gotten fifteen days in solitary for allegedly trying to bribe an officer, but by using an actual punishment he'd received for a mundane, friendly action, he was able to win readers to his side. Letters from strangers calling for his release started finding their way to the parole board, and Leopold began to believe that he could use publicity as a way to enhance his image without the negative slant and inaccuracies that had plagued his early dealings with the press.

Behind the scenes Mike led the effort on Leopold's behalf, hosting meetings where Leopold's friends pooled ideas for whom to solicit letters from, debated which aspects of Leopold's life should be highlighted and which hidden, and searched for jobs they could secure for him in the event of his release. William Friedman, a lawyer and longtime friend of the family, gave legal advice, though the group decided that Leopold should go before the board unrepresented, so as not to differentiate him from other convicts.

Before the parole hearing, Mike left snowy Chicago behind for a Caribbean vacation, but even thousands of miles away, he couldn't stop working on his brother's case. On one of their stops he and his wife met Dr. George Watson, a political science professor who taught in Chicago. As they chatted, Mike brought up his hopes for Leopold's parole, and his belief that if a medical project could offer Leopold a job outside of the continental United States the probability of parole seemed very good. Watson, a Quaker, knew of another peace church with its headquarters in the Chicago area that sponsored medical missions around the world. This was how Leopold's team came to know Harold Row, executive secretary of the Brethren Service Commission for the Church of the Brethren.[13]

The Church of the Brethren is a Protestant sect of Christianity known for its focus on acts of service, pacifism, forgiveness, and acceptance regardless of past sins, so they seemed a perfect fit for a supposedly reformed convict. As soon as Mike got back to the States, Row met the Lebold brothers (Mike and Sam had changed their names in 1934) for dinner and they explained Leopold's case. Row was moved by their petition and offered up what seemed an ideal job: a laboratory technician in a hospital located in the mountains of Puerto Rico.[14] The pay would be minimal, the conditions quaint and isolated, but these were aspects the brothers saw as positives. Famous for his wealth, it would be great for Leopold's image if he were to work for $10 a month, and his brothers hoped the isolation would keep Leopold from publicity and allow him to slowly get used to life on the outside, without becoming overwhelmed or tempted toward anything unsavory.

The decision to sponsor Leopold was not initially embraced by all Brethren members, including those stationed where Leopold would be relocating in the event of his release. Responding to concerns from project director Homer Burke, Harold Row wrote: "I know it is somewhat of a risk relative to Public relations, and I know it is somewhat a bold thing to do. However, I think the Christian Church is called upon doing the right thing even when it costs something." He assured Burke that Leopold was rehabilitated and had a wholesome personality with no prison-learned "anti-social habits" like homosexuality.[15] With this new development Leopold's chances for parole looked much improved, but it also forced an issue Leopold had avoided discussing publicly since 1924: his religious beliefs.

The Brethren being a Christian organization was not the problem; the Puerto Rican project focused on medical rather than spiritual service and accepted volunteers from all religious backgrounds including atheists. But when the job was submitted to the parole board, questions about Leopold's beliefs were sure to come up and he needed a plan for how to answer them.

A few years previously Father Weir had observed of Leopold: "You shun real philosophy for fads and shirk religious study for fear of disturbing the encasement you have built up around your mind. . . . You fear what others would say if you changed your views. They would not think you the great man you imagine they think you are." He also blamed loyalty to Loeb and the pact they had made before his death to abstain from religion for his continuing atheism. Perhaps hoping to jar him out of this, Weir considered informing Leopold of Loeb's ambivalence toward him at the end of his life, writing: "About three weeks before Dick's death I spoke to him and he let me know things confidentially that he asked me not to divulge, not even to you."[16] Leopold responded that he was interested to know Loeb's thoughts, and spent five pages walking Weir explicitly through his relationship to faith:

> I can think of nothing I should desire more, not even my freedom, than to be able sincerely to believe in a personal, omnipotent, benevolent Deity. . . . I too am sure I should find joy and peace and help if only I could sincerely believe. And I have tried. Believe me I have tried—tried with all the sincerity and hope and goodwill of which I am capable. . . . I have tried to attain belief by study, by prayer, and by attempts (not always too successful) to become a better man and therefore one who would be more acceptable to God if He exists. I sincerely do not see what else I cando [*sic*] except to keep hoping and keep trying. I could say I believed, but that would be but to add one more sin to those with which I am already burdened. Hypocrisy or intellectual dishonesty is surely not the way out.[17]

Perhaps realizing that Loeb wasn't the reason for his lack of faith, Weir didn't divulge his confession. Despite daily prayer, decades of religious study, and the kindness of religious men like Weir, Leopold simply could not believe. But as with many facets of his life, appearances mattered more than the truth. Once he had been unwilling to lie about his beliefs, but now hypocrisy was the least of his concerns. The week before his hearing an interview came out in which Leopold claimed that though he questioned his faith after his mother died, "I believed in God then and I do now."[18] With the public warily coming around to this new Leopold being presented to them, he and his supporters could only hope it would be enough when tested before the board.

After years of preparation, Leopold's first parole hearing was held on January 8, 1953. Three members of the Parole and Pardons Board sat behind a folding table in Stateville's chapel, listening closely as nine witnesses spoke on his behalf, a mix of sociologists and professors who had known him in prison and pre-prison friends who came to vouch for the change they'd seen in him over the decades. Dr. Carl Winters called Leopold "the most completely rehabilitated person I ever have known." He testified that in prison Leopold developed "a sincere desire to be of greater help to the world on the outside."[19] Marvin Sukov, William Byron, Helen Williams, and Dr. J. B. Rice confirmed this, each giving their personal assessment of the projects they'd worked alongside Leopold on, while rabbi Irving Melamed testified to Leopold embracing his Jewish faith. No family members spoke, but Bal was on hand to coordinate and arrange transportation for those witnesses who had come from out of town.

After the witnesses had finished Leopold was brought out. He stood before the board members in his gray-striped prison shirt, a pair of reading glasses in a case protruding from his front pocket, the number which had become his name printed bold and black in the middle of his back. When asked to explain his original crime, Leopold admitted:

> That was 29 years ago, and in all truth I am still unable to make sense out of it or provide a motive. It was a damn fool stunt by a child, a child without judgement. I could furnish a good many reasons why I am different today. I am like the burnt child who shuns fire . . . I was a wild, irresponsible, smart alec kid. Now I am mature, as mature as I shall ever be.[20]

The Franks family remained neutral, one spokesperson stating: "Members of our family feel we should not take a stand one way or the other as to Nathan Leopold. Whatever the parole board decides we will consider as proper. We have no bitter feeling against Leopold."[21] State's Attorney John Gutknecht was one of two people who opposed Leopold's plea. Discounting Leopold's witnesses as "professional do-gooders, sob sisters and pseudo-scientists who dare to predict what God alone knows will happen to the emotions of an individual."[22]

"Society owes him nothing," Gutknecht continued. "He has merely repaid in a small measure the debt he owed to the memory of Franks, aye, even to the memory of Loeb, his dupe."[23] As a final warning he called into question the reality of Leopold's transformation: "You can understand the motive of a man who kills a policeman to escape arrest. . . . But this is a murder committed for mental stimulation by one of the highest IQs ever to occupy a cell in this prison."[24] Leopold's friends, family, and hundreds of citizens were praising Leopold for the important projects he was involved in, but these were often the same people who had been blindsided by his crime in 1924. Back then Leopold had also been a gifted student whom no one would suspect of murder, so how could anyone judge what he was capable of now?

On May 15 Victor Knowles, chairman of the parole board, addressed a gathering of reporters and announced their decision: Leopold was denied parole, and his case would be continued for twelve years, stating that new evidence would have to be produced for Leopold to be granted another parole hearing before 1965. Fielding questions from reporters after the announcement, Knowles said that Leopold's rehabilitation was very much in question, as he was seen as a "con man" who knew how to work the system to get what he wanted without breaking the rules.[25] Robert Crowe, now long retired from public life, called the decision "a triumph for justice and decency."[26]

Called into Ragen's office to hear the news, Leopold betrayed no emotion by either his expression or his statement: "I am naturally somewhat disappointed. I had hoped the board would see fit to parole me, but since it hasn't, I can accept its decision as gracefully as possible and hope that some time a board will feel my debt is paid."[27] He even had the notice that announced his twelve-year continuance framed, and it joined the photos and letters that hung on the x-ray lab's walls. When writing to friends about the result in the weeks that followed, however, he was somewhat more revealing:

> I don't intend to let it embitter me nor to deprive me of my sanity. This is a possibility I had always reckoned with, and while the death of my hopes has not been painless, seeing a possibility turn into a fact will not change me fundamentally. I am determined that it shall not. . . . This seems like an appropriate time to take stock of myself and to reevaluate all my fundamental viewpoints, opinions and beliefs.

Toward this end he wrote to Weir, seeking guidance:

> You mentioned a conversation with Dick some three weeks before his death. You said that you had tried to moralize your right to tell me about it and would write me if you ever thought it proper. I just don't want you to forget, Padre, and I mention it now because it is an important time for me, if I am to reach any sound conclusions, to have any data available.[28]

When Weir responded he ignored Leopold's request, telling him to focus on the future, perhaps afraid of what this emotionally compromised Leopold may do if confronted with Loeb's final thoughts. Perhaps for the best, as in the wake of the board's decision, Leopold found himself more isolated than ever.

It had been Bal, rather than Mike, who had coordinated the parole hearing because Mike's health had become increasingly fragile in the last year. After the board's decision he flew to Florida for a rest but had a heart attack a few weeks into his vacation. He had another once back in Chicago, and Leopold was particularly distressed thinking that the effort Mike had expended on his behalf had contributed to his worsening condition. Through the summer, though they exchanged a few letters, Mike was too sick to make the journey to Stateville, and Leopold missed his counsel. Friedman was out of the country; and though Sam visited every three weeks, Leopold lamented that "things are so disorganized that I can't for the life of me see any glimmer of hope in the foreseeable future."[29]

With little outside assistance, a suggestion that friends had been making to him for decades finally seemed a viable option: writing an autobiography. Leopold assured Mike that the book "WOULD BE VERY CAREFULLY CALCULATED TO BE HELPFUL. . . . It would definitely NOT be conceited or self-praising—it would very carefully be kept general, objective, descriptive."[30] In addition to the image enhancement, he had faith that the book would sell well on notoriety alone and earn him a substantial paycheck, enough that he could gain financial independence from his brothers. Embracing the power of publicity, he hoped to make his case seem bigger than himself:

> It seems to me that we have exactly two choices: to do nothing, or to carry this issue to the people. To do that we have to tie my case up, I think, with some broad social principle. As an individual, I am insignificant, but as the symbol of s [*sic*] principle my case might be made to arouse the interest of lots of people. . . . Perhaps my case can be tied up to the philosophy of rehabilitation versus revenge in penology.[31]

Writing the book was an exercise in balance: Leopold trying to seem down-to-earth, yet pushing his accomplishments, inserting enough rule-breaking to be believable, but not too much to seem incorrigible. As he wrote, he passed his chapters to Warden Ragen for approval, extremely conscious that if he wanted it published it was not just his own reputation he had to look out for, but the prison's as well.[32]

When Leopold wrote Mike in early November, he discussed his troubles with writing and potential parole strategies, ending it: "I, too, find this sitting and waiting no easy chore. What makes it endurable is the knowledge that with you out there no possibility is going to be overlooked. That means a lot. Here's hoping that you will make steady and rapid progress and that you will soon be entirely well again."[33]

The letter would be the last Leopold sent to his older brother. He died on November 12 at the age of 58, and for some time Leopold was inconsolable. He wrote to a friend a few days after Mike's death: "He was so much more than a big brother to me—ever since I can remember he has been my counselor, champion and confidant. With his going the sun has gone down for me and I haven't yet been able to get the grip on myself I know he would want me to. I just don't have the manhood and the strength of character he had."[34]

Later that week Bal promised Leopold that though "I know I can't take Mike's place as far as you are concerned—no one can, but I shall try."[35] While Bal would take over some of Mike's duties—sending letters when Leopold had used up his weekly allotment, visiting regularly, rallying the family, and mediating between Leopold and Sam—it was Ralph Newman who would, in Leopold's mind at least, do the most to fill Mike's shoes. Newman had been Mike's best friend, and after his death Newman became Leopold's literary agent, acknowledging that initially this was done more "for Mike than affection for Babe."[36]

In his grief, Leopold threw himself into writing, finishing the first typed draft of his book by the end of February 1954.[37] As chapters circulated among his family and friends, author Meyer Levin wrote to Leopold announcing that he had been commissioned to write a novel about his crime and asked for his cooperation. Leopold panicked, consulting various legal avenues he could take to stop Levin's book before it was written, until Levin suggested co-authoring a book. Leopold considered the offer, if only so he could stop the fictional book and have some control over the tone of whatever emerged from their collaboration.[38]

In April, Levin and Newman visited Leopold for an hour, but Leopold firmly stuck to business matters during their discussion, steering the conversation to royalties and editorial details every time Levin made inquiries about his feelings or personal life.[39] After the meeting Leopold remained conflicted, afraid that Levin would lack the sympathy he was looking for, stressing that "my only purpose is to do what I can to ameliorate public opinion."[40] After a couple of weeks Leopold decided to shelve the book idea and Levin was turned down as a collaborator. However, Leopold could do nothing to stop him from writing his fictional take.

16

PAROLE

A s the new year of 1955 dawned, Leopold began looking to shake himself out of stagnation. After several years together, Leopold's thirty-
year-old punk William Carr had been paroled in December. Carr was
taken on as Leopold's assistant in the x-ray lab after coming to Stateville in
1950 for a series of auto thefts. Before he left, Carr noted that Leopold had
become set in his ways: eating, bathing, walking the yard, and watching
TV at the same times every day, moody if his routine was disturbed. Carr
was reluctant even to stop playing handball with Leopold, though he knew
it wasn't good for his health, because he sensed the aging con needed the
stability.[1] He's "more sensitive than most people know," Carr said to a reporter.[2] When Carr was paroled Leopold sent him $200 (around $2,500 in
2023) as a going-away present before turning back to the changes he must
make in his own life.[3]

To get away from the hospital building where he'd spent fourteen
years, Leopold secured a job as a bookkeeper in the prison's Business Office. This new position meant that he was put back with the general population and once again had to abide by the regular prison rules and routine.
He now worked just outside the prison walls in an administration building
where he could mingle with civilians. Securing this job implied that he
was trusted, but Leopold was not happy with the assignment. He did everything possible to secure a transfer back to the x-ray lab, as "I found the
work there much more stimulating than what I am doing now. And quite
frankly, the creature comforts: better food, a better bed, etc., mean a great
deal."[4] His efforts were unsuccessful.

Leopold wasted no time filling Carr's shoes once in the Business Office. Twenty-one-year-old Paul Henry had been arrested with a group
of five men in 1952 after they committed a series of burglaries. On one

of their last jobs Henry and his partners beat the homeowner when he wouldn't reveal the location of his valuables. Escaping with only a watch and $1.38, they left the homeowner on the ground, and, though taken to the hospital, he died eight days later.[5] Following a short trial, Henry was sent to Stateville with a sentence of twenty-five to life.

In 1954 Henry took one of Leopold's German correspondence courses and midway through 1955 they became cellmates. Soon Henry's name began appearing in the expense ledger Leopold kept, noting books, a camera, and other small items that Leopold was gifting him.[6] In November Leopold began paying him outright, at first $30 a few times a year, then $50, up to $150 (which is equivalent to about $1,700 in 2023) in 1957, all sent to Henry through Helen Williams and Ralph Newman.[7] Henry, a handsome veteran with wavy brown hair and blue eyes, was a catch, especially to Leopold, for whom little details like a missing finger and a first-degree murder conviction were inconsequential.

As with Leopold's other relationships, he shared the money he received from his family for goods from the commissary and encouraged Henry to continue his education. Once as a treat for "Paulie," who had never had lobster before, Leopold "persuaded the officer who ran the Commissary, to put Richelieu brand canned lobster on the list of items. It was horribly expensive (about a dollar a can and we weren't allowed to spend more than five dollars), but there are situations when you need luxuries more than you do necessities. Prison is one of them."[8] In return, Henry used his position in the kitchen to cook for Leopold, sneaking him steaks and other delicacies from the officers' better food supply.

Two years into their relationship Leopold wrote Henry into his will; $1,000 was set aside for William Carr, while of the remainder of his estate, two-thirds would go to David Fulford and one-third to Henry.[9] Throughout the relationship, Leopold remained in regular contact with Dave Fulford, who often told stories and sent pictures of his growing family. It was during one of these updates when Fulford wrote of his sixteen-month-old son: "At the time he was born there existed in my mind the question of a name for him. We were tempted to name him Nathan Leonard; but since he is to be the last of the Mohicans, Mother and I decided there really should be a junior."[10]

Leopold replied:

> I don't know when I've ever been so flattered, Davie, as when you wrote me that you considered naming Davie Jr. after me. That is certainly the greatest compliment I've ever received in my life . . . if you

don't mind, I'll take the same proprietary interest in little Dave as if his name were Nate. I'll certainly take enormous pleasure from watching his progress and development from a distance. . . . Should I be fortunate and get out of here, perhaps I could help a little in assuring little Dave's education. Should I die in here, I have made provision in my will to leave you half my estate, with the suggestion that you might use the money for the education of your children.[11]

He embraced the role he'd given himself, sending each of Fulford's children presents for their birthdays and Christmas, but especially interesting himself in Davie Jr. Frequently he ended his letters to Fulford asking him to give an extra hug to "my boy," requested photos and drawings, and even asked Fulford to bring him on a visit so Leopold could meet him, though this failed to occur.[12] Fulford did all he could to repay Leopold, gathering signatures on a petition to free him and sending letters to the board when he came up for parole.[13]

Inspired by the sympathetic publicity Leopold's case had been getting, authors began turning to the story for inspiration. From 1956 to 1957, three fictional books exploring the 1924 crime were published, and leading the charge was Meyer Levin, who combined extensive research with a healthy helping of Freudian theory to produce his best-selling novel, *Compulsion*. In interviews, Levin revealed he had attended the University of Chicago with Leopold and Loeb and, though at the time he had never met either murderer and despite being in Europe for the entirety of the trial, Levin said he had covered it as a reporter. Levin's claimed intimacy with the case convinced thousands of readers that his version of the story was the truth.

In *Compulsion*, Loeb is represented by a character named Artie Straus, a teenager who is possibly a delusional schizophrenic, has likely killed several people in addition to the Bobby Franks character, shows extreme contempt for the Leopold character, and persuades him into their joint murder. Leopold is represented by Judd Steiner, a deeply disturbed teenager who dreams of being Artie's slave and reluctantly goes through with the murder with the subconscious hope that through the act he will be able to kill the girl inside of himself, releasing him from his effeminate traits and homosexuality.[14]

A reporter character in *Compulsion* who stood in for Levin mused to himself before interviewing Judd in prison: "What I wrote about him . . . might have a good deal to do with whether or not he would be released."[15] Levin may have been correct; it was in fiction that the new truth Leopold was peddling finally struck a chord with the public. Many readers wrote to Leopold, Levin, and the governor, explaining that *Compulsion* had given them insight into the case and led them to favor Leopold's release. Levin was even allowed to speak at Leopold's clemency hearing in 1957, to advocate for his freedom.

The success of *Compulsion* got *Life* magazine involved. In 1957 they published a photo-heavy article discussing the book paired with shots of Leopold teaching, giving blood, browsing the library, and working on his autobiography. "I can look into my own heart and soul," Leopold said to a nation of readers, "and know positively that I could and would become a useful, decent, law-abiding citizen."[16] *Life*'s wide circulation introduced even more people to Leopold the humanitarian, and, as a bonus, letters from half a dozen publishers arrived as soon as they saw the reference to Leopold writing a book, eager for a sample. After a healthy bidding war, Leopold accepted an advance of $16,000 (equivalent to about $170,000 in 2023) from Doubleday and began working with editors to clean up his manuscript to ensure it would make the best impression possible on the reading public.

Against his judgment, his editors convinced him to add some chapters about 1924, but Leopold insisted on starting the narrative immediately after he and Loeb had committed the crime, so he wouldn't have to describe it. While Leopold wanted readers to see how he had changed, starting with such a brutal act may have made him seem completely irredeemable. Other than the added chapters, the bulk of the book remained relatively unchanged; Leopold had been telling the story of his life in prison for years and knew which stories people responded well to. His editors noted he had a bit of a blind spot when it came to his rap-partner, however.

Leopold's original manuscript only had good things to say about Loeb, and he was advised to cut many long, effusive passages about him, as well as stories of their sending each other secret messages and breaking rules.[17] Pages revealing Loeb's flaws were added to tarnish the pristine image Leopold had painted, including a eulogy where Leopold praised his good qualities while reminding readers one last time that "there persisted in his makeup, to the very day of his tragic death, an element of the demoniac."[18]

For many years Leopold wouldn't discuss Loeb in relation to their crime, explaining:

> The matter of relative degree of guilt is one I have carefully avoided bringing up. In the first place, I have always felt that, regardless of who was the leader in the matter, Dick and I are equally guilty. And with Dick dead and unable to defend himself, I have been unable to bring myself to say anything about it. I know that Dick, himself, would want

me to use whatever facts would be to my advantage. But in spite of that it strikes me as disloyal and not in good taste.[19]

Yet by 1957, that had changed. Leopold could see the tide of public opinion was turning and against the advice of Bal and Weir, when Leopold petitioned another hearing with the parole board, for the first time he laid the blame squarely on Loeb's shoulders. "The crime was conceived by Loeb, planned by Loeb, and, in the main, carried out by Loeb," Leopold declared. "I participated at his request."[20]

As Leopold worked to build a better public image, he was denied parole hearings several times. He had cycled through a couple of lawyers, growing tired of William Friedman and then of prison lawyer Varian Adams. Considering them not aggressive enough, Leopold felt compelled to try his own schemes for garnering public interest. Ralph Newman suggested that Leopold meet a friend of his, a well-known civil lawyer who had been friends with Mike, was a Clarence Darrow enthusiast, and had written several times in favor of Leopold's release. Leopold agreed, and on May 16, 1957, Leopold met Elmer Gertz.

Gertz was charmed by Leopold's manner and surprised by his candidness, as he aired familial gripes with cousins who had abandoned him and dismissed the Bachrach brothers, who had been part of his defense team with Darrow, as men "whose sole qualifications as criminal lawyers was that they belonged to the Standard Club with my father."[21] While his first meeting with Leopold was ostensibly about his autobiography, after a long chat Leopold said that if Adams's latest parole effort failed, he wanted Gertz to represent him for the next attempt.[22]

While Adams remained Leopold's lawyer on paper, Gertz rapidly took the reins, working almost exclusively on his case and giving Leopold all the attention Leopold thought he deserved. With Gertz's approval, Leopold launched a widespread letter campaign, asking hundreds to write to the parole board and governor on his behalf, and continued giving interviews to sympathetic reporters. Gertz began courting Leo Lerner, whose chain of newspapers covered most of Chicago, leading to half a dozen interviews, articles, editorials, and a poll asking readers if they thought Leopold should be freed. With some help from Leopold nudging friends to send in ballots, these positive poll results were also sent to the parole board, indicating that 84 percent of Chicagoans favored a release for Leopold.[23] Not everyone was so enthusiastic about these tactics: watching from the sidelines Bal wrote about Leopold, "I cannot help but feel that he is a publicity seeker and will always seek publicity."[24]

With the way public opinion was heading, it was decided that Leopold should try to get his sentence commuted, rather than asking yet again for parole. A commutation would shorten his sentences or remove them completely, allowing him a quick release and a way to circumvent the period of parole supervision he would otherwise have to endure.

This hearing was granted, and before the board Leopold's old friend Abel Brown cemented the new version of Loeb in the public consciousness: "Loeb was a leader, aggressive, crafty, smart, Leopold was definitely a follower. Loeb induced Leopold to make the tragic mistake of his life. . . . I mean no disrespect for the dead when I told you that Loeb died as he lived, a violent death." Leopold praised this speech, writing to Brown: "It is only now, 21 years after Dick's death and on my fifth attempt for freedom that I have been able to bring myself to come close to saying some of the things that are true. You said them clearly, unequivocally, forcefully. THEY HAD TO BE SAID ONCE."[25]

For the first time the editorials and articles appearing in the papers after his hearing were more positive than negative. They repeated the points of Leopold's witnesses, leaning into the story of his rehabilitation and his role as Loeb's follower. Therefore, when it was announced on July 30 that the executive clemency was denied, the team was not too disheartened. The parole board seemed to be paving his way to freedom with their recommendation that "if and when he is released from the penitentiary it should be on parole."[26]

Leopold and Henry celebrated the loss by throwing a "No-Commutation Party" in their cell. Invitations complete with detailed menus, boasting the crab, shrimp, and sausage canapés they would be serving, were sent to Gertz and Newman as well as to prisoners who were more likely to attend.[27] A month after the commutation was denied, Gertz filed another petition, for parole this time, and in mid-November it was announced that Leopold would get another parole hearing on February 5, 1958.

A few days before the hearing, Leopold wrote that he was feeling "surprisingly calm—calm and hopeful. . . . If we are so supremely fortunate as to succeed this time, it will always be my feeling that the major part of the victory will be attributable to the July hearing. It will be something in the nature of a delayed reaction,"[28] In anticipation of the day, he sent out gifts to those he saw as having helped him the most, set to arrive on the day of the hearing.[29]

His most prized possession, the letter he had received from Albert Einstein, he bestowed to Ralph Newman. Toward Newman, he wrote that his admiration, affection, and gratitude "are as deep and as genuine and as great as my heart and my soul are capable of harboring."[30] To Gertz he sent the few letters he had received from Clarence Darrow, connecting the two in a way that Gertz certainly found flattering:

> Just after Judge Caverly handed down his decision that September day in 1924, I turned to Mr. Darrow and told him that I didn't know whether to thank him or to forgive him for saving my life. I still don't know, Elmer.
>
> For up to now it hasn't been a life he saved, in contradistinction to an existence. It is you who, if we are successful, will have given me back my life. It is you who will have given meaning to what Mr. Darrow did so many years ago.
>
> For if you succeed I may still have the opportunity of justifying my existence of making of it a life.[31]

Unlike his idol Darrow, who used hardly any notes during his time defending Leopold, Gertz had scripted everything meticulously. Every statement made by himself and the witnesses at Leopold's hearing had been scrutinized and edited by him. After their many witnesses and a lengthy statement from Gertz, the opposition spoke, but even that had become muted over the years.

State's Attorney Benjamin Adamowski said that though Leopold would likely be successful on parole, this case was too newsworthy to treat lightly. He worried that freeing Leopold would increase crime and decrease the public's opinions of the parole board. This time Robert Crowe was not able to add his voice to the opposition; he had died on January 18.[32]

Leopold followed this with a carefully prepared explanation of his own: "I admired Richard Loeb extravagantly, beyond all bounds. I literally lived and died on his approval or disapproval. I would have done anything he asked, even when I knew he was wrong, even when I was revolted by what he suggested."[33] Even though Loeb had done the actual killing, Leopold claimed that his remorse for the crime was "the strongest emotion I have ever had. It is with me constantly."[34] He wrapped up by saying:

> Gentlemen, you see before you today not the arrogant, conceited, smart-Alecky kid of nineteen, who came to prison. I am an old man, a broken man, who humbly pleads for your compassion. . . . All I want in this life is a chance to prove to you and the people of Illinois, what I

know in my own heart to be true, that I can and will become a decent, a respected and law abiding citizen, a chance to find [redemption] for myself by service to others.[35]

He was then turned over to questions from members of the board. He stated that he had been offered a job and housing in Puerto Rico, where he hoped he could "get lost" and stay far away from people who knew of his name and crime. When asked about notoriety and the danger of publicity he replied, "Don't you see that would be the worst thing in the world? My goodness, all I want, if I am so lucky as to ever see freedom again, is to try to become a humble little person."[36] After a few more questions he was dismissed, and the hearing was concluded. All there was left to do was await the board's decision.

On February 20 Warden Ragen called Leopold into his office and informed him he had just gotten off the phone with the governor. On March 13 he would be a free man: he was getting his parole. Leopold's statement to reporters after hearing the news perfectly outlined the tone he was trying to set: "I am grateful first of all to God. For men can do only what God permits them to do. . . . I am acutely conscious that more than my own future hangs in the balance. Thousands of prisoners, especially long-term prisoners, look to me to vindicate the rehabilitation theory of imprisonment. I will do my best not to fail in that trust."[37] Letters of congratulation poured in from friends, family, and strangers, and Leopold attempted to reply to as many as possible.

With his release less than a month away, Leopold frantically began planning: he hoped to visit Rosehill cemetery to see the graves of his parents, Aunt Birdie, and Mike. Bal would still be in California, where he was recovering from a stroke, and Sam was scheduled to be in Florida on business, so their reunion would have to wait. Mike's widow, Peg, offered to put him up, but he declined, determined to protect her from publicity. Still, Leopold longed to meet the Fulfords, young Davie especially, as the four-year-old was the "only family I've ever had or am likely to have."[38] Gertz discouraged a face-to-face meeting with Dave Fulford, as this would be an immediate breach of his parole regulations that forbade men on parole from contacting ex-convicts, but he promised to see what he could do about the Fulford children.

Before his release, Leopold made sure to add himself to Paul Henry's mailing list under the name William Eiss, Henry's actual uncle, but with Dave Fulford's address.[39] Leopold and Henry could send their letters to

Fulford who would pass them on, with the prison censors none the wiser. Leopold was pleased by the ruse, writing to Fulford: "I should be somewhat more reluctant to call on you for this service if we hadn't done just the same for you many years ago. This strikes my sense of poetic justice, and tickles me probably beyond the real importance of the matter. Makes me feel good all over!"[40]

On March 2 Leopold opted to eat dinner in the officer's kitchen where Henry was a cook, and where Leopold had been manufacturing reasons to visit so he could get better food for months. This time when his absence in the dining hall was noticed, Leopold was ordered to spend three days in the hole. Being manacled to the bars was a thing of the distant past, and as Leopold received diabetic meals and was able to get cigarettes, this was not a terrible punishment. It seemed the prison authorities were as interested in good publicity as Leopold was, as his punishment was not leaked to the press.[41] He was sitting in the hole when his autobiography was published on March 6.

Too late to influence the parole board as had been its goal, the book still went far to bolster Leopold's public image during his release, and over the next half-century would cement the narrative he had been trying to achieve. While some reviews were lukewarm, calling it boring and white-washed, most praised him for his insight and the way he had improved the lives of so many The book was quite popular, selling nearly 28,000 copies in its first four months, making the *New York Times* Best Seller List for 14 weeks and eventually being serialized, translated, and reprinted several times.[42] Fan mail began pouring in by the hundreds, from readers who were touched by his tale and saw him as completely rehabilitated.

V

FREEDOM

17

A NEW LIFE

On March 13, 1958, reporters crowded the wide stone steps leading up to Stateville's gatehouse, with their notebooks in hand. Video crews from television stations waited at a distance, their cameras focused on a pair of double doors under a sign reading "Illinois State Penitentiary." When a short middle-aged man, dressed in a gray hat and long overcoat appeared a little after ten in the morning, they were ready.

Leopold stepped out into the cool spring day as a free man for the first time in over thirty-three years. He removed his hat, revealing dark brown hair carefully combed back from a receding hairline, and approached a cluster of microphones erected on the steps of the gatehouse. Reporters eagerly surrounded him, snapping pictures and shouting questions. Leopold pulled out a prepared speech and unfolded it, waiting for the crowd to quiet before he began reading. He was rehearsed and detached-sounding as he pleaded with the crowd to show restraint and give him some peace.

> I appeal as solemnly as I know how to you, and to your editors, and to your publishers, and to society at large to agree that the only piece of news about me is that I have ceased to be news.
>
> I beg, I beseech you and your editors and your publishers to grant me a gift almost as precious as freedom itself—a gift without which freedom ceases to have much value—the gift of privacy.[1]

As he wrapped up, he was bombarded with more questions from the swarm. Asked if he felt free, he smiled, replying: "No, I'm a little hemmed in at present."[2] Reporters laughed at the quip as he waited impatiently to leave.

After inmates are released from prison, most enter into a parole period where they are monitored by a parole officer and have limited freedoms. For Leopold this would last for five years, followed by a hearing to determine if he should be released to total freedom. Leopold would have to obey the usual parole restrictions: he couldn't leave the county without permission, drink, own a gun, or communicate with convicts or ex-convicts, but his notoriety won him an additional caveat. At no point during this parole period was he allowed to seek publicity, be interviewed, or publish.[3] If any of the conditions were violated, Leopold was in danger of being sent back to prison, where public opinion was unlikely to give him a second chance at freedom.

Replacing his hat, Leopold was led by Gertz to a white Oldsmobile parked on the wide gravel drive, where Ralph Newman waited at the wheel. Cameras continued to click and reporters rushed to their cars along with them. With Newman, Leopold, and Gertz all in the front seat, they began their journey back to Chicago, about a dozen cars holding reporters trailing behind them.

As Newman's car sped onto the highway, a blue Cadillac raced past the reporters and pulled up beside them, Leopold and the driver within gesturing to each other before Newman pulled ahead. Reporters were intrigued, one describing the incident as a perilous high-speed chase in which the Cadillac driver "seemed to bear a grudge against someone in the car," and shook his fist at the occupants.[4] Actually, the Cadillac was driven by Dave Fulford. Forbidden by Gertz from a more intimate visit with Leopold, Fulford at least wanted to share a wave with his old friend before his departure.[5]

In an attempt to lose the caravan of reporters tailing them, Newman sped excessively, and the high speeds combined with the stress of the day caused Leopold to be violently ill. As Newman pulled over to let Leopold out, the reporters stopped as well, taking pictures of the man who continued to terrify hundreds, as he bent over retching in a ditch. The process was repeated several times, every car stopping and starting at the whim of Leopold's stomach. Finally they made a detour into Oak Park, a Chicago suburb, where Leopold retreated into Ralph Newman's home in the hopes of quieting his stomach.

With reporters persistently camping outside the Newman house, it was clear that anonymity was not something Leopold was entitled to yet. In a *Chicago Sun-Times* editorial, the newspaper defended the right of reporters to detail Leopold's activities on parole. Though they respected his wish for privacy, they maintained that anonymity was something he would have to earn. Until then, "The public will be entitled to know how the man whose sentencing judge said he should never be set free is faring outside of prison."[6]

Hoping for some privacy, Leopold decided to stay at Abel Brown's apartment, rather than the hotel he had booked. Not to be deterred, reporters followed him in, camping in the hallways as Brown's neighbors gathered to gossip and provide refreshments for the newsmen.[7] Stepping through the crowded halls, Peg Lebold met Leopold for the first time outside of a visiting room.[8] Leopold spent the next several hours calling Bal and Sam, but his family was disturbed when he also called ex-convict ex-lovers Frank Sandiford and Dave Fulford.

Soon joining the little party were Elmer Gertz's wife, their young adult son, and daughter, along with the three Fulford children.[9] By the time he was released, the kids were thirteen, nine, and four years old and eager to meet the "Uncle Nate" they had heard so much about. In between more phone calls from friends and family and a dinner of sukiyaki, Leopold chatted with the children and played blocks on the floor with Davie.[10] Leopold told Helen Williams: "I'm entirely sure I picked the right kids to 'adopt.'" He described the short time he spent with them as "heart-balm" that "erased the whole preceding thirty years."[11]

The following morning, with reporters undaunted by the wait still lining the halls, it was clear that the private visit Leopold had wanted to make to the graves of his family members would have to be postponed. Instead, he accompanied Gertz on a walk through Lincoln Park, flinching at the speeding cars and marveling at the many changes that had appeared during his years away.[12] Several times they were stopped by passersby, who wanted to shake Leopold's hand and wish him well.[13] Walking past a group of children playing baseball, Leopold remarked to Gertz that it had been thirty-four years since he was last able to see a group of kids at play. Presumably both tactfully failed to mention that the last time Leopold had seen children playing ball he had murdered the umpire.

After their walk, Leopold and Gertz returned to the Brown's apartment and readied themselves for the flight. Peg Lebold came over again to say goodbye and to caution Leopold against breaking his parole restrictions. For the sake of the family as well as his newfound freedom, she made him promise that he would have no more contact with any cons or ex-cons until his parole period was up.[14] It took him less than two weeks to break this promise.[15]

As his family watched Leopold take his first steps into the free world after more than thirty-three years away, even the most optimistic were unsure how it would play out. After they had poured so much time and effort into helping him attain his freedom, all they asked was that he spend the rest of his life constructively within the bounds of the law, or at least not immediately throw all those sacrifices in their faces. For a man who had spent his entire adult life in a maximum-security prison after committing cold-blooded murder, this seemed a relatively tall order, and even those who purported to believe fully in his rehabilitation felt that someone must be there to shelter and closely monitor him as he entered this new stage of his life.

At 8 p.m. the night after his release from prison, Leopold flew to New York and from there caught a 3:30 a.m. plane for Puerto Rico.[16] Despite his worries about his previous carsickness, he felt fine on the plane rides and was clear-headed when he arrived in San Juan around noon on Saturday. Joining Leopold on his flight was Harold Row, a man Leopold had recently added to his personal hagiography, calling him one of the two living saints he knew.[17] Greeted at the airport by more reporters, Leopold gave a short speech in Spanish thanking them for accepting him on their island. From there they drove the three hours to the remote mountain village of Casta-ñer where the Brethren hospital was located.

The Brethren's presence in Puerto Rico began in 1942 with the erection of a hospital and recreation center and the establishment of a material assistance program.[18] From there they expanded, creating a high school and small industries program. They stressed local involvement and their goal was to eventually leave and have Puerto Ricans running the programs they put in place. By the time Leopold arrived dozens were working for the project, most of them volunteers who came for summers or a year or two at a time. Most members lived on the project property in Casa Grande and Casa Larga, wooden apartment complexes close to the hospital, which had been converted from old CCC barracks.

As the car made its final turns up the winding mountain road, a sense of excitement grew among the project community. Doctors peeked out of window, and patients craned their necks from their beds as off-duty project members gathered outside to get the first glimpse of their new member. With families lining the upper porch of Casa Grande, the children present recalled that they didn't know who the man stepping out of the car in the late afternoon sun was, but there was the sense that he was someone famous and important.[19]

Leopold and Row were greeted by Ralph Townsend, the hospital administrator, who gave them a tour of the project where Leopold would live and work. He was introduced to the people who would become his friends and colleagues and shown to his small apartment in Casa Larga. With locking doors and his own bathroom, it was more luxury than he'd had in years. Leopold was delighted by the nature he could see from his window, from the distant mountains to the gardenia bush by his porch. He quickly made the interior of his room his own, displaying pictures of his deceased family members and, without a cellmate to clean for him, instantly amassing clutter.[20]

His new world was bigger than anything he'd seen in the past three decades but small enough that everyone hoped he wouldn't be overwhelmed. The village of Castañer, on the central western side of the island, was so tiny that it didn't appear on many maps. The surrounding area consisted mainly of small villages and scattered homes with most living below the poverty line. Despite its limited staff and resources, the hospital served about one hundred thousand people, providing pro bono and sliding scale medical and social services for the municipalities of Adjuntas, Yauco, Maricao, and Lares.[21]

After touring the project and recovering from the excitement of his first days outside of prison, Ralph Townsend and Harold Row took Leopold back to San Juan to shop and introduce Leopold to his parole supervisor, a man named Angel Umpierre, who impressed Leopold as a fine person with a kind interest in him.[22] It was Sr. Umpierre to whom Leopold would give monthly reports on his progress, and to whom he would write when he needed permission to ride in vehicles and travel outside of Castañer. As he needed to travel outside the county frequently in his work, he asked and received blanket permission for these rights less than two weeks after his release.[23]

He was also introduced to several Jewish residents of the island and the local rabbi, who invited Leopold to attend the annual public Seder at the Caribe-Hilton Hotel.[24] Leopold had been waiting for a negative reaction, for someone to reject him or react negatively to his freedom. He was surprised when, not only in Chicago but in Puerto Rico as well, people seemed either indifferent or genuinely happy to have him free. He reported to his friends: "In San Juan I had the exciting experience of hearing a man who didn't recognize me tell another what a fine thing he thought it was that I had been released and how happy he was that I had chosen Puerto Rico as my home."[25]

Part of what enabled Leopold to earn the goodwill of the community was his location. As Umpierre put it, "We Puerto Ricans could not feel terribly involved in a cause celebre that had occurred 2,000 miles and thirty-four years away." He encouraged Leopold "to think of his coming here as beginning a new life, as being born all over again; and to forget about a past few people here knew of anyway."[26]

Tuesday evening Harold Row left for his home in Illinois, satisfied that Leopold was properly situated and in good hands. Waiting to see him off at the airport, Leopold was overcome with emotion by the new life he had been given, in his mind thanks in large part to Row. He stared hard into some display cases in the airport's waiting area, hoping the others wouldn't notice the tears that welled in his eyes.[27]

Aware of the curiosity around his adjustment, Leopold was quick to assure acquaintances of his love for the island:

> Puerto Rico should be spelled PARADISE. The countryside is unbe-
> lievably lovely; the natural beauty is exceeded only by the kindness and
> generosity of the inhabitants. Here on the Project we have as devoted
> a group of men and women as could be found anywhere. They've
> welcomed me with open arms and vie with one another to make me
> feel at home.[28]

Despite the glowing assurances, he did not find the beginning of his life in Puerto Rico as easy as he made it seem. While he was able to converse with continental Americans who spoke fluent Spanish, "let me get into a conversation with one of the Puerto Ricans, and I almost have to draw pictures!"[29] Learning to distinguish Puerto Rican accents and slang was a decidedly different experience from the European Spanish he had seen in textbooks and what he had practiced with Mexicans in Stateville. Worse, he immediately began to have difficulties with his new job.

Assigned to work as a lab technician, he found he had forgotten most of what he once knew and struggled to re-learn everything, frustrated when he wasn't catching on as quickly as he felt he should be.[30] He'd never worked with women or children; even with reading glasses he was having trouble reading the lab results; and the lab equipment was different than what he had used in prison a decade previously. Two weeks into his freedom he mused: "I seem to have some sort of mental block. I fumble on things I should know well. . . . At the moment I have serious doubts as to whether I'll be able to hold down the job."[31]

Though the hospital staff saw few flaws in his work, after two months they allowed him to switch to pharmaceutical and x-ray work, where he felt more comfortable.[32] While this helped some, he continued to put increasing pressure on himself, trying to answer not only the backlog of correspondence he'd accrued in prison, but also the hundreds of fan letters coming in from those who were reading his book. Often he would stay up until the early morning at his typewriter, trying to make it through the day on a few hours of sleep.

Aware that his job performance was only part of the adjustment process, Leopold was determined not to be isolated. He reached out to the staff and volunteers on the project, and they went out of their way to be gracious and generous with their time. The group of volunteers living on the project lived lives dedicated to the service of humanity and God and could be very strict about abstaining from vices. Brethren members didn't smoke, drink, dance, or play cards—in some ways living under stricter conditions than Leopold had behind bars. As he wasn't part of their church, Leopold was not held to the same standards, and he made no attempt to hide his drinking and chain-smoking, but the project members accepted it, just as they had accepted his past.

Leopold lived next door to Dr. Gerald Church, his wife, Joanne, and their children.[33] They invited him on a picnic soon after his arrival and when the group found a pleasant spot to set their blanket, the older children played as Joanne held her six-week-old baby, Holly, in her arms. Joanne recalled: "I was very busy, I had four little children, I was preparing food and I asked Nate to hold Holly as I laid out the rest of the food. He looked at me with such astonishment, tears came to his eyes immediately. He said: 'You'd trust me to hold your new little baby?'"[34]

The trust Joanne had shown in him with that casual request stayed with Leopold; he wrote proudly of the event to his friends and held it up as an example of the goodwill the Brethren exuded. "The little [Church] girls and also the Townsend children want to adopt me as a 'Grandpa,'" Leopold reported to Helen Williams. "Now I'm all for the idea of adoption, but I bristle a little at the generation they chose. 'Uncle' would have pleased me better."[35] Though the Church family left the island two months after Leopold's arrival, more families quickly took their place and Leopold made sure to get to know them all. Of the many project children I interviewed, all had fond memories of the man who showed interest in their activities and was quick to give them a kind word and a piece of candy.

The families Leopold bonded with fussed over him, patching his clothes, providing home-cooked meals, and making sure his lack of life skills would continue to go unchallenged. Still, there was another group that intrigued him: the young single nurses. At fifty-three, Leopold was usually several decades older than the eligible ladies on the project, but he didn't let that deter him. It would be in his overwhelming best interest to straighten up, as his relationship with Loeb, the suspected sexual nature of the Franks crime, and spending the majority of life in prison meant there was still a lot of speculation about his sexuality. While Leopold was still in his custody, Warden Ragen had pulled him aside and "told me—very diffidently and with much hemming and hawing—just before I left that he didn't think the Board would mind if I laid a broad occasionally."[36]

Leopold took each of the nurses out and began to supplement this growing heterosexual image by entertaining some of the female fans his notoriety had brought him. These women began to visit him just four months after his release, Leopold showing them around Castañer and San Juan. Far from proving himself a Lothario, Leopold mocked these women to friends, bemoaning their prudishness and calling one "homely as a mud fence."[37] "Most of these letter-writing dames," he complained, "turn out to be old bags that want to marry you or that cream in their jeans at sight of you."[38] His fans told a different story, complaining about his lack of affection and the infrequency of his kisses.[39]

Beyond enhancing his heterosexual image, these women flattered his ego and gave him far more tangible incentives to continue communication. Concerned about his small paycheck, boxes of snacks, toiletries, clothes, books, and cartons of cigarettes were soon arriving at Leopold's door. Some even gave him checks, which he encouraged, writing to these gullible women of his quaint living conditions without explaining the extent of his finances. After his father's death, Sam and Mike had taken out $50,000 in life insurance policies, so they could financially support Leopold while they were alive, and the money from the policies would go into a trust after they had died. Mike's trust paid Leopold around $1,200 a year (equivalent to about $12,400 in 2023) and Sam matched that, paying out of pocket every January.[40] With Leopold getting free room and board and including the more than $10,000 he still had from the sale of his book, he was not in quite the desperate straits he allowed his fans to believe.

In the fall of 1958 Leopold intended to attend San Juan's largest public Seder with around three hundred other Jewish families. But, fearing publicity, he went instead to a private Seder at the apartment of a rabbi, where he met Gertrude "Trudi" García de Quevedo. Originally from Baltimore, in the 1940s Trudi Feldman and her sister Anita Faure began taking yearly cruises to Puerto Rico. On one of these trips Trudi met and married Manuel García de Quevedo, a Puerto Rican doctor.[41] Faure got a job with the army and both sisters resettled on the island. When Dr. García de Quevedo died in 1947, Trudi decided to remain in her new home and opened a flower shop in San Juan to support herself.

When she met Leopold for the first time Trudi was intrigued. "At first Nathan was like a child learning to walk," she recalled. "He seemed to need help badly."[42] Trudi extended an open invitation to visit her the next time he was in San Juan but did not expect him to take her up on the offer. "He was not shy," she observed. "But he was plainly reluctant to meet people and uncertain about accepting invitations."[43]

As Leopold played up this straight persona, he was more covertly trying to set up meetings he was more likely to consummate. Less than a year after his release, he tried to convince Dave Fulford and his son to come down for a visit, all expenses paid. Hinting that Fulford could share his bed, Leopold more overtly stated: "I have in mind renewing our friendship of 20 years ago ON EXACTLY THE SAME TERMS. After all, what's 20 years? And I've seen you only once in all that time, and then at a distance. *I hope you understand exactly what I mean by that.*"[44] Fulford hedged for a couple of letters, saying he didn't want to take advantage of Leopold's generosity, but when pressed he replied: "It certainly has been many years since we have seen each other, and I am sure our feelings to see each other are mutual. On the other point in question, *I think I'm so old.*"[45] Fulford never made the journey and Leopold would have to scratch this particular itch elsewhere.

Aside from these human connections, Leopold was ecstatic when, a couple of months after his arrival on the island, he was allowed to adopt a black five-week-old puppy when one of the project doctor's pets had a litter. He named the puppy Bill and recalled that he was "the very first creature I had in my brave new world of free men . . . here was a living being of my very own: one I could hug and pet and love."[46] Though exhausted after days in the lab and nights spent at his typewriter, those first weeks Leopold was often up during the night cleaning up after Bill and holding him when he cried. "I should have my head examined," he wrote to his niece, "I'm hardly able to take care of myself, and here I take on an additional responsibility. But he is so darn cute and affectionate."[47] Bill quickly became devoted to Leopold as well, chasing after him when he left the project and waiting for him outside the lab, where he wasn't allowed inside.

Standing on the precipice of the remainder of his life, with the eyes of the world on him, Leopold had to consider his public persona very carefully. Despite what he'd told the parole board, he wasn't cut out for a quiet, safe life outside of larger society and the many pleasures he'd become accustomed to. In August he wrote to his family that if his life was to have a meaningful message it "MUST imply a slow, gradual, but steady return to normal living."[48] Seeking a job that would be more interesting, Leopold campaigned for and was granted the position of Brethren social worker on January 1, 1959.

As his first unofficial assignment Leopold took a three-day vacation with a teenager who worked part-time in the lab, under the pretense of taking him for a scholarship interview at the University of Puerto Rico. The rest of the time, Leopold reported, they lounged on the beach and enjoyed scenic plane rides across the island. No justification for his personally accompanying the boy or of the vacation they took around the brief interview was offered. This trip was a long time coming; he'd planned a similar vacation in October with "my favorite lab boy," without the pretext of an interview, but had to postpone it after temporarily blinding himself when he tripped in the dark and hit his eye on a table.

The project members noticed nothing suspicious in this trip; Leopold was now a social worker and he had been taking an interest in high school kids since he arrived. He went to dinner with the lab boys, took groups of teenagers to a local carnival, opened his apartment for afterschool coffee meetings, and helped with the high school yearbook. One boy, who worked in the lab during high school, recalled Leopold fondly and was grateful that Leopold had helped him get a job and a scholarship. "Anytime you needed help he was there. . . . He was the nicest guy I ever worked with."[49]

In 1958 Leopold got to know a sixteen-year-old named Tony, whose family was in considerable financial straits. His father was disabled and unable to find consistent work, so Leopold must have seemed like a miracle when he found a job for Tony and offered to help his younger sisters get scholarships once they graduated. As Leopold integrated himself into Tony's life, the relationship became sexual, but at that point there was little Tony would have been able to deny the man who had been so generous.

As Leopold had learned in prison, he courted Tony and many other Puerto Rican teenagers with gifts, jobs, and the promise of a better life. Perhaps he enjoyed the inequal dynamic reminiscent of his old fantasies of being a benevolent king to fawning slaves. He assuredly enjoyed the power that came from pursuing the young and destitute and the gratitude that came from his extravagant gifts. It had been decades since Leopold had a relationship with someone he considered his equal, and by the time of his release he seemed very comfortable trading money and gifts for sex and companionship with minors.

Leopold's new job as a social worker made these crimes easier to conceal, and he found that he enjoyed the other facets of the position as well. Three days a week Leopold worked in an office, helping families negotiate medical care and mental health services and attaining government aid.[50] The other two days Leopold did casework in people's homes, the fifty-three-year-old diabetic climbing steep hills and shuffling along dirt roads as he wasn't allowed to drive. Despite the physical difficulties, he found the work absorbing and preferred to travel around talking to people rather than always being stuck behind a desk punching a clock. Outside of work he took on several extra projects: fundraising for the new hospital the project was trying to build, setting up a community vegetable garden, and looking for land to build a vocational school for juvenile delinquents.

On the evening of January 5 Leopold was pulled into another project. He had already shown a willingness to get into costume, when he donned a hat, a nurse's red pajama pants, a white cloth beard, and stuffed a pillow under his shirt to hand out presents during the project's Christmas party. But to most Puerto Ricans, Día de los Reyes Magos, or Three Kings Day, was winter's true gift-giving holiday. For several years the Puerto Rican employees who worked on the project had collected gifts and distributed them to the homes of nearby children on the eve of Three Kings Day. This year Leopold joined them. Donning robes and paper crowns the group set out on horseback with jeeps full of presents trailing behind. They distributed about nine hundred presents in eight hours.[51]

On March 8, the project held its cornerstone laying ceremony for the new hospital they were planning to build. The current one was nearly

Leopold handing out candy for Día de los Reyes Magos (Three Kings Day) in 1969.
Photo courtesy of Larry Miller.

twenty years old, with termites eating through the small wooden structure and flyswatters in the surgical ward. So close to the anniversary of his release from prison, Leopold used this event as a framing device for how far he had come since Stateville. He wrote to friends and family about the event:

> I ate my dinner that Sunday at the table with the Governor's lady, the President of the Senate, the Speaker of the House and his wife, our own Executive Secretary, and the Administrator of the Project and his wife. Last March 8 I had my lunch from the floor in The Hole at Stateville. Who doesn't believe in fairy tales? They just got Cinderella's sex wrong![52]

This was Leopold's first introduction to the island's political elite, and over lunch, governor Luis Muñoz Marín's wife, Dona Inés, engaged Leopold in discussions about building a boy's school for juvenile offenders. The next week he was invited to La Fortaleza, the governor's mansion, where the deal was discussed further, and Leopold elaborated on his own similar plans, involving negotiating the sale of the land from Robert Claiborne, an elderly retired teacher and politician with a large farm on the outskirts of Maricao.

Claiborne had invited Leopold to visit his property soon after Leopold's arrival on the island, promising quiet and privacy.[53] Leopold and a Brethren chaperone took Claiborne up on his offer in October, spending the night in the house with Claiborne's pack of asthmatic dogs and a couple of houseboys. The following February Claiborne invited Leopold to meet his wife while she was visiting from the States, though the houseboys would be gone. Leopold replied: "As to the boys' being there, I had hoped to be able to make it sometime when they were there . . . because I am interested in some of the things you mentioned on my last visit and would welcome the opportunity of going into them further."[54]

After the cornerstone ceremony, Claiborne and Leopold began to discuss the idea of a vocational school, though Claiborne was mostly interested in getting free labor to help his struggling farm. He complicated things with an aversion to delinquents, the government or religious interference, and only wanted boys fourteen and younger—the same ages he preferred for his houseboys.[55] With all of Claiborne's parameters the idea soon withered, but a friendship had been struck between the men who recognized that they both had a fondness for teenage boys.

Though Leopold was careful about his image, this readjustment was not without its public stumbles. In the fall of 1958 Leopold and Elmer Gertz began seriously considering suing Meyer Levin, claiming that *Com-*

pulsion appropriated Leopold's property rights to his story. Initially Leopold was skeptical, writing to Gertz: "There seems little point in going ahead with suits . . . if all I will get is a lot of publicity and no cash!"[56] But promising a quick and hefty settlement and the right to edit the film version that was in production, Gertz convinced Leopold to go forward, and the suits were served to Levin in October 1959.

Immediately Leopold was bombarded with backlash; his family and friends criticized him, news articles and editorials pointed to this move as proof that Leopold had lied about his rehabilitation and was only after money. Most importantly, some parole board members voted that this move violated the anti-publicity clause in his parole agreement. Less than a month after filing the suits, Leopold wrote to Gertz proposing they drop it, hoping that an about-face would erase most of the damage. While he mourned the loss of the potential monetary gain and a perceived blow to his masculinity if it looked like Levin had scared him, his freedom mattered far more.[57]

Gertz responded with several long letters detailing why they needed to keep on. He assured Leopold that he had better judgment than any of Leopold's friends, and explained that if Leopold recanted, the parole board would view Leopold as impulsive and wonder if they'd been wrong to parole him. Ultimately putting his friendship on the table, Gertz stated: "My professional judgment and reputation are at stake, to say nothing of the thousands of dollars worth of time both I and Gordon have invested to the exclusion of other fee-producing matters. You would, indeed, be leaving me high and dry."[58] As the publicity faded and the board decided Leopold hadn't violated his parole, Leopold agreed to let things lie. Gertz was placated and the lawsuits began their slow journey through the courts.

Despite this blip, it seemed that Leopold was doing well in his new life, but after thirty-three years in prison, Leopold remained pessimistic. In 1958 he wrote:

> Thanks for your consoling remarks about whether my life was wasted. I'm afraid it was tho. I didn't, for instance, marry and raise a family. I didn't make a success in the law or in business. I did not attain a respected position in the community. What very little I have been able to accomplish is entirely by the way—nothing of any importance at all, and much of it done, I'm afraid, simply in preference to the alternative—boredom.[59]

As Leopold looked to the future, these values would help shape what he made of the remainder of his life.

18

EMERGING FROM SECLUSION

When Leopold was released from prison, his parole officer told him that he was "only two days old," and needed much guidance and support.[1] A year after his release it seemed Leopold had reached his late teens; once again he was considering going away to college.

Despite the accelerated start he had received in his education, Leopold had never progressed beyond a bachelor's degree and this lack rankled him, especially as he came into daily contact with doctors on the project. He took the entrance exam for medical school at the University of Puerto Rico, but decided to get a master's degree in social work, as he wasn't sure he'd live through all the years that medical school entailed.[2]

Feeling obligated to the Brethren for the part they had played in his release, and perhaps feeling guilty that he was planning to abandon them after only a year, Leopold threw himself into fundraising for their new hospital with his customary vigor. It took him some time to look up Trudi after their initial visit, but once he did, she proved an indispensable ally. She was happy to use her knowledge of the Jewish residents and businesses on the island for his fundraising campaign, sending out a letter pleading for funds that Leopold had drafted over her signature.[3] They began meeting nearly every time Leopold came to San Juan.

As he increased his activity and in anticipation of his schooling in the fall, Leopold applied for a driver's license. Gertz objected, fearing what would happen if he got in a car accident and not wanting to annoy the parole board by asking for this favor. "Please don't push your good fortune," he wrote, but Leopold ignored his concerns.[4] Angling for a way of expediting the process and ensuring he passed his test, he wrote to local businessmen, hoping he could find someone with high enough connections willing to pull strings for him.[5]

He also sought alternate ways of paying for a car, considering getting the Brethren to finance it, with the claim that he would come back after school and use it while working for them.[6] Ultimately he only had to write to his fans that he was "saving every penny," because he desperately needed a car and they gladly sent him money without being asked.[7] When one woman sent $2,000 (equivalent to about $21,000 in 2023), he turned her name over to the Brethren, hoping she would also finance a four-figure donation for the new hospital.[8] Leopold used money from the same fan to take Tony's sisters shopping for school clothes in his new Volkswagen Beetle, on one of his many visits to see the teenager.[9]

Despite misgivings from the chancellor of the School of Social Work, who thought Leopold's enrollment was a publicity stunt, Leopold was eventually accepted. Hearing the good news, more checks rolled in from fans for his "Educational Fund."[10] In August he completed his transformation to college student by moving into an apartment with a classmate. Every Monday through Wednesday he would get on a bus and ride the two miles to campus, an oasis of greenery and Spanish-style stone among the modern businesses and highways of San Juan. Leopold stuck out just as obviously among the young Puerto Rican women who were his classmates in the female-dominated field of social work. The instruction was in Spanish, which he claimed to understand most of the time, except with one professor "who mumbles and talks like a machine gun at the same time."[11]

Unfortunately for Leopold, this return to university wasn't all he had hoped. "This social work racket is for the birds," he complained three weeks into the semester. "They assign an enormous amount of reading, but so far I haven't come across a single solid concept you can get your teeth into. Nothing but words and platitudes."[12] Still, Leopold conceded to friends that it wasn't all bad, bragging about dating a twenty-year-old classmate.[13]

Despite the playboy posturing, Leopold spent a good deal of time with Trudi, their fundraising eventually turning into personal conversations and dates. In June 1960 he wrote to Ralph Newman:

> I am, for the first time, seriously considering marrying Trudi García. . . .
> As far as I'm concerned I'm anything but "in love." That is, I'm not
> especially attracted romantically. However I do like Trudi a lot and I
> think we would be compatible. Some of the time I feel that I would
> like the stability and comfort of a home; then other times I'm not at all
> sure I want to give up my freedom of movement.

Trudi is far more anxious about this whole thing than I; she's pushing pretty hard. I'm afraid she is in love. She understands about the terrific publicity to which she is likely to be subjected but claims not to mind particularly. I've also told her that there is considerable likelihood that I may want to pop off to Africa or some other unlikely place. She thinks that's fine—wants to go along! In fact, I've tried to picture all the unpleasant things that might come up and all the possible disadvantages. She still wants to go ahead.

One point she stresses strongly is that she believes the Parole Board would approve heartily of my getting married and that this might increase chances of getting my final discharge. While I certainly don't want to get married as a means to an end, I think I have to consider very carefully what attitude the Board would take—whether pro or con.[14]

Leopold even tried to put Trudi off by telling her their marriage would be sexless, as his diabetes made him impotent, but she refused to be discouraged.[15] On top of these conditions within their relationship, she also had to stand against external pressures, as outside of Castañer it was clear that not everyone was so willing to accept Leopold. When apartment hunting with him she had seen firsthand how tenants would complain and landlords who had once been friendly closed their doors once they realized who Leopold was.[16] Worse, anonymous letters began arriving at her door:

So. . . . You are finally getting a RICH husband. How can you think of sleeping with a man who has blood on his hands. . . . an innocent child's blood. Your hunger for a man must have been very great.

We are sick of the sight of you . . . both of you. Take your lover and get off the island . . . both of you. We tremble when that murderer looks at one of our children.[17]

Though the messages shook her, they did not deter her from her goal of settling down with Leopold.

Ignoring his lackluster classes and uncertain relationship with Trudi, during his first school year Leopold continued pouring much of his excess energy into the Brethren's hospital campaign.[18] He wrote a script for a documentary raising awareness of the project, once again paying tribute to Loeb by crediting Ricardo Lawrence as the author.[19] Writing and sending hundreds of letters begging for donations, he chafed at the parole restrictions that kept him from signing his own name, as he was sure that using his notoriety would make the funds easier to raise.[20]

By the end of his first school year, Leopold was able to see this project completed. Between government assistance and donations, $207,000 was raised to build and outfit the modern building.[21] The hospital's dedication took place on May 22, 1960. Leopold and Trudi watched from the crowd as Harold Row praised all of those who helped make their dream a reality.[22] The little hospital was extremely successful, offering surgeries and dental and social work services to thousands every year who otherwise would have no way to afford it.

After a summer in Castañer helping the new hospital get settled, Leopold returned to school, taking courses in the medical and social work programs at the same time. He vastly preferred the school of medicine, commenting snidely that in contrast to his social work classes, he may actually learn something there.[23] But, turned down for a traineeship he had hoped would allow him to pay for medical school without having to ask his brothers for money from his trust, he reluctantly returned to social work.

While he had little respect for the classroom side of social work, he reveled in the casework that got him into the field. Every semester he far exceeded his required number of hours and was assigned to work with hundreds of people, leading discussions in medical clinics, community organizing to get residents of a slum transferred to a new housing project, and doing individual casework.[24] Every few months he would write to friends of a new case that had captured his interest, fixating particularly on a fifteen-year-old named José he was assigned in late 1960.

Leopold wrote of his case: "My guess is that kid is either going to turn out to be one of the greatest scientists or doctors of this generation or else one of the most notorious juvenile delinquents since me. For he's threatened to kill his father! In my view, he stands right at the cross-roads. And the responsibility is mine."[25] Within a month Leopold was considering adopting José and had decided to fund his college education.[26] He was proud the following year when "Joie" sent him a Father's Day present, especially as by then their relationship had become sexual.[27]

While he spent all of his time on a case as long as it interested him, as soon as that wavered the client would be relegated to a minimum amount of attention, likely with little understanding of what they had done to cause the abrupt shift. This happened with a mute boy Leopold focused on for months, getting him appointments with doctors all over the island and spending time with his family, before Leopold deemed him "a mental defective" and inserted himself into José's life instead.[28] Leopold's professors noted with concern that "there is a tendency to over identification in some instances," and in one case were disturbed that "he made use of influential people to reach a psychologist on behalf of a client."[29] Despite the overreach, they praised his enthusiasm and administration skills and didn't stop him from getting personally acquainted with his cases.

To fill his already packed schedule, Leopold also taught math classes in the university's night school. Getting approved had been a struggle; Gertz had to appeal to the parole board personally, and there was a university rule against allowing felons to teach. But Leopold had maintained a friendship with the governor's wife, so her husband personally made sure that his appointment went through.[30]

Two nights a week Leopold could be found in a small classroom with half as many textbooks as were needed, lecturing about algebra in a mix of English and Spanish.[31] A man who observed Leopold's class remarked that his students "were a wonderful group to be teaching simply because they were so anxious to learn. They were all very happy with Leopold simply because he was imparting the knowledge."[32] Leopold's class was so enthusiastic about him that after their first semester when they learned they would be getting a new teacher for Math 101 they signed a petition and marched as a group to the head of the night school, demanding that Leopold teach the next section as well.[33] This was granted.

Not everyone was so comfortable with Leopold, however. Though his brothers wrote to him regularly, things were always touch-and-go with Sam. When he and his wife visited in 1960, Leopold filled their days with dinners, sightseeing, and gatherings with friends, determined to prove his adjustment and keep them from fighting, though this was unsuccessful.[34] After a tumultuous final evening together, Leopold complained: "Why Sam feels he has to take a 2,000 [mile] trip to make me feel bad and to recriminate over things of 35 years ago I haven't figured out. He seems to feel that it is incumbent upon him to keep punishing me."[35]

While Leopold still wasn't sure about marrying Trudi, he did add another lady to his family: a terrier mutt he brought off the street and named Sue. Bill had been deemed too large for apartment living, so he stayed first with Tony's family, and then with José's. Leopold was delighted with his replacement, sending out postcards with Sue's picture on the front and a message he'd written from her perspective describing their whirlwind romance on the back: "A week ago Thursday Nathan invited me to supper; Friday we started going steady; and Saturday we got hitched—at least I went to live in his place," "Sue" explained, and signed each card with her inky pawprint.[36]

Completing his unconventional family, Leopold was in regular contact with the Fulfords and Paul Henry. Henry would soon be eligible for a parole hearing, and as Leopold and Gertz helped him prepare, Henry reiterated his gratitude for his former cellmate, referencing a Kipling poem Leopold had given him. "You know, it's taken the last five or six years of my life to fully understand the implication of that word 'friend.' Now that you've shown me what it really means, it is doubtful that I will ever have but the one I have now since loyalty of this degree is not so common as that."[37] When asked where he'd like to be paroled to, Henry replied that maybe it was just the dreamer in him, but "maybe you will remember the talks we had," about joining Leopold in Puerto Rico.[38] Henry was assured that a job would be waiting for him in Castañer.

Never one for monogamy, Leopold still made semi-frequent visits to Robert Claiborne and his houseboys, sometimes bringing along young guests who Claiborne claimed were his social work cases. While planning a visit in 1961, Leopold asked if a boy named Ivan was still working for him. Claiborne responded that Ivan had left, but perhaps Leopold could bring the same boy he had during his last visit (likely José, as he was from the town mentioned and Leopold had taken him to Maricao earlier that year) and leave him at the farm:

> I'd greatly appreciate it if you could bring for MY NEED and YOUR PLEASURE some 14 to 15 [year old] beautiful and intelligent as the boy from Caguas.
>   The poorer they are, the worse shoes, the least family connections, the better for me: they will stay in proportion to prosperity of family.
>   You'd solve an unsolvable to date problem for me if you found one. And if so he'd be here for your recreation. Nothing asked but responsibility. reading and writing . . . cooking, washing dishes and floors and clothes. And of course thin, lovely, and "sex in face" like boy Caguas, and Ivan we have lost.[39]

Outside Claiborne's farm and his many boys scattered around the islands, Leopold combed San Juan's plazas and beaches for hustlers. When Leopold's gay friend Henry Johnson visited for his annual winter vacation, the pair set each other up, Leopold offering Castañer boys while Johnson used his decades of Puerto Rican cruising experience to find locals for Leopold.[40] Johnson recalled "he'd get very impatient if we didn't find somebody immediately," and that he preferred "younger ones, much younger."[41]

Leopold was certainly not the only gay man who had his sights set on boys below the age of consent, and for those so inclined, Puerto Rico in the 1960s offered something of a buffet. One reporter from a gay magazine noted that in Puerto Rico: "The relaxed atmosphere is most dramatically demonstrated in the casual way young numbers (under 15) go brazenly hustling around. I am sure there are laws against child molesting, but if there are, they must be the most ignored laws on the island."[42]

While cruising Leopold used a fake name, though this wasn't always enough to protect him.[43] He got a scare in early 1960 when a tabloid hinted cheekily: "Nathan Leopold of Loeb and Leopold fame has been giving individual lectures on leading a normal life—to cute teen-age Puerto Rican boys who visit him in his hotel room in San Juan."[44] The article was sent anonymously to the parole board, prompting a damage control visit by Harold Row. Leopold wrote to family and friends that he was "disturbed" and "sickened" by the accusations, revealing that he'd been afraid of an attack of this nature since he was paroled.[45] Yet he wasn't afraid enough to stop, continuing these clandestine activities after his friends and family assured him that no one believed the article's outrageous implication.

As his social sphere expanded and his reputation in the community grew, Leopold considered trying to get an early discharge from parole. "Why am I so anxious to get off parole?" he asked rhetorically. "Certainly I've had it easy enough: the restrictions on my liberty have been minimal. The parole authorities here in Puerto Rico are extremely permissive,"[46] Leopold admitted. But he worried about blackmail connected to his trysts, wanted desperately to travel the world, and couldn't get his social work license until his parole had gone through. Perhaps most importantly: he still felt caged. When he and Loeb had written a parole manual in the 1930s, they acknowledged that "The time you have to spend on parole is just as much a part of your sentence as the time you spent in the institution."[47] Leopold was eager to put that sentence far behind him.

Harold Row argued Leopold's case before the parole board and dozens of letters glowing with praise from his new colleagues, professors, and the governor arrived to provide anecdotal evidence of his success. Brethren social worker John Forbes praised Leopold's "great devotion to duty and a high standard of excellence in his work . . . he has been and still is rewarding the project with excellent suggestions, intelligent perceptions and just plain hard work."[48] Trudi claimed: "He has made himself respected, loved and admired by all who have come in contact with him—from the highest officials in Government circles to the poorest farmer in the country. This, because he gives so unstintingly of himself in every possible way; nothing is too much or too difficult for him to accomplish when it means helping a person in need."[49]

Despite the praise, the parole board saw no reason to cut Leopold's parole short and he was forced to concede serving his entire five years.

"Those bastards are often not governed by logic," he complained bitterly. He admitted to Gertz that he had considered offering them a bribe, "but in my case I'm about convinced that would be suicide."[50] Gertz failed to acknowledge this remark.

When the board denied his release, they threw him a bone by permitting him to marry. A potential marriage could no longer be used as leverage to gain an early release, but Leopold agreed to marry Trudi regardless. He longed for a home, someone to cook and clean for him, as well as the respectability and cover that he would gain with a wife. Without telling anyone their plans, on February 5, 1961, Leopold, Trudi, her sister Anita, and Señor and Señora Angel Umpierre (along with Leopold's terrier, Sue) drove up to Castañer where Umpierre performed a simple ceremony.

Announcement cards from one of Trudi's brothers were sent out to friends and family, and everyone managed to keep the marriage a secret for two days before a friend of Trudi's alerted the press. Congratulations were universal, and Gertz wrote him that his marriage "is one of the most remarkable events from a human viewpoint of which I have any knowledge. Certainly, thirty-seven years ago, nobody would have dreamed of such a climax to your life."[51]

Directly after the wedding Leopold and Sue moved to the antique-filled second-floor apartment in San Juan's Santurce district that Trudi had been living in since she'd been widowed. He brought little furniture of his own, but a study was set up for him where he could continue his nightly chore of keeping up with correspondence and writing reports, with lockable filing cabinets for letters, photo albums, and journals he'd rather Trudi didn't stumble across.

To cap off this façade of success, after two years of classes he disdained, hundreds of hours of fieldwork, and a thesis on alcoholism he disagreed with, on June 2, 1961, Leopold received a master's of social work degree. He attended the convocation "with my entire family: Trudi, Sue Dogg, and José."[52] After sitting for hours in the sun watching seemingly endless speeches and handshakes, the little group headed off to the Caribbean coast, borrowing a beach house and boat from friends to spend the weekend relaxing and deep-sea fishing. Leopold snapped a photo of his self-described family, José and Trudi smiling in sun hats with Sue in Trudi's arms as they prepared to step onto a little red yacht waiting beside the dock.[53]

After graduation, Leopold took a series of temporary jobs, until he was hired as a research associate by sociologist Howard Stanton. Leopold would be assigned a field of study, read what had been written on the subject, interview the field's leaders and identify the gaps in knowledge. His department would then fund people to research to fill those gaps and further the field.[54] Leopold was thrilled with the position; he spent much of his time traveling and talking with interesting, intelligent people, and the high turnover of subjects ensured he never got bored. "I think this job may very well be what I want to do for the next x years," he wrote to Gertz after his first week.[55] He and Stanton even applied for a grant from the National Institutes of Health that would allow them to do a three-year study tracing the transmission of parasites on the island, though they didn't expect the organization to meet their $125,000 price tag.[56]

When not on the job, Leopold maintained his high energy and output characteristic of him. He was treasurer of the Natural History Society of Puerto Rico, compiled data on the birds of Puerto Rico, fundraised for Castañer's medical co-op, and gave lectures on social work to visiting students.[57]

Capping off these accomplishments, Leopold was ecstatic to receive a telegram from Gertz in February 1962 announcing that Paul Henry was approved to be paroled to Castañer.[58] Leopold immediately wrote Henry advising him to buy nothing and accept no gifts from his family, as Leopold wanted to provide him with everything he needed once he arrived: "Ideally, you should leave there in your prison suit, clutching only a toothbrush, a comb, and a razor, preferably in a brown paper sack."[59]

Not everyone was so comfortable with the arrangement, however. Though Gertz had facilitated Henry's release, he worried that it may jeopardize Leopold's parole if the authorities ever caught wind of them seeing each other. After several remarks along this line, Leopold had enough. Far more candid than usual, in ten pages of type Leopold argued for his right to see Henry and aired the many personal grievances with Gertz that he'd bottled up over the years.

> You and I, I think, are the two vainest, most conceited humans I've ever met in that same career. Like me, you tend to arrogate unto yourself all the credit for anything good that happens and to disclaim responsibility for anything that blows up in our face. . . . You, again like me, lap up praise and adulation and publicity, even when your good sense tells you it's bologna. . . . And of course you, again like me, rationalize like a sonofabitch. Everything either of us does is always done, of course, for the very noblest motives. Unfortunately we've both got brains enough generally to be able to put up a pretty convincing story.

Leopold took this opportunity to admit that he had not been following his parole regulations since his release, specifying that he drank, stayed out after curfew, communicated with prisoners and ex-prisoners, went to brothels, and owned weapons.

And that ain't all, Butch. I intend to continue violating these provisions whenever the occasion arises. . . . . I wonder if you don't agree that some laws—and this includes rules and regulations of administrative boards—are morally wrong and SHOULD be disobeyed. . . . I consider some of the parole regulations too damn silly for words and too damn much nuisance even to attempt to obey. I think they are morally wrong in my case.

Once these annoyances were out of the way he addressed the matter that had triggered the letter: Paul Henry.

I have looked forward for years to just this consummation. During the past weeks or months my sense of anticipation has heightened. Since news of Paul's parole to Puerto Rico, it has reached fever heat. I'm not going to be deprived of one of the most exquisite pleasures in my life. I let you talk me out of seeing Dave Fulford, on March 13, 1958; I'm not going to let you talk me out of seeing Paul whenever I regard it as safe.

If they are so concerned about Paul's and my seeing each other, they'd better deprive him of his chance and parole him to Sioux City, Iowa, where he can learn to make rattan furniture, or put me under house arrest. Because, unless they do something of that nature, I am going to see Paul whenever I think I can safely do so, and they can pound their "ground rules" up their ass sideways.[60]

Gertz, far from getting angry, replied: "I have the feeling that I have read a masterpiece—not of literature, but, as Henry Miller would say, of life."[61] Fortunately for Gertz, the problem solved itself. At the last minute, the board decided to parole Henry to his family in Iowa and a job with the Salvation Army. Leopold sent rapid-fire letters to Gertz advising possible avenues of changing the board's decision. If a few hundred dollars to the right parole official didn't work,[62] then maybe Harold Row could argue that Castañer had been counting on his help and it would be the ideal place to keep him out of further trouble.[63] The board was unmoved.

Henry was paroled on March 29 and to ease Leopold's disappointment, Henry called him hours after his release. After the call Leopold wrote: "I've just come back from the phone after talking to you and I'm so excited I'm shaking."[64] Though he had dreamed of outfitting Henry personally, money, clothes, and other gifts began arriving for him in Iowa. The pair kept up their correspondence, Henry's letters detailed his new job, good relationship with his parole agent, and a burgeoning romantic relationship. Leopold was happy with these updates and after three months he advised strongly that Henry not attempt to come to Puerto Rico.[65] Though he doubtless would have enjoyed his company, Leopold encouraged his partners to find wives if they desired them, and seemed content not to relocate Henry from what seemed to be much-needed stability.

With Henry in Iowa and José having abruptly relocated to be with his mother in New Jersey, Leopold cast around for somewhere to channel his paternal urge. It landed, thankfully, on someone he wasn't interested in sexually: David Fulford Jr. In June 1962 Leopold hosted the eight-year-old for a ten-day visit. He was hypervigilant, noting every sneeze and headache, but despite Leopold's concerns over his health, he reported that:

> Davie is, to all appearances, having the time of his life. I have tried to keep him busy with varied activities as much as is humanly possible. We've been to the beach at Luquillo, to the tropical rain forest on El Yunque, to Morro Castle and La Fortaleza in Old San Juan, to Chico Park, the amusement park, and to Castañer, where we spent yesterday going up a 3,000 foot peak near the Hospital in a jeep, catching butterflies and going on a picnic.[66]

Trudi was apparently unenthusiastic about their houseguest and much less eager than Leopold to add a child into their lives.[67] But Leopold was "delighted with him" and happy to finally get to know the boy he considered at least partially his own.[68] As March 13, 1963, approached, there seemed to be only one thing missing from Leopold's life: freedom from parole. As there had been almost nothing but positive reports about Leopold's life since his release from prison, there seemed little reason for the board to make an exception in what was typically an automatic procedure but as Leopold complained to a friend, "where I am concerned you can never tell what will happen."[69]

19

FREEDOM

In the early morning of March 13, 1963, five years from the day Leopold had been released from prison, the Illinois Parole Board announced that they would be recommending the end of his parole. The governor of Illinois stated that Leopold "has set an example of rehabilitation and service."[1] In response, a flurry of newspaper articles and radio broadcasts revealed that the public was generally well-disposed to this move; one editor claimed that hereafter Leopold would "be cited as a leading example of prisoner rehabilitation," and filled several paragraphs extolling all the good works he had done.[2] Gertz stated to reporters that "I do not think there ever has been a more successful parole,"[3] and wrote to state officials claiming that "the parole system of the state has been strengthened as never before by this one case."[4]

Leopold was not around to hear his virtues being sung across the country, as he had skipped town the day before. He told no one but the friends he anticipated meeting where he was going, even leaving Trudi in ignorance so she could not have his destination bullied out of her. That, and if he did tell her where he planned to spend his first days of freedom, she may have raised a few objections.

Early on March 12 Leopold drove to Claiborne's secluded farm on the outskirts of Maricao.[5] In that disconnected farmhouse without the benefit of a radio or phone, he was safe from publicity but also unable to hear confirmation that he had been paroled. It was not until the next morning when he drove to the nearby coastal city of Mayagüez that he saw newspaper headlines in the stands declaring the parole board's decision, his first bit of proof that he would soon be completely free for the first time in thirty-eight years.[6] He immediately set out to make the most of it.

In Mayagüez Leopold met up with Henry Johnson at Arturo's, a hotel that catered to wealthy, older gay men. While most of Puerto Rico's gay life at the time centered around a few streets in Old San Juan, Arturo's offered a more scenic and secluded alternative to the bars and beaches of the city. The hotel sat in the mountains overlooking the Atlantic Ocean, offering a communal bar area as well as individual guest cottages which dotted the lush landscape and ensured the privacy of their occupants.[7] Nightly the hotel's manager would drive into the city to pick up boys interested in working, taking the most attractive volunteers back with him and leaving them to the mercy of the guests.[8]

When Leopold's release was announced Trudi braved the onslaught of reporters at their door alone, stating that her husband was out of town doing work for the Health Department.[9] She read a statement he had prepared for the occasion, in which he thanked those who helped him and said he was determined "to prove by my entire future life that the kindness, friendship and opportunities lavished on me have not been bestowed in error."[10]

Despite the work Trudi was doing to build the foundation of their lives together, Leopold seemed to have little interest in sharing his celebration with her. Two days after he left, with the phone still ringing off the hook and well-wishers popping by, Trudi sat down to voice her concern to Gertz. "Nathan left Tuesday morning," she wrote, "and I rather hoped I'd hear from him last night but, so far, nary a word."[11] Leopold spent the next four days breaking sodomy laws and embracing Arturo's motto: "Relax, you have just entered paradise."[12]

On March 29 Leopold's release papers arrived and were presented to him by the chairman of the Puerto Rican Parole Board, indicating that he was legally completely free. The chairman made a ceremony out of handing over the documents, and he assured Leopold that his freedom was "honorably won by you and based on the patience, courage, faith and love for other people shown by you."[13] Leopold had nothing but praise for the Puerto Rican parole officials who had handled his case. After his release he wrote to thank his first parole agent, who he admitted, "consistently treated me more like an indulgent uncle than as an official."[14]

This attitude was typical of the department's approach to Leopold's case, in every instance allowing him as much freedom and as little supervision as possible. This hands-off approach enabled Leopold's near-constant violations of his parole to go either unnoticed or dismissed as unimportant. He would be moving on with their full support and trust soundly behind him, the officials seem convinced that he had been rehabilitated through their minimal attempts at guidance.

But there was one thing even the Puerto Rican parole officials had not allowed him to do while he had been on parole: travel. As soon as his release papers arrived, Leopold applied for a passport, and when the employee wasn't being helpful, he expedited the process "by telling her my name and suggesting that my case was a trifle unusual and that perhaps she had seen some things about me in the paper! Worked too!"[15] While waiting for his passport to arrive Leopold planned an extended vacation to Europe, several years in length, which he hoped to spend getting a PhD in between sight-seeing excursions.

To Leopold's great surprise, shortly before he planned to leave for his trip, he received word that the National Institutes of Health had approved the grant funding for the three-year parasite project he and Stanton had proposed. Though originally slated to begin in June, Leopold was letting nothing stop his vacation, so he postponed the start of the project for five months. With the new time constraint to consider, he made plans for a more realistic trip.

Four and a half months in length, it would begin with a cruise followed by an extended tour around Europe and the Middle East. More than a simple vacation, symbolically it was to make up for the trip to Europe he had planned to take in the summer of 1924, that Grand Tour-esque rite of passage into adulthood that his arrest had "delayed for some time," as he flippantly put it.[16]

Moving beyond a sense of recovering what he had lost, it seemed that Leopold hoped this vacation would be able to usher in a new era of his life. Upon his return he had a steady, interesting job and money from his trust fund to look forward to.[17] Now that he had successfully completed parole, his brothers agreed he could handle his own money. Before he received this reward, however, he apparently felt the need to leave some socially undesirable aspects of his life in the past. When Leopold left Puerto Rico the life-long chain smoker finally bent to his doctor's wishes and pledged to give up cigarettes.[18] Then, the day he and Trudi left the island, Leopold added a codicil to his will that removed all the monetary gifts he had previously promised to his prison lovers. Instead, everything would be left to Trudi, then when she died, to the Church of the Brethren Service Commission.[19]

It was a non-smoking and seemingly devoted Leopold who set off in mid-May with Trudi at his side, beginning their trip in Philadelphia where Leopold met most of his wife's family for the first time.[20] The family and its notorious addition got to know each other for a few days before the couple flew to New York, where they would catch a cruise ship and join a tour group that would guide their first thirty days of travel.

Once they reached Europe, enthusiastic postcards began arriving for friends and family tracking their journey through France, Switzerland, Italy, Austria, and beyond. The guided tour they had signed up for led them to new locations nearly every day, and though Leopold enjoyed himself immensely, he admitted, "We've seen so much so fast that it tends to become jumbled."[21] At the end of June their supervised tour ended and they slowed things down, striking out in a rental car to explore England and Germany.[22]

Along their self-guided journey the Leopolds never wanted for comfort, staying with hospitable friends or in the best hotels every night. They took in entertainment as varied as stripteases at The Crazy Horse cabaret and leisurely walks around the grounds of Versailles. One night Leopold particularly enjoyed attending a Lumiere ceremony at the Notre Dame Cathedral that relayed the history of the church and "Played to a huge audience standing across the Seine."[23] Though slowed by herniated discs in his spine and clogged arteries that forced him to rest every few blocks, he let nothing stop him from seeing and experiencing as much as possible.

In his search for a new beginning, Leopold seemed to be having trouble leaving past habits behind. He started smoking again soon after they made it to Europe, and Paul Henry was a recipient of some of his many postcards. As he followed Leopold's travels, Henry remarked to Gertz that he was proud Leopold had finally been able to take this trip: "After all the suffering Nate went through, he deserves a real fling at living."[24] In the middle of the trip Henry wrote Leopold to announce that his first child had been born. Though he had just cut Henry from his will, Leopold now reconsidered, mulling over the possibility of setting up a fund for the child's education as he had for David Fulford Jr.[25]

The Leopolds' adventures continued across the countries, sitting in for a session of the House of Lords at the invitation of a baroness, touring a German castle with his prison friend Heinrich Hammer, and being woken in the early morning by a border skirmish in Jerusalem. After Israel the couple began to retrace some of the steps of their journey so they could spend more time in cities that had especially caught their fancy, and it was here that Leopold passed a milestone in his life.

During a stretch of the journey between Rome and Florence, Leopold estimated by "certain esoteric calculations of my own," that the pleasure he'd gotten out of paroled life made up for the pain of prison. He could finally say with certainty that he was glad he hadn't killed himself in 1924.[26]

The Leopolds ended their vacation with two and a half weeks in Portugal and Spain, where Trudi fractured her ankle and was forced to rest. Undeterred, Leopold went spelunking and to a bullfight while she remained in their hotel room, her leg in a cast.[27] On October 6 the couple landed once more in Puerto Rico, their trip of a lifetime coming to an end at last.

As he caught up with the mountain of correspondence that had accumulated in his absence, Leopold wrote happily about their travels and the sights they had seen and sent special thanks to all the friends who had hosted them. Going off the content of these letters, his vacation seems fairly mundane, comprising a rotating batch of restaurants and tourist attractions. When writing to Henry Johnson, however, he cheekily alluded that even with Trudi along, his trip had not been without some good gay fun, "notably in Austria, Germany, Egypt, Greece, Italy, Spain and Portugal."[28] After several countries worth of wear-and-tear, his "wimpus," the sex-assistive device he used when his diabetes made maintaining an erection difficult, had been worn out and he had to order more.[29]

Shortly after his return he began to correspond with the first of many young international pen pals, this one a seventeen-year-old cook named Friedl he had met in Germany. Leopold courted the boy from afar, sending him checks and paying for him to take Spanish lessons with Hammer in case he decided he'd like to move to Puerto Rico. In return Leopold asked for photos and a promise to meet him the next time he was in the country. Despite the apparent intimacy, it took several years before Leopold trusted the boy enough to reveal his first name, until then telling him that it was "Bill."[30]

In his other life, where he lived quite openly as former child-murderer Nathan Leopold, everything seemed to be falling into place. In mid-October his trust fund was turned over to him, and between that, his salary, and additional money coming in from stocks and other property, he had around $121,000, equivalent to over a million in 2023.[31] Once the transfer was complete, he wrote to Bal: "Today, the 42nd anniversary of Mother's death, is a singularly appropriate day for me to express my thanks. . . . You have always been a perfect brother."[32] Likewise, the onset of his new project gave him a heightened sense of purpose. He wrote dramatically: "The curtain is about to rise on what may well be the most important and the most interesting thing I have ever undertaken."[33]

There had already been several interventions by the Puerto Rican Department of Health to improve living conditions and stop the spread of parasites. Leopold and other researchers noticed that while sanitary conditions improved as long as researchers were monitoring the situation, once they left things quickly shifted back to the way they had been before the intervention. In light of these failures Leopold's research team decided to take a more sociological approach to the problem. In their proposal for the project, the group of researchers explained:

> Despite knowing the dangers of parasitic infection and, further, the means of avoiding it, people continue to act in ways favoring the spread of infection. The usual explanation of the non-indigenous investigator is either that the people are ignorant or that they are lazy. These answers appear to the author too facile. . . . Perhaps it is we who are ignorant— ignorant of the cultural traits and the unconscious drives which prevent people from following the course of procedure they know, intellectually, to be the safe one.[34]

Pursuant to this, being able to see how the parasites were transmitted was deemed essential to their project. The team's first task was trying to discover safe ways to trace the parasites as they traveled from host to host. This would occupy Leopold for the next several months.

Still high off his international jaunt and eager to visit his home city, less than two weeks after his return from abroad Leopold began making plans to leave again, hoping to attend a joint meeting of the American Society of Parasitologists and the American Society of Tropical Medicine being held that year in Chicago. He anticipated negative reactions from his brothers over this decision, but he was determined to get back to the city, and thought this a great occasion to do so.[35]

As predicted, Sam was against Leopold coming, worrying that his infamous brother coming to town "might undo everything Mike and I accomplished over the last thirty years in the changing of the spelling of our name. . . . Do you think it would please [Mother] to have you come to Chicago for this meeting and possibly create very unpleasant publicity which could reflect adversely on the future generation?"[36]

After waiting a few days to let his anger subside, Leopold responded. He detailed professional reasons why he wanted to go to the conference, then tried to logically explain his perspective on how to handle the publicity that continued to trail him:

> We have waited 39 years and five months in the vain hope that people would eventually forget about me. . . . I'm ready to give up the whole approach.
>
> If we can't succeed by lying doggo, the only other possibility that occurs to me is to try to substitute a different public image of me, by mind-

ing my business, by living modestly and retiringly, AND BY TRYING TO WIN A PLACE FOR MYSELF BY CONSTRUCTIVE EFFORT. And that's what I've tried to do. . . . Given a chance, it is just possible that I can someday change my public image from heinous murderer to the guy that did something about parasitosis in Puerto Rico.[37]

This hardly relieved Sam's concerns, and because Sam "pitched a bitch," as Leopold put it, he decided to compromise by coming to Chicago but arranging for private meetings with other parasitologists rather than attending the conference itself.[38]

The day before his departure he and Trudi hosted a party that added yet another project to Leopold's already laden plate: the administration of a social service fund for Castañer. Since leaving his position with the Church of the Brethren, Leopold maintained a fondness for the people who had welcomed him back into the world. A small social service fund already existed and was used by medical social workers to help patients or their families cover minimal costs. As usual, Leopold was not content with minimal. He envisioned running his own fund for the people of Castañer, inflated by huge fundraisers that would enable him to pay for surgeries, medical equipment, and offer scholarships to local high schoolers. To kick things off he had already begun planning for his first event: a benefit fashion show in San Juan to take place early the following year.

He revealed these plans at his little gathering, its guests assumedly selected with this in mind. In attendance was Mollie Parnis, a dress designer especially well known for her skill in outfitting First Ladies. She agreed to donate a dress that could be raffled off in conjunction with the event.[39] Ana Santisteban, who ran a modeling academy and produced the Miss Puerto Rico beauty competition, was also among the guests and agreed to act as master of ceremonies for the show.[40] His party was a success and as he prepared to return to the city of his childhood—and his crime—he may have been bolstered by the numerous projects he now saw as potential roads to his redemption in the eyes of the public.

Leopold arrived in Chicago late on November 3 and though ostensibly in town for work, he planned to spend the bulk of his time catching up with family and friends. The day after he arrived in town, Elmer Gertz and his wife picked him up and drove him to Rosehill cemetery so he could visit the graves of his family members, some of them for the first time. The sprawling cemetery on Chicago's North Side had long been popular among prominent local families, its inhabitants including the Loebs, Frankses, and most of Leopold's extended family. As Leopold stood before his parent's graves beneath a stately oak "to utter lonely prayers (the Aramaic <u>Kaddish</u>) and to deposit sprigs of flowers,"[41] his victim's body lay on its marble slab in a mausoleum just seven hundred feet up the winding road.

The following day Bal hosted a family dinner, attended by Sam and all Leopold's nieces and nephews who were in town. Leopold reported to Trudi that though relations were "a little strained in some quarters," it had been a very pleasant evening.[42] On November 6 Leopold was driven up to the Chicago suburb of Elgin, where Harold Row lived and the headquarters of the Church of the Brethren were located.

There he spoke before a Brethren staff meeting and got "a chance to mumble a few words of thanks for the bounty, the charity—yes, the love—showered on me."[43] As a favor to this group that had done so much for him, Leopold allowed himself to be interviewed for an article in the Brethren's internal periodical: *The Gospel Messenger.*

"What lies behind your own zeal for humanitarian service?" he was asked.

Nathan Leopold in 1963, addressing a staff meeting at Church of the Brethren headquarters in Elgin. Photo originally published in *The Gospel Messenger* magazine, © Church of the Brethren. Used by permission.

"I didn't know I had any," he quipped. Then more seriously he replied: "Well I like people. I feel I have a debt to repay and this is perhaps one way to start doing it. Besides, I am utterly selfish and believe in my mother's motto: 'Happiness is not a perfume you can sprinkle upon others without getting a few drops on yourself.' I am avid for the drops."[44]

These were the answers he had been giving since he had begun crafting his rehabilitated image in prison, but there were some changes to his script. His freedom from parole and his assurance that this interview would only be for the Brethren allowed him to make jokes and admit to selfishness and vice. When asked "What personal disciplines do you maintain?" He replied: "Well, I never drink when I can't get it. I never overeat if I don't like the food being served, I never smoke after I run out of cigarettes."[45] Despite listing his indulgences to the teetotal Brethren members, the interview came off well and he was invited to attend the annual Brethren conference the following year.

After the interview concluded, Row had a surprise for Leopold. He and his wife drove him through the peaceful streets to the nearby Elgin Audubon Museum, which closed for repainting. After Leopold had been sentenced and shipped off to prison, the majority of his collections, containing around three thousand ornithological pieces along with various other natural odds and ends, had been donated here.

Curator Howard Gusler met the group and gave them a tour. As Gusler was pointing out pieces of Leopold's collection he admitted that "just for a test, I deliberately pointed out wrong birds, but he caught me every time! I think it's very remarkable to remember his own collection after all these years."[46] "I guess I'm more of a sentimental cuss than I'm willing to admit—even to myself," Leopold related after the visit. "Seeing some of those specimens after 39 years—seeing some of the B.C. cards in my own handwriting brought me near to tears. It was an experience I'll never forget."[47]

Following the tour of the exhibit rooms, the group descended into the basement storage, where among the taxidermy and other anthropological pieces Leopold noticed a sailfish he had donated along with his birds. As its top fin had been broken off and lost, it was not deemed acceptable for display and spent its time doing little more than gathering dust. Row noted that seeing the fish there "moved him very deeply."[48] Not long after Leopold and the Rows had thanked Gusler and left the museum, Leopold began to question Row about the possibility of getting the fish back.

After his trip through Elgin, Leopold was driven back to Chicago, as the tropical medicine conference was starting, and the meetings he scheduled

(l-r) Nathan Leopold, Howard Gusler, Harold Row, and Leona Row in 1963, looking at birds Leopold donated to the Elgin Audubon Museum. Photo originally published in *The Gospel Messenger* magazine, © Church of the Brethren. Used by permission.

were approaching. Though the conference and opportunity to confer with colleagues was supposed to be the point of the trip, in the many letters Leopold wrote describing his time in Chicago to friends and family, he failed to mention which scientists he met with or what they discussed.

After his parasite business was completed, Leopold saw a variety of friends, including David Fulford and "Davie" Jr. Leopold admitted that he had a great time seeing the whole family, but "above all—my own little Davie."[49] Leopold spent the next afternoon alone with "Big Dave," driving out to Stateville. Along the way Leopold tried to convince Fulford that it wasn't too early to enroll Davie in colleges in anticipation of his 1973 high school graduation. The time he was able to spend reacquainting himself with Fulford he especially valued, assuring him "it really meant a great deal to me, Fellow."[50]

For Leopold's last day in Chicago, Gertz and his wife picked him up from his hotel in the morning and at his direction, drove him around to his old haunts. Leopold started with the location of the first house he had ever lived in, on Michigan Avenue. They found that it had been torn down, but the nearby houses that had once been occupied by his maternal aunts remained. From there it was off to his elementary schools in order, before he directed them to return him to the Hyde Park neighborhood where he had spent his teen years. They drove by the lot where the Leopold house had once stood, the Loeb home, still standing and in good repair, and the Harvard School, which Gertz noted was "once attended by Leopold and then by the ill-fated Bobby Franks."[51]

Gertz appeared moved by the experience of indulging his friend's nostalgia. He wrote to another client: "It was a sentimental journey, particularly impressive because Leopold has an outer surface that is restrained and sometimes cold and even cynical."[52] He may have been surprised to learn that Leopold had taken a very similar trip with his prison friend William "Bill" Evans just two days earlier. As with Gertz, Leopold had directed Evans to take him to all his old homes, including Wildwood, as well as his schools, relaying to friends that the first trip had been "a real, nostalgic, sentimental holiday," without mentioning that it had apparently been so satisfying that he had felt the need to take it twice.[53]

After six days in Chicago, Leopold flew to New York. After avoiding direct confrontations with reporters in Chicago, he was aggravated to see a cameraman waiting to take his picture when he landed. "I restrained myself from kicking the camera out of his hands," he wrote.[54] Leopold quickly got his mind off the publicity because José had also come to Idlewild to welcome him to the city.[55] When José moved to the United States in 1962 and got into trouble by eloping with a young girlfriend, Leopold had advised him on how to duck the law and escape her father's rage. Proud to see one of his protégés married and independent, he spent much of his time in New York with the couple, one afternoon taking them for a tourist view of the city from atop the Empire State Building.[56]

Leopold's time in New York was packed; one evening going to six nightclubs as newspaper columnist Leonard Lyons's guest, another attending a cocktail party thrown for him by Mollie Parnis. Among the other guests of this gathering were Dr. William Hitzig (an acquaintance of Leopold's who had gained some prestige after aiding victims of Hiroshima), along with an assortment of other prominent doctors, publishers, and an explorer.[57] In this age of cocktail parties, having a child-murderer-turned-parasitologist in attendance was just one more curiosity to spice up the night.

When he was not sightseeing with teenagers or rubbing elbows with celebrities, Leopold returned to his hotel room in the luxurious Plaza Hotel, which overlooked Central Park. There he was amused by his new pets: two baby turtles and two baby alligators were given to him by Ralph Newman. Still small enough to manage easily, he fed the reptiles flies and steak, cheerfully anticipating Trudi's negative reaction once he smuggled them home.[58] Luck was in her favor, however: the alligators died on the flight back to Puerto Rico. Leopold preserved them in alcohol and added the two little turtles, dryly named Ralph-T-1 and Ralph-T-2, to the household, which they shared with Sue Dogg.

Once home Leopold began tackling the mountain of correspondence that built up whenever he went on vacation. There had been a few small articles announcing his presence in the city, but nothing excessive, and the photos taken of him in the New York airport had not been published. Leopold wrote happily that he would "chalk it up to my Guardian Angel, who pretty generally rides on my left shoulder and smooths things out for me."[59] Unbeknownst to Leopold, while he was in New York a two-page interview with him had been published in the *Chicago Tribune*.

The Brethren's Director of News Service Howard Royer was to blame for this leak. When a friend from the *Tribune* had called up Royer looking for Leopold, Royer offered to share the article he was writing as long as they agreed not to publish it before Leopold left the city. To assure them of the credibility of his source, Royer included a transcript of Leopold's interview.[60] The interview, interspersed with bits from Royer's original article, was front-page news two days later.

Though family and friends were a little off put by some of the phrases Leopold used, most agreed the interview wasn't too bad, and how could it be, as it had been intended for use in a church paper. To many friends it seemed good that Leopold had broken the ice with the article and returned to Chicago with relatively little fanfare. Leopold reacted rather differently.

"I'M NEVER GOING TO TRUST ANOTHER HUMAN BEING AS LONG AS I LIVE," he wrote to Evans shortly after his return.[61] After seeing the article for the first time he became violently upset and started drinking. Weeks later he wrote to friends: "I'm drunk—have been drunk for 24 hours and expect to stay drunk indefinitely." After several paragraphs of ranting he stated:

> I realize that I'm acting like an eight-year old who has just been told there ain't no Santa Claus. Know why? 'cause that's the way I feel.
>
> The last time someone destroyed my "simple, child-like faith, when I was 17 and my mother died. I decided that (a) either there was no God or, if there was, I didn't want anything further to do with the son-of-a-bitch. I think the murder of 1924 was not too indirectly connected.
>
> But Joe Mother-fucker at Stqteville [*sic*] and his minions have done an A-number 1 job of rehabilitating me . . . I probably won't kill a single solitar7 [*sic*] soul this time.[62]

His reaction seems out of proportion to what appears to have been an innocent mistake. Yes, he placed the Brethren on a pedestal and was hurt to be disappointed by them, but he perhaps revealed the real source of his anger when discussing the situation with Evans:

> Judas, traditionally, got only 30 pieces of silver for putting the finger on Christ, but you know how the cost of living has spiraled in the last 1930 years. I could have got anywhere from $2,000 to $5,000 had I been willing to give the TRIB an exclusive on that interview. I hope Royer did at least as well. If he didn't, he's stupid as well as being a son-of-a-bitch.[63]

Despite his wealth, Leopold was plagued by paranoia about money, apparently because he lived off a trust fund and had made so little himself. He longed to make a large amount of money of his own volition, preferably in one masterful swoop. And barring the lawsuit he had pending against *Compulsion* (still endlessly wending its way through a series of appeals), trading in on his notoriety was the most likely way he believed he could accomplish that. By taking that opportunity from him, in Leopold's eyes Royer had not only betrayed his trust, he had also robbed him.

The end of the year had been difficult for Leopold, with Royer's "betrayal," followed by several deaths that touched his life, starting with President Kennedy's assassination on November 21 and ending on November 25, when his dog, Sue, was killed by a car while he was attending the funeral of a nurse in Castañer. Morosely he asked Evans: "Can you blame me for feeling that Tragedy is stalking ever closer? So a Merry Christmas to you too. And let's hope the New Year is better than this one. IT COULD HARDLY BE WORSE."[64]

20

NOTORIETY BECOMES CELEBRITY

Every year since Leopold's release from prison, no matter where he was living on the island, he had returned to Castañer to help pass out thousands of toys for Three Kings Day. The year 1964 was no exception; he and his friend, radio personality Sally Jessy Raphael, had been working for months to collect toys and donations.[1] When Leopold got into his white Ford Counsel and began his drive, he knew he would soon be slipping on a robe with a towel over his head secured by a gold paper crown and leading a brigade of gift-laden jeeps around the rural countryside.

That particular year he left behind Trudi, who used the privacy to write to Gertz of an altercation she had with Leopold shortly before his departure, pleading for advice on how to handle her often volatile husband. Gertz admitted he too had concerns about Leopold; he'd been disturbed by Leopold's focus on his imagined financial loss from the *Tribune* article. However, hoping to get Trudi to understand and sympathize, Gertz offered some thoughts on the nature of his lashing out:

> He is in rebellion against all of his physical difficulties, including par-
> ticularly his diabetes. His rebellion takes the form of excessive drinking,
> overeating, dissipation generally. Half of the time he thinks that life is
> worth while [*sic*] and the other half of the time he says the hell with it
> and looks forward to his exit. It is unfortunate that you must bear the
> brunt of this. You are a very great and wonderful woman and you must
> do nothing that adds to his woes, hard as it is to bear. If he collapses,
> then you and all of us will suffer thereby.[2]

Gertz wasn't the only one to notice Leopold ignoring his health; doctors on the project remembered that he would avoid taking insulin, sometimes until he was on the edge of going into a diabetic coma.[3] When asked why he continued to smoke despite the adverse effects on his health, he answered: "Suppose I could live X number of years smoking, and *exist* X number of years plus eight by not smoking. I prefer just X number of years."[4] This was a philosophy he'd lived by since he was a teenager, and presumably the thirty-three years he spent in prison only heightened his sense of urgency to experience as much pleasure and as little pain as possible with the time he had remaining. It meant that he pushed his body past its limits, but also that when things were going badly for him, he tended to lash out in frustration over the wasted time.

Matters were not helped when on January 20, Paul Henry was arrested for theft in Iowa. Just as he had before his first arrest, Henry found himself in debt and looking for a quick way to make money; he and several other men committed a series of at least 21 robberies around Sioux City. He was sentenced to serve 10 years, with the understanding that when that sentence was completed, he would be taken back to Illinois to serve additional time for breaking his parole.

Leopold declared himself "heart-sick" when he heard the news, finding it difficult to believe that a man he had put so much faith in could blindside him so severely. Perhaps mixed in was slight guilt, as the month before he had sent Henry a letter pressuring him to pay the legal fees he owed Gertz, fees Leopold only told Henry he'd be responsible for after he'd been released.[5]

Shortly before Henry's arrest, when Leopold was planning to visit him during a trip to the States, Leopold wrote about their reunion: "I feel constrained to repeat a question I wrote you once shortly before your release, when you were still planning to come to Castañer. Your answer that time was most satisfactory. The question, you remember, had to do with activities associated with 435 Fourth Street. Please let me know whether things still stnad [*sic*] as they always did."[6] This was code: in Stateville they had shared cell #435 in F-House. Henry had not answered Leopold before he went to prison, so behind bars, Henry asked his aunt to pass on a message: "'Everything is the same!'" she quoted. "He said 'Uncle Bill' will understand."[7]

Evidently Leopold did, and despite his disappointment and Gertz's advice, he decided to stay in contact with his old flame. This time, rather than continuing to write Henry as his uncle, they decided it would be safer to switch to a new alias. Leopold wrote instead as his Aunt Anita Faure, using Trudi's sister as a cover and with Gertz's Illinois address so as not to arouse suspicion. In line with gay customs of the time, letters between them or in reference to Leopold from this period refer to Leopold using female pronouns and "Aunt."

Despite the blips caused by bad publicity, Henry's imprisonment, and his own emotional instability, Leopold's life was soon reaching a post-prison high. He began collecting birds, nests, eggs, and insects again, even buying a large freezer just for dead birds waiting to be taken to the taxidermist. He had his sailfish sent from the Elgin Museum, repaired, and mounted in his study. As his Kirtland's Warbler group made a similar journey from Chicago's Field Museum to his living room, the apartment he shared with Trudi was slowly becoming a museum to Leopold's past.

A picture of his brother Mike and his mother's motto about happiness hung above the bed.[8] A picture of a teenaged Loeb, likely the same one that had graced his x-ray lab in prison, sat on his dresser. A framed photo of Clarence Darrow reclined in the living room alongside one of his former girlfriend, Susan Lurie.[9] When asked about the photos Trudi shrugged and said that her husband was a complicated man with a past that these people had all been a part of.[10] When Leopold was asked about Loeb's photo he answered, somewhat more tellingly, that though Loeb had ruined his life, "he was really a swell guy, the best friend I ever had."[11]

Trudi was not immune to the nostalgic home makeover: a share of Leopold's mother's pearls, loaned to her from Bal's wife, hung around her neck and Leopold even attempted to get a Phi Beta Kappa key to give to her, reliving the high school tradition of giving your fraternity pin to a girl to indicate you were going steady. Though the fraternity board denied his request for an extra key,[12] a childhood friend of Leopold's who worked at the University of Chicago was able to supply him with a replacement.[13] In many ways he had never left behind the teenager he'd been when his life halted in 1924, as he wrote to Weir on his sixtieth birthday: "According to Cicero, or one of those jokers, today at 4:00 PM, CST I become a senex [a wise old man]. How silly can you get? I'm still an arrested adolescent!"[14]

At home he was "wallowing in sentiment," but Leopold was still actively cultivating a future and legacy that would live beyond him. In early 1964 he attempted to become the director of a small museum that the biology department of the University of Puerto Rico maintained. This would give him some status as well as a place to store the many new birds he was acquiring without having to donate them and give up ownership.[15]

Harold Heatwole, who helped administer the museum with two other faculty volunteers, didn't think the little collection needed a director. They especially didn't need Leopold, "who lacked professional expertise and, at best, had only a trivial understanding of avian biology," according to Heatwole.[16] Though he and Leopold attended meetings of the Natural History Society of Puerto Rico together, Heatwole disdained the praise and celebrity status other Club members gave him. "I didn't believe he was still a threat to society," Heatwole recalled, "but he was still a con artist and an insufferable egoist."[17]

Denied the museum position, Leopold was keen to prove his expertise in other ways. When he had arrived on the island in 1958, he noticed immediately that there were no field guides for the region or even a consistent list of birds that could be found there. Deciding to fill this gap in the literature, Leopold worked for three years and in early 1964 he published the "Checklist of the Birds of Puerto Rico and the Virgin Islands" through the University's Agricultural Experiment Station.[18] Leopold was proud of the booklet, despite recommending it as a cure for insomnia to his non-ornithologist family and friends.[19]

More important than the checklist, which would live on only within a small group of birders, Leopold hoped to alter his public image by pulling focus away from his past crime and into the present. To this end, in February he spent two weeks with actor, director, and Brethren member Don Murray, who had shown an interest in purchasing the film rights for his autobiography. Leopold was convinced that Murray, who had cowritten, coproduced, and starred in the film *The Hoodlum Priest*, about a prison chaplain's compassionate work with convicts, would not sensationalize his crime and would make a sensitive, dignified picture. Murray paid $1,000 (equivalent to about $9,700 in 2023) for the rights and anticipated that, once he secured funding, the movie would come out in the fall.[20]

In Murray's screen treatment Tony, the teenager Leopold had started sleeping with soon after he arrived in Puerto Rico, was essential in showing Leopold's generosity. In the treatment, Leopold gets Tony a job, which improves the fortunes of his whole family. Much of the rest of the focus is spent on the burgeoning romance between Leopold and Trudi. Together these concepts culminate in the film's final moment, with Trudi in Leopold's arms on their way to Europe as Tony waves from the docks.

Tears fill Leopold's eyes as he says: "For-for the first time I'm truly, completely glad I wasn't hanged. For the first time, I-I believe Darrow was—was right."[21] The audience would be expected to cry into their popcorn and have their hearts warmed by the happiness of a man they once disdained. Impressed by Murray's vision for the movie, Leopold wrote to Harold Row:

> In the back of my mind right along has been the hope that if the picture is well done and is sympathetic, laying more emphasis on the constructive side than the other, this is perhaps the greatest opportunity I'll ever have to alter my "public image." Let's face it: to a large majority of the

people in the world I am a heinous murderer. . . . Perhaps here is the opportunity to add something to that picture—to be remembered not only for the crime but also for the rehabilitation.[22]

As Murray worked to get funding, Leopold settled into finding a balance between his private pleasures and the positive public image he was cultivating. He'd been looking forward particularly to Easter weekend, as he wrote to Henry Johnson about his plans to buy time with hustlers: "I'm like a kid in a candy store with a nickel to spend—and they all look so good!"[23] When the holiday came he reported that:

> J and I wound up with another young fellow we met Saturday night— a fellow named Jerry—a Continental. We all went home together. Sunday, Easter, we went to Dick's, but none of the rest showed up by mid-afternoon when I had to go home, I've seen Jerry a couple of times since, but Johnnie only once. . . . My only trouble now seems to be time, not material.[24]

Shortly after Easter, Leopold's methods of blending rehabilitating his image with illicit pleasures developed a new dimension. The Castañer Community Social Service Fund Leopold had been toying with had finally gotten off the ground. Vaguely the fund claimed it would "meet urgent, direct human needs, for which no other funds exist," within the Castañer community.[25]

Leopold's first big fundraising event was a fashion show and raffle, sponsored by the mayor of San Juan. On April 11 the fundraiser commenced, on a raised runway erected in the Grand Ballroom of the Ponce de Leon hotel. Four Puerto Rican designers exhibited their collections and items were raffled off; the highest prize, a Mollie Parnis dress, was awarded to an infant.[26] The event raised over $3,000 (equivalent to about $29,000 in 2023), and Leopold used the money to buy a wheelchair, purchase layettes for babies born in Castañer hospital, and create a local fund administered by Castañer's social worker.[27]

Capping this triumph, on April 15, after five years, a judge granted a summary judgment in Leopold's favor in his *Compulsion* lawsuit. Though quickly appealed, Leopold hoped for a settlement of around $150,000 (equivalent to over one million dollars in 2023) and basked in happy imaginings of the life he could lead with enough money for the house, yacht, and year-long vacations he craved. For now, he would have to settle for another month-long trip to the States, but even that was a victory. Only a year ago such a trip had been a point of contention between him and his family; now he was determined not to be kept from anywhere he wanted to go or anyone he wanted to see.

He and Trudi began their vacation in Flint, Michigan, where Trudi visited one of her sisters and Leopold went off to chase more nostalgia. As he described it: "I deposited my good wife and the next morning took off for northern Michigan to see my other love, the Kirtland's Warbler."[28]

From Michigan they traveled to Chicago, where Leopold's family welcomed them with open arms. Bal and Sam's son Don threw them parties, as did their friends Helen Williams, Leo Lerner, and Harold Gordon. Leopold's fan Jeanne Hall wanted to do something special and hosted an all-day gathering with dozens of guests at her cottage on Lake Winnebago in Wisconsin.[29] He made sure to reserve an afternoon to see the Fulford children, announcing proudly that he "Managed to get two ice cream sodas, a hot dog, and a piece of cake down Davie. God love him, he's a honey—a real, all-American boy."[30]

For a change of pace, on June 17 Leopold accepted an invitation to the Playboy Mansion, where he was escorted to the VIP room for a chat with Hugh Hefner. What was supposed to be a brief meeting became a three-hour conversation covering an array of topics in "a rare display of brilliance not often seen or heard."[31]

After their talk Hefner wrote to Leopold:

> I had looked forward to our meeting with what was something probably not far removed from curiosity, but that blossomed forth—a few minutes after I sat down—into an uncommon interest in you—as a most remarkable human being—and in your really refreshing openness, personal insight, and individual reactions to a variety of subjects covered in our too-brief meeting.[32]

Leopold was flattered, replying:

> Your honesty is refreshing, Hef! All too often in my daily doings it has become obvious to me that I have been able to gain entree to certain people I wished to see chiefly because they wanted to convince themselves at first hand whether the horns were visible and there was an external tail. But few have the grace, or the courage, or the sincerity to admit it.[33]

They traded publications, Leopold sending Hefner his autobiography and checklist, Hefner sending a free subscription to *Playboy* and several back issues. Leopold really did read the magazine for the articles, and they occasionally enlightened him on legal matters. Reading one a few years later, Leopold was affronted to find that evidence taken without a warrant was inadmissible in court, and confessions were voided if police refused suspects' access to lawyers. Recalling the dubious practices of Crowe's team in 1924, Leopold asked Gertz: "Am I right in thinking that if my case were to take place now I could not have been convicted? If so, it seems a darn shame that I wasted 33 years, sixm [*sic*] months and two days as Uncle Joe Ragen's guest!"[34]

To cap off the Midwestern leg of their trip, Leopold and Trudi caught a plane to Lincoln, Nebraska, for the Brethren annual conference. Surrounded by a semicircle of reporters and cameras, here Leopold was able to speak publicly about penology and capital punishment for the first time, to a pacifist audience he knew would be receptive. Prisons, he declared, were "100% ineffective," in rehabilitating inmates. Leopold said he knew "maybe half a dozen people who were rehabilitated," and it happened in spite of, rather than because of, prison.[35]

After a month their trip ended in New York. Trudi, Leopold, "my little PR protégé" José, and his wife, Maria, strolled around the World's Fair, taking in the sights one hundred feet up in the Swiss sky ride, eating from the international food carts, and harshly judging the Puerto Rican section of the Caribbean pavilion.[36] Leopold also made time to meet with Austin MacCormick, the assistant director of the Federal Bureau of Prisons, "to get a little more help for Paulie."[37] After the meeting he wrote optimistically: "The case looks a little less hopeless to me now, and I'm sleeping better."[38]

The couple returned home on the morning of July 1, and Leopold didn't waste a minute before writing to thank those he'd visited for their hospitality. "The whole trip was delightful but EXHAUSTING," he wrote Bal. "Now I'll have to take a vacation from my vacation."[39] True to his prediction, he was hardly back to work before he began to feel the itch to leave again, writing to a friend:

> I got bored recently and decided I need a change of scene; so I'm off for Europe on a fast, flying trip, on Aug. 31. I even managed, belatedly, to think up a couple of good plausible reasons for the trip: I have to consult some experts in toxicology and pharmacology at WHO [World Health Organization] in Geneva about a problem in my project, and I want to look over the Universities of Geneva, Marburg and Hamburg with an eye to doctoral possibilities for me. But those are just good reasons—not the real one.[40]

The "real one" he wrote to Henry Johnson, was "to see a friend in Germany. Remember the photo I once showed you?"[41] This "friend" was the now nineteen-year-old Friedl, the cook he had met on his last international trip.

Outside of his teenage trysts, Leopold did meet with professionals in Europe who were finally able to help him with his parasite project. After a year of not being able to figure out how to safely track their transmission, he was advised he try feeding test subjects fluorescent dye covered with thyron. As the parasites were spread through contact with fecal matter, after a few days he would be able to look for the dye under a UV light around the home to see where transmission may be occurring.[42]

When he returned to Puerto Rico, Leopold began the long process of finding a dye that would be safe to ingest. He tested first on dogs, then on himself and his research associates to ensure there were no ill effects and to see if the dye would be visible and when it would pass. Once this was approved, Leopold and Trudi made a Styrofoam hat covered in six-inch florist stakes that were draped with a waist-length black cloth.[43] Wearing this, Leopold would carry a UV lamp and move through the homes and yards of his test families, checking for any traces of dye. "I look like a

Nathan Leopold (3rd from left) and friends paying tribute to The Beatles during a Caribbean cruise in 1965. Photo courtesy of Ron Martinetti.

mythical monster," Leopold reported. "I suspect the mothers are using me as the bogey-man to scare their children into behaving."[44]

One of Leopold's assistants during this process was José. He, his wife, and their new daughter had moved back to the island and Leopold hired him to give him an income. He also paid for the young family's doctors' visits, shots, contraception, and meals out of the Castañer Community Social Service Fund.[45] That same fund paid $90 (equivalent to about $900 in 2023) for the removal of a tattoo for Johnny, one of Leopold's regular hookups, in December 1964. Attempting to justify this to the doctor he'd hired, Leopold wrote:

> The matter of removing the tattoo may have struck you as trivial, and you may have wondered why I should bother you for such a minor matter. The fact is that Johnny was well on the way toward major delinquency when it became possible to find employment for him in a beauty salon. His employer, however, made it a condition that the tattoo be removed.
>
> So you see that in his case the operation was a matter of considerable importance: your kindness may well have given this boy's life a totally different direction.[46]

He signed this letter "Nathan Leopold, ACSW Social Worker," possibly indicating that he was Johnny's social worker, or representing himself as such to provide some explanation for why he was paying the boy's bill with money from a social service fund associated with the Church of the Brethren's Castañer Hospital.[47] Neither Johnny or José were from Castañer, and they were the first instances in what would become a habit of Leopold using the fund as a personal piggy bank for his "protégés."

As time went by Leopold became increasingly comfortable with publicity and began using his notoriety to enter into the conversations around capital punishment and prison reform. In January his article, "Imprisonment Has No Future in a Free Society," was published in a criminology journal edited by famous criminologist Hans Mattick. His article detailed his arguments against imprisonment and his opinion that it failed to deter crime or rehabilitate inmates. Instead, Leopold encouraged psychiatric help, familial support, and youth programs to cut down on crimes before they occurred.[48]

That same month Leopold flew to Toronto for a televised interview about capital punishment for the program *This Hour Has Seven Days*. His interviewer, Patrick Watson, recalled that "his soft-spoken courtesy and steady, emotionless blue eyes were riveting."[49] When the cameras were rolling Watson asked:

Watson: Why did you and Richard Loeb kill Bobby Franks?

Leopold: I'd rather not answer.

Watson: Can you give us no insight into that?

Leopold: I'm not going to.[50]

"Calm," Watson recalled of that moment. "Not a flicker of those eyes. The studio was electrically silent."[51] Reactions to this interview were favorable, one article declaring that "Apart from demonstrating the reformability of one man, Leopold is a living argument for enlightened parole policies."[52] With his expertise cemented, Leopold began regularly lecturing to universities on penology, capital punishment, and juvenile delinquency.[53]

When his brothers pushed back against the increasing publicity, Leopold acknowledged that so much public attention may not be wise. However:

> I feel so strongly on certain causes, such as abolition of the death penalty and prison reform that it is a little difficult to remain silent. I think there is a real chance of a breakthru on these matters in the near future and, since people seem willing to listen to me and to publish what I write on these subjects, I think I'd be something of a coward not to say my piece.[54]

By this point he was at least adept at deciding what should become part of his public persona and what should be kept hidden. Though he publicly said nothing bad about Stateville or its officials, when Bill Evans sent him a clipping regarding Joseph Ragen's resignation from the prison, Leopold replied that he wanted two more news clippings from Evans: "The first would announce Joe's death—preferably in agony, and the second, that a State-appointed commission drove a stake thru his heart before burial. We can't afford to have him visiting us again after death!"[55]

By this time public opinion had gone far enough in Leopold's favor that he was thinking about joining the Church of the Brethren. As he explained:

> I should like very much to give the Church of the Brethren a boost, if I can. My conversion would certainly not go unnoticed! But I want to be very careful not to do them any harm. . . . There will be a certain number who will vilify the Brethren. They'll say this was all part of the bargain, or that it is a forced conversion, or that they proselyted me.[56]

As far as his personal religious beliefs factored into it: "Actually, I don't have any: I suppose if I had to stick a label on myself it would read Agnostic. But this I do believe and always have: that the important part of any religion to me is the ETHICS and not either the theology or the ritual."[57] Leopold never did publicly convert, though the idea remained, as did that of using his notoriety to further causes he believed in.

In mid-September 1965, after two years, Leopold's parasite project at last had a breakthrough when a trace of their dye was detected in the field for the first time, reinvigorating Leopold's excitement for the project. But less than a week later he was forced to resign and check into the hospital for spine surgery to remove two herniated discs.[58] After a month of rest he took a position with the Urban Renewal Agency, a much more sedentary position which didn't involve wandering up hills or crawling under homes looking for dye.

But once Leopold was back on his feet, he regretted leaving his parasites. His new job had strict hours and this inability to be "master of my own time" made him consider retiring and going full time into Brethren Volunteer Service.[59] He pleaded with Row to find him a placement outside of the country, but international relations with the United States were strained because of the Vietnam War, and Leopold, as a middle-aged, married, Jewish man, was not seen as a desirable fit for most missionary settings, which favored the young, Protestant, and unencumbered.

To combat the boredom with his new job, Leopold put together another fashion show fundraiser for the Castañer Community Social Service Fund, showcasing the work of Puerto Rican designer José Berga de Lema. The front of the fundraiser's program had a photo and description of the Castañer hospital, though much of the money raised would never see the town of Castañer, let alone the hospital.[60] Despite snidely commenting that de Lema was a "psychopath" and "queer as a three-dollar bill," Leopold was happy with the cocktail parties attached to the event where he rubbed elbows with senate presidents and the governor's wife in their mansion overlooking the San Juan Harbor. He was also pleased with the $4,500 he netted (equivalent to about $42,750 in 2023) despite the exorbitant hotel and airfare bills of de Lema and his guests.[61]

By the year's end, it was becoming obvious that Leopold's attempts to refocus the narrative of his life were working beyond what anyone could have hoped for. In 1965 Great Britain outlawed the death penalty, and Leopold's rehabilitation story had been used as an example in favor of the act when the case was being heard before the House of Lords.[62] He was now a sought-after lecturer, newspapers raved about "The New Life of

Nathan Leopold," and no matter where he went in the world he was sure to find friends who would open their homes and lives to him.

This shift in perception was not completely comfortable, however. Leopold wrote: "I was never quite the monster the papers used to portray me as; I am certainly not now the selfless philanthropist and the outstanding scientist they depict me. This is very embarrassing to me. . . . I sometimes wonder whether any of my colleagues suspect me of courting this kind of thing."[63]

21

HIGH LIFE

On the evening of July 13, 1966, twenty-four-year-old Richard Speck was angry and aimless. He had recently lost his job at Inland Steel (the company owned by Leopold's uncle, Philip Block), and was having trouble finding another. After a day in the bars Speck took out some of that aggression: raping and robbing a woman he'd been drinking with. But it wasn't enough. Armed with a gun he'd stolen from her, he broke into a townhouse on the south side of Chicago where nine student nurses were sleeping. Only one escaped alive. Within days Speck was apprehended after a failed suicide attempt and sent to Cook County Jail to await trial.

On the day of Speck's arrest Leopold was cut open from chest to hips, his intestines resting beside him on an operating table in Michigan. While in Flint visiting Trudi's sister, he had decided to take advantage of the highly rated doctors in the area and got an aortogram for a look at his arteries. "While I was still on the x-ray table, higher than a kite . . . the doc asked whether I'd like to see the film. Even in that condition I realized that I had to have surgery, and NOW."[1] His left iliac artery was completely blocked, and a right femoral artery was well on its way.

While recovering from his bilateral aortofemoral bypass, Leopold had plenty of time to read newspaper stories about Speck's case. A couple of weeks after the murders Leopold was asked by a friend to consider writing a book about it. Rather than focusing on the crime, he decided that if he accepted, his book would spend much of its time exploring a fictionalized version of Speck's life in prison. Leopold imagined he could use Speck's celebrity to bring attention to his own ideas on penological issues, told through fictional anecdotes.[2]

Keeping the idea in mind, Leopold wasn't about to let major surgery get in the way of finishing his vacation. After a couple of weeks of recovery,

Leopold was back on his feet and flying to New York, where he'd arranged to have some LSD dropped off. Coached by his "anchor man" Leonard Rayner, the gay son of a couple Leopold was friends with, he spent several hours "in inner-space" babbling to Trudi and Ralph Newman over the phone and getting frustrated by belly-dancing vases.[3] Disappointed that he didn't have an electrocardiograph or at least a tape recorder to help document the trip, nevertheless: "I feel that I did get some new insights; I felt that I was peeling off, one by one, the poses, affectations, conditioned attitudes acquired during a lifetime of conditioning. . . . But I didn't <u>quite</u> get to the last one."[4]

Written last-minute the morning after his LSD trip, his prospective outline of the Speck book is jarringly self-concerned. The first three pages cover Leopold's history, the rest goes through the aspects of prison life Leopold wanted to discuss, most of which mirror the story Leopold told of his own life. He would have Speck get close to prison chaplains and find religion, teach in the prison school, get experience working with medicine and help cure a disease.[5] He pitched the outline the same morning it was written, but it was turned down.

He maintained a glancing interest in the case anyway, and several months later he remarked to fellow murderer Bill Evans that despite Speck's high body count, Leopold bet he would receive a light sentence or asylum time. "Seems you can get it cheaper wholesale," he joked. "Maybe that is where we made our respective mistakes!"[6]

The loss of the Speck book meant little, as when he got back to the island he got a much more enticing job offer. A previous boss offered Leopold a ninety-day position as project director and principal investigator to study leprosy and the living conditions of those suffering from the disease.[7] Agreeing quickly, in part to get him away from his "dull as dishwater" Urban Renewal job, Leopold began spending his days in the field, tracking down and interviewing ex-patients and their relatives around the island.[8]

Outside of work, with his position within the local B'nai B'rith chapter, Leopold used his social work skills to fight for those afflicted with leprosy to keep the land they lived on rather than being sent to a tuberculosis ward and connecting them with the University Hospital so they would have better and more frequent medical care.[9] He admitted that after work "I often stay awake half the night while the various parts churn around in my head, finally falling into some kind of order."[10] He had a theory about asymptomatic leprosy carriers, which again filled him with dreams that he "might get famous," for a monumental contribution to science.[11]

Despite his enthusiasm for his new job, Leopold was still trying to get assigned to work in another country through the Brethren Service Commission. For a while it looked as though Poland would come through, so Leopold began reading Polish newspapers, and planned to lease his apartment and sell off much of the furniture. At this, Trudi balked. She had previously been on board with the idea of following Leopold around the world, but the prospect of shedding everything she owned made her reconsider. When Harold Row broke the news that Poland had rejected him as they were looking for young, single volunteers, Leopold quipped that though he probably couldn't get anyone to believe his age was twenty-six instead of sixty-two, he *could* represent himself as single, as Trudi would be staying behind.[12] Row promised to keep looking for another placement.

Shortly before Christmas that year, Leopold got an unexpected call. "When I answered it the voice at the other end said, Hello, Nathan, this is Roy Cohn."[13] They knew each other slightly; they'd met at a party Leonard Lyons had thrown a couple of years previously.[14] Leopold felt a connection to the controversial lawyer, describing him as "a brilliant guy, but an egomaniac. My chief objection to him is that in '54 [during the Army-McCarthy hearings] he looked more like me in '24 than I did myself, and there is still a rather strong resemblance. Psychologically, too, I fear. He's an awful show-off."[15]

That resemblance came into clearer focus when Leopold and Trudi spent an evening with Cohn, barbequing and cruising the San Juan harbor on Cohn's yacht.[16] In many ways Cohn was living an ideal version of a life Leopold thought he could have attained had he not gone to prison. Cohn was a gifted lawyer who mingled among the most powerful men in the country, known for generosity among his friends, ruthlessly tearing down his enemies, and, until his disbarment in 1983, always staying one step ahead of the law. After their evening together Leopold noted that he and Cohn had something else in common: "Roy gives every indication of being what we genteelly call in Spanish a pato [homosexual] (which really means 'duck'). He's got the cutest crew of four aboard his palatial yacht, and the two or three boy-friends he was traveling with also gave every indication."[17]

Whether Leopold discussed this particular similarity with Cohn or not is unclear, though in one letter a year into their friendship Leopold called Cohn "angel" and signed off with "Love," showing a distinct lack of the gruff heterosexuality that characterized his letters to straight friends.[18] Whatever the relationship, Cohn helped Leopold with his own con, donating over $3,000 (equivalent to about $27,800 in 2023) to Leopold's social service fund and hosting a fundraising benefit dinner in his home in 1968. Soon after the dinner, though, Cohn was indicted on five counts of bribery, conspiracy, and extortion, and ignored Leopold's requests for the money he raised.[19] He was facing up to thirty-five years in jail and $35,000 in fines if found guilty and had enough on his plate to worry about without Leopold pestering him for a few thousand dollars.

While happy to work behind the scenes for the Castañer hospital and his social service fund, Leopold always kept an eye on his public image. In 1967 Leopold's friend Leonard Rayner pitched his version of a Leopold movie. Though skeptical of his abilities, Leopold gave him a six-month contract for the film rights of his autobiography. Writer Alfred Allan Lewis turned out a treatment and it was sent to prospective producers. Similar to Don Murray's vision, this movie would also focus on Leopold's life in Puerto Rico and use Tony as an example of Leopold's generosity and interest in helping the downtrodden. Thematically it would be about Leopold overcoming adversity and the prejudices people had against him to find a full and happy life of social service work and love.[20] Leopold was "much impressed," by the effort, and told Gertz that "there is complete meeting of the mind[s] as to tone, mood, etc."[21]

Though Rayner pitched the movie hard, in March 1968 he came back to Leopold with some harsh realities: Leopold's expectations were getting in his own way. Leopold was trying to tie in a sequel book deal with the movie and asking for a $25,000 advance (equivalent to about $214,250 in 2023), which Rayner warned was way out of line and had already cost them a deal. Rayner was also frustrated that Leopold wanted to show himself as being universally liked. Rayner warned: "Unless a movie can show naked honesty and really deep insights into the subject there is no market. I feel that you are not ready to delve into your own emotions, negative feelings etc. to the point where an exciting film portrayal could be drawn. You want to project a particular image and in most cases not based on reality."[22]

Leopold ignored this criticism and sold the rights to someone else, who also failed to find funding. Leopold was fine with deception and had no interest in showing the public his true thoughts or actions. The persona he'd built for himself was functioning as beautifully as he had crafted it to.

In June 1967 he and Trudi left for another long vacation beginning in the States. In Oregon, for the annual Brethren conference, Leopold was honored by the church for his "dedicated service of heart, hand and mind on behalf of humankind."[23] This was followed by two and a half months abroad touring around Asia, Europe, and the Middle East. Leopold was

Nathan and Trudi Leopold on vacation in Haiti in 1968. Photo courtesy of Larry Miller.

particularly impressed with the extravagant Villa Sajuana along the Straits of Johor in Singapore, where their tour group watched "a group of Malay dancers wearing beautiful traditional costumes present Malay folk dances on the lawn."[24]

Not content with the visit itself, shortly after his return he wrote to the man who owned the Villa and asked him to pass on a letter to the young man named Saadon who had waited on them.[25] Based on Singapore's child labor laws, he was likely between thirteen and sixteen years old, as he was old enough to occasionally dance and serve at the Villa, but complained that he was too young to get full-time employment. Leopold advised the boy that if he fancied writing back:

> I would like to send you money from time to time. . . . In the back of my mind is the thought that perhaps, someday, you would want further education. If this turns out to be the case, perhaps I could help you get into the United States and help with the money you would need. This depends, of course, on your desires and also on how our friendship progresses.[26]

Saadon responded favorably, so Leopold began to send him checks and asked Saadon to have photos taken in his work uniform and sent to

Leopold.[27] This sexual tourism and souvenir collecting was by now old hat for Leopold; every trip he'd taken he collected more pen pals, still maintaining ties with Friedl from Germany, a blind boy in Norway, and a Chinese boy he called Bamboo, though he still spent plenty of time cruising closer to home.

In 1967 the Puerto Rican Supreme Court upheld its sodomy law, but in practice, Puerto Ricans were fairly lax, and Old San Juan was a popular winter vacation destination for gay continentals. Crammed into a few streets in the city were more than a dozen gay establishments, with more arriving every year. Leopold soaked in the variety; he spoke glowingly of Main Street, a relaxed afternoon piano bar favored by "mature and more elite gay people."[28] "Quite a joint!" he enthused to Henry Johnson. "Lots of our friends go there. You must try it next trip."[29] If he wanted to cut loose, he could also be found at The Finale, where between cheap drinks late into the night he could "drink, dance, cruise, or neck (or grope) with the nicest looking natives or tourists in town."[30] While he couldn't take his conquests home, he easily found other arrangements, sometimes renting out rooms in town long term.[31]

Leopold hadn't had steady, full-time employment in several years, and as various job opportunities fell through, Leopold went back to Brethren and asked to be paid for what he had been doing for free for the past decade: fundraising. After several long discussions, Leopold was hired part time as an administrative assistant, and it was agreed that his social service fund and his fundraising for the hospital would remain separate, allowing him to continue funneling the social service funds wherever he saw fit.[32]

As Leopold explained: "It is I who am the Fund. I collect all the moolah and I MAKE ALL THE DECISIONS on disbursements. I have a second signature on the checks just to demonstrate to all and sundry that I'm not dipping my fingers into the till for questionable purposes. . . . I simply lay before him the checks he is to countersign, which he meekly does."[33] He was still free to host his elaborate benefit events, going all out the following month with a Celebrity Night in the San Jeronimo Hilton's Grand Ballroom featuring acts playing at all the local clubs, including Diana Ross and the Supremes.[34]

For his salaried position, Leopold fundraised and used his connections in San Juan to help facilitate the hospital. If necessary, he organized patient transfers to specialists in the city. Sometimes this put him in a complicated position. Part of Leopold's professional life involved navigating the world of social work and psychology's current views of treatment involving queer patients. In 1969 the National Institute of Mental Health stated that "For most workers in the field, the prevention of the development of a homosexual orientation in an individual child or adolescent is seen as one of the most important goals."[35]

In 1968, a Brethren doctor wrote to Leopold that he had a teenage patient who he wanted to be transferred to the University's Psychiatric Division, as the patient "demonstrate[s] transvestism and transsexualism and in the past some tendency to homosexuality. He needs direction reorienting his role development."[36] Though only asked to set up an appointment, upon receiving the letter Leopold immediately offered to personally oversee the case and chauffeur the patient the three-hour round trip to the psychiatrist. He promised to "keep an eye on him" in college and offered his long-term, personal social work services.[37] Perhaps he did this out of compassion for a child caught in the wheels of a homophobic and transphobic system, or maybe he was just hoping to secure a new sexual partner.

Still, despite harsh laws and medical jargon, an understanding and acceptance for homosexuality was developing. In 1967 England struck down its law against sodomy, and Leopold was delighted to discover through a *Playboy* article that in 1964 Illinois had also changed its sodomy law to something "a bit less archaic."[38] When a friend confided about the mental anguish he and his wife were going through after their son came out, Leopold assured him that "world opinion in these matters is changing rapidly and I am sure that [he] can look forward to a less unpleasant life than would have been the case a generation ago."[39]

Happy with his new job and especially with the freedom it offered, Leopold spent a lot of time traveling and pursuing his personal projects. In January 1968, shortly after he was hired, he went back to Illinois to catch up with family and friends. He made sure to make time to see Davie Fulford, spending one afternoon taking "his boy" out for ice cream and buying him a case for his guitar. As Leopold admitted before Davie took his second trip to stay with Leopold in Puerto Rico, "I want the youngster to like me, and I'm not one bit above trying to <u>buy</u> his affection!"[40]

Exemplifying just how far he had come since his parole, on this trip he and Bill Evans were invited back to Stateville, where the warden led them on a grand tour of their "alma mater." Several times the warden halted the tour, gathered prisoners together and asked the ex-cons to offer words of encouragement and advice. Leopold joked "I never thought I'd grow up to be a paradigm!"[41] The high point though was the chance the visit afforded him to talk with Paul Henry in person for the first time in ten years. Leopold assured Henry that he and Row were working toward his parole, and they hoped to have him out by August at the latest.[42]

From Illinois Leopold flew to New York, where he attended his usual round of parties, Broadway shows, and dinners. On January 21 he was one of thousands who attended a speech by Maharishi Mahesh Yogi at Madison Square Gardens, who was famous at the time for his position as spiritual advisor to The Beatles. Following the lecture, Leopold was invited to a more exclusive group discussion in the yogi's flower-strewn room at the Plaza Hotel and concluded the night with a private séance. Leopold was less than impressed by the evening, complaining that "all he does is mouth a lot of tired old platitudes!"[43] He noted that author and activist Allen Ginsberg, also in attendance, dominated the conversation.[44] Ginsberg's account of the discussion confirms this wordiness, Ginsberg admitting: "I sat at [Maharishi's] feet and literally started yelling at him . . . spoke for half an hour almost, challenging, arguing."[45]

Leopold didn't see José and his wife on this trip, explaining somewhat perfunctorily that they'd lost touch a couple of years earlier and he no longer knew where José was living "nor do I care very much."[46] Evidently, the boy he had once called a son and considered legally adopting was out of the family.

On March 10, in anticipation of the tenth anniversary of his release from prison, Leopold wrote nearly identical letters to Harold Row, Elmer Gertz, and Ralph Newman; three men he credited with doing the most to help him regain his freedom. Leopold concluded that "the past ten years, from my point of view, have been superb. I really don't see how they could have been any happier." As for society: "From the point of view of the statistics of parole violation, I qualify as a 'success.' But honestly, I think it has gone a bit farther than just that. My case may have had a profound influence on the whole theory of parole. And I've done a few things in the professional field that I think needed doing."[47]

Still hoping to sell his version of parole success to the world, when his friend Douglas Lyons got a job at Doubleday, Leopold asked Lyons to pitch his new autobiography, which he planned to title "Grab for a Halo." In addition to describing his years after prison and persona philosophy, he wanted to discuss "The Anti-Hero Legend":

> For some forty years, I was perhaps the most hated human being in the US. Gallons of printer's ink and reams of paper have gone into the description of my wickedness, my depravity, my un-humanness. One day the pendulum began to swing. It has now swung as far to the right as it used to be to the left. One recent article about me, dated Dec.

19, 1965, which went to hundreds of newspapers over UPI, starts off:
"Some people say he is a saint."

Now this, to me, is as nauseating as was the earlier "Hate Leopold"
genre. It is just as exaggerated, just as untrue, just as phony, as was the
earlier material.

Not many people, perhaps, have experienced in their own life-time
this shift from exaggeration on one side to equal exaggeration on the
other. I should like to poke gentle fun at this human tendency. I should
like to pierce the balloon.[48]

He warned Lyons that the book may be a hard sell; he was still asking
for an advance of $25,000, with half to be paid before he wrote anything.
He explained that though he had tried in the past to write the book in his
spare time, his job and social life always got in the way. So, he would need
the money to rent a house on another Caribbean island and he imagined
that there, with no distractions, he would finally be able to buckle down
and write. Doubleday was uninterested.

Unwilling to try writing at home, Leopold instead used his ample free
time to focus on his hobbies and social life. On March 31 he left home at
3:30 in the morning, so he and a couple of assistants could trek for hours
through a dense section of the Caribbean National Forest. Finally, they
reached the location his scouts had told him about: the nesting site of a
Puerto Rican parrot, which had been critically endangered for decades. In
the mid-1960s, scientists in Puerto Rico began studying the bird, trying to
help save its waning population.

Leopold was happy to do his part, on a ladder hastily constructed from
saplings, Leopold climbed up and "measured the tree every which way,
took pictures, and even took a picture, with flash, down the four foot long
nesting cavity! I'm told now that it may be the only photograph of a nest
of the PR Parrot extant! How I hope it turned out!"[49]

In May 1968 Leopold finally convinced Trudi to move out of the
apartment she'd lived in since the death of her first husband. The two
purchased a more upscale condo, and while Leopold enjoyed a short vacation to the Virgin Islands, snorkeling and sunning himself on the beach,
Trudi supervised the movers, unpacked, organized, and decorated their
new home.[50]

With no regular job to hold him on the island, Leopold began planning
a solo trip around Europe and Asia, writing happily to Bal: "I'm looking
forward to this trip enormously. It will be very varied and kaleidoscopic."
In addition to spending some time at a Brethren mission in India, "I'm
also going to try to see all the dives of Cairo, Kabul, Singapore, Bangkok,

Hong Kong, and Tokyo. I've been gathering information furiously. This time there will be no maiden school teachers and I expect to see something more than natural bridges and Moghul monuments!"[51]

He was helped in his planning by his friend William Conner, a gay writer of Asian travel guides. Happy to tap Conner's knowledge, in each of the countries he planned to visit Leopold asked for recommendations for gay bars and baths, prostitutes to look up, and hotels to stay in. He was especially eager to visit a "he whorehouse" in Taipei, which he had heard described as "expensive but well worth it."[52] Even in Honolulu, though he would be staying with straight friends, "so my cruising activities may be a trifle curtailed," he asked for places to visit in case he was able to slip out for a night or two.[53]

In anticipation of his trip, Leopold checked in with Saadon, the boy from Singapore he'd met the year before. He asked if the boy would be able to show him lively places around the city, assuring him that "Naturally, I would pay you very well for your time."[54] In case Saadon didn't understand, he emphasized that he wanted them to spend a lot of time together and share a hotel room, writing bluntly: "You'll have to help make up for my wife's absence!"[55]

He needn't have worried; Saadon promised to show Leopold "the gay world" of Singapore and assured him that "I know that you have chosen your way of life and that it is fun for you and surely for me. I know that it would be great sport to go to some of the bars, see some of the people and have a ball."[56] With this confirmation that Saadon was on the right page, Leopold made hotel reservations and continued to send the boy $20 (equivalent to about $200 in 2023) checks at regular intervals as he waited to meet him again. As a bonus, during his planning Leopold got the news that Paul Henry would be paroled to Puerto Rico right before Leopold returned home.[57]

His trip began in late August and would last until October and seems a perfect microcosm of Leopold's post-paroled life: his tendency to flit around seeking new experiences and old favorites while balancing deftly his hidden pleasures with the scientific and academic.

He began in Northern Europe, visiting a blind boy he'd corresponded with for years, bemoaned the lack of functioning Roman Orthodox churches, and took in a Chopin recital in the composer's home country.[58] He then made his way into the Middle East, visiting holy sites and caves, and making friends with a young Turk in Tehran who was "very friendly and accommodating," before touring archaeological dig sites around Ghazni in Afghanistan.[59] The day after returning from the dig, "I had dinner at the Staff House of the American Embassy, with some very interesting AID and State Dept. people. A delightful experience."[60]

He continued East, staying for a week in Singapore to enjoy the company of Saadon and other boys introduced to him through Conner.[61] Between these pleasant visits and private massages, Leopold toured leprosariums and boy's reform schools.[62] Afterward he jumped at the chance to join a friend of Abel Brown's on a tour of camps and military bases in Vietnam.[63] In Tokyo he met with a physician who had succeeded in culturing leprosy in a test tube, which Leopold was itching to try replicating once he returned home.

He finished his trip in the States, meeting with his old friend Ferris Laune in Hawaii, before going to Los Angeles and finally Chicago. He was touched when Sam threw him a party, which Leopold noted was the first time he'd ever been in Sam's home. He wrote to Brown: "Maybe (and I fervently hope so) this betokens a change in relations between Sam and me. I would dearly love to be friends with him, to have a real brother."[64] Leopold certainly tried to get this gratitude across to Sam, thanking him three times in one letter, and saying that the high point of his time in Illinois "was certainly your party."[65]

While he was in Chicago Paul Henry was released from prison, and talked on the phone, but decided to wait just a bit longer until they could reunite in Puerto Rico.[66] Henry's wife had divorced him shortly before his release, so he would be unencumbered when he arrived. Leopold capped his trip by flying to Philadelphia where Trudi was recovering from cataract surgery with her family, and the couple returned home together at the end of October.

As soon as he returned, Leopold drove up to Castañer to stay with Paul for four days. Leopold finally got a chance to personally take him shopping and began supplementing his $15/month salary with an additional $50 (equivalent to around $450 in 2023).[67] After the trip Leopold wrote to Row: "I am so thrilled and happy over Paul Henry's reception, accommodations, acceptance and very rapid acclimatization on the Project that I am fairly bubbling over."[68] Project employee Marie Brubaker reported to Row that "Paul Henry is a fine young man and seems to be fitting into the project very well. He's being transferred to the Lab and that pleases him for that is what Nate did and Nate is his idol."[69]

For the next few months Leopold's letters to friends and family were hardly complete unless he included some mention of the young man he credited himself for getting out of prison. He was further elated when a month later he attended Tony's wedding, described to Bal as "my very finest protegé, a Puerto Rican lad, now 26, whose case I've been handling for nearly ten years."[70] In early December he revealed to Gertz that he was beginning to get depressed, but there was plenty to keep him distracted for the moment.[71]

As the year ended, Leopold focused increasingly on trying to put together his largest ever fundraising event for his social service fund: a Sammy Davis Jr. concert. The celebrity had been helping Leopold's cause since 1957 when he spoke on a radio program advocating his release from prison.[72] The pair had met backstage after a performance of Davis's play *Golden Boy* in 1964 and had kept up an acquaintanceship since.[73] When Leopold learned that Davis would be on the island for three weeks with other shows, Leopold pounced on the opportunity. "You have several times expressed your desire to do something really big for Castañer Hospital," Leopold wrote Davis. "Here's your chance!"[74] Davis accepted, and Leopold began to plan for what he imagined would be an enormous windfall of money.

On January 12, after weeks of scheduling problems, the Sammy Davis Jr. benefit concert was staged. Despite the star power, the concert didn't draw as large a crowd as Leopold had hoped because Davis's changing schedule meant they couldn't settle on a date or start advertising until a couple of weeks ahead of time, and they were forced to book it for the same day as the Super Bowl. Still, largely through donations rather than ticket sales, Leopold managed to raise $7,000 (equivalent to about $57,000 in 2023). He celebrated with a long weekend in Castañer with Paul Henry. Leopold was already spinning grand plans for Henry's future, imagining that in a year he would get him a job managing a fast-food chain.[75]

After returning from his visit, Leopold wrote to Harold Row: "I've been doing a lot of thinking recently about how very happy I am and how I hardly seem to have an unsatisfied wish or ambition." He summarized the sources of his happiness: his health, his home, the amount of traveling he was able to do, his medical and ornithological work, and, of course, Paul Henry's parole. "With that having turned out so well, I really can't think of anything further I really want very badly."[76] He seemed content with his life and excited for the future as he looked forward to the coming year.

It wouldn't be long until that mood evaporated.

22

DECLINE AND DEATH

Soon after the benefit concert, the depression that had been lurking over Leopold finally settled. Expounding on his dip in mood, he observed: "I've always been a manic-depressive personality, I guess. Any work I do is always accomplished in the manic phases; in the depressive ones I just vegetate. Fortunately, the manic phase is apt to last years, while the depressive phase is usually a matter only of weeks, or at most, months. But they sure do occur at inconvenient times!"[1]

Unfortunately for Leopold, on January 2, Luis Ferré and the New Progressive Party took over from the long incumbency of Puerto Rico's Popular Democratic Party. With fewer funds being allocated to research and no more political connections, Leopold found himself struggling to find a job. With no project or employment to distract himself, he was unable to pull himself out of his slump as he had in the past.

The *Compulsion* case was also a persistent thorn in his side, exacerbated by his financial paranoia brought on by not having employment. "Shocked and horrified" to receive a bill for $969 for xerox copies (equivalent to about $8,000 in 2023), Leopold wrote to his lawyers: "Again I am assailed by grave doubts. . . . We've been in the courts now nine and a half years and, at the present writing, we have gotten just they should minimize their losses and get out.

As Leopold became increasingly withdrawn, Trudi wasn't faring any better. Sick from a series of illnesses, she was continually trying new medications and treatments, and her eyes had gotten so bad that she was afraid to leave home alone.[2] The same Leopolds who had once been so social and active within their community had retreated to the confines of their condominium. As the months went by Leopold even stopped writing letters with his customary frequency, minimizing contact with friends and family.

While they still had house guests, instead of happily taking them on tours of the islands, Leopold was annoyed at the intrusion.[3]

In March, Trudi left for more consultations with her ophthalmologist in the States, leaving Leopold alone and complaining that there was no one to cook or clean for him.[4] A few days after she left, Leopold journeyed up to Castañer and Marie Brubaker quickly became alarmed. Unbeknownst to Leopold she wrote to Harold Row that "I consider him in a precarious position and unless he gets some help I fear for him."[5] Paul Henry was more outspoken, opining to Brubaker that especially with the way he drank and smoked, he didn't expect Leopold to live out the year. Row, however, had deeper concerns. When Leopold went to the States to pick up Trudi he learned that Row had prostate cancer, which was very likely to be terminal. The impending loss of one of his most ardent champions deepened Leopold's depression further.

After half a year of unemployment, Leopold secured a job teaching summer classes for the private Commonwealth High School in San Juan. Leopold was hired back in the fall and taught remedial science and math five mornings a week, but by mid-September the schedule had already proved to be too much, and Leopold turned in his resignation.[6] He complained that he didn't like the textbooks he had to teach from and that he couldn't get the students to behave. A holdover from his prison-learned philosophy against stool pigeons, he refused to send kids to the principal, so he had no way to discipline them.[7] One of his students recalled that "He was a very sweet, elderly man. . . . He never raised his voice, and kids used to say you could get away with murder in his class. We liked him a lot."[8]

According to Leopold, the school administration refused his resignation and worked instead to alter his course load. He taught less and began to give teacher orientations and tutor children individually to help them prepare for College Board exams. While this worked better for him, he still disliked it, complaining that the kids were "horribly stupid," and he felt he was accomplishing nothing in his attempts to teach them.[9] He was also not particularly qualified to teach science. Though he was eventually made head of the science department, he'd taken almost no classes in the discipline after high school and acknowledged that he didn't understand most of the exhibits in the school's science fair.[10]

Though the work left him exhausted, he felt unable to leave. He was reluctant to dip into money from Mike's trust fund, leaving nearly $40,000 untouched[11] (equivalent to about $325,000 in 2023) as he complained that he struggled to pay grocery bills.[12] He was exaggerating, but his pride made him feel he had to spend only the money he earned whenever possible.

Depressed and dissatisfied, in October Leopold wrote to Harold Row that Bal was in the hospital, but if Bal were to die soon, at least he had led a good life. "He and Dodie have had a long and happy life together—they have been married over 45 years, and they have eight lovely grandchildren. He has won the respect and admiration of the community; all in all, his life has been a most satisfying and rewarding one."[13] It is hard not to contrast this with Leopold's own life.

Unlike Bal, Leopold was stuck in a loveless and suffocating marriage, with no children of his own. He saw Davie Fulford as something resembling a son, but he had only seen the boy a handful of times and had not heard from him in months. There were also his lovers, those men he called protégés and sons, but most of those relationships had not lasted, and all were at least partially transactional. Professionally he'd never stuck with anything long enough to see it through to a meaningful conclusion and his current job left him cold. Though he had certainly changed his reputation and gathered a dedicated group of friends, still he knew logically that his crime and infamy were what he would be remembered for. With no PhD, movie, or second book and so many of his glorious plans failing to materialize, what had he really accomplished?

Still, the darkness couldn't last forever, and in late October he reported to Henry Johnson that after "floundering in a rather deep depression since last winter. . . . I think it is beginning to lift a bit the past couple of weeks."[14] Paul Henry helped with this shift; Leopold began visiting him at the project nearly every weekend and celebrated Thanksgiving there with Henry and his fiancée, Virginia. On December 20, accompanied by the vocal talents of the project's executive director, Leopold walked Virginia down the aisle and gave her away to Henry.[15] After the wedding Leopold wrote to Row: "I am very happy for Paul, Harold, and my heart is very full. . . . I feel supremely confident that he will earn his discharge from parole and that we can turn our backs on the past and look forward hopefully and confidently to a brighter future."[16]

In early April, Marie Brubaker was happy to report to Harold Row that on his most recent weekend visit to Castañer Leopold looked much improved.[17] She relayed that Paul had made a steak dinner, as "he wanted to bring a little nostalgia to Nate for the steaks he fixed for him and sneaked to him in Stateville."[18]

In May 1970, after eleven years and many rounds through the court system, the Supreme Court of Illinois ruled against Leopold in the *Compulsion* lawsuit. The judge declared that Leopold did not have a right to privacy as his crime was part of the historical record and because he had consented to publicity through his autobiography and interviews. "Having encouraged public attention," the judge explained, "he cannot at his whim withdraw the events of his life from public scrutiny."[19] His lawyers could have taken the matter to the US Supreme Court, but Leopold was tired of the expense, and Gertz and Gordon were similarly exhausted.[20] This loss, expected and perhaps a relief to finally have behind him, did not overly deter Leopold, and his spirits continued to rise.

In June the Leopolds took another trip, first to Michigan to see wild Kirtland's Warblers, then set off for the South Pacific. In Australia Leopold petted kangaroos and koalas in an animal sanctuary and drove fifty miles to see a platypus for the first time. He drank kava and toured a leprosarium in Fiji, was wowed by the isle of Moorea off of Tahiti, walked on a glacier, and marveled over a cave filled with glowworms in New Zealand.[21] Trudi followed dutifully behind, packing and unpacking their suitcases, often sitting out the more strenuous excursions, before ending their trip back to the States. In Washington, Leopold and Row struggled over the increasingly dark developments about Row's cancer, and Leopold presented Row with an icon he had bought during his travels.[22]

With the possibility of Row's death looming over him, Leopold felt pressured to attempt to convey how he felt about the man before it was too late:

> Harold, my respect, my admiration, and, yes, my love for you have grown steadily every day since that first meeting. . . . You took a poor, bedraggled pup, who had not been with his fellow-men for more than 33 years, and in a few short months restored his pride, his self-respect, his view of the world . . . you folk saved my life as truly as if you had saved me physically from drowning—and in a more fundamental, more real sense.[23]

Soon after his arrival back on the island, Leopold secured a position with the Commonwealth Department of Social Services where he was tasked with putting together research plans and evaluating grant proposals. Relieved not to be forced back to teaching, he planned to hire some of his favorite boys for prime positions beneath him, and he was extremely pleased to be making $1,000 a month.[24] "My job continues to enchant me," he reported to Row, "this is the kind of thing I ought to be doing."[25] He even began trading lessons as he had decades ago in Stateville, his new coworker teaching him Basque while Leopold instructed him in statistics.

He began again to give interviews and speak on panels when the organizers agreed to meet his increasingly large financial requirements. On September 11 (which Leopold was quick to mention was the forty-sixth anniversary of his journey to Stateville),[26] Leopold joined a deputy defense attorney, prison superintendent, and judge for the panel discussion "The Human Cage: An Analysis of Our Prisons," at the Bench-Bar Convention of the Philadelphia Bar Association in Atlantic City.[27]

His prepared lecture focused on sexual assaults in the Philadelphia prison system and sheriffs' vans, concluding that as the sheriff knew of the prevalence of rapes that occurred in the backs of unsupervised police vans, an indictment should be made for his being an accessory before the fact to homosexual gang rape. "If a person coerced another to enter a cage full of lions known to be ferocious, and the latter were clawed to death by the beasts, would not the former be guilty of manslaughter?"[28] Leopold advised that police officers be present in vans and for judges to visit the prisons in their districts so they had a realistic view of the places they were sending the men in their power.[29]

Leopold was building himself back up both professionally and in his intimate relationships. After years of sparse letters and a couple of brief vacations, in October, Davie Fulford opened up to Leopold and discussed his troubles, his fears about school, and a perception that he was different from other kids. He ended the letter: "You care so much about other people you are to [sic] good to be true, like someone out of the bible."[30]

Leopold, touched, wrote him seven pages in reply. He was quick to clarify Fulford's assessment: "I don't care about all other people; just some special ones. And you are one of the most special. I love you very dearly, you know, and have since the day you were born. I have kind of imagined you, for 17 years now, as the son I never had."[31]

Eager to maintain the relationship and apparently with no understanding of how to accomplish that outside of monetary coercion, he warned Fulford that one good letter doesn't earn an inheritance, and Davie's continued attitude and actions toward him would determine if he would be included in Leopold's will or not.[32]

The relationship with his "son" on the rise, Leopold was also spending an increasing amount of time with the other "adopted sons" and "protégés," who had come to represent the family he had failed to find with his wife. Leopold was determined to make the second anniversary of Paul's release from prison a special occasion, inviting Paul and Virginia to spend the weekend in San Juan. The first night they were in town, the two married couples went to see *The Boys in the Band*, a movie about a group of gay friends celebrating a birthday. Putting on an affronted and moralizing tone when he wrote of the incident to Harold Row, he commented: "WELL! It turned out to be a story about a group of 'boys' in a homosexual 'band,' not musical as we had naively believed it might be. It was pretty horrid, and, married or not, I wonder if Ginnie is old enough to be exposed to that sort of thing. Don't see it; it's disgusting."[33]

Despite his claims of disgust, apparently the group sat through the entire movie, then the wives were dropped off and Leopold took Henry out on the town. The following day he flew the couple to St. Thomas where they rented a Volkswagen, filled up on banana and strawberry daiquiris, and relaxed on the white sand beaches of Sapphire Bay. When they returned to Puerto Rico, Leopold took the party out to dinner, ordering lobster for Paul, then to the casino. The couple left the following day and Leopold was very satisfied with how the "GREAT EVENT" had come off. That night he wrote to Row: "I am probably the most selfish person in the world: I never do anything except for my own, personal pleasure. And I can't remember when anything has given me so much pleasure as making this little jaunt possible for them and introducing them to new experiences. That's really living."[34]

Row was touched by his account, writing: "I know you enjoy so much doing things for others. In fact your life in the period that I have known you has been filled unbelievably full of doing things for others, especially those who have hardly any hope otherwise. This has caused me and others to think of you as a Puerto Rican saint. I grant you, a very unorthodox saint, but nevertheless an authentic one."[35]

Leopold's relationships were not without their troubles, however. On November 2 Leopold's "favorite protégé" Tony turned down Leopold's invitation to meet up that week and refused any further monetary gifts, explaining that while he was grateful for the help Leopold had given in the past, he was an adult now and owed himself to his wife.[36] Leopold was less than pleased, responding,

> I thank you for all the kindness you have shown me during 11½ years. It is too bad that you came to this new conclusion at this moment, since I intended to let you go completely of my own will on the day of your 30th birthday. . . . Only a year or so more to go and that way it would have been so much nicer. . . . Very often in the past you called me your second father and that always made me proud, very proud. Well, it is always sad to lose a favorite son.[37]

Sixteen when they met, Tony had spent nearly half of his life in Leopold's debt. Leopold had found him his job, talked to his boss when he wanted a raise or a change in schedule, frequently supplied him with money, and his social service fund had put his sisters through college. It must have been extremely difficult to deny this father figure the access to his body that had drawn Leopold to him and granted him and his family such rewards over the years. Despite Leopold's nuclear reaction, Tony had only attempted to end the sexual side of the relationship, and evidently they found a way to patch things up. Four months later Leopold stopped by Tony's home to chat and wrote happily that he spent the visit holding his nearly one-year-old "grandson" on his lap.[38]

As 1970 came to a close, Leopold continued to ride his high, buying himself a parrot as a birthday present (and naming him Bill, of course).[39] Still enthusiastic about wild birds, Leopold stayed in touch with some of the island's ornithologists. When visiting ornithologist Herbert Raffaele called to tell him about being the first to record seeing a Caspian tern on the island, Raffaele recalled Leopold said: "Oh my god, we have to go collect it!"[40] Raffaele said that was impossible as the bird was in a heavily populated area of San Juan, but Leopold grabbed his gun and insisted they go out. When they tracked down the tern, Raffaele was relieved that it was too far out in the mudflats of the San Juan Harbor for Leopold to shoot.

As Raffaele spent more time in the field with Leopold, his continuous talk about his image wore on the young ornithologist. Raffaele recalled that "he showed little concern about helping the people. . . . My sense was that he was completely doing this stuff in order that when this next movie came out, he would look and smell great. He'd become a crusader, he was a very egocentric guy, very concerned about his image."[41]

As his final year began, Leopold found himself looking ever more toward his adopted family, his will, and his legacy. During Leopold's previous visit to the States, Row introduced the idea that Leopold should donate his personal papers to an institution after his death.[42] This pleased Leopold's sense of importance and in early December, after Trudi had worked on putting them in order for a month, the "Leopoldiana" was shipped to the Chicago Historical Society.

Leopold continued his habit of driving to see the Henry family in Castañer every other weekend. After one such "unusually pleasant week end," he wrote that "Paul and Virginia are such a joy to me: they quite take the place of the son and daughter I never had. Only I'm sure they spoil me far more than my own would!"[43] Leopold was delighted when Henry was released from parole in early February, and with him both successful in his work and happily married, Leopold was able to take pleasure in the knowledge that at least one of his protégés seemed well-adjusted.

Evidently the Henrys were not the only people Leopold was going to the project to see. In January 1971 Leopold wrote to Harold Row that he planned to pay for the medical school tuition of a bright, young hospital orderly named Eliud.[44] He was also making plans to take the teenager on a three-week European getaway.[45] Even among the relatively naïve and trusting Brethren members, this association raised some eyebrows. Unsure of how to address the situation, they remained silent.[46]

On April 7 Leopold's plans came crashing down around him when he was hospitalized for a coronary occlusion. After a lifetime of excesses, it seemed that his body was catching up with him. Trudi visited the hospital several times a day, bringing him lunch and keeping him company. After one visit she sat down to respond to a worried letter from Gertz inquiring about Leopold's health.[47] She updated him on Leopold's condition, but she felt the need to dig a little deeper, revealing her relationship with her husband and his psychology as she had never done before.

> You know I've had problems with him before but as long as I remained with him he's had a cloak of respectability over him. I find I can't and dont want to continue with him. . . . Everything has deteriorated to a point that I must have OUT, and I'm fully aware that this may destroy him. But, I must think of myself also—I have no wish to be destroyed and that's what he's doing to me.
>
> You know we're taking separate vacations; on his proposed trip to Europe he's taking with him an 18 or 19 year old boy from Castañer, as his guest. I've pleaded with him not to do this because on this Bridge-water College (Brethren) tour, there may be many people who will recognize him and wonder about his so-called protegee, and it might just unleash an avalanche of criticism hearkening back to 1924 and his unholy alliance with Dick L. . . . My very superior husband laughed at me and is continuing with his arrangements for the tour. . . . I hate to say this but he isn't one bit different than he was in 1924; his activities continued throughout his Stateville days, and started here a month after he arrived in 1958, and are continuing presently. I've confronted him with what he is and he laughs at me and says I'm a paranoid schizo-phrenic. Naturally, when confronted, he lies but I have such damning evidence that he doesn't have a leg to stand on. I hope with all my heart that I never [*sic*] need to use this. I don't wish to hurt him but I long since ceased to love him and don't have a particle of respect for him.
>
> A half hour ago Paul came in from Castañer and I sent him over to the hospital for a visit. Paul, incidentally, could be termed the leader of

the "Boys in the Band," since his arrival on the Island, but he's only one of many and while I don't have any real evidence on the youngster he's taking to Europe (he also hopes to put this boy through Medical School), I haven't even met the boy and have no wish to, it's pretty obvious. . . . Perhaps, between us, we can think of something or some way to handle this without too much hurt. The fact that I'm writing to you would be unpardonable to him, with his perverted sense of loyalty according to the hoodlum code, but he's sick to the point of no return.[48]

Gertz tried to put her off, promising they'd speak about it in three months once they saw each other in person.[49] Instead of waiting, Trudi reached out to another mutual friend. "We're planning a separation," she informed Harold Row, and they wanted to do it "very quietly, without any fanfare which could prove disastrous, and an appointment for him in Europe or wherever a vacancy exists, would prove to be the ideal solution."[50]

Leopold was released from the hospital on April 21 but overextended himself and ignored the doctor's orders, so two weeks later he was sent back. Lying in his hospital bed he assured Row: "Only the good die young: so I'll be here quite a spell yet."[51] From his bed he wrote to Ralph Newman of his grand plans for the still unwritten "Grab for a Halo." Unlike the sanitized version of his life that he had been attempting to peddle for the last decade, he envisioned this new book as much more personal and revealing.

Parts autobiography, philosophical text, and primer on topics ranging from the psychology of tropical Hispano American apathy to abolishing prisons, he imagined it as very different tonally than his first book because he wouldn't have to constantly be wary of things that may hurt his parole chances or the warden. "Last time I wrote 'the truth and nothing but the truth,'" he claimed. "This time I can write 'the whole truth'!"[52]

And never one to stop while he was behind, Leopold was planning yet another book. He envisioned his new project as a collection of unfiltered interview transcripts with prisoners, aiming for a "frank, informative book, shocking or, at least, certainly disturbing."[53] No topics would be out of bounds: sex, crime, education, revenge on society, homosexuality, remorse or lack thereof would all be looked at frankly and in detail. He planned to insert himself into the narrative as a participant, rather than just an observer.[54] As his health declined, it seemed that Leopold was feeling more open to the idea of exposing the more controversial elements of his life to the world.

In the beginning of July, Leopold reluctantly canceled the European portion of his trip on doctor's orders, while stubbornly holding onto the States. Oxygen tank in tow, he flew to see Row in Washington before journeying to Chicago, lasting only a few days before he was admitted to the hospital. There, the news of Row's death reached him, and he insisted to his doctor that he needed to attend Row's funeral and see Davie Fulford in California. Denied both requests, Leopold seethed from his hospital bed, where "he agitated himself and everyone around him."[55]

On August 4, Leopold was discharged from the hospital and picked up by the Stroms, a family he had made friends with when trying to gain parole. That afternoon, at his request, they drove him to where he used to go birding in the Calumet Swamp district. He directed them to the intersection of 108th Street and Avenue F, the same intersection mentioned in his 1924 confession as the place where he and Loeb had turned into the swamp and started toward the body disposal site.[56] Standing with the Strom family on that summer afternoon, he was about a mile from the location where he had pushed and kicked the body of Bobby Franks into a railroad culvert forty-seven years earlier. "It's all built up now," he wrote to Abel Brown, "I would never have recognized it."[57]

After the field trip, the Stroms took Leopold to the Brethren headquarters in Elgin where he had "the most satisfactory interviews" about setting up a foreign volunteer assignment. His interviewer recalled that though Leopold repeatedly said he wanted the assignment so that he could repay his debt to the Brethren, "I have the feeling that there is a great ego need in Nathan Leopold that yearns for fulfillment."[58] He cautioned Leopold that the only remote possibility available was a position in Nigeria that wouldn't be open for a year. Despite this, the interviewer noted Leopold's optimism about the future, and Leopold wrote to friends: "I really think it will go thru as I wish within the next few months."[59]

After his meeting, the Stroms delivered Leopold to the Gertz apartment, where he talked incessantly to Gertz and his wife, chain-smoking as he watched the birds by their window feeder. After retiring early, around one in the morning he woke Gertz in distress. "Frankly," Gertz recalled, "we did not think he would survive the trip from our home to the hospital. It was a nightmare."[60] After ten days in the hospital he flew to New York before returning home.

Leopold rested for a week and then spent four days in Castañer, but on August 19, the day after his return to San Juan, Trudi wrote to friends and family to inform them that Leopold was back in the hospital, his lungs again filling with fluid. "I think he's finally convinced that he must take proper care of himself or his condition will worsten [*sic*] and will kill him."[61] Trudi visited him twice a day and brought home-cooked meals, hoping to stimulate his flagging appetite.

Despite Trudi's care and visits from Paul Henry, on August 29 Leopold's heart failed and he died after ten days in Mimiya Hospital.[62] Trudi described his last moments: "He asked me for his 'vomit cup.' I had my right arm behind him, to support him, and my left hand held the cup—a few seconds later he was gone, at 8:45 p.m." She said a prayer, kissed his lips, and waited for the doctors to step in.[63]

As had been his wish, Leopold's eyes were removed and donated to an eye bank, Trudi noting that one was given to a man and the other a woman, "so Nate's final act brought sight to two strangers."[64] Though he had wanted to be buried with the rest of the family in their Rosehill plot, Sam "somewhat curtly, told me I should make other plans."[65] Not wanting to be buried anywhere but beside his parents and Mike, he opted to donate his body to science instead.

For most of his life Leopold had tried to look at death rationally and professed to be unafraid to face it. In prison Leopold became enamored with the novel *Beyond Life* by James Branch Cabell, reading it more than two dozen times. He was particularly taken with Cabell's commentary on the flawed nature of humanity and the point of existence: "'Muddling through to an epitaph' is Cabell's—to me—very beautiful, very striking metaphor for the course of human life. . . . Death is there for all of us. It's the ultimate destination of all in nature, and we do the best we can on the way, and sometimes that best isn't very good."[66]

CONCLUSION

As with all other major events in his life, Leopold's death could scarcely go by without a huge outpouring of publicity. Governor of Puerto Rico Luis Ferré pushed the narrative determinedly toward the side of redemption when he stated to the press: "The story of Nathan Leopold is one that must confirm the faith and intrinsic goodness of the human being. His story, that of a man who committed a crime in his youth, who fulfilled the punishment imposed on him by society and left prison regenerated to serve humanity with a great spirit of sacrifice and generosity . . . his story clearly shows that there is kindness in the heart of every man."[1]

Trudi gave reporters a few sweet sentiments about her deceased husband, calling him "one of the most gentle people I've met in my life."[2] She remained protective of him, so when Gertz wrote her about an author who hoped to do an article about Leopold's life for *Reader's Digest*, she hastily replied: "You surely know how unwise it would be to have newsman delving and prying into the past. Let his present image which is fine and good, and which I worked so hard to create, remain."[3]

Despite trying to maintain a positive public face, in the weeks after Leopold's death, Trudi was surrounded by reminders of her late husband's infidelities. One of the first things she did after Leopold died was tear up the picture of Loeb he had kept in their home.[4] When going through the papers in his study, she found a dated list Leopold had kept of the men he'd had sex with.[5] But it was when the contents of Leopold's will were divulged that her determination to continue covering for Leopold crumbled.

In 1966, Leopold had drafted a will that left everything to Trudi, but his last will, written without her knowledge two months before his death, radically altered that. There were large monetary gifts included for Dave Fulford, Paul Henry, Eliud, and the most substantial gift for Tony, which would leave him with the Leopolds' condominium and the remainder of his estate after Trudi had died.[6] To lose so much to these men was too much to swallow. She contested the will less than a month after Leopold had died, and the legal battle that ensued dragged on for several years.[7]

As her case languished in court, Trudi's opinion of her husband continued to deteriorate, and eventually she began planning a tell-all style book of her own. If published, the book surely would have severely damaged the reputation Leopold had built.[8] However, she still hadn't finished by 1975, when author Hal Higdon published *The Crime of the Century*, the first nonfiction book to cover the Leopold-Loeb crime and hearing in a narrative, nonbiased, and detailed manner. Though Higdon had wanted to write about Leopold's life after prison, Trudi was looking to protect her market, so she told friends not to speak to him and threatened to sue Higdon if he quoted from Leopold's book or letters.[9] Trudi eventually enlisted the help of an author when it became clear that she couldn't finish her book alone, but when she died in 1987 her version of her life with Leopold remained unfinished and untold. Yet even with everyone connected to the crime gone, interest in the Leopold-Loeb case never really died.

Starting in the 1980s and continuing to the present day, dozens of fictional adaptations of the lives of Leopold and Loeb have emerged. And though the focus is almost always on the crime and trial, the work Leopold did to rehabilitate his image undoubtedly paid off. In 1924 he was seen as the dominant mastermind, and the "suggestible" Loeb was his "unwilling victim."[10] The story has now completely reversed, as playwright Stephen Dolginoff explained about his musical adaptation: "Leopold was so in love and so willing to do anything for Loeb that he finds himself being led down a horrible path."[11]

Much of this change in perception around Leopold's character has been credited to his supposed rehabilitation, but the question remains, was he really rehabilitated? In 1961 Leopold wrote: "Rehabilitation, to me, is an altering of the basic attitudes of a person. It is reflected in his conduct because, by and large, his conduct is a reflection, an acting-out of his basic ways of viewing the world."[12] By his own definition then, thirty-three years in prison and thirteen years of freedom had not rehabilitated the killer.

The Leopold who emerged from prison had a larger waistline and less hair than the one who had entered, but internally little had changed. He enjoyed the same poems and hobbies, retained the same ego, still considered Loeb his best friend, and even held a candle for the same girl. More importantly, throughout his entire life Leopold retained the philosophical ideas that he had used to justify killing Bobby Franks. Psychiatrists in 1924 noted that he often spoke about being a hedonist, and one explained: "He considers his own individual pleasure paramount to everything else. . . . He says that murder is a very small matter to weigh in the balance of his pleasure."[13] Less than a year before his death Leopold confirmed that this mindset was unchanged, writing: "I am what they call an individual hedonist, a fellow who believes that his <u>own</u> pleasure is the only good in the world."[14]

It was this philosophy that allowed him to manipulate money from vulnerable women, constantly cheat on his wife, commit statutory rape and charity fraud, all without a hint of remorse. He may not have killed again, but fundamentally he remained the same as the teenager who had murdered Bobby Franks on that sunny May afternoon in 1924.

ABBREVIATIONS

ARCHIVAL COLLECTIONS

ALPL   Abraham Lincoln Presidential Library
CBA   Church of the Brethren Archives
   RLP   Row-Leopold Papers
   PRR   Brethren Service Commission: Puerto Rico Records
CHM   Chicago History Museum
   NFLP   Nathan F. Leopold Papers
   HHP   Hal Higdon Papers
CIS   Cranbrook Institute of Science
   CISDP   Cranbrook Institute of Science Director's Papers
ISA   Illinois State Archives
   JDC   James Day Clemency File
   NLC   Nathan Leopold Clemency File
LC   Library of Congress
   CDP   Clarence Darrow Papers
   EGP   Elmer Gertz Papers
   JBMP   John Bartlow Martin Papers
NA   National Archives
   RSEH   Records of St. Elizabeth's Hospital
NRL   Newberry Research Library
CDMLSCUA, NUL   Charles Deering McCormick Library of
   Special Collections and University Archives
   HSHP   Harold S. Hulbert Papers
   LLC   Leopold and Loeb Collection
   RLP   Richard Loeb Papers

UCB   University of California Berkeley, Bancroft Library
ISP   Irving Stone Papers
JALP   John A. Larson Papers
**UCL, SCRC   University of Chicago Library, Special Collections
   Research Center**
BGSP   Bernard Glueck Sr. Papers
EWBP   Ernest Watson Burgess Papers
UI, SC   University of Iowa Iowa, Special Collections
PNL   Papers of Nathan Leopold
UM   University of Michigan
BHL   Bentley Historical Library
UW, AHC   University of Wyoming, American Heritage Center
AHGC, LLF   Alvin H. Goldstein Collection, Leopold-Loeb File

NAMES

Certain names have been changed or omitted to help preserve the privacy
of those individuals.

ADB	Adolf and Doris Ballenger
AGB	Adolf Gerhard Ballenger
AKB	Abel and Kathryn Brown
AMB	Abel Marchand Brown
CRD	Clarence and Ruby Darrow
CSD	Clarence Seward Darrow
DEF	David Edward Fulford Sr.
DLF	David and Lavila Fulford
EG	Elmer Gertz
EMG	Elmer and Mamie Gertz
EW	Eligius Weir
FML	Foreman Michael Lebold
GFL	Gertrude Feldman Leopold
HHW	Harriet Helen Williams
HMH	Hugh Marston Hefner
HSJ	Henry Stoddard Johnson
LL	Leonard Lyons
LSL	Leonard and Sylvia Lyons
NFL	Nathan F. Leopold Jr.
NGL	Nathan and Gertrude Leopold

PH	Paul Henry
RAL	Richard Albert Loeb
RGN	Ralph Geoffrey Newman
RWC	Robert Watson Claiborne
SEL	Samuel and Eleanor Lebold
SNL	Samuel Nathan Lebold
WBE	William and Betty Evans
WGS	William Grant Stratton
WHR	William Harold Row
WLR	William and Leona Row
WME	William Mortimer Evans

NEWSPAPERS

CDJ	*Chicago Daily Journal*
CDN	*Chicago Daily News*
CEA	*Chicago Evening American* and *Chicago American*
CEP	*Chicago Evening Post*
CHA	*Chicago Herald-American*
CHE	*Chicago Herald and Examiner*
CST	*Chicago Sun-Times*
CT	*Chicago Tribune*
JEHN	*Joliet Evening Herald-News*
NYT	*New York Times*
SEP	*Saturday Evening Post*
SLPD	*St. Louis Post-Dispatch*
SRN	*Sheridan Road News-Letter*
UHSD	*University High School Daily*

NOTES

INTRODUCTION

1. Aidem—Palazzo Pitti—Firenze tickets and Incontri Con La Musica program, 22/12, NFLP, CHM.

2. NFL to CSD, Undated, 1/3, CDP, LC.

3. NFL to RGN, 9.29.1963, 42/2, NFLP, CHM.

4. "Leopold Case as an Example," *Decatur Daily Review,* 3.15.1963.

CHAPTER 1

1. Nathan Leopold, "The Delinquent Boy and the Adult Criminal," 20/17, NFLP, CHM.

2. Paul Gilbert and Charles Lee Bryson, *Chicago and Its Makers* (Chicago: Felix Mendelsohn, 1929), 1037.

3. Report of South Side Ladies Sewing Society, *Annual Report of the United Hebrew Charities of Chicago v4-11* (1892–1899).

4. NFL to Walter Darling, 7.18.1964, 6/1, NFLP, CHM.

5. "At the Altar," *Chicago Inter-Ocean,* 6.12.1892.

6. NFL to HHW, 2.8.1958, 14/16, LLC, CDMLSCUA, NUL.

7. US Census Bureau, Thirteenth Census of the United States: 1910–Population Schedule, 3229-3223 Michigan Avenue, Chicago, Illinois.

8. Karl M. Bowman and H. S. Hulbert, *Report of Preliminary Neuro-Psychiatric Examination: Nathan Leopold,* 45, 4/1, LLC, CDMLSCUA, NUL.

9. Bowman and Hulbert, *Report of Leopold,* 4.

10. Ibid., 4–5.

11. Ibid., 4.

12. Ibid., 16.

13. Nathan F. Leopold Jr., *Life Plus 99 Years* (New York: Doubleday, 1958), 170.

14. H. S. Hulbert, "The Franks Case: Psychiatric Data, Interpretation and Opinion (Nathan Leopold)," 6, 2/1, HSHP, CDMLSCUA, NUL.

15. Bowman and Hulbert, *Report of Leopold*, 7–8.

16. Ibid., 32.

17. NFL to Joan and Jerome Cohen, 8.27.1970, 14/12, NFLP, CHM.

18. Hulbert, *Franks Case (Leopold)*, 2.

19. NFL to AKB, 8.24.1970, 3/12, NFLP, CHM.

20. Statements of Nathan F. Leopold, Jr. and Richard Albert Loeb, 259–60, HSHP, CDMLSCUA, NUL.

21. John Bartlow Martin, "Murder on His Conscience: Part One," *SEP*, 4.2.1955, 18.

22. John Bartlow Martin, "The Nathan Leopold Story," 20, 149/3-11, JBMP, LC.

23. Bowman and Hulbert, *Report of Leopold*, 34.

24. Ibid., 36.

25. *Illinois vs. NFL and RAL*, 2296–97.

26. Bowman and Hulbert, *Report of Leopold*, 34.

27. Hulbert, *Franks Case (Leopold)*, 3

28. Bowman and Hulbert, *Report of Leopold*, 32–33.

29. "Report of Dr. William A. White. A Psychiatric Diagnosis and Interpretation of the Two Defendants," 13, 2/1, HSHP, CDMLSCUA, NUL.

30. Bowman and Hulbert, *Report of Leopold*, 44.

31. White, *A Psychiatric Diagnosis*, 13.

32. Martin, *Nathan Leopold Story*, 16.

33. Interview with Don Lebold, 2/7, HHP, CHM.

34. Ibid.

35. NFL to EG, 3.4.1962, 20/20, LLC, CDMLSCUA, NUL.

36. Florence Westheimer to NFL, 7.14.1958, 19/21, NFLP, CHM.

37. Leopold, *Life Plus*, 31.

38. "Another Sale," *SRN*, 11.23.1900.

39. "Wildwood," *SRN*, 5.24.1901.

40. "Highland Park," *SRN*, 3.15.1901.

41. Elliot Miller and Jean Sogin, "Highland Park as a Summer Resort," Highland Park Public Library, 2.17.2016.

42. NFL to Laura Chase, 1.31.1959, 5/5, NFLP, CHM.

43. NFL to Katherine Hirsch, 6.11.1958, 13/2, NFLP, CHM.

44. "Fire Destroys Large Wildwood Residence," *Highland Park Press*, 12.31.1914.

45. "Official Real Estate Transfers," *Highland Park Press*, 3.11.1920.

46. Reuben H. Donnelley, *Lakeside Annual Directory of the City of Chicago* (Chicago: Lakeside Press, 1910), 108.

47. Bowman and Hulbert, *Report of Leopold*, 23.

48. "Death Notices," *CT*, 3.7.1911.

49. Bowman and Hulbert, *Report of Leopold*, 17.

50. Ibid., 18.

51. Ibid., 20.

52. Ibid., 18.

53. Ibid., 24.

54. Martin, *Murder Part One*, 86.

55. Bowman and Hulbert, *Report of Leopold*, 23–24.

56. *Illinois vs. NFL and RAL*, 495.

57. NFL to Walter Darling, 7.18.1964, 6/1, NFLP, CHM.

58. Richard Blodgett, *Federal Paper Board at Seventy-Five* (Connecticut: Greenwich, 1991), 90.

59. Ibid., 91.

60. John William Leonard, *Who's Who in Engineering* (New York: John W. Leonard Co. 1922), 94, 763.

61. Morris Paper Mills, *The Morris Story*.

62. "Residence Property," *The Economist*, 10.9.1915.

63. "Roofs and Realty," *Chicago Inter-Ocean*, 1.3.1886.

64. Martin, *Nathan Leopold Story*, 20.

65. Bowman and Hulbert, *Report of Leopold*, 20–21.

66. Harvard School for Boys, *Harvard School Review* (Chicago: 1920), 8–9.

67. John J. Schobinger, *Fifty Years in the Harvard School* (1925).

68. Bowman and Hulbert, *Report of Leopold*, 24–25.

69. Transfer Certificate of High School Credits, 1/8, NFLP, CHM.

70. *Harvard School Review* (1920).

71. Camp Highlands, *Dinglebat* (Sayner, WI: 1917), 38.

72. Martin, *Nathan Leopold Story*, 25–26.

73. Edward Howe Forbush, *Some Under-Water Activities of Certain Waterfowl* (Boston: Wright & Potter, 1922), 20.

74. NFL to Jean Parker, 8.18.1966, 16/8, NFLP, CHM.

75. Bernard Glueck, "Psycho-Analytic Reflections on Two Homicides," 42, 1/5, BGSP, SCRC, UCL.

76. Katherine Hirsch to NFL, 4.22.1958, 13/2, NFLP, CHM.

77. Colin Sanborn to EG, 1.28.1958, 38/3, LLC, CDMLSCUA, NUL.

78. *Illinois vs. NFL and RAL*, 479.

79. Martin, *Nathan Leopold Story*, 19.

80. "Our Frontispiece," *Wilson Bulletin* (March 1923).

81. Martin, *Nathan Leopold Story*, 20–21.

82. Nathan F. Leopold Jr., "General Notes: Yellow-Crowned Night Heron at Chicago," *Auk* (April 1918)· 477.

83. James D. Watson, George Porter Lewis, and Nathan F. Leopold Jr., *Spring Migration Notes of the Chicago Area* (1920).

84. "Recent Literature: Spring Migration Notes of the Chicago Area," *Auk* (October 1920): 616.

85. Bowman and Hulbert, *Report of Leopold*, 18–19.

86. Ibid., 19.

87. NFL to EG, 6.24.1957, 11/7, LLC, CDMLSCUA, NUL.

88. Bowman and Hulbert, *Report of Leopold*, 54.

89. Ibid., 65.

90. Bernard Glueck et al.,"Joint Report: Nathan F. Leopold Jr. and Ricard Loeb," 21, 1/2, Bernard Glueck Sr. Papers, SCRC, UCL.

91. Bowman and Hulbert, *Report of Leopold*, 66–67.

92. Ibid., 55.

93. Ibid.

94. Ibid.

95. "Psycho-Analytic Reflections on Two Homicides," 7.

96. Vice Commission of Chicago, *The Social Evil in Chicago* (Chicago: Gunthorp-Warren, 1911), 298.

97. Harvey Warren Zorbaugh, *The Gold Coast and the Slum: A Sociological Study of Chicago's Near North Side* (Chicago: University of Chicago Press, 1929), 100–101.

98. Ibid.

99. Statements of NFL and RAL, 264.

100. Army Registration Cards for Adolf G Ballenberg and Foreman N Leopold (1917).

101. Leonard, *Who's Who*, 94, 763.

102. University of Michigan, *Michiganensian* (Ann Arbor: 1919), 156.

103. Martin, *Nathan Leopold Story*, 95.

104. War Record of American Jews: Foreman Nathan Leopold.

105. Bernard Glueck, "A Psychiatric Diagnosis and Interpretation of the Two Defendants," 18, 2/1, HSHP, CDMLSCUA, NUL.

106. NFL to DEF, 4.17.1955, 33/35, NFLP, CHM.

107. Bowman and Hulbert, *Report of Leopold*, 40–41.

108. *Illinois vs. NFL and RAL*, 1496–97.

109. Ibid.

CHAPTER 2

1. William A. White, Notes, 17, 418/37, RSEH, NA.

2. Morris Robert Werner, *Julius Rosenwald: The Life of a Practical Humanitarian* (New York: Harper & Brothers, 1939), 67–68.

3. "Society," *Sentinel*, 11.3.1911.

4. Marion R. Stadeker, "Meeting of Chicago Jewish Committee for Palestinian Welfare," *Sentinel*, 1.2.1914.

5. "Suffragists Plan Chicago Campaign," *Chicago Inter-Ocean*, 5.11.1913.

6. "Society," *Sentinel*, 7.2.1915.

7. "Awards at the South Shore Country Club Horse Show, Chicago June 21, 22, 23, 1917," *Saddle and Horse Show Chronicle*, 12.16.1917–1.30.1918.

8. Karl M. Bowman and H. S. Hulbert, *Report of Preliminary Neuro-Psychiatric Examination: Richard Loeb*, 12, 4/2, LLC, CDMLSCUA, NUL.

9. Ibid., 31–33.

10. Ibid., 72–75.

11. The Editor, "Humanity," *Richard's Magazine* (March 1916): 15.

12. Theodore Roosevelt to RAL, 5.8.1916, Scrapbook 5, Julius Rosenwald Papers, SCRC, UCL.

13. Bowman and Hulbert, *Report of Loeb*, 6.

14. "Marion Ascoli Speaks of Her Childhood and Memories of Loeb-Leopold," *Chicago Jewish History*, Spring 1995, 14.

15. Bowman and Hulbert, *Report of Loeb*, 34–35.

16. Ibid., 82.

17. Dan Pollock, "How a Freshman Officer Became a Murderer," *Midway*, 6.11.1968.

18. Ibid.

19. *"Dick Loeb Leads Frosh in Cheers,"* UHSD, 4.11.1918.

20. "Freshmen Elect Officers," *UHSD*, 1.16.1918.

21. "Scientist Nearly Killed!" *UHSD*, 12.21.1917.

22. Leopold, *Life Plus*, 26.

23. *Illinois vs. NFL and RAL*, 1859–60.

24. Bowman and Hulbert, *Report of Loeb*, 24.

25. "Members and New Applicants Invited to Campus Dinner," *Daily Maroon*, 1.20.1920.

26. Bowman and Hulbert, *Report of Loeb*, 80–81.

27. Ibid., 17.

28. White, *A Psychiatric Diagnosis*, 16.

29. White, *Notes*, 17.

30. Martin, *Nathan Leopold Story*, 35.

31. Ibid., 38.

32. Glueck et al., *Joint Report*, 45.

33. NFL to Katherine Strom, 4.3.1959, 18/14, NFLP, CHM.

34. White, *A Psychiatric Diagnosis*, 14.

35. Martin, *Nathan Leopold Story*, 32.

36. "Dr. Hall's Report on Loeb," *CHE*, 8.11.1924.

37. NFL to John Pick, 12.19.1957, 37/6, NFLP, CHM.

38. *Illinois vs. NFL and RAL*, 1869.

39. Glueck, *Psycho-Analytic Reflections*, 1.

40. *Illinois vs. NFL and RAL*, 1867.

41. Ibid., 1452.

42. Ibid., 1450.

43. Harold Hulbert, "Abstract of the Preliminary Neuro-Psychiatric Examination of Nathan Leopold," 4, 2/1, HSHP, CDMLSCUA, NUL.

44. Glueck, *Psycho-Analytic Reflections*, 1.

45. Bowman and Hulbert, *Report of Leopold*, 13.

46. Ibid., 82–83.

47. Ibid.

48. Hall, *Report on Loeb*.

49. Dorothea Vent to Members of the Chicago Ornithological Society, 12.12.1922, 1/1, Benjamin T. Gault Papers, Peggy Notebaert Nature Museum.

50. Martin, *Nathan Leopold Story*, 31.

51. Ibid.

52. Jesse Lowe Smith Diary 1921, Highland Park Public Library.

53. Wilhelm Miller, "Bird Gardens in the City," *Country Life in America* (August 1914).

54. "New Angles to Slayers' Character Revealed," *Huntington Herald*, 8.5.1924.

55. Ibid.

56. Nathan F. Leopold Jr. vs. Meyer Levin et. al., *Deposition*, 57, (1960). 6/35, Robert Bergstrom Papers, NRL.

57. "Tell New Loeb-Leopold Plot," *CDJ*, 8.30.1924.

58. Ibid.

59. University of Chicago, *Cap and Gown* (1919), 204–207.

60. NFL to HHW, 10.14.1958, 19/12, NFLP, CHM.

61. Statements of NFL and RAL, 244.

62. Glueck, *A Psychiatric Diagnosis*, 23.

63. White, *A Psychiatric Diagnosis*, 16.

64. Bowman and Hulbert, *Report of Leopold*, 16.

65. Hulbert, *Franks Case (Leopold)*, 10.

CHAPTER 3

1. RAL to Recorder, 7.15.1921, Box 10, College of Literature, Science and the Arts, BHL, UM.

2. Bowman and Hulbert, *Report of Loeb*, 27.

3. Hal Higdon, *Leopold and Loeb: The Crime of the Century* (New York: G. P. Putnam's Sons, 1975), 20.

4. *Illinois vs. NFL and RAL*, 1951.

5. Bowman and Hulbert, *Report of Leopold*, 28.

6. Notes on Compulsion (1960), 32/1, NFLP, CHM.

7. Lillian Ross, *Here But Not Here: A Love Story* (New York: Random House, 1998), 40.

8. Leopold, *Life Plus*, 130.

9. "Obituary," *Sentinel*, 10.21.1921.

10. Leopold, *Life Plus*, 241.

11. *Illinois vs. NFL and RL*, 1324–25.

12. "Women Reveal How Leopold Ruled Birds," *CDN*, 6.25.1924.

13. Glueck, *Psycho-Analytic Reflections*, 7.

14. Official Students' Directory (Ann Arbor: University of Michigan, 1921), 238, 241.

15. Bowman and Hulbert, *Report of Leopold*, 89–90.

16. *Illinois vs. NFL and RAL*, 1771.

17. Interview with Max Schrayer, 2/7, HHP, CHM.

18. Statements of NFL and RAL, 516.

19. "Loeb on Stand in Ream Case," *CEA*, 1.4.1927.

20. Bowman and Hulbert, *Report of Leopold*, 59.

21. *Illinois vs. NFL and RAL*, 1451.

22. *Decennial Anniversary and Initiation*, Myron Chon Scrapbook, BHL, UM.

23. *Illinois vs. NFL and RAL*, 4333.

24. Interview with Max Schrayer, 2/7, HHP, CHM.

25. Charles V. Slattery, "Loeb's Sweetheart Lies, Crowe Says," *CHE*, 8.8.1924.

26. Clayton Smith, *Tales by the Fireside* (Charlevoix: Trapper Cabin Press, 1996), 14.

27. Martin, *Nathan Leopold Story*, 41.

28. Ibid.

29. Howard Whitman, "The College Fraternity Crisis Part One," 9, *Collier's*, 1.8.1949.

30. "Spotlight Vaudeville!" *The Michigan Daily*, 1.19.1921.

31. Bowman and Hulbert, *Report of Leopold*, 29.

32. "Differed in College Life," *New York Times*, 6.2.1924.

33. White, *Notes*, 19.

34. Bowman and Hulbert, *Report of Leopold*, 61.

35. Statements of NFL and RAL, 260.

36. Ibid.

37. Bowman and Hulbert, *Report of Leopold*, 30.

38. University of Chicago transcript for Nathan Freudenthal Leopold Jr., 2/9, RLP, CBA.

39. Martin, *Nathan Leopold Story*, 26.

40. NFL to Patricia and William Stein, 7.7.1968, 3/1 NFLP, CHM.

41. Bowman and Hulbert, *Report of Leopold*, 45.

42. "New Link in Franks Evidence is Uncovered," *CHE*, 6.27.1924.

43. NFL to Jean Parker, 9.25.1966, 16/8, NFLP, CHM.

44. Morrow Krum, "Find U. of C. Co-ed Friend of Leopold," *CT*, 6.2.1924.

45. Ibid.

46. Bowman and Hulbert, *Report of Leopold*, 51.

47. Leopold, *Life Plus*, 30.

48. Bowman and Hulbert, *Report of Leopold*, 31.

49. "Chicago Anglers Are Lucky on First Trip," *Miami News*, 4.2.1923.

50. NFL to Jeanne Hall, 3.11.1959, 12/15, NFLP, CHM.

51. NFL to Patricia and William Stein, 7.7.1968, 3/1 NFLP, CHM.

52. "Youngest Senior Graduates at 17," *Michigan Daily*, 6.3.1923.

53. "Editorial: Tap and Reveille," *Michigan Daily*, 6.18.1923.

54. *The Kirtland's Warbler in Its Summer Home*, James McGillivray Collection, CHM.

55. NFL to Katherine Friedman, 6.22.1923, 16/38 CISDP, CIS.

56. Nathan Leopold, "The Kirtland's Warbler in Its Summer Home," *Auk* (January 1924): 55.

57. Ibid., 58.

58. Statements of NFL and RAL, 439.

59. Bowman and Hulbert, *Report of Leopold*, 37.

60. White, *A Psychiatric Diagnosis*, 17.

61. "Dr. William Healy's Report (Richard Loeb)," 1, 2/1, HSHP, CDMLS-CUA, NUL.

62. University of Chicago transcript, Richard Albert Loeb.

63. H. S. Hulbert, "The Franks Case: Psychiatric Data, Interpretation and Opinion (Richard Loeb)," 10, 120/1, EGP, LC.

64. Higdon, Interviews with Schrayer, Mayer, and Brown, 2/7, HHP, CHM.

65. Virginia Gardner, "Eleven Years After the Crime of Loeb and Leopold," *CT*, 5.19.1935.

66. White, *A Psychiatric Diagnosis*, 16.

67. Groves B Smith, "Parole Progress Report," 1.27.1948, 4, NLC, ISA.

68. White, *A Psychiatric Diagnosis*, 25.

69. Statements of NFL and RAL, 423.

70. Ibid., 427.

71. Ibid., 426.

72. Ibid., 426.

73. Ibid., 430–31.

74. Ibid., 431–32.

75. Ibid., 433.

76. T. S. Palmer, "The Forty-First Stated Meeting of the American Ornithologist's Union," *Auk* (January 1924): 129.

77. *Illinois vs. NFL and RAL*, 1503–504.

CHAPTER 4

1. Bowman and Hulbert, *Report of Leopold*, 95.

2. Bowman and Hulbert, *Report of Loeb*, 87–88.

3. Ibid., 89.

4. Ibid.
5. Bowman and Hulbert, *Report of Loeb*, 90.
6. Ibid., 95.
7. *Illinois vs. NFL and RAL*, 1449–50.
8. Bowman and Hulbert, *Report of Loeb*, 46.
9. Glueck, *A Psychiatric Diagnosis*, 24.
10. White, *A Psychiatric Diagnosis*, 18.
11. Glueck, *A Psychiatric Diagnosis*, 25.
12. Hall, *Report on Loeb*.
13. Hulbert, *Abstract of Leopold*, 25.
14. Ibid., 26.
15. Bowman and Hulbert, *Report of Leopold*, 111.
16. Bowman and Hulbert, *Report of Loeb*, 122.
17. Bowman and Hulbert, *Report of Leopold*, 35.
18. Ibid., 101.
19. White, *Notes*, 19.
20. Hulbert, *Abstract of Leopold*, 27.
21. "Crowe Tells Jury How Three Boys Escaped Franks' Killers," *CDJ*, 6.4.1924.
22. Bowman and Hulbert, *Report of Loeb*, 103.
23. White, *A Psychiatric Diagnosis*, 7.
24. Hall, *Report on Loeb*.
25. White, *A Psychiatric Diagnosis*, 18.
26. *Illinois vs. NFL and RAL*, 1869.
27. Bowman and Hulbert, *Report of Leopold*, 33.
28. *Illinois vs. NFL and RAL*, 208.
29. Statements of NFL and RAL, 391.
30. Bowman and Hulbert, *Report of Leopold*, 10.
31. Helen Rose, *Just Make Them Beautiful* (California: Dennis-Landman, 1976), 21.
32. "'Likely and Ready to Hang,' Writes Leopold," *CEA*, 8.2.1924.
33. Rose, *Just Make*, 21.
34. *Illinois vs. NFL and RAL*, 1451–52.
35. Bowman and Hulbert, *Report of Loeb*, 99.
36. Statements of NFL and RAL, 297.
37. Identification Card, 4/2, HSHP, CDMLSCUA, NUL.
38. White, *Notes*, 10.
39. Leopold, *Life Plus*, 28.
40. Statements of NFL and RAL, 202.
41. *Illinois vs. NFL and RAL*, 145.
42. Statements of NFL and RAL, 49–50.

CHAPTER 5

1. Ibid., 448.
2. Ibid., 55.
3. Ibid., 215–16.
4. Ibid., 58.
5. Ibid., 217.
6. Ibid., 219.
7. NFL to Melinda Holub, 7.11.1964, 3/6, NFLP, CHM.
8. Interviews with Robert Asher and Joseph Eisendrath, 2/7, HHP, CHM.
9. *Harvard School Review* (1924), 108.
10. Christopher Meindl, *In Search of History: Leopold and Loeb: Born Killers*, History Channel (1998).
11. Statements of NFL and RAL, 220–21.
12. Ibid., 5.
13. Bowman and Hulbert, *Report of Loeb*, 108.
14. Statements of NFL and RAL, 63.
15. Ibid.
16. Ibid., 64–65.
17. Ibid., 65.
18. Ibid., 34–35.
19. Ibid., 6.
20. George Johnson to Sir, 5.21.1924, 2/8, HSHP, CDMLSCUA, NUL.
21. Statements of NFL and RAL, 68.
22. Ibid., 25.
23. Ibid., 69.
24. Ibid., 70.
25. Ibid., 71.
26. Leopold, *Life Plus*, 27–28.
27. Statements of NFL and RAL, 72.
28. Ibid., 3–4.
29. Inquest on the Body of Robert E. Franks, 5.23.1924, Cook County Medical Examiner's Office.
30. Statements of NFL and RAL, 8.
31. Ibid., 29.
32. *Illinois vs. NFL and RAL*, 74–75.

CHAPTER 6

1. Leopold, *Life Plus*, 28–29.
2. "Believe Moron Killed Boy," *CDJ*, 5.23.1924.
3. Gene Flack, "Slain by Gag, Coroner Finds," *CHE*, 5.24.1924.

4. *Illinois vs. NFL and RAL*, 95.

5. J. McCann, D. Reay, J. Siebert, B. G. Stephens, & S. Wirtz, "Postmortem Perianal Findings in Children," *American Journal of Forensic Medicine and Pathology*, (December 1996): 289–98.

6. "Gray Auto Murder Clue," *CEP*, 5.23.1924.

7. "Franks Slayer Sends Wreath to Bier," *CHE*, 5.26.1924.

8. *Illinois vs. NFL and RAL*, 1328–29.

9. Ibid., 390.

10. Flack, *Slain by Gag*.

11. Inquest on the Body of Robert E. Franks, 5.23.1924, Cook County Medical Examiner's Office.

12. Bowman and Hulbert, *Report of Leopold*, 105.

13. Leopold, *Life Plus*, 29.

14. Statements of NFL and RAL, 231–232.

15. Leopold, *Life Plus*, 30.

16. *Illinois vs. NFL and RAL*, 692.

17. "Are They Sane? Fathers Ask," *CT*, 6.7.1924.

18. Nathan Leopold "May 25, 1924," 4/2, HSHP, CDMLSCUA, NUL.

19. Leopold, *Life Plus*, 33–34.

20. *Illinois vs. NFL and RAL*, 441–42.

21. Ibid., 445.

22. "State to Use Leopold's Girl Friend in Proving His Sanity," *CDJ*, 6.2.1924.

23. *Illinois vs. NFL and RAL*, 468.

24. Ibid., 47.

25. Statements of NFL and RAL, 186.

26. Ibid., 397–404.

27. Leopold, *Life Plus*, 35.

28. *Illinois vs. NFL and RAL*, 483.

29. Leopold, *Life Plus*, 37.

30. Ibid., 38.

31. Statements of NFL and RAL, 190.

32. *Illinois vs. NFL and RAL*, 461–62.

33. Statements of NFL and RAL, 425.

34. Ibid., 434.

35. "Shake Leopold-Loeb Alibi," *CT*, 5.31.1924.

36. Statements of NFL and RAL, 242–43.

37. *Illinois vs. NFL and RAL*, 56.

38. Leopold, *Life Plus*, 43.

39. Maurine Watkins, "Big Experience Either Way, Is Nathan's View," *CT*, 5.31.1924.

40. "Poison Discovered in Leopold Boy's Room," *CHE*, 5.31.1924.

41. *Illinois vs. NFL and RL*, 391.

42. Ibid.

43. Howard G. Mayer, "Writer with Lads Heard Bold Tale of Denial," *CEA*, 5.31.1924.

44. Interview with Howard Mayer, 2/7, HHP, CHM.

45. "Youth Retain Friends' Faith during Their Long Ordeal," *CT*, 5.31.1924.

46. Adele Loeb to Mr. and Mrs. Fies, 5.31.1924, RLP, CDMLSCUA, NUL.

47. "Flattery and Sentiment Brought Slayers' Confessions, Prosecutors Reveal," *CHE*, 6.10.1924.

48. Statements of NFL and RL, 459.

49. Joseph P. Savage, *A Man Named Savage* (New York: Vantage Press, 1975), 85.

50. Nathan Leopold, draft of *Life Plus 99 Years*, 46–47, 24/2, NFLP, CHM.

51. Statements of NFL and RL, 449–478.

52. Ibid., 486.

53. Ibid., 489–90.

54. Interview with Ethel Cronson, 2/8, HHP, CHM.

55. *Illinois vs. NFL and RAL*, 716.

56. Ibid., 195.

57. Ibid., 199.

58. Ibid., 62.

59. Ibid.

60. Ibid., 923–25.

61. Statements of NFL and RAL, 249.

62. Ibid., 75.

63. Leopold, *Life Plus*, 50.

64. Ibid., 48.

CHAPTER 7

1. "Young Leopold Asks Hughes for Chance to Commit Suicide," *CDJ*, 5.31.1924.

2. Genevieve Forbes, "Old Fashioned Discipline Need of Leopold Jr.," *CT*, 6.2.1924.

3. *Illinois vs. NFL and RAL*, 478–79.

4. Morrow Krum, "'This'll Be the Making of Me,' Says Loeb Boy," *CT*, 6.2.1924.

5. Ibid.

6. Larry Smith, "Blames Partner for Killing Boy Kidnap Victim," *Akron Beacon Journal*, 6.2.1924.

7. Statements of NFL and RAL, 170–95.

8. Ibid., 265, 276.

9. Martin, *Nathan Leopold Story*, 50.

10. Leo M. Glassman, *Biographical Encyclopedia of American Jewry* (New York: Maurice Jacobs & Leo M. Glassman, 1935), 21–22.

11. Statements of NFL and RAL, 168.

12. Leopold, *Life Plus*, 50–51.

13. "Final Ransom Note Found on Train in East; Winds Up Plot," *CDN*, 6.2.1924.

14. Ibid.

15. "Leopold and Loeb Jailed," *CEP*, 6.2.1924.

16. "Identifies Loeb in Moron Gland Attack on Midway," *CDJ*, 6.2.1924.

17. "Franks Story to Jury," *CDJ*, 6.3.1924.

18. "Loeb Turns 'Teacher,'" *CDN*, 6.3.1924.

19. Leopold, *Life Plus*, 54.

20. Clarence Darrow, *The Story of My Life* (New York: Charles Scribner's Sons, 1932), 231.

21. James Doherty, "Quick Trial for Boy Slayers," *CT*, 6.3.1924.

22. Statements of NFL and RAL, 265.

23. Leopold, *Life Plus*, 53.

24. Chicago Community Trust, *Reports Comprising the Survey of the Cook County Jail* (Chicago: Calumet Publishing Co., 1922), 78–79.

25. Ibid., 74.

26. "Franks Case Perjury Fought," *CDN*, 6.4.1924.

27. Leopold, *Life Plus*, 57.

28. "Witnesses Called by Grand Jury in Franks Murder," *CEP*, 6.3.1924.

29. "Tracy Bullet Fits Pistol of Franks Killers," *CDJ*, 6.3.1924.

30. "Slain in Auto Near Midway," *CT*, 11.26.1923.

31. Melvin Lindenthal Wolf, Form 18, 5.7.1924, Chicago Medical Examiner's Office.

32. Winifred Black, "Winifred Black Calls Loeb the Faun and Leopold the Svengali," *CHE*, 6.12.1924.

33. Bowman and Hulbert, *Report of Leopold*, 144.

34. Ibid., 3.

35. "Diagnostic Report for Mr. Bachrach and Mr. Darrow from Doctor Hulbert on Nathan Leopold," 2, 2/1, CDMLSCUA, NUL.

36. Mary Field Parton, 1924 Agenda, June 17, 58/5, Margaret Parton Papers, University of Oregon Library.

37. Glueck, *A Psychiatric Diagnosis*, 12.

38. Glueck et al., *Joint Report*, 10.

39. Ibid.

40. White, *Notes*, 19.

41. *Illinois vs. NFL and RAL*, 1508.

42. White, *Notes*, 19.

43. Leopold, *Life Plus*, 49.

44. Hall, *Report on Loeb*.

45. White, *Notes*, 9–10.

46. Hall, *Report on Loeb.*

47. RAL to Anna and Albert Loeb, 7.28.1924, 420/3, ISP, BL, UCB.

48. Leopold, *Life Plus*, 50.

49. Glueck et al., *Joint Report*, 10.

50. "Diagnostic Report for Mr. Bachrach and Mr. Darrow from Doctor Hulbert, on Richard Loeb," 10, 2/1, HSHP, CDMLSCUA, NUL.

51. Anna Loeb to Thomas Loeb, 6.13.1924, RLP, CDMLSCUA, NUL.

52. Bowman and Hulbert, *Report of Leopold*, 35.

53. *Illinois vs. NFL and RAL*, 2029.

54. Ibid., 1322–23.

55. *Leopold. vs. Levin*, Deposition (1960), 189–90.

56. Ibid., 92.

57. Bowman and Hulbert, *Report of Loeb*, 67.

58. "Loeb Second Cousin of Boy He Kidnaped," *CHE*, 6.1.1924.

59. "Crowe Attacks Franks' Killers' 'Insane' Defense," *CT*, 7.18.1924.

60. Salmon Levinson to J. Reuben Clark, 6.18.1924, 56/12, Salmon Levinson Papers, SCRC, UCL.

CHAPTER 8

1. Lindsay Denison, "Dickie Loeb's Soul Poisoned by Leopold, as Adventure in Crime, Neighbors Believe," *Springfield Missouri Republican*, 6.8.1924.

2. Perry M. Lichtenstein, "Alienist Calls Leopold 'A Moral Monstrosity,'" *Times* (Munster, Indiana), 7.5.1924.

3. Denison, *Dickie Loeb's.*

4. Observer, "Vignettes of Main Characters in the Franks Trial," *CEP*, 7.28.1924.

5. "Concludes Tests of Franks Killers," *CEP*, 6.17.1924.

6. Paul Y. Anderson, "A Visit to Leopold and Loeb in the Chicago Jail and Their Conversations with Reporters," *SLPD*, 7.21.1924.

7. Ibid.

8. Ibid.

9. "Leopold Spurns Insanity Defense," *CHE*, 6.18.1924.

10. Clarence Darrow to Paul Darrow, 7.20.1924, Clarence Darrow Collection, University of Minnesota Law Library.

11. Walter Bachrach to Adolf Meyer, 2.6.1925, 1/130/1, Johns Hopkins.

12. Martin, *Nathan Leopold Story*, 69.

13. "Slayers Blase in Courtroom," *CDJ*, 7.21.1924.

14. "Slayers Josh Reporters," *CDN*, 7.23.1924.

15. Ibid.

16. "Police Guard at Doorway," *CDJ*, 7.23.1924.

17. George R. Holmes, "Loeb Boy Aided in Solving Franks Case," *Mount Vernon Daily Argus*, 7.25.1924.

18. Arthur Brisbane, "Today," *CHE*, 7.30.1924.

19. "Franks Slayers Listen Unmoved to Death Demand," *New York Evening Post*, 7.23.1924.

20. *Illinois vs. NFL and RAL*, 21.

21. "Franks on Stand," *CEP*, 7.23.1924.

22. *Illinois vs. NFL and RAL*, 67.

23. Ibid., 89–90.

24. US Census Bureau, Fifteenth Census of the United States: 1930—Population Schedule, Drake Hotel, Chicago, Illinois.

25. Mary G. Baker Eddy, *Science and Health with Key to the Scriptures* (Boston: E. J. Foster Eddy, 1895), 185.

26. "Let Law Take Its Course, Says Franks, Father of Slain Boy," *CDJ*, 5.31.1924.

27. *Illinois vs. NFL and RAL*, 161.

28. James Glassner to Mrs. Glassner, 7.29.1924, 7/90, Arthur and Leila Weinberg Papers, NRL.

29. "Franks on Stand," *CEP*, 7.23.1924.

30. Glueck et al., *Joint Report*, 42.

31. "Heat in Courtroom about All That Bothers Loeb and Leopold; Otherwise They Feel Fine," *CT*, 7.24.1924.

32. Ruth Hamerman, "High School Miss Gives Impressions of Franks Trial," *CEP*, 8.18.1924.

33. "Bars Can't Keep Slayers From Perfect Sunday," *CT*, 7.28.1924.

34. "Boys Not Angry at Friends Who Have Testified," *Oakland Tribune*, 7.25.1924.

35. Tyrrell Krum, "Slayers Spurn Sympathy," *CT*, 7.26.1924.

36. *Illinois vs. NFL and RAL*, 1773.

37. RAL to Anna and Albert Loeb, 7.28.1924, 420/3, ISP, BL, UCB.

38. Leopold, *Life Plus*, 67.

39. *Illinois vs. NFL and RAL*, 400.

40. Ibid., 494–95.

41. Leopold, *Life Plus*, 68.

42. "Killers Staked Human Prey," *CDJ*, 6.4.1924.

43. *Illinois vs. NFL and RAL*, 584.

44. "Lively Session Cheers Up Both Boys, Bored Before," *CDN*, 7.30.1924.

45. Leopold, draft of *Life Plus* 66, 24/2.

46. Henry Valance, "The Coal Bin," *The Birmingham News*, 6.14.1924.

47. "Bare Sensational Crimes of Leopold, Senior," 8.1.1924 and Karl Reeve, "Leopold Shop Mangles Child" 8.3.1924, *Chicago Daily Worker*.

48. Rev. W. M. Sykes, "Evolution," *Presbyterian Standard*, 9.16.1924.

49. 1924 Day Book, July 26, Box 2, Edwin Herbert Lewis Papers, SCRC, UCL.

50. Edwin Herbert Lewis, *Sallie's Newspaper* (Chicago: Hyman-McGee, 1924).

CHAPTER 9

1. *Illinois vs. NFL and RAL*, 978–79.

2. William White to Walter Bachrach, 8.7.1924, 418/27, RSEH, NA.

3. Horace Wade, "Teddy Bears in Arms Appeal to Horace," *CEA*, 8.7.1924.

4. "Dickie Joyous over Girl Pals' Loyalty; So Babe Is Happy, Too," *CDJ*, 8.7.1924.

5. *Illinois vs. NFL and RAL*, 1331.

6. Ibid., 1488.

7. Glueck, *A Psychiatric Diagnosis*, 14.

8. "Leopold Jokes about Being Hanged with Reporter," *CEA*, 8.4.1924.

9. Ibid.

10. *Illinois vs. NFL and RAL*, 1450.

11. *CDN*, 8.4.1924.

12. *Illinois vs. NFL and RAL*, 1483.

13. Glueck, *A Psychiatric Diagnosis*, 12.

14. *Illinois vs. NFL and RAL*, 1452–53.

15. Paul Y. Anderson, "Death Preferable to Loss of Dignity, Says Leopold," *SLPD*, 8.4.1924.

16. Ibid.

17. *Illinois vs. NFL and RAL*, 1677.

18. Ibid., 2924.

19. William Anthony M'Guire, "Playwright Finds Franks Case Drama Lies in Father's Tragedy," *CHE*, 8.12.1924.

20. *Illinois vs. NFL and RAL*, 2656.

21. Walter Bachrach to William Healy, 8.14.1924, 418/27, RSEH, NA.

22. "Starts Plea to Hang Leopold and Loeb," *CDN*, 8.19.1924.

23. "Noose, Not Mercy, State Asks," *CEA*, 8.20.1924.

24. "'It's Too Much,' Says Franks, Quitting Vigil at Trial First Time," *CDJ*, 8.21.1924.

25. *Illinois vs. NFL and RAL*, 3685–86.

26. "Sorry for Boys in Plot-Loeb," *CDJ*, 8.21.1924.

27. *Illinois vs. NFL and RAL*, 3878.

28. Ibid., 4045.

29. Ibid., 4038.

30. Ibid., 3941–42.

31. Ibid., 3976–77.

32. Ibid., 4112–13.

33. Leopold, *Life Plus*, 73.

34. "Speeches Will End Today," *CT*, 2.9.1898.

35. John Ashenhurst, "'Hang Them Like Mad Dogs'-Crowe," *CEA*, 8.16.1924.

36. *Illinois vs. NFL and RAL*, 4187.

37. "Babe's Sorry Trial's Over," *CDJ*, 8.28.1924.

38. *Illinois vs. NFL and RAL*, 4229–30.

39. Ibid., 4329–30.

40. Ibid., 4365.

41. "Caverly Ponders; Boys Joke," *CEA*, 8.29.1924.

42. Leopold, *Life Plus*, 59.

43. Anderson, "Death Preferable."

44. Leopold, *Life Plus*, 73.

45. Ibid., 73–74.

46. *Likely and Ready*.

47. NFL to June Matheson, 6.25.1958, 15/5, NFLP, CHM.

48. William Cullen Bryant, *Poems* (Boston: Russell, Odiorne, and Metcalf, 1834), 21–22.

49. *Likely and Ready*.

50. "Judge Caverly's Decision," *CEP*, 9.10.1924.

51. Ibid.

52. Leopold, *Life Plus*, 78.

53. Ibid., 79.

54. "Slayers Order 3-Inch Steaks to Celebrate," *CEA*, 9.10.1924.

55. NFL to CSD, Undated, 1/3, CDP, LC.

56. Ibid.

57. "Darrow Got $65,000 from Loeb, Leopold," *Boston Daily Globe*, 12.31.1927.

58. William Weinfeld, "Income of Lawyers, 1929–48," *Survey of Current Businesses* (August 1949): 18.

59. "Killers May Do World Good," *CDJ*, 9.17.1924.

CHAPTER 10

1. Leopold, *Life Plus*, 80.

2. "Slayers' Trip from Jail to Prison," *CT*, 9.12.1924.

3. *Report of the Commissioners of the Illinois State Penitentiary at Joliet for the Two Years Ending September 30, 1898* (Springfield: Phillips Bros., 1901), 11.

4. "The Workings of the Indeterminate-Sentence Law and the Parole System in Illinois" (1928), 153.

5. Leopold, *Life Plus*, 82.

6. Ibid., 84.

7. Martin, *Nathan Leopold Story*, 70.

8. "Killers Weep in Prison," *CDJ*, 9.12.1924.

9. Charles V. Slattery, "Slayers Are Meek in Convict Garb," *CHE*, 9.13.1924.

10. Willis C. O'Rourke, "Bar Loeb from Seeing Leopold," *CEA*, 9.12.1924.

11. "Girl Friends Write to Loeb," *CDJ*, 9.16.1924.

12. Leopold, *Life Plus*, 97–98.

13. "The Adaptation of Nathan Leopold," 4, 1/4, NFLP, CHM.

14. Walter B. Martin to NFL, 1.9.1960, 15/4, NFLP, CHM.

15. *Adaptation*, 11.

16. Ibid., 9

17. Joliet Discharge Register, 243.204, Illinois State Archives.

18. Intelligence Ratings for the Fiscal Years 1944–1955, Joliet-Stateville, Box 5, JRP, ALPL.

19. "Dr. William Healy's Report (Nathan Leopold)," 1, 2/1, HSHP, CDMLS-CUA, NUL.

20. Ibid., 8.

21. "Leopold, Loeb, Ask to Teach in Prison School," *CEP*, 9.20.1924.

22. Leopold, *Life Plus*, 86.

23. Martin, *Nathan Leopold Story*, 90.

24. "Mrs. Loeb Held in Charlevoix," *CDJ*, 9.24.1924.

25. Leopold, draft of *Life Plus*, 53, 25/1.

26. RAL to CRD, 4.15.1926, 1/3, CDP, LC.

27. Walter B. Martin to NFL, 1.9.1960, 15/4, NFLP, CHM.

28. "Mrs. Loeb Visits Prison, Sees Dick as Felon for First Time," *CT*, 10.7.1924.

29. Richard Loeb, "Lesson 18," *English A: Elementary Principles of Grammar and Letter Writing*, 3.

30. Anna Loeb to CRD, 10.7.1924, 1/3, CDP, LC.

31. Leopold, *Life Plus*, 118.

32. "'Dickie' Loeb Breaks under the Strain," *Times* (Munster, Indiana), 11.3.1924.

33. Leopold, *Life Plus*, 124.

34. Leopold, draft of *Life Plus*, 53, 25/1.

35. Susan Lurie to NFL, 11.17.1924, 2/1, NFLP, CHM.

36. Susan Lurie to NFL, 12.9.1924, 2/1, NFLP, CHM.

37. Martin, *Nathan Leopold Story*, 174.

38. Leopold, *Life Plus*, 126–27.

39. Walter B. Martin, "The Development of Psychoses in Prison," *Journal of Criminal Law and Criminology* (Fall 1927): 409.

40. Leopold, draft of *Life Plus*, 77, 25/1.

41. Ron Martinetti, *Crazy Bird: Nathan Leopold and the Crime of the Century* (unpublished manuscript, 2022), 240.

42. Leopold, *Life Plus*, 135.

43. Joseph F. Fishman, *Sex in Prison* (New York: National Library Press, 1934), 92.

44. John Bartlow Martin, "Murder on His Conscience: Part Two," *SEP*, 4.9.1955, 65.

45. Ibid., 71.

46. Leopold, *Life Plus*, 137.

47. *Workings of the Indeterminate*, 62.

48. "Capone Is Praised Highly by Pastor," *Reading Times* (Reading, PA), 1.2.1934.

49. Martinetti, *Crazy Bird*, 242.

50. Leopold, *Life Plus*, 140.

51. Ibid., 143.

52. Birdie Schwab to NFL, 1.11.1926, 2/9, NFLP, CHM.

53. Leopold, *Life Plus*, 147.

54. "Capture Four of Gang That Killed Klein," *JEHN*, 5.6.1926.

55. "State to Wind up Its Case This Afternoon," *JEHN*, 11.19.1926.

56. Leopold, *Life Plus*, 154.

57. Ibid., 155.

58. "Two Convicts to Testify in Own Defense," *JEHN*, 11.21,1926.

59. "Jury May Get Murder Case Early Friday," *JEHN*, 11.24.1926.

60. Ibid.

61. "Leopold, Citing Prison "Ethics" Refuses to Talk," *JEHN*, 11.22.1926.

62. "Link Jail Break to Pardons," *CT*, 5.7.1926.

63. "Leopold and Loeb Hear Doctor Tell of Bad Surgery," *CDN*, 1.5.1927.

64. Genevieve Forbes Herrick, "Leopold Denies Mutilation of Taxicab Driver," *CT*, 1.6.1927.

65. "Report Ream Suit against Loeb and Leopold Settled," *CT*, 9.18.1927.

66. "Loeb, In Prison, Takes Latin at Columbia U. By Correspondence," *CT*, 11.3.1927.

CHAPTER 11

1. Illinois Association for Criminal Justice, *The Illinois Crime Survey* (Chicago: Blakely Printing Company, 1929), 763.

2. Leopold, *Life Plus*, 173.

3. Martinetti, *Crazy Bird*, 261.

4. Martin, *Murder Part Two*, 65.

5. NFL to Gladys Erickson 11.15.1955, 34/52, NFLP, CHM.

6. Leopold, draft of *Life Plus*, 160, 25/1.

7. Leopold, *Life Plus*, 174.

8. Leopold, draft of *Life Plus*, 146, 25/1.

9. AMB to NFL, 11.26.1930, 1/7, NFLP, CHM.

10. Leopold, *Life Plus*, 179.

11. Martin, *Nathan Leopold Story*, 174.

12. Leopold, *Life Plus*, 180.

13. Leopold, draft of *Life Plus*, 152, 25/1.

14. Leopold, draft of *Life Plus*, 153–54, 25/1.

15. Ibid., 164.

16. Ibid., 133–34.

17. Ibid., 134–35.

18. Leopold, *Life Plus*, 183.

19. Prison Register: Nathan Leopold, ISA.

20. Ibid.

21. Leopold, *Life Plus*, 183.

22. Ibid., 184.

23. Ibid.

24. Ibid.

25. Ibid., 186.

26. "Leopold, Loeb Placed at Hard Labor in Prison," *CT*, 10.17.1930.

27. Leopold, *Life Plus*, 185.

28. Ibid.

29. Ibid.

30. FML to NFL, 10.17.1930, 1/20, NFLP, CHM.

31. Ibid.

32. John A. Larson and Herman M. Adler, "A Study of Deception in the Penitentiary," *Institution Quarterly* (June 1925): 137–38.

33. John A. Larson, Notes, 3, Carton 2, JALP BL, UCB.

34. Leopold, draft of *Life Plus*, 191A, 25/1.

35. "Protest Plan for Pardoning 600 Convicts," *CT*, 10.28.1929.

36. Leopold, *Life Plus*, 201.

37. Julio Chileno Coroner's Report, Will County Coroner's Office.

38. Martin, *Murder Part Two*, 71.

39. Leopold, *Life Plus*, 200.

40. Joseph Coakley Coroner's Report, Will County Coroner's Office.

41. Leopold, *Life Plus*, 203.

42. Martin, *Murder Part Two*, 71.

43. Ibid.

44. "1,700 Convicts Locked in Cells Supperless as Finale of Riot," *JEHN*, 3.15.1931.

45. Leopold, *Life Plus*, 204.

46. Ibid., 205.

47. "Troops on Guard at Joliet," *CT*, 3.19.1931.

48. William Hart, "Reporter Tells How Riot Was Quickly Halted," *JEHN*, 3.19.1931.

CHAPTER 12

1. Leopold, *Life Plus*, 208.

2. Ibid., 213.

3. Ibid., 226.

4. Ibid., 216.

5. Ibid., 220.

6. Leopold, draft of *Life Plus*, 161, 25/1.

7. James B. Jacobs, *Stateville: The Penitentiary in Mass Society* (Chicago: University of Chicago Press, 1977), 25.

8. Illinois Prison Inquiry Commission, *The Prison System in Illinois* (Springfield: 1937), 140.

9. Joe Cioni, *True Facts of the Prison (Stateville)*, Box 5, Joseph Ragen Papers, ALPL.

10. Martin, *Nathan Leopold Story*, 218–20.

11. Leopold, *Life Plus*, 221.

12. Leopold, draft of *Life Plus*, 265, 25/1.

13. Ibid., 264.

14. Leopold, *Life Plus*, 243.

15. RAL to NFL, 11.19.1931, 1/7, NFLP, CHM.

16. Martin, *Nathan Leopold Story*, 244.

17. John Stone, "Murder Photos Shatter Nerve of Loeb Slayer," *Chicago Daily Times*, 1.31.1936.

18. Paul Warren, "Nathan Leopold: Penitentiary Pygmalion," *Village Voice*, 10.28.1971.

19. Interview with Victor and Jean Neilson, 10.8.–10.9.1936, 135/2, EWBP, SCRC, UCL.

20. Leopold, *Life Plus*, 286.

21. Leopold, draft of *Life Plus*, 220, 25/1.

22. NFL to EG, 5.26.1964, 11/5, NFLP, CHM.

23. Vida and Trevlyn Clinkunbroomer to NFL, 1/7, NFLP, CHM.

24. Plan for High School Correspondence Courses under the Direction of Prof. Taylor, PNL, SC, UI.

25. NFL to Gladys Erickson, 11.17.1955, 34/52, NFLP, CHM.

26. Leopold, *Life Plus*, 226.

27. Edwin A. Lahey, "Leopold in Own Story at Quiz," *CDN*, 2.1.1936.

28. "Report of the Stateville Correspondence School From January 1, 1936 to December 31, 1936," 55/4, Sheldon Glueck Papers, Harvard Law Library.

29. *1936 Report of Stateville.*

30. A. L. Bowen, "Nineteenth Annual Report of The Illinois Department of Public Welfare" (State of Illinois, 1936), 492.

31. Loeb, *English A: Lesson 18*, 3.

32. Leopold, *Life Plus*, 230–31.

33. Anna Loeb to Abraham Cronbach, 2.7.1935, 3/1, Abraham Cronbach Papers, American Jewish Archives.

34. Leopold, *Life Plus*, 286.

35. Ferris F. Laune, *Predicting Criminality: Forecasting Behavior on Parole* (Evanston, IL: Northwestern University, 1936), 11.

36. Ibid., 12.

37. Ibid., 20.

38. Ibid., 22.

39. NFL to Edwin Sutherland, 6.19.1934, 25/6, LLC, CDMLSCUA, NUL.

40. Virginia Gardner, "Eleven Years after the Crime of Loeb and Leopold," *CT*, 5.19.1935.

41. Record of Correspondence Courses, Folder 1, PNL, SC, UI.

42. NFL to HHW, 10.26.1931, Folder 1, PNL, SC, UI.

43. "Einstein Here, Not Relatively, But in Flesh," *CT*, 5.3.1921.

44. NFL to Albert Einstein, 11.14.1933, 33/31, NFLP, CHM.

45. Albert Einstein to NFL, 1.5.1934, Albert Einstein Archives, Hebrew University of Jerusalem.

46. Albert Einstein to Ernest Zeisler, 6.7.1936, Albert Einstein Archives, Hebrew University of Jerusalem. Translation from AGB to NFL, 7.2.1936, 33/8, NFLP, CHM.

47. NFL to Hazel Peters, 3.1.1962, 16/31, NFLP, CHM.

48. Martin, *Murder Part Three*, 198.

49. NFL to Gerald Burd, 9.20.1962, 3/14, NFLP, CHM.

50. Martin, *Murder Part Three*, 198.

51. RAL [As Paul J. Fitzgibbon] to Columbia University and NFL [As Paul J. Fitzgibbon] to Walter B. Clark, 10.27.1933, 1/8, NFLP, CHM.

52. NFL to EG, 6.7.1961, 19/15, LLC, CDMLSCUA, NUL.

53. *Journal of Criminal Law and Criminology*, 27/2 (1936): 207–13.

54. Ibid., 214–18.

55. Martin, *Murder Part Three*, 198.

CHAPTER 13

1. Gladys A. Erickson, *Warden Ragen of Joliet* (New York: E. P. Dutton, 1957), 42–43.

2. Ibid., 61.

3. Joseph Ragen, "Leopold as I Knew Him" 15/7, LLC, CDMLSCUA, NUL.

4. John Bartlow Martin, Ragen Notes, 3, 150/8, JBMP, LC.

5. Leopold, *Life Plus*, 265–66.

6. Parole Prediction Report: James Day, 1.12.1942, JDC, ISA.

7. John A. Swanson to John C. Cranor, 2.13.1932, JDC, ISA.

8. "Jury Accuses Loeb's Slayer," *JEHN*, 1.29.1936.

9. Erickson, *Warden Ragen*, 80.

10. Leopold, *Life Plus*, 266.

11. Ibid.

12. Ibid., 267.

13. Eligius Weir, Untitled memoir, 124, Franciscan Providence of the Sacred Heart Archives.

14. Ibid.

15. Martin, *Murder Part Three*, 198.

16. Leopold, *Life Plus*, 268.

17. Ibid., 270.

18. Associated Press photograph, 1.30.1936.

19. "Jury Hears Day's 'Murder Excuse,'" *CEA*, 6.1.1936.

20. Edwin Lahey to Alexander Woollcott, 2.6.1936, Rare Book Room, Hamilton College.

21. John Larson, Notes, 4, Carton 2, JALP, BL, UCB.

22. Erickson, *Warden Ragen*, 78.

23. Virginia Gardner, "Eleven Years Ago Next Tuesday," *New York Daily News*, 5.19.1935.

24. "Loeb Slain in Convict Plot, Quiz Indicates," *CHE*, 2.1.1936.

25. Leopold, *Life Plus*, 275.

26. Martin, *Nathan Leopold Story*, 274.

27. "Loeb Fate Shock to Darrow," *CEA*, 1.28.1936.

28. "Loeb Case Sidelights," *CDN*, 1.29.1936.

29. "Suffered Enough, Says Family," *CHE*, 1.29.1936.

30. NFL to EW, 12.10.1965, 19/7, NFLP, CHM.

31. HHW to NFL, 1.29.1936, 2/15, NFLP, CHM.

32. NFL to HHW, 2.3.1962, 19/12, NFLP, CHM.

33. *Orlando Sentinel*, 1.29.1936.

34. "Along El Camino Real with Ed Ainsworth," *Los Angeles Times*, 1.30.1936.

35. "Loeb Private Bath Probe," *Times-Union (Albany, New York)*, 1.30.1936.

36. "Day Trial Will Open Tomorrow," *JEHN*, 5.24.1936.

37. NFL to Miss Geller, 5.17.1964, 126/8, EGP, LC.

38. NFL to Courtland Van Vechten, 5.19.1958, 19/1, NFLP, CHM.

39. Nathan Leopold, "The Good Hoodlum," 12/6, EWBP, SCRC, UCL.

40. NFL to EW, Undated, 34/45, NFLP, CHM.

41. Leopold, *Life Plus*, 276.

42. "Leopold in Own Story at Quiz," Edwin A. Lahey, *CDN*, 2.1.1936.

43. "Courtroom Filled as Attorneys Make Final Pleas," *JEHN*, 6.4.1936.

44. Edwin A. Lahey, "Convict Day Tells Jury Why He Killed Loeb," *CDN*, 6.3.1936.

45. Edwin A. Lahey, "Day's Defense Makes Final Plea to Jury," *CDN*, 6.4.1936.

46. "Acquit Day, Judge Pleased," *CEA*, 6.4.1936.

47. Joseph Schwab to Hal Higdon, 11.3.1974, 3/2, HHP, CHM.

48. "Day Acquitted; Must Serve Ten Years, Says Ragen," *JEHN*, 6.5.1936.

49. Ibid.

50. "Conduct Record: James Day," 1.2.1942, JDC, ISA.

CHAPTER 14

1. Martin, *Murder Part Three*, 198.

2. Leopold, *Life Plus*, 278.

3. John Bartlow Martin, "Murder on His Conscience Part Four," *SEP*, 4.23.1955, 136.

4. Martin, *Murder Part Three*, 198.

5. Weir, *Memoir*, 122.

6. Bowman and Hulbert, *Report of Loeb*, 123.

7. Martin, *Murder Part Three*, 197.

8. Martin, *Murder Part Two*, 65.

9. Warren, *Pygmalion*.

10. Ferris F. Laune to Whom It May Concern, 5.9.1936, 1/17, NFLP CHM.

11. Leopold, *Life Plus*, 282.

12. James J. Doody and J. D. Meaux to John E. Rees, 4.10.1941, Folder 2, PNL, SC, UI.

13. Edward J. Farrant to HHW, 4.30.1941, Folder 1, PNL, SC, UI.

14. "Stateville Correspondence School Pushes Beyond State Borders," *Joliet-Stateville Time*, October, 1941.

15. Inquiry Commission, *The Prison System*, 275.

16. November 19 booklet, 1/7, NFLP, CHM.

17. Leopold, *Life Plus*, 244.

18. Ibid.

19. Warren, *Pygmalion*.

20. Ibid.

21. Ibid.

22. Ron Martinetti, in discussion with the author, September 2021.

23. NFL to Gladys Erickson, 11.18.1955, 34/52, NFLP, CHM.

24. E. F. Lindquist to NFL [as Paul J. Fitzgibbon], 2.22.1940, Folder 2, PNL, SC, UI.

25. Head Instructor, "Education in Prison and Success on Parole," Monograph Series Number 1, 1941.

26. John Bartlow Martin, Leopold Jacket Notes, 31, 150/6, JBMP, LC.

27. Leopold, draft of *Life Plus*, 314, 23/1.

28. Francis Sandiford, "Only the Damned," *Tangents* (October 1966): 11.

29. Leopold, *Life Plus*, 297.

30. Leopold, *Life Plus*, 300.

31. Sandiford, *Only the Damned*, 11.

32. Martin, *Murder Part Three*, 201.

33. Ibid.

34. Ibid.

35. Paul Warren, "Nathan Leopold: Compelled to Atone," *Village Voice*, 11.4.1971.

36. Leopold, *Life Plus*, 301.

37. Prison Register: Nathan Leopold, ISA.

38. Leopold, draft of *Life Plus*, 160–61, 25/1.

39. Offense record, Institutional Jacket: Nathan Leopold, Illinois Department of Corrections.

40. NFL to HHW, 8.3.1958, 19/12, CHM, NFLP.

41. Pardon Board Visitors Hearing, 4.12.1949, 5, NLC, ISA.

42. NFL to HHW, 8.3.1958, 19/12, NFLP, CHM.

43. Charles C. Purvis, "Half His Life in Prison," *Daily News* (New York), 9.6.1942.

44. Herbert C. Morton, "Leopold Termed 'Genius' by Medic," *St. Paul Pioneer Press*, 1.10.1953.

45. Leopold, *Life Plus*, 319.

46. Ibid., 325.

47. Clay G. Huff to EG, 1.7.1958, 38/3, NFLP, CHM.

48. Karen M. Masterson, *The Malaria Project: The U.S. Government's Secret Mission to Find a Miracle Cure* (New York: Penguin Group, 2014), 278.

49. Ibid.

50. "Malaria and the Inmates," *Joliet-Stateville Time*, April 1947.

51. Ibid.

52. NFL to J.Ll.J. Edwards, 3.11.1967, 6/6, NFLP, CHM.

53. Nuremberg Military Tribunals, 9125–9133 and 9212–9231.

54. "Malaria Research Report: Script of Broadcast over WGN," 1.3.1946, 20/13, NFLP, CHM.

55. Ragen, *Leopold as I*.

56. NFL to EW, Undated, 1/7, NFLP, CHM.

57. FML to NFL, 1.9.1948, 1/20, NFLP, CHM.

58. Ibid.

59. Ibid.

60. Petition for Executive Clemency, Received 1.12.1948, NLC, ISA.

61. FML to Board of Pardons and Parole, 2.20.1948, 2/4, NFLP, CHM.

62. Ibid.

63. NFL to Marvin Sukov, 1.14.1958, 13/22, LLC, CDMLSCUA, NUL.

64. Martin, *Nathan Leopold Story*, 395–96.

65. NFL to HHW, 5.17.1953, 34/48, NFLP, CHM.

66. Leopold, *Life Plus*, 347.

67. Martin, *Nathan Leopold Story*, 395.

68. John Bartlow Martin, Leopold Jacket Notes, 28, 150/6, JBMP, LC.

69. Prison Register: Nathan Leopold, ISA.

70. Ibid.

71. Interview with Gene Lovitz, 2/7, HHP, CHM.

72. Ibid.

73. Anonymous to the Governor and State Pardon Board, 2.19.1949, NLC, ISA.

74. Leopold, *Life Plus*, 341.

75. George Wright, "Leopold Seeks Shorter Term in Parole Plea," *CT*, 4.23.1949.

76. DEF to Board of Paroles and Pardons, 7.9.1949, NLC, ISA.

77. Illinois State News, "News Release," 9.22.1949, NLC, ISA.

78. Leopold, *Life Plus*, 344.

CHAPTER 15

1. Leopold, *Life Plus*, 345.

2. Ibid.

3. Richard A. Lawrence and Lloyd Ohlin, "A Comparison of Alternative Methods of Parole Prediction," *American Sociological Review* (June 1952): 268–274.

4. NFL to Marvin Sukov, 2.19.1952, 34/42, NFLP, CHM.

5. NFL to Courtlandt Van Vechten, 6.29.1952, 34/43, NFLP, CHM.

6. Bob Considine, "On the Line," *Times-Union (Albany, New York)*, 4.22.1950.

7. Ibid.

8. Gladys Erickson, "Offers to Spy Against Reds," *Chicago Herald American*, 8.22.1952.

9. NFL to HHW, 4.25.1970, 19/12, NFLP, CHM.

10. Alvin Goldstein, Draft of "Nathan Leopold Asks for Mercy," LLF, AHGC, AHC, UW.

11. Alvin Goldstein to Al Offer, Undated, LLF, AHGC, AHC, UW.

12. Nicholas Shuman, "Nathan Leopold's Story—With His O.K.," *CDN*, 1.3.1953.

13. NFL to WHR, 1.8.1966, 17/4, NFLP, CHM.

14. WHR to Parole Board, 1.6.1953, 30/1, LLC, CDMLSCUA, NUL.

15. WHR to Homer Burke, 1.10.1953, 3/1, RLP, CBA.

16. EW to NFL, 12.19.1948, 34/45, NFLP, CHM.

17. NFL to EW, Undated, 34/45, NFLP, CHM.

18. Shuman, "Nathan Leopold's Story."

19. James Doherty, "How Leopold Asked Parole," *CT*, 1.9.1953.

20. "Leopold Tells Why He Should Be Free," *CHA*, 1.9.1953.

21. "Board in Shuffle May Hit Leopold," *CHA*, 1.10.1953.

22. Doherty, *How Leopold*.

23. "'We Owe Leopold Nothing': Gutknecht," *CDN*, 1.8.1953.

24. Doherty, *How Leopold*.

25. "Leopold Parole Bid Denied," *CT*, 5.15.1953.

26. "Leopold's Parole Plea Turned Down," *CST*, 5.15.1953.

27. *Parole Bid Denied*.

28. NFL to EW, 5.24.1953, 34/45, NFLP, CHM.
29. NFL to HHW, 9.27.1953, 34/48, NFLP, CHM.
30. NFL to FML, 9.10.1952, 1/20, NFLP, CHM.
31. NFL to HHW, 7.19.1953, 34/48, NFLP, CHM.
32. NFL to Joseph Ragen, 6.26.1953, 34/28, NFLP, CHM.
33. NFL to FML, 11.1.1953, 33/59, NFLP, CHM.
34. NFL to RGN, 12.1.1953, 34/23, NFLP, CHM.
35. AGB to NFL, 11.18.1953, 33/8, NFLP, CHM.
36. RGN to Hal Higdon, 3.17.1975, 3/1, HHP, CHM.
37. NFL to Emma Peggy Lebold, 2.28.1954, 33/59, NFLP, CHM.
38. NFL to HHW, 3.21.1954, 34/48, NFLP, CHM.
39. Interview with Meyer Levin, 2/8, HHP, CHM.
40. NFL to RGN, 4.18.1954, 34/23, NFLP, CHM.

CHAPTER 16

1. John Bartlow Martin, William Carr Interview Notes, 51, 150/7, JBMP, LC.
2. Ibid.
3. Expense ledger, 28/6, NFLP, CHM.
4. NFL to Joseph Ragen, 9.23.1955, 35/2, NFLP, CHM.
5. Indictment for Murder, Files of the Criminal Court, 52-1218, Archives, Richard J. Daley Center.
6. Expense ledger, 28/6, NFLP, CHM.
7. NFL to HHW, 1.22.1956, 35/2, NFLP, CHM.
8. NFL to WLR, 10.25.1970, 3/3, RLP, CBA.
9. Last Will and Testament of Nathan F. Leopold Jr., June 1957, 8/7, LLC, CDMLSCUA, NUL.
10. DEF to NFL, Undated, 33/35, NFLP, CHM.
11. NFL to DEF, 4.17.1955, 33/35, NFLP, CHM.
12. NFL to DEF, 9.11.1955, 35/1, NFLP, CHM.
13. DEF to WGS, 6.11.1957, NLC, ISA.
14. Meyer Levin, *Compulsion* (New York: Simon & Schuster, 1956).
15. Ibid., 495.
16. "Nathan Leopold after 32 Years," *Life*, 3.25.1957.
17. NFL to AGB, 5.2.1954, 124/6, EGP, LC.
18. Leopold, *Life Plus*, 269.
19. NFL to EW, 12.2.1954, 34/45, NFLP, CHM.
20. Application for Executive Clemency, 1957, NLC, ISA.
21. Elmer Gertz, *A Handful of Clients* (Chicago: Follett, 1965), 10.
22. Notes on First Meeting with N.F.L., Jr., 11/3, LLC, CDMLSCUA, NUL.
23. Leo A. Lerner to WGS, 10.29.1957, Leo A. Lerner Papers, Special Collections Research Center, Syracuse University Libraries.

24. AGB to RGN, 4.4.1957, 43/3, NFLP, CHM.

25. NFL to AMB, 7.24.1957, 33/15, NFLP, CHM.

26. Pardon Board to Governor, July 1957, 403.012, ISA.

27. Menu of No-Commutation Party, 40/9, NFLP, CHM.

28. NFL to AMB, 2.1.1958, 34/52, NFLP, CHM.

29. NFL to EG, 2.2.1958, 1/3, RLP, CBA.

30. NFL to RGN, 2.2.1958, 41/2, NFLP, CHM.

31. NFL to EG, 2.2.1958, 1/3, RLP, CBA.

32. "Bob Crowe, of Leopold Fame, Dies," *CEA*, 1.20.1958.

33. Parole and Pardon Board Stenographic Verbatim Report: Nathan F. Leopold Jr., 2.5.1958, 3, 33/4, LLC, CDMLSCUA, NUL.

34. Ibid., 5.

35. Ibid., 7–8.

36. Ibid., 15.

37. "Statement," 2.20.1958, 35/5, NFLP, CHM.

38. NFL to Lavila Fulford, 35/1, 2.20.1958, NFLP, CHM.

39. NFL to HHW, 5.12.1959, 19/12, NFLP, CHM.

40. NFL to DEF, 2.6.1959, 6/21, NFLP, CHM.

41. NFL to HHW, 4.12.1959, 19/12, NFLP, CHM.

42. Timothy Seldes to NFL, 6.25.1958, 43/9, NFLP, CHM.

CHAPTER 17

1. NFL to Ladies and Gentlemen, 32/4, LLC, CDMLSCUA, NUL.

2. Joseph Egelhof, "Illness Mars Leopold's First Day on Parole," *CT*, 3.14.1958.

3. Parole Agreement, 2.20.1958, 18/25, NFLP, CHM.

4. Hugh Hough, "Leopold Ill, Staying on Gold Coast," *CST*, 3.14.1958.

5. NFL to HHW, 3.19.1958, 19/12, NFLP, CHM.

6. "Leopold's Request for Privacy," *CST*, 3.14.1958.

7. "Swank Apartment Building in Tizzy over Leopold Visit," *CDN*, 3.14.1958.

8. Nathan Leopold, *Grab for a Halo*, 21–22, 7/4, LLC, CDMLSCUA, NUL.

9. NFL to AKB, 3/10, NFLP, CHM.

10. NFL to David Fulford Jr., 7.7.1958, 6/21, NFLP, CHM.

11. NFL to HHW, 3.19.1958, 19/12, NFLP, CHM.

12. Ray Brennan, "Leopold Takes Last Look at City," *CST*, 3.15.1958.

13. Ibid.

14. NFL to DEF, 4.16.1958, 6/21, NFLP, CHM.

15. NFL to Mary and Frank Johnston, 3.31.1958, 13/16, NFLP, CHM.

16. NFL to HHW, 3.19.1958, 19/12, NFLP, CHM.

17. NFL to Donald and Patricia Lebold, 1.30.1965, 14/3, NFLP, CHM.

18. Statement by WHR, 1/1, RLP, CBA.

19. Joyce Groff Pérez, in discussion with the author, November 2018.

20. AGB to NFL, 9.19.1958, 2/24, NFLP, CHM.

21. Statement by WHR, 1/1, RLP, CBA.

22. NFL to AGB, 3.22.1958, 2/24, NFLP, CHM.

23. NFL to Angel Umpierre, 3.21.1958, 18/25, NFLP, CHM.

24. NFL to AGB, 3.22.1958, 2/24, NFLP, CHM.

25. NFL to Mary and Frank Johnston, 3.31.1958, 13/16, NFLP, CHM.

26. Al Hine, "Not a Saint, But a Servant," 3–4, 7/8, LLC, CDMLSCUA, NUL.

27. NFL to WHR, 9.15.1970, 3/3/, RLP, CBA.

28. NFL to Mary and Frank Johnston, 3.31.1958, 13/16, NFLP, CHM.

29. NFL to Heinrich and Etta Hammer, 3.29.1958, 12/17, NFLP, CHM.

30. NFL to WHR, 3.22.1958, 1/2, RLP, CBA.

31. NFL to Emma Peggy Lebold, 3.28.1958, 14/4, NFLP, CHM.

32. Ralph Townsend to WHR, 5.12.1958, 1/21, PRR, CBA.

33. NFL to HHW, 3.28.1958, 19/12, NFLP, CHM.

34. Joanne Church, in discussion with the author, March 2019.

35. NFL to HHW, 3.28.1958, 19/12, NFLP, CHM.

36. NFL to PH, 3.29.1962, 126/3, EGP, LC.

37. NFL to HHW, 8.3.1958, 19/12, NFLP, CHM.

38. NFL to WME, 7.9.1965, 6/10, NFLP, CHM.

39. June Matheson to NFL, 8.1.1958, 15/5, NFLP, CHM.

40. NFL to SNL and AGB, 1.21.1961, 2/25, NFLP, CHM.

41. GFL to WGS, 12.8.1960, 19/10, LLC, CDMLSCUA, NUL.

42. Harry Mursh, "Widow Tells Love for Leopold," *CEA*, 1.19.1961.

43. Ibid.

44. NFL to DEF, 2.6.1959, 6/21, NFLP, CHM. The last sentence was kept in Leopold's original italics and translated from Spanish.

45. DEF to NFL, 3.16.1959, 6/21, NFLP, CHM. The italicized portion was translated from Spanish.

46. NFL to Marvin Snell, 10.18.1963, 18/4, NFLP, CHM.

47. NFL to Joan Cohen, 5.16.1958, 5/10, NFLP, CHM.

48. NFL to Boys, 8.1.1959, 41/20, NFLP, CHM.

49. Brethren employee, in discussion with the author, February 2019.

50. NFL to Viola Westfall, 2.24.1959, 19/8, NFLP CHM.

51. NFL to WHR, 1.10.1959, 1/3, RLP, CBA.

52. NFL to Katherine Strom, 4.3.1959, 18/14, NFLP, CHM.

53. RWC to NFL, 4.9.1958, 5/8, NFLP, CHM.

54. NFL to RWC, 2.2.1959, 5/8, NFLP, CHM.

55. RWC to Virginia Claiborne, 3.14.1959, Box 21, Papers of Robert Watson Claiborne, Special Collections, University of Virginia Library.

56. NFL to EG, 5.18.1958, 16/6, LLC, CDMLSCUA, NUL.

57. NFL to EG, 10.28.1959, 8/6, NFLP, CHM.

58. EG to NFL, 10.30.1959, 8/6, NFLP, CHM.

59. NFL to Ruth Credland, 9.8.1958, 5/20, NFLP, CHM.

CHAPTER 18

1. NFL to Angel and Señora Umpierre, 3.18.1963, 18/25, NFLP, CHM.
2. NFL to HHW, 5.12.1959, 19/12, NFLP, CHM.
3. NFL [as GFL] to Friend, 3.26.1959, 1/3, RLP, CBA.
4. EG to NFL, 3.9.1959, 8/2, NFLP, CHM.
5. NFL to Norman Parkhurst, 2.12.1959, 16/9, NFLP, CHM.
6. NFL to WHR, 4.27.1959, 1/3, RLP, CBA.
7. NFL to Viola Westfall, 2.15.1959, 19/8 NFLP, CHM.
8. NFL to Hazel Peters, 3.6.1959, 16/28, NFLP, CHM.
9. NFL to HHW, 1.6.1960, 19/12, NFLP, CHM.
10. NFL to Cathleen Siterley, 8.29.1959, 18/1, NFLP, CHM.
11. NFL to HHW, 8.22.1959, 19/12, NFLP, CHM.
12. NFL to RGN, 9.5.1959, 15/24, NFLP, CHM.
13. Ibid.
14. NFL to RGN, 6.22.1960, 41/25, NFLP, CHM.
15. Dr. Henry Johnson, interview by Ernie Potvin, 9.27.1983, ONE Archives, University of Southern California.
16. NFL to WHR, 8.16.1960, 1/4, RLP, CBA.
17. Anonymous to GFL, Undated, 20/23, LLC, CDMLSCUA, NUL. Ellipses and spaces are present in the original.
18. Ralph Townsend to WHR, 11.2.1959, 1/3, RLP, CBA.
19. Ricardo Lawrence, "Documental Para el Hospital Castañer," 8/7, NFLP, CHM.
20. NFL to EW, 12.3.1959, 19/7, NFLP, CHM.
21. Anonymous to The Friends of the New Castañer General Hospital, 4.27.1960, 18/25, LLC, CDMLSCUA, NUL.
22. Remarks of WHR, 1/17, PRR, CBA.
23. NFL to WHR, 8.16.1960, 1/4, RLP, CBA.
24. Field work evaluations, 1960 and 1961, 34/4, LLC, CDMLSCUA, NUL.
25. NFL to Cathleen Siterley, 12.3.1960, 18/1, NFLP, CHM.
26. NFL to EG, 1.5.1961, 19/15, LLC, CDMLSCUA, NUL.
27. Ron Martinetti, in discussion with the author, May 2022.
28. NFL to HHW, 3.23.1960, 19/12, NFLP, CHM.
29. Field work evaluations, 1960 and 1961, 34/4, LLC, CDMLSCUA, NUL.
30. Luis Muñoz Marín to WGS, 9.7.1960, 34/2, LLC, CDMLSCUA, NUL.
31. NFL to All, 8.20.1960, 41/25, NFLP, CHM.
32. Interview with Ephriam London, 2/8, HHP, CHM.
33. Myriam to Domingo Marrero, 11.16.1960, 1/4, RLP, CBA.
34. NFL to EG, 3.15.1960, 18/17, LLC, CDMLSCUA, NUL.
35. NFL to HHW, 3.23.1960, 19/12, NFLP, CHM.
36. NFL [as Sue Dogg de Leopold] to WHR, Undated, 1/8, RLP, CBA.
37. PH to NFL [as Uncle Bill], 2.21.1960, 86/7, EGP, LC.
38. PH to NFL [as Uncle Bill], 5.15.1960, 86/7, EGP, LC.

39. RWC to NFL, Undated, written on NFL letter of 6.14.1961, 5/8, NFLP, CHM.

40. Johnson interview, 1983.

41. Ibid.

42. Alejandro Martinez, "Puerto Rico a Gay Playland but Can Be Dangerous," *The Advocate*, 9.29–10.12.1971.

43. Johnson interview, 1983.

44. Your Hollywood Reporter, "Night Life in Chicago: Thru the Keyhole," 1.8–1.15, 1960.

45. NFL to WHR, 2.29.1960, 1/4, RLP, CBA.

46. NFL to WHR, 9.5.1960, 1/4, RLP, CBA.

47. George T. Scully, *A New Day . . . and How to Make It* (Illinois: Department of Public Welfare, 1934), 23.

48. John Forbes to Illinois Parole and Pardons Board, 8.29.1960, 34/2, LLC, CDMLSCUA, NUL.

49. GFL to Illinois Parole and Pardons Board, 8.30.1960, 34/2, LLC, CDMLS-CUA, NUL.

50. NFL to EG, 3.15.1960, 18/17, LLC, CDMLSCUA, NUL.

51. EG to NFL, 2.8.1961, 9/4, NFLP, CHM.

52. NFL to RGN, 6.1.1961, 42/1, NFLP, CHM.

53. Photo 093E, 39/18, LLC, CDMLSCUA, NUL.

54. NFL to Boys and Girls, 1.16.1962, 14/8, NFLP, CHM.

55. NFL to EG, 12.24.1961, 20/16, LLC, CDMLSCUA, NUL.

56. NFL to EG, 4.5.1963, 21/19, LLC, CDMLSCUA, NUL.

57. NFL to Editor of the *Caribbean Journal of Science*, 9.20.1961, 15/3, NFLP, CHM.

58. EG to NFL, 2.26.1960, 20/19, LLC, CDMLSCUA, NUL.

59. NFL [as William Eiss] to PH, 3.1.1962, 20/19, LLC, CDMLSCUA, NUL.

60. NFL to EG, 3.4.1962, 20/20, LLC, CDMLSCUA, NUL.

61. EG to NFL, 3.8.1962, RLP, CBA.

62. NFL to EG, 3.9.1962, 20/21, LLC, CDMLSCUA, NUL.

63. NFL to EG, 3.26.1962, 20/23, LLC, CDMLSCUA, NUL.

64. NFL to PH, 3.29.1962, 126/3, EGP, LC.

65. NFL to PH, 5.26.1962, 20/26, LLC, CDMLSCUA, NUL.

66. NFL to DLF, 6.24.1962, 7/2, NFLP, CHM.

67. HHW to EG, 8.12.1962, 21/2, LLC, CDMLSCUA, NUL.

68. NFL to DLF, 6.30.1962, 7/2, NFLP, CHM.

69. NFL to RGN, 1.1.1963, 42/2, NFLP, CHM.

CHAPTER 19

1. Otto Kerner to EG, 3.26.1963, 315/46, Otto Kerner Papers, ALPL.

2. "Leopold Case as an Example," *Decatur Daily Review*, 3.15.1963.

3. "Nathan Leopold Freed from Parole; Tells Gratitude, Plans," *CST*, 3.14.1963.

4. EG to George J. Stampar, 3.13.1963, 21/14, LLC, CDMLSCUA, NUL.

5. NFL to WLR, 2.16.1963, 1/7, RLP, CBA.

6. Johnson interview, 1983.

7. John Francis Hunter, *The Gay Insider USA* (Stonehill Publishing, 1972), 560.

8. Johnson interview, 1983.

9. Horst Buchholz, "Granted Full Freedom, Leopold Voices Gratitude," *Hartford Courant*, 3.14.1963.

10. Nathan Leopold, Untitled Statement, 21/12, LLC, CDMLSCUA, NUL.

11. GFL to EG, 3.14.1963, 21/16, LLC, CDMLSCUA, NUL.

12. Hunter, *Gay Insider*, 560.

13. Ramón Pérez de Jesús to NFL, 4.1.1963, 1/7, RLP, CBA.

14. NFL to Angel Umpierre, 3.18.1963, 18/25, NFLP, CHM.

15. NFL to EG, 3.19.1963, 21/17, LLC, CDMLSCUA, NUL.

16. "Nathan Leopold, Real-Life Subject of 'Compulsion,' Leaves," *Jerusalem Post*, 8.29.1963.

17. AGB to NTL, 9.25.1963, 2/25, NFLP, CHM.

18. NFL to HSJ, 10.10.1963, 13/15, NFLP, CHM.

19. Codicil to the Last Will and Testament of Nathan F. Leopold, Jr., 5.20.1963, 8/9, LLC, CDMLSCUA, NUL.

20. Itinerary of Mr. & Mrs. N. F. Leopold, 21/22, LLC, CDMLSCUA, NUL.

21. NGL to WLR, 7.19.1963, 1/7, RLP, CBA.

22. NFL to WLR, 6.25.1963, 1/7, RLP, CBA.

23. NFL to EG, 7.8.1963, 22/2, LLC, CDMLSCUA, NUL.

24. PH to EMG, 9.6.1963, 86/10, EGP, LC.

25. NFL to EG, 9.9.1963, 22/5, LLC, CDMLSCUA, NUL.

26. NFL to RGN, 9.29.1963, 42/2, NFLP, CHM.

27. GFL to EG, 10.1.1963, 22/6, LLC, CDMLSCUA, NUL and NFL to LSL, 10.7.1963, 14/24, NFLP, CHM.

28. NFL to HSJ, 10.10.1963, 13/15, NFLP, CHM.

29. NFL to RGN, 10.8.1963, 42/2, NFLP, CHM.

30. Letters between NFL and Friedl, 13/25, NFLP, CHM.

31. NFL to WHR, 11.22.1963, 17/1, NFLP, CHM.

32. NFL to AGB, 10.17.1963, 2/25, NFLP, CHM.

33. NFL to EG, 10.7.1963, 22/7, LLC, CDMLSCUA, NUL.

34. Nathan F. Leopold, Howard R. Stanton, and José F. Maldonado, "Proposed Methodology for Isolating and Altering Components of Human Behavior Related to Parasite Transmission," 5/9, LLC, CDMLSCUA, NUL.

35. NFL to EG, 10.16.1963, 22/8, LLC, CDMLSCUA, NUL.

36. SNL to NFL, 10.22.1963, 14/9, NFLP, CHM.

37. NFL to SNL, 10.27.1963, 14/9, NFLP, CHM.

38. NFL to EG, 10.27.1963, 22/9, LLC, CDMLSCUA, NUL.

39. Castañer Community Social Service Fund Benefit Program, 1964, 4/12, NFLP, CHM.

40. NFL to Caleb Frantz, 11.3.1963, 1/1, PRR, CBA.

41. EG to Henry Miller, 12.2.1963, 22/12, LLC, CDMLSCUA, NUL.

42. NFL to GFL, 11.5.1963, 22/9, LLC, CDMLSCUA, NUL.

43. NFL to WLR, 11.12.1963, 1/7, RLP, CBA.

44. WHR: Rough Copy of Interview, 2/12, RLP, CBA.

45. Ibid.

46. Howard Gusler to WHR, 11.29.1963, 1/8, RLP, CBA.

47. NFL to WLR, 11.12.1963, 1/7, RLP, CBA.

48. WHR to Howard Gusler, 11.27.1963, Box 1/7, RLP, CBA.

49. NFL to DLF, 11.19.1963, 7/2, NFLP, CHM.

50. NFL to DLF, 11.19.1963, 7/2, NFLP, CHM.

51. EG to Jack Friedman, 11.11.1963, 22/10, LLC, CDMLSCUA, NUL.

52. EG to Henry Miller, 12.2.1963, 22/12, LLC, CDMLSCUA, NUL.

53. NFL to HHW, 11.22.1963, 19/12, NFLP, CHM.

54. NFL to WLR, 11.12.1963, 1/7, RLP, CBA.

55. Ibid.

56. Ibid.

57. Ibid.

58. NFL to RGN, 11.11.1963, 42/2, NFLP, CHM.

59. NFL to Donald Lebold, 11.13.1963, 14/3, NFLP, CHM.

60. Howard Royer to NFL, 1.15.1964, 16/26, NFLP, CHM.

61. NFL to WME, 12.15.1963, 6/10, NFLP, CHM.

62. NFL to EG, 11.18.1963, 10/21, NFLP, CHM.

63. NFL to WME, 12.15.1963, 6/10, NFLP, CHM.

64. Ibid.

CHAPTER 20

1. NFL to Sally Jessy Raphael, 12.6.1963, 4/2, NFLP, CHM.

2. EG to GFL, 1.8.1964, 126/8, EGP, LC.

3. Larry Miller, in discussion with the author, December 2021.

4. Leonard Lyons, "The Rehabilitation of Nathan Leopold," *SEP*, 6.1.1963, 68.

5. NFL to PH, 12.5.1963, 126/4, EGP, LC.

6. NFL to PH, 12.5.1963, 126/4, EGP, LC.

7. Ruth Jensen to EG, 3.20.1964, 126/7, EGP, LC.

8. NFL to AGB, 5.4.1964, 2/26, NFLP, CHM.

9. Peter Rose, *Guest Appearances and Other Travels in Time and Space* (Athens: Ohio University Press, 2003), 195.

10. Lyons, *Rehabilitation*, 68.

11. Rose, *Guest Appearances*, 196.

12. Richard Nelson Current, *Phi Beta Kappa in American Life* (New York: Oxford University Press, 1990), 173–74.

13. NFL to Parker Hall, 9.5.1961, 12/16, NFLP, CHM.

14. NFL to EW, 11.19.1964, 19/7, NFLP, CHM.

15. NFL to SEL, 1.21.1964, 14/10, NFLP, CHM.

16. Harold Heatwole, email message to author, October 14, 2018.

17. Ibid.

18. NFL to SEL, 4.24.1964, 14/10, NFLP, CHM.

19. NFL to HMH, 7.4.1964, 12/21, NFLP, CHM.

20. NFL to RGN, 2.11.1964, 42/2, NFLP, CHM.

21. Don Murray, "Beyond the Night," 41, 6/7, LLC, CDMLSCUA, NUL.

22. NFL to WHR, 2.24.1964, 17/2, NFLP, CHM.

23. NFL to HSJ, 4.4.1966, 13/14, NFLP, CHM.

24. NFL to HSJ, 5.8.1964, 13/14, NFLP, CHM.

25. NFL to Duane Steiner, 4.25.1966, 4/10, NFLP, CHM.

26. NFL to EG, 4.24.1964, 11/3, NFLP, CHM.

27. NFL to Brethren, 1.9.1965, 4/10, NFLP, CHM.

28. Lincoln, Nebraska, Interview, 1964, 2/12, RLP, CBA.

29. NGL to Friends, 6.3.1964, 42/2, NFLP, CHM.

30. NFL to AKB, 7.5.1964, 3/11, NFLP, CHM.

31. Jeanne Hall, "Woman Confidential," *Chicago Daily Defender*, 8.18.1964.

32. HMH to NFL, 6.29.1964, 12/21, NFLP, CHM.

33. NFL to HMH, 7.4.1964, 12/21, NFLP, CHM.

34. NFL to EG, 3.26.1966, 23/13, LLC, CDMLSCUA, NUL.

35. Marjorie Marlette, "Leopold: Prison 100% Ineffective in Rehab," *Lincoln Evening News*, 6.27.1964.

36. NFL to Strom family, 7.8.1964, 18/15, NFLP, CHM.

37. NFL to Leona and Betty Jo Row, 7.1.1964, 3/2, RLP, CBA.

38. Ibid.

39. NFL to ADB, 7.1.1964, 2/26, NFLP, CHM.

40. NFL to WME, 8.18.1964, 6/10, NFLP, CHM.

41. NFL to HSJ, 7.29.1964, 13/15, NFLP, CHM.

42. NFL to EG, 9.30.1964, 22/21, LLC, CDMLSCUA, NUL.

43. NFL to WHR, 6.2.1965, 2/1, RLP, CBA.

44. NFL to EW, 9.11.1965, 19/7, NFLP, CHM.

45. NFL to Duane Steiner, 10.19.1964, 4/3, NFLP, CHM.

46. NFL to Walter Benavent, 12.19.1964, 4/3, NFLP, CHM.

47. NFL to Brethren, 1.9.1965, 4/10, NFLP, CHM.

48. Nathan F. Leopold Jr., "Imprisonment Has No Future in a Free Society," *Key Issues* (1965): 24–32.

49. Patrick Watson, *This Hour Has Seven Decades* (Toronto: McArthur & Company, 2004), 250.

50. *This Hour Has Seven Days*, CBC, 1.3.1965.

51. Watson, *This Hour*, 250.

52. "The Reformed Thrill Killer," *Toronto Star*, 1.5.1965.

53. "Mr. N. Leopold Speaks," *Inter American Review*, 2.17.1965.

54. NFL to RGN, 3.8.1965, 42/2, NFLP, CHM.

55. NFL to WME, 7.9.1965, 6/10, NFLP, CHM.

56. NFL to HHW, 8.19.1964, 19/12, NFLP, CHM.

57. Ibid.

58. NFL to Howard Stanton, 9.16.1965, 19/21, NFLP, CHM.

59. NFL to WME, 12.2.1965, 6/10, NFLP, CHM.

60. "Benefit Cocktail Party-Fashion Show," 11.28.1965, 4/1, NFLP, CHM.

61. NFL to AGB, 12.5.1965, 2/26, NFLP, CHM.

62. House of Lords Official Report, 12.17.1969, 1145.

63. NFL to WHR, 1.8.1965, 17/4, NFLP, CHM.

CHAPTER 21

1. NFL to Robert McCandles, 8.19.1966, 15/9, NFLP, CHM.

2. NFL to Jean Parker, 8.18.1966, 16/8, NFLP, CHM.

3. Ibid.

4. Ibid.

5. N. F. Leopold, "Tentative Plan, Content and Method of Handling of Possible Book," 42/2, NFLP, CHM.

6. NFL to WBE, 10.23.1966, 6/10, NFLP, CHM.

7. NFL to HHW, 9.30.1966, 19/12, NFLP, CHM.

8. Ibid.

9. NFL to Jean Parker, 9.25.1966, 16/8, NFLP, CHM.

10. Ibid.

11. NFL to EG, 1.13.1966, 23/19, LLC, CDMLSCUA, NUL.

12. NFL to WHR, 10.1.1966, 2/1, RLP, CBA.

13. NFL to LSL, 12.21.1966, 14/24, NFLP, CHM.

14. LL to NFL, 10.24.1963, 14/24, NFLP, CHM.

15. NFL to HHW, 11.17.1964, 19/12, NFLP, CHM.

16. NFL to LSL, 12.21.1966, 14/24, NFLP, CHM.

17. NFL to WME, 2.2.1967, 6/10, NFLP, CHM.

18. NFL to Roy Cohn, 2.25.1968, 5/1, NFLP, CHM.

19. NFL to LL, 12.4.1968, 14/24, NFLP, CHM.

20. Alfred Allen Lewis, "The Nathan Leopold Story," 6/8, LLC, CDMLSCUA, NUL.

21. NFL to EG, 9.24.1967, 23/23, LLC, CDMLSCUA, NUL.

22. Leonard Rayner to NFL, 5.20.1968, 16/19, NFLP, CHM.

23. "Boy Killer Honored By Church," *Detroit Free Press*, 6.26.1967.

24. John C. Caldwell, "Far Pacific Travel Guide" (New York: John Day Company, 1966), 274.

25. NFL to Saadon bin Ghani, 10.5.1967, 17/8, NFLP, CHM.

26. Ibid.

27. NFL to Saadon bin Ghani, 10.26.1967, 17/8, NFLP, CHM.

28. Jerry Roberts, "Gay Bars abound in San Juan," *Advocate*, 5.13–5.26.1970.

29. NFL to HSJ, 9.5.1966, 13/14, NFLP, CHM.

30. Hector Simms, "Stoned in San Juan," *Gay*, 5.25.1970.

31. NFL to HSJ, 9.5.1966, 13/14, NFLP, CHM.

32. NFL to WHR, Undated, 17/6, NFLP, CHM.

33. NFL to Douglas Lyons, 5.3.1968, 14/24, NFLP, CHM.

34. Tony Beacon, "Exclusively Yours," *San Juan Diary*, 2.16.1968.

35. National Institute of Mental Health, "Final Report of the Task Force on Homosexuality," 10.10.1969, 14.

36. Warren Heffron to NFL, 3.28.1968, 4/6, NFLP, CHM.

37. NFL to Warren Heffron, 5.26.1968, 4/7, NFLP, CHM.

38. NFL to HMH, 8.5.1964, 12/21, NFLP, CHM.

39. NFL to William Willoughby, 3.21.1968, 19/14, NFLP, CHM.

40. NFL to HHW, 4.21.1968, 19/12, NFLP, CHM.

41. NFL to AKB, 1.21.1968, 1/5, HHP, CHM.

42. NFL to WHR, 2.1.1968, 17/6, NFLP, CHM.

43. NFL to ADB, 1.25.1968, 3/1, NFLP, CHM.

44. Ibid.

45. Allen Ginsberg, "The Maharishi and Me," *Los Angeles Free Press*, 4.19.1968.

46. NFL to HHW, 2.1.1967, 19/12, NFLP, CHM.

47. NFL to EG, 3.10.1968, 24/2, LLC, CDMLSCUA, NUL.

48. NFL to Douglas Lyons, 6.24.1968, 14/24, NFLP, CHM.

49. NFL to ADB, 4.3.1968, 3/1, NFLP, CHM.

50. NFL to WME, 6.9.1968, 6/11, NFLP, CHM.

51. NFL to ADB, 8.7.1968, 3/1, NFLP, CHM.

52. NFL to William Conner, 8.6.1968, 5/14, NFLP, CHM.

53. NFL to William Conner, 7.19.1968, 5/14, NFLP, CHM.

54. NFL to Saddon Bin Ghani, 2.21.1968, 17/8, NFLP, CHM.

55. NFL to Saddon Bin Ghani, 3.15.1968, 17/8, NFLP, CHM.

56. Saadon Bin Ghani to NFL, 3.28.1968, 17/8, NFLP, CHM.

57. NFL to HHW, 9.7.1968, 19/12, NFLP, CHM.

58. NFL to WHR, 9.16.1968, 2/2, RLP, CBA.

59. NFL to HSJ, Undated, 13/15, NFLP, CHM.

60. NFL to WLR, 9.29.1968, 2/2, RLP, CBA.

61. NFL to William Conner, Undated, 5/14, NFLP, CHM.

62. NFL to EW, 12.8.1968, 19/7, NFLP, CHM.

63. NFL to AKB, 11.6.1968, 3/12, NFLP, CHM.

64. Ibid.

65. NFL to SEL, Undated, 14/11, NFLP, CHM.

66. NFL to HHW, 12.19.1968, 19/12, NFLP, CHM.

67. NFL to EMG, 12.8.1968, 24/6, LLC, CDMLSCUA, NUL.

68. NFL to WHR, 11.4.1968, 17/6, NFLP, CHM.

69. Marie Brubaker to WLR, 11.24.1968, 2/3, RLP, CBA.

70. NFL to AGB, 11.11.1968, 3/1, NFLP, CHM.

71. NFL to EMG, 12.8.1968, 24/6, LLC, CDMLSCUA, NUL.

72. Gervase Brinkman to Sammy Davis Jr., 3.25.1957, 34/52, NFLP, CHM.

73. NFL to LL, 11.12.1964, 14/24, NFLP, CHM.

74. NFL to Sammy Davis Jr. 8.11.1968, 6/2, NFLP, CHM.

75. NFL to WLR, 11.22.1968, 2/3, RLP, CBA.

76. NFL to WHR, 1.19.1969 2/3, RLP, CBA.

CHAPTER 22

1. NFL to EMG, 12.8.1968, 24/6, LLC, CDMLSCUA, NUL.

2. NFL to SHJ, 10.28.1969, 13/14, NFLP, CHM.

3. NFL to Ellis Shenk, 2.26.1969, 4/8, NFLP, CHM.

4. NFL to AGB, 3.25.1969, 3/1, NFLP, CHM.

5. Marie Brubaker to WLR, 3.30.1969 2/3, RLP, CBA.

6. NFL to EG, 9.20.1969, 24/8, LLC, CDMLSCUA, NUL.

7. NFL to HHW, 9.18.1969, 19/12, NFLP, CHM.

8. George Gamester, "Kind Old Teacher Spent 34 Years in Class by Himself," *Toronto Star*, 9.12.1991.

9. NFL to WBE, 12.14.1969, 6/11, NFLP, CHM.

10. NFL to WBE, 3.14.1970, 6/11, NFLP, CHM.

11. Walter C. Rundin Jr. to EG, 10.17.1972, 7/21, LLC, CDMLSCUA, NUL.

12. NFL to AKB, 10.9.1969, 3/12, NFLP, CHM.

13. NFL to WLR, 10.25.1969, 17/7, NFLP, CHM.

14. NFL to HSJ, 10.28.1969, 13/14, NFLP, CHM.

15. NFL to WLR, 12.22.1969, 17/7, NFLP, CHM.

16. Ibid.

17. Marie Brubaker to WLR, 4.13.1970, RLP, CBA.

18. Ibid.

19. Leopold v. Levin 45 Ill. 2d 434 (1970).

20. Harold Gordon to NFL, 6.1.1970, 12/5, NFLP, CHM.

21. NFL to AKB, 8.24.1970, 3/12, NFLP, CHM.

22. Leona Row to NGL, 8.26.1970, 17/7, NFLP, CHM.

23. NFL to WHR, 9.15.1970, 3/3, RLP, CBA.

24. NFL to WLR, 11.7.1970, 17/7, NFLP, CHM.

25. NFL to WLR, 9.27.1970, 3/3, RLP, CBA.

26. NFL to EG, 9.18.1970, 24/9, LLC, CDMLSCUA, NUL.

27. Philadelphia Bar Association, press release, 8.23.1970, 3/3, RLP, CBA.

28. Nathan F. Leopold, "Philadelphia Bar Association," 9.11.1970, 3/3, RLP, CBA.

29. Mike Willmann, "Bond Hits 'Rantings' of Agnew, Hoover," *Philadelphia Inquirer*, 9.12.1970.

30. David Fulford Jr. to NFL, Undated, 7/3, NFLP, CHM.

31. NFL to David Fulford Jr. 10.17.1970, 7/3, NFLP, CHM.

32. Ibid.

33. NFL to WLR, 10.25.1970, 3/3, RLP, CBA.

34. Ibid.

35. WHR to NFL, 10.29.1970, 3/3, RLP, CBA.

36. Tony to NFL [translated by Anita Faure], 11.2.1970, 8/2, LLC, CDMLS-CUA, NUL.

37. NFL to Tony [translated by Anita Faure], 11.5.1970, 8/2, LLC, CDMLS-CUA, NUL.

38. NFL to WLR, 2.1.1971, 3/4, RLP, CBA.

39. NFL to WLR, 10.2.1970, 3/3, RLP, CBA.

40. Herbert Raffaele, in discussion with the author, July 2020.

41. Ibid.

42. NFL to EMG, 8.15.1970, 3/3, RLP, CBA.

43. NFL to WLR, 1.18.1971, 3/4, RLP, CBA.

44. NFL to WLR, 3.28.1971, 3/4, RLP, CBA.

45. Ibid.

46. Brethren member, in discussion with the author, January 2019.

47. EG to GFL, 4.9.1971, 24/12, LLC, CDMLSCUA, NUL.

48. GFL to EMG, 4.11.1971, 24/12, LLC, CDMLSCUA, NUL.

49. EG to GFL, 4.19.1971, 24/12, LLC, CDMLSCUA, NUL.

50. GFL to WLR, 4.19.1971, 3/4, RLP, CBA.

51. NFL to WLR, 5.9.1971, 3/4, RLP, CBA.

52. NFL to RGN, 5.9.1971, 42/3, NFLP, CHM.

53. Ibid.

54. NFL to RGN, 6.17.1971, 42/3, NFLP, CHM.

55. Elmer Gertz, *To Life* (New York: McGraw-Hill, 1974), 196.

56. NFL to AKB, 8.15.1971, 24/14, LLC, CDMLSCUA, NUL.

57. Ibid.

58. Kenneth McDowell to Hazel Peters, 8.6.1971, 2/3, RLP, CBA.

59. NFL to AKB, 8.15.1971, 24/14, LLC, CDMLSCUA, NUL.

60. EG to HHW, 9.3.1971, 477/8, EGP, LC.

61. GFL to Friends and Family, 8.19.1971, 42/3, NFLP, CHM.

62. Certificado de Defunción, Nathan Leopold Foreman.

63. GFL to Family and Friends, 9.10.1971, 24/16, LLC, CDMLSCUA, NUL.

64. Ibid.

65. NFL to ADB, 10.7.1970, 3/1, NFLP, CHM.

66. *Leopold. vs. Levin*, Deposition (1960): 274–75.

CONCLUSION

1. "Leopold's Body Given to School," *Times-Advocate (Escondido, California),* 9.1.1971.
2. "Leopold 'Atonement' over, Widow States," *CT*, 8.31.1971.
3. GFL to EG, 9.13.1971, 24/16, LLC, CDMLSCUA, NUL.
4. Johnson Interview, 1983.
5. Ron Martinetti, in discussion with the author, September 2021.
6. Last Will and Testament of Nathan F. Leopold, 6.23.1971, 8/10, LLC, CDMLSCUA, NUL.
7. Harvey B. Nachman to EG, 9.20.1971, 7/18, LLC, CDMLSCUA, NUL.
8. Louise Spall to GFL, 2.21.1976, 477/8, EGP, LC.
9. GFL to Hal Higdon, 3.20.1975, 3/1, HHP, CHM.
10. Charles A. Bonniwell, "Expert Analyzes Characteristics of Slayers of Young Franks," *San Francisco Examiner*, 6.7.1924.
11. Susan Daniels, "Musical Recreates Brutal Tale of 1920's Chicago Murderers," *Jewish Advocate*, 1.21.2005.
12. NFL to Timothy Seldes, 8.27.1961, 42/1, NFLP, CHM.
13. White, *A Psychiatric Diagnosis*, 21.
14. NFL to David Fulford Jr. 10.17.1970, 7/3, NFLP, CHM.

BIBLIOGRAPHY

This will include collections and works that were consulted during the writing but may not have been cited directly in the book.

ARCHIVAL COLLECTIONS

Abraham Lincoln Presidential Library

Henry Horner Papers, Joseph Edward Ragen Papers, Otto Kerner Papers.

Chicago History Museum

Hal Higdon research papers on the Leopold and Loeb case, James McGillivary Collection, Nathan F. Leopold Papers, Nathan Kantrowitz research papers on Stateville penitentiary.

Church of the Brethren Archives

Brethren Service Commission: Puerto Rico Records, Row-Leopold Papers.

Library of Congress

Clarence Darrow Papers, Elmer Gertz Papers, John Bartlow Martin Papers.

Illinois State Archives

Clemency Files, Institutional Jackets, Joliet Prison Photos, Parole and Pardon Files, Prison Registers for Joliet-Stateville, Menard, and Pontiac.

Charles Deering McCormick Library of Special Collections and University Archives, Northwestern University

Harold S. Hulbert Papers, Leopold-Loeb Collection, Richard Loeb Papers.

University of Chicago Library, Special Collections Research Center

Bernard Glueck Sr. Papers, Edwin Herbert Lewis Papers, Ernest Watson Burgess Papers, Hyde Park Historical Collection, Julius Rosenwald Papers, Nathan F. Leopold Collection, Salmon Levinson Papers.

Other Collections

American Art Archives, American Jewish Archives, Charlevoix Historical Society, Chicago Film Archives, Chicago Public Library, Columbia University Library, Connecticut State Library, Cook County Medical Examiner's Office, Cranbrook Institute of Science, Elgin Public Museum, Field Museum, Franciscan Providence of the Sacred Heart Archives, Gerber/Hart Library and Archives, Hamilton College Rare Book Room, Harvard Law Library, Hebrew University of Jerusalem Albert Einstein Archives, Highland Park Public Library, Johns Hopkins Chesney Archives, Library of Michigan in Lansing, Manchester University, National Archives, National Library of Medicine, Newberry Research Library, ONE Archives, Peggy Notebaert Nature Museum, Richard J. Daley Center Archives, Spertus Institute, Sterling Morton Library, Syracuse University Libraries Special Collections Research Center, University of Illinois Rare Book and Manuscript Library, University of California Berkeley Bancroft Library, University of Iowa Special Collections and Archives, University of Michigan Bentley Historical Library, University of Minnesota Law Library, University of Oregon Library, University of Texas Harry Ransom Center, University of Virginia Library, University of Wisconsin American Heritage Center, Will County Archives, Will County Coroner's Office.

INTERVIEWS CONDUCTED BY THE AUTHOR

Joanne Church, Harold Heatwole, and Herbert Raffaele.

BOOKS

Blodgett, Richard. *Federal Paper Board at Seventy-Five.* Connecticut: Greenwich, 1991.

Bryant, William Cullen. *Poems*. Boston: Russell, Odiorne, and Metcalf, 1834.

Camp Highlands. *Dinglebat*. Sayner, Wisconsin, 1917–1919.

Current, Richard Nelson. *Phi Beta Kappa in American Life*. New York: Oxford University Press, 1990.

Darrow, Clarence. *The Story of My Life*. New York: Charles Scribner's Sons, 1932.

Donnelley, Reuben H. *Lakeside Annual Directory of the City of Chicago*. Chicago: Lakeside Press, 1910.

Erickson, Gladys A. *Warden Ragen of Joliet*. New York: E. P. Dutton & Co., 1957.

Fishman, Joseph F. *Sex in Prison*. New York: National Library Press, 1934.

Forbush, Edward Howe. *Some Under-Water Activities of Certain Waterfowl*. Boston: Wright & Potter, 1922.

Gertz, Elmer. *A Handful of Clients*. Chicago: Follett, 1965.

———. *To Life*. New York: McGraw-Hill, 1974.

Gilbert, Paul, and Bryson, Charles Lee. *Chicago and Its Makers*. Chicago: Felix Mendelsohn, 1929.

Glassman, Leo M. *Biographical Encyclopedia of American Jewry*. New York: Maurice Jacobs & Leo M. Glassman, 1935.

Harvard School for Boys. *Harvard School Review*. Chicago, 1916–1925.

Higdon, Hal. *Leopold and Loeb: The Crime of the Century*. New York: G. P. Putnam's Sons, 1975.

Laune, Ferris F. *Predicting Criminality: Forecasting Behavior on Parole*. Evanston, IL: Northwestern University, 1936.

Leonard, John William. *Who's Who in Engineering*. New York: John W. Leonard Co., 1922.

Leopold, Nathan. *Checklist of Birds of Puerto Rico and the Virgin Islands*. Río Piedras: University of Puerto Rico Agricultural Experiment Station, 1963.

———. *Life Plus 99 Years*. New York: Doubleday, 1958.

Levin, Meyer. *Compulsion*. New York: Simon & Schuster, 1956.

Lewis, Edwin Herbert. *Sallie's Newspaper*. Chicago: Hyman-McGee, 1924.

Loeb, Richard. *English A: Elementary Principles of Grammar and Letter Writing*.

Masterson, Karen M. *The Malaria Project: The U.S. Government's Secret Mission to Find a Miracle Cure*. New York: Penguin Group, 2014.

Morris Paper Mills. *The Morris Story*.

Official Students' Directory. Ann Arbor: University of Michigan, 1921.

Richard's Magazine. March 1916.

Rose, Helen. *Just Make Them Beautiful*. California: Dennis-Landman, 1976.

Rose, Peter. *Guest Appearances and Other Travels in Time and Space*. Athens: Ohio University Press, 2003.

Ross, Lillian. *Here but Not Here: A Love Story*. New York: Random House, 1998.

Savage, Joseph P. *A Man Named Savage*. New York: Vantage Press, 1975.

Schobinger, John J. *Fifty Years in the Harvard School*. 1925.

Scully, George T. *A New Day . . . and How to Make It*. Illinois: Department of Public Welfare, 1934.

Smith, Clayton. *Tales by the Fireside*. Charlevoix: Trapper Cabin Press, 1996.

University of Chicago. *Cap and Gown*. Chicago: 1918–1924.

University of Michigan. *Michiganensian*. Ann Arbor: 1919, 1922–1923.

Vice Commission of Chicago. *The Social Evil in Chicago*. Chicago: Gunthorp-Warren, 1911.

Watson, James D., Lewis, George Porter, and Leopold, Jr., Nathan F. *Spring Migration Notes of the Chicago Area*. 1920.

Watson, Patrick. *This Hour Has Seven Decades*. Toronto: McArthur & Company, 2004.

Werner, Morris Robert. *Julius Rosenwald: The Life of a Practical Humanitarian*. New York: Harper & Brothers, 1939.

Zorbaugh, Harvey Warren. *The Gold Coast and the Slum: A Sociological Study of Chicago's Near North Side*. Chicago: University of Chicago Press, 1929.

ARTICLES

Cronbach, Abraham. "My Contacts with Nathan Leopold." *American Judaism* (January 1959).

Day, James. "Why I Killed Richard Loeb." *True Detective* (May 1960).

Day, James, and Spurrier, Harry. "I Killed Dickie Loeb!" *Master Detective* (November 1936).

Day, James, and Stephens, Barry. "Why I Killed Richard Loeb." *Detective Story* (September 1942).

Huff, Ray. "Is Parole Prediction a Science?" *Journal of Criminal Law and Criminology* 27/2 (1936).

Lanne, William F. "Parole Prediction as Science." *Journal of Criminal Law and Criminology* (Fall 1935).

Larson, John A., and Adler, Herman M. "A Study of Deception in the Penitentiary." *Institution Quarterly* (June 1925).

Lawrence, Richard A., and Ohlin, Lloyd. "A Comparison of Alternative Methods of Parole Prediction." *American Sociological Review* (June 1952).

Leopold, Nathan. "General Notes: Yellow-Crowned Night Heron at Chicago." *Auk* (April 1918).

———. "Reason and Instinct in Bird Migration." *Auk* (January 1923).

———. "The Kirtland's Warbler in Its Summer Home." *Auk* (January 1924).

———. Communicated by Ferris F. Laune. "The Scientific Status of Parole Prediction." *Journal of Criminal Law and Criminology* 27/2 (1936).

———. "Imprisonment Has No Future in a Free Society." *Key Issues* (1965).

Lyons, Leonard. "The Rehabilitation of Nathan Leopold." *SEP*, 6.1.1963.

"Marion Ascoli Speaks of Her Childhood and Memories of Loeb-Leopold." *Chicago Jewish History* (Spring 1995).

Martin, Walter B. "The Development of Psychoses in Prison." *Journal of Criminal Law and Criminology* (Fall 1927).

Miller, Wilhelm. "Bird Gardens in the City." *Country Life in America* (August 1914).

Martin, John Bartlow. "Murder on His Conscience: Part One." *SEP*, 4.2.1955.

————. "Murder on His Conscience: Part Two." *SEP*, 4.9.1955.

————. "Murder on His Conscience Part Three." *SEP*, 4.16.1955.

————. "Murder on His Conscience Part Four." *SEP*, 4.23.1955.

"Nathan Leopold after 32 Years." *LIFE*, 3.25.1957.

"Our Frontispiece." *Wilson Bulletin* (March 1923).

Palmer, T. S. "The Forty-First Stated Meeting of the American Ornithologist's Union." *Auk* (January 1924).

Pollock, Dan. "How a Freshman Officer Became a Murderer." *Midway*, 6.11.1968.

"Recent Literature: Spring Migration Notes of the Chicago Area." *Auk* (October 1920).

Royer, Howard E. "Nathan Leopold Calls on the Brethren." *The Gospel Messenger*, 2.1.1964.

Sandiford, Francis. "Only the Damned." *Tangents* (October 1966).

Simms, Hector. "Stoned in San Juan." *Gay*, 5.25.1970.

NEWSPAPERS

Advocate, Akron Beacon Journal, Times-Union (Albany, New York), Birmingham News, Boston Daily Globe, Chicago Daily Defender, Chicago Daily Journal, Chicago Daily News, Chicago Daily Times, Chicago Daily Worker, Chicago Evening American, Chicago Evening Post, Chicago Herald American, Chicago Herald Examiner, Chicago Inter-Ocean, Chicago Sun-Times, Chicago Tribune, Daily Maroon, Daily News (New York, New York), Decatur Daily Review, Detroit Free Press, The Economist, Hartford Courant, Highland Park Press, Huntington Herald, Inter American Review, Jerusalem Post, Jewish Advocate, Joliet Evening Herald News, Joliet-Stateville Time, Lincoln Evening News, Los Angeles Free Press, Los Angeles Times, Miami News, Michigan Daily, Mount Vernon Daily Argus, New York Daily News, New York Evening Post, New York Times, Oakland Tribune, Orlando Sentinel, Philadelphia Inquirer, Presbyterian Standard, Reading Times, Saddle and Horse Show Chronicle, San Francisco Examiner, San Juan Diary, Sentinel, Sheridan Road News-Letter, Springfield Missouri Republican, St. Louis Post-Dispatch, St. Paul Pioneer Press, Times (Munster, Indiana), Times-Advocate (Escondido, California), Toronto Star, University High School Daily, Village Voice.

REPORTS

Bowen, A. L. "Nineteenth Annual Report of The Illinois Department of Public Welfare." State of Illinois, 1936.

House of Lords Official Report, 12.17.1969.

Illinois Association for Criminal Justice. *The Illinois Crime Survey.* Chicago: Blakely
Printing Company, 1929.

Illinois Prison Inquiry Commission. *The Prison System in Illinois.* Springfield: 1937.

National Institute of Mental Health. "Final Report of the Task Force on Homosexuality," 10.10.1969.

Report of South Side Ladies Sewing Society, *Annual Report of the United Hebrew
Charities of Chicago v4-11* (1892–1899).

Report of the Commissioners of the Illinois State Penitentiary at Joliet for the Two
Years Ending September 30, 1898. Springfield: Phillips Bros. 1901.

Report of the Stateville Correspondence School from January 1, 1936 to December
31, 1936, 55/4, Sheldon Glueck Papers, Harvard Law Library.

US Census Bureau, Census of the United States: 1860–1950.

The Workings of the Indeterminate-Sentence Law and the Parole System in
Illinois (1928).

PSYCHIATRIC REPORTS

Bowman, Karl M., and Hulbert, H. S. *Report of Preliminary Neuro-Psychiatric Examination: Nathan Leopold,* 4/1, LLC, CDMLSCUA, NUL.

Bowman, Karl M., and Hulbert, H. S. *Report of Preliminary Neuro-Psychiatric Examination: Richard Loeb,* 4/2, LLC, CDMLSCUA, NUL.

Glueck, Bernard. "A Psychiatric Diagnosis and Interpretation of the Two Defendants." 2/1, HSHP, CDMLSCUA, NUL.

———. "Psycho-Analytic Reflections on Two Homicides." 1/5, BGSP, SCRC,
UCL.

———. "Psycho-Analytic Reflections on Two Youthful Murderers." 1/3, BGSP,
SCRC, UCL

Glueck, Bernard, Hamill, Ralph C., Healy, William, and White, William A. "Joint
Report: Nathan F. Leopold Jr. and Ricard Loeb." 1/2, Bernard Glueck Sr.
Papers, SCRC, UCL.

Hall, James Whitney. "Dr. Hall's Report on Loeb." *CHE,* 8.11.1924.

"Dr. William Healy's Report: Nathan Leopold Jr." 2/1, HSHP, CDMLSCUA,
NUL.

"Dr. William Healy's Report (Richard Loeb)." 2/1, HSHP, CDMLSCUA, NUL.

Hulbert, Harold. "Abstract of the Preliminary Neuro-Psychiatric Examination of
Nathan Leopold." 2/1, HSHP, CDMLSCUA, NUL.

———. "Diagnostic Report for Mr. Bachrach and Mr. Darrow from Doctor Hulbert on Nathan Leopold." 2/1, CDMLSCUA, NUL.

———. "Diagnostic Report for Mr. Bachrach and Mr. Darrow from Doctor Hulbert, on Richard Loeb." 2/1, HSHP, CDMLSCUA, NUL.

Hulbert, H. S. "The Franks Case: Psychiatric Data, Interpretation and Opinion
(Nathan Leopold)." 2/1, HSHP, CDMLSCUA, NUL.

———. "The Franks Case: Psychiatric Data, Interpretation and Opinion (Richard Loeb)." 120/1, EGP, LC.

White, William A. "Report of Dr. William A. White. A Psychiatric Diagnosis and Interpretation of the Two Defendants." 2/1, HSHP, CDMLSCUA, NUL.

LECTURES

Miller, Elliot, and Sogin, Jean. "Highland Park as a Summer Resort." Highland Park Public Library, 2.17.2016.

LEGAL DOCUMENTS

Nuremberg Military Tribunals.

People of the State of Illinois vs. Nathan F. Leopold Jr. and Richard Loeb.

Statements of Nathan F. Leopold Jr. and Richard Albert Loeb.

UNPUBLISHED MATERIAL

Joseph Austrian memoirs, CHM.

"The Adaptation of Nathan Leopold." 1/4, NFLP, CHM.

Martinetti, Ron. *Crazy Bird: Nathan Leopold and the Crime of the Century.* Unpublished manuscript, 2022.

TELEVISION

This Hour Has Seven Days, CBC, 1.3.1965.

Meindl, Christopher. *In Search of History: Leopold and Loeb: Born Killers*, History Channel, 1998.

SECONDARY SOURCES

Baker Eddy, Mary G. *Science and Health with Key to the Scriptures.* Boston: E. J. Foster Eddy, 1895.

Caldwell, John C. "Far Pacific Travel Guide." New York: John Day Company, 1966.

Chicago Community Trust. *Reports Comprising the Survey of the Cook County Jail.* Chicago: Calumet Publishing, 1922.

Damron, Bob. "Bob Damron's Address Book." San Francisco: 1968–1972.

Ginsberg, Allen. "The Maharishi and Me." *Los Angeles Free Press*, 4.19.1968.

Guild Press Ltd. "International Guild Guide." Washington, DC: Guild Press, 1964–1972.

Hunter, John Francis. *The Gay Insider USA*. New York: Stonehill Publishing, 1972.

Jacobs, James B. *Stateville: The Penitentiary in Mass Society*. Chicago: University of Chicago Press, 1977.

Ragen, Joseph, and Finston, Charles. *Inside the World's Toughest Prison*. Springfield: Charles C. Thomas, 1962.

Weinfeld, William, "Income of Lawyers, 1929–48." *Survey of Current Businesses* (August 1949).

Whitman, Howard, "The College Fraternity Crisis Part One." *Collier's*, 1.8.1949.

INDEX

ABOUT THE AUTHOR

Erik Rebain is an archivist who works for the *Chicago Tribune* and Chicago History Museum. He has spent seven years researching the life of Nathan Leopold in over 200 archival collections across the United States. In his free time, Erik volunteers for the Gerber/Hart Library and Archives. He lives in Chicago with a cat named Newt.

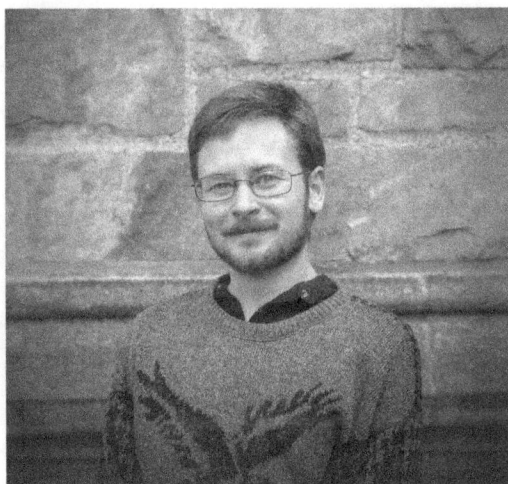

Erik Rebain. Photo © Katie and Christian Flickinger.